# STUDIES IN
# JEWISH BABYLONIAN ARAMAIC

# HARVARD SEMITIC MUSEUM PUBLICATIONS

Lawrence E. Stager, General Editor
Michael D. Coogan, Director of Publications

# HARVARD SEMITIC STUDIES

W. Randall Garr, Jo Ann Hackett, and John Huehnergard, editors

# STUDIES IN
# JEWISH BABYLONIAN ARAMAIC

*Based upon Early Eastern Manuscripts*

by
## Matthew Morgenstern

EISENBRAUNS
Winona Lake, Indiana
2011

# STUDIES IN JEWISH BABYLONIAN ARAMAIC
# BASED UPON EARLY EASTERN MANUSCRIPTS

by

Matthew Morgenstern

Printed in the United States of America

www.eisenbrauns.com

**Library of Congress Cataloging-in-Publication Data**

Morgenstern, Matthew, 1968–
    Studies in Jewish Babylonian Aramaic based upon early Eastern
    manuscripts / by Matthew Morgenstern.
              p.   cm. — (Harvard Semitic studies ; 62)
    Includes bibliographical references and index.
    ISBN 978-1-57506-938-8 (hardback : alk. paper)
        1. Aramaic language—Grammar.   2. Aramaic language—
    Dialects—Iraq—Babylonia.   3. Aramaic language—Dialects—Yemen
    (Republic).   I. Title
        PJ5302.M68   2011
        492′.29—dc22
                                                                            2010045385

The paper used in this publication meets the minimum requirements of the American
National Standard for Information Sciences—Permanence of Paper for Printed Library
Materials, ANSI Z39.48-1984.⊗™

*For my parents*

# Table of Contents

# Preface

This book has been long in the making, and over the course of my work on it I have benefited from the support and advice of friends and colleagues.

I first addressed issues of Jewish Babylonian Aramaic in PhD dissertation written under the supervision of Professor Moshe Bar-Asher. Professor Bar-Asher's expertise in the complexities of manuscript-based linguistic studies is apparent in his own research. His publications serve as a model for integration of precise descriptive data with a wider analytical perspective.

Professor Steven Fassberg and Dr James Nathan Ford read drafts of this book and provided both encouragement and direction. The editorial team at Harvard Semitic Studies—Professors John Huehnergard, Randall Garr and Michael Coogan—have expended great energies to ensure the uniformity of this complex work. The special fonts used in this book were kindly created by Shai Heijmans, M.A. The text was copyedited by Aaron Hornkohl, M.A., whose outstanding attention to detail saved me from many embarrassing errors.

Rabbi David Ebner introduced me to study of the Babylonian Talmud. The late Dr Michael Weitzmann and Professor Jonas Greenfield were my first teachers of Aramaic philology, and it was through their faith in me that I embarked on my present career.

I am grateful to my wife for her love and help over the many years. My children, who have been competing with Aramaic for as long as they can remember, undertook numerous tasks to facilitate the appearance of this book, in particular, the preparation of computerized materials and general office management.

This book is humbly dedicated to my parents, without whose support it would never have been published.

# Abbreviations

**BDB**—F. Brown, S. R. Driver and C. A. Briggs, *A Hebrew and English Lexicon of the Old Testament* (Oxford: Clarendon Press, 1906).

**EEMss**—Early Eastern Manuscripts.

**Geon**—L. Ginzberg, *Geonica II: Genizah Studies* (New York: The Jewish Theological Society of America, 1909)—cited by document, folio, and line number.

**Gil**—M. Gil, *In the Kingdom of Ishmael* (Tel Aviv: Tel Aviv University and Jerusalem: The Bialik Institute, 1997)—cited by document, folio, and line number.

**GK**—B. M. Lewin, *Ginze Qedem* (6 volumes; Haifa and Jerusalem, 1922–1944 [published by the editor])—cited by page and line number.

**GR**—*Ginza Right,* according to H. Petermann, *Thesaurus sive Liber magnus vulgo "Liber Adami" appellatus opus Mandaeorum summi ponderis* (Leipzig: P. O. Weigel, 1867).

**GS**—L. Ginzberg, *Genizah Studies in Memory of Doctor Solomon Schechter II: Geonic and Early Karaitic Halakah* (New York: The Jewish Theological Seminary of America, 1929)—cited by page and line number.

**Hark**—A. Harkavy, *Responsen der Geonim (zumeist aus dem X–XI. Jahrhundert)* (Studien und Mittheilungen aus der Kaiserlichen Oeffentlichen Bibliothek zu St. Petersburg: Vierter Theil; Berlin, 1887)—cited by page and line number.

**HGP**—*Sefer Halachot Gedolot, Codex Paris 1402* (Jerusalem: Makor Press, 1971)—cited by page and line number of facsimile edition.

**HPS**—*Sefer Halachot Pesuqot by Rav Jehudai Gaon, Codex Sassoon 263* (Jerusalem: Makor Press, 1971)—cited by page and line number of facsimile edition.

**HR**—A. L. Shlosberg, הלכות פסוקות או הלכות ראו [*Halakhot Pesuqot or Hilkhot Re'u*] (Versailles: Cerf et fils, 1886).

**JBA**—Jewish Babylonian Aramaic.

**LPT**—S. Abramson, Rabbi Shmuel b. Chofni, *Liber Prooemium Talmudis* (Jerusalem: Mekize Nirdamim, 1990).

**MHD** — S. Fisch, *Midrash Haggadol on the Pentateuch: Deuteronomy* (Jerusalem: Mossad Harav Kook, 1972).

**MHE** — M. Margulies, *Midrash Haggadol on the Pentateuch: Exodus* (Jerusalem: Mossad Harav Kook Publishing, 1956).

**MHG** — M. Margulies, *Midrash Haggadol on the Pentateuch: Genesis* (Jerusalem: Mossad Harav Kook Publishing, 1947).

**MS** — Aramaic magic texts in the Martin Schøyen Collection. Cited courtesy of Professor S. Shaked.

**RBA** — Rabbinic Babylonian Aramaic.

**TGAs28** — S. Assaf, *Geonic Responsa from Geniza MSS* (Jerusalem: Darom, 1928) — cited by document, folio, and line number.

**TGAs42** — S. Assaf, *Geonic Responsa* (Jerusalem: Mekize Nirdamim, 1942) — cited by document, folio, and line number.

**TOJ** — The Aramaic of Targum Onqelos to the Torah and Targum Jonathan to the Prophets, cited according to A. Sperber, *The Bible in Aramaic* (Leiden: Brill, 1959–73) unless otherwise stated.

**Talmudic Manuscripts**

Only brief bibliographical references are provided here for the Tamudic manuscripts. Further details may be found in M. Krupp, "Manuscripts of the Babylonian Talmud," in S. Safrai (ed.) *The Literature of the Sages* (Compendia rerum Iudaicarum ad Novum Testamentum 2:3; Assen/Maastricht: Van Gorcum and Philadelphia: Fortress Press, 1987), pp. 351–61.

**Col** — Columbia X893-T141.

**Esc** — Escorial G-I-3.

**Firk** — Firkovitch.

**Fl8** — Florence II-I-8.

**Fl9** — Florence II-I-9.

**Fr** — Frankfurt MS Barth 107.

**G** — Geniza fragments (see relevant discussions).

**Gö3** — Göttingen 3.

**H165** — Hamburg 165.

**J** — Jerusalem, Yad Harav Herzog.

**JTS15** — Jewish Theological Seminary 15.

**JTS108** — Jewish Theological Seminary 218 (= Enelow 319).

**JTS218** — Jewish Theological Seminary 218 (= Enelow 270).

**JTS1623** — Jewish Theological Seminary 1623 (= Enelow 271).

**K9** — Köln 9.

**L400** — London 400.

**M95** — Munich 95.

**Macerata** — Macerata archive 725-6.

**MG594** — Moscow Guenzburg 594.

**O23** — Oxford Opp. Add. fol. 23.

**O51** — Oxford Bodl. heb. e. 51.

**V115** – Vatican 115.

**V117** — Vatican 117.

# CHAPTER 1
# Introduction

## 1.1 The Purpose of This Book

The purpose of this book is twofold. The first aim is to clarify many individual points pertaining to the grammar of the types of Jewish Babylonian Aramaic employed in Rabbinic sources, i.e., the Talmud and post-Talmudic (Geonic) Babylonian Rabbinic literature. To distinguish this form of Aramaic from others employed by Jews in Babylonia, I have employed the term Rabbinic Babylonian Aramaic (henceforth: RBA).[1] As will be outlined in the following pages, recent advances in the study of this corpus of literature, the identification of earlier and more accurate manuscript sources, and a reexamination of previous published materials have conjoined to demonstrate the necessity of reconsidering the data presented in the currently available works. In parallel, the recent upsurge in publication of contemporaneous Aramaic epigraphic sources—primarily the Aramaic magic bowls—has provided us with a rich treasure of new sources which further illuminate the subjects under discussion.

The present work may be regarded as the continuation of a research project that I began with my 2002 Hebrew University dissertation, "Jewish Babylonian Aramaic in Geonic Responsa—Studies in Phonology, Verb Morphology, Pronouns, and Style." The two works differ greatly in their scope and aim. The dissertation aimed at providing a detailed and comprehensive linguistic description of the responsa, and at answering some fundamental questions regarding the language of the Babylonian Geonim and its relationship to that of the Babylonian Talmud. The present study addresses more general questions about research into RBA grammar, and is based upon a wider variety of sources: Talmud manuscripts, Geonic responsa, the *Sheʾiltot,* and the Geonic legal compendia, i.e., *Halachot Pesuqot* and *Halachot Gedolot.* In contrast to the former work, which presented the evidence from the Geonic works in an exhaustive

---

[1] When the abbreviation RBA is employed in this book, it refers exclusively to the Aramaic found in these Rabbinic sources. Other forms of Aramaic current in Babylonia are always indicated explicit, e.g., the Aramaic of Targum Onqelos or the Aramaic of the magic bowl texts.

manner, the present work, though based upon a comprehensive study of these varied sources, generally presents representative examples.

However, beyond the simple (and often not so simple) presentation and analysis of the linguistic data, this monograph has a secondary methodological agendum, which runs through most of the work: I aim to demonstrate that only a small number of manuscript sources maintain the language of the Talmud in its pristine state. The Babylonian Aramaic language that emerges from these manuscripts differs in numerous points of detail from all later, predominantly European sources. Accordingly, these sources must be the primary base for any description of RBA. Lest this statement seem obvious, it must be emphasized that in practice, this principle has not been followed in many of the studies on this dialect, a fact which has led to some serious misunderstandings regarding its details.

Chapter 2 surveys the history of research into RBA, and provides an assessment of the various publications' merits and desiderata. I have endeavored to indicate their contributions as well as their shortcomings. However, since the primary aim of the chapter is to indicate the current needs of research, particular emphasis has been given to those aspects in which the various studies are weak.

While I have striven to allow my evidence to speak for itself, it will become clear that one of my aims is to dispel some misapprehensions regarding the role of the Yemenite traditions—written and oral—in reconstructing the linguistic realities of Babylonian Aramaic. To anyone acquainted with the research literature on the field, it will be clear that my position is thus contrary to that of the late Prof. Shelomo Morag, who greatly emphasized the value of the Yemenite traditions in the study of this dialect. This is a fundamental methodological question, which profoundly affects our understanding of the grammar of RBA. Accordingly, chapter 3 is devoted to a detailed description of differences between the early manuscripts and the Yemenite oral and written traditions. In order to achieve this, it has been necessary to clarify many of the finer points of Babylonian Aramaic grammar. It is hoped that those researchers to whom the debate about the historical validity of Yemenite reading tradition is of secondary interest will nevertheless find here an up-to-date account of research on many topics of RBA grammar.

Chapter 4 considers the complex issue of linguistic variation in RBA texts. It is claimed that none of the explanations of this phenomenon so far presented in the research literature can account for the wide scope of this variation found in any given source. However, underlying all the interchanges appears to be a lack of a standard literary language in which Babylonian Rabbinic literature was formulated.

Chapter 5 examines the structures of the direct object as they emerge from accurate manuscript sources. It is demonstrated that, while less vulnerable to scribal change than morphology, the syntax of RBA also needs reevaluation based upon the best manuscript sources. In particular, it is shown that since the currently available reference works were based primarily on the printed editions of the Talmud, their descriptions of the direct object structures are inaccurate, because only the best manuscripts employ a consistent and systematic pattern of direct object marking. In addition, the chapter demonstrates that the Hamburg manuscript of *Neziqin*, rightly regarded as an important source for the history of the Talmud text, has undergone linguistic editing which has greatly reduced its value as a linguistic witness.

At this juncture it is worth emphasizing the distinction between a good linguistic witness and a good textual witness. The focus throughout this study has remained strictly linguistic; I do not presume to comment on the validity of the readings or on the historic development of the Talmud text, except regarding issues that directly relate to the topic at hand. In such cases I have attempted to address these matters according to my understanding of recent research in the field. None of the contemporary Talmudic research that I have read contradicts my basic contention that only a tiny number of manuscripts at our disposal can be regarded as genuinely reflecting the Babylonian Aramaic idiom. How, why, and where the language became corrupted is a subject that must be addressed by researchers of the history of the Talmud text. Such an undertaking would require the mapping of development of the text through dozens of manuscripts, a momentous task that lies beyond the scope of the present monograph, and extends well beyond my own fields of inquiry. It is a topic that should ideally be addressed by a competent research group.

My research into RBA has continued over a period of more than ten years, since I began to gather materials for my doctoral dissertation up to the present time. I now feel that my work has reached a stage where I can present a report of my findings, in the hope that this will encourage and guide further research into these dialects. However, this study does not claim to be the final word on this language, and I am certain that future research will allow for additional clarifications of some of the topics discussed herein. For example, I have not addressed the important issue of the unique idiom in which the six tractates of the Talmud that were not studied in the Babylonian academies are written.[2]

---

[2] See Epstein, *Grammar*, pp. 14–16. Breuer, "Karetot," represents a valuable contribution to the study of the language of these tractates.

As this book goes to press, several significant developments are taking place in the field of Babylonian Aramaic research. First, hundreds of
Aramaic magic bowls, the majority of which are written in the Jewish
script, are awaiting publication. There can be no doubt that accurate editions of these texts will significantly enrich our understanding of the historical development of forms of Aramaic employed by the Jews of Babylonia.[3]

In parallel, the ongoing work of identifying and grouping the Geniza
manuscripts of Babylonian Rabbinic literature is reaching a critical stage,
with the imminent publication of a comprehensive catalog of this material in the framework of the Friedberg Genizah Project.[4] The long-term
plan of scanning the various fragments and placing those digital images
on the internet will allow researchers to have immediate access to these
sources at a speed unthinkable in previous generations. The digitization
of sources such as the Jerusalem manuscript of *Sanhedrin* and *Makkot* allows the researcher to check textual readings on the basis of clear photographs without having to leave his or her desk, while the computerized
databases of the Academy of the Hebrew Language and the Jewish Theological Seminary's Saul Lieberman Institute for Talmudic Research enable
one to search accurate transcriptions of scores of manuscripts with a
speed that was unthinkable ten years ago.

## 1.2 Note on the Citations and Translations

I have had some doubts regarding the correct length of the citations and
the detail to be provided in the translations. It has often been necessary
to cite grammatical forms in their context in order to prove my point.
Furthermore, since many of the examples are drawn from manuscripts
that remain either unpublished or hard to locate, it could not be assumed
that the reader would have access to the original Aramaic text, and accordingly the citations are somewhat lengthier than those found in some
linguistic publications.

However, since much of RBA literature is of a technical nature, and
comprises interpretations of earlier legal statements often presented in a
highly elliptic style, the lengthier the citation, the more difficult it becomes to translate word-for-word. Occasionally, a brief explanation has
been added in the footnotes to direct the reader regarding the overall

---

[3] See in particular my articles, Morgenstern, "Moussaieff Collection" and "Non-
Standard Spellings."

[4] This project aims to catalogue and digitize the entire contents of the Cairo Geniza.

context of a legal discussion. Nonetheless, since the emphasis in this work is primarily grammatical, no attempt has been made to explain the texts in more detail than a simple understanding of the words requires, even though this may leave the reader somewhat baffled.

The translations provided are my own, though I have made some use of M. Sokoloff's *Dictionary of Jewish Babylonian Aramaic*, M. Jastrow's *Dictionary of the Targumim, the Talmud Babli and Yerushalmi, and the Midrashic Literature*, and the Soncino translation of the Babylonian Talmud to aid me in finding concise and felicitous translations of the often technical Talmudic terms. Occasionally elegance has been sacrificed for the sake of expediency, especially when it was necessary to make the translation follow the structure of the Aramaic text in order to highlight a specific point. This is particularly marked in the chapter on direct objects, wherein the direct object structures in Aramaic have been rendered wherever possible into parallel direct object structures in English.

All the examples cited within this work are accompanied by cross-references to the source from which they are drawn. Wherever possible, they have been cited according to manuscript facsimiles or editions that reproduce the manuscripts line-by-line. Since all of the printed transcriptions have been collated from the original manuscripts or from clear photographs, the readings presented here may differ from those found in printed editions. In the field of Jewish studies, Talmud manuscripts are traditionally cited by reference to the city in which they are currently held and a catalog number, e.g., Hamburg 165 refers to Staats- und Universitätsbibliothek, Hamburg codex 165, a Spanish manuscript of the Babylonian Talmud, *Neziqin*. This system has been followed in citing such manuscripts (employing an initial for the city name, e.g., H165 for Hamburg 165), while full manuscript references are provided in the list of abbreviations. Evidence for the Yemenite reading tradition, which is cited widely in this study, is taken primarily from S. Morag's *Babylonian Aramaic: The Yemenite Tradition: Historical Aspects and Transmission, Phonology, The Verbal System* (henceforth "Morag, *YT*") and Rabbi ʿAmr's hand-vocalized edition of the Babylonian Talmud (henceforth "ʿAmr"). For technical reasons, the fricative (*rapē*) and gemination (*šadda*) diacritical marks employed in Morag's transcriptions have been omitted. In no place does their omission affect the argument at hand.

When a Talmudic source is quoted in a Geonic work, the Talmudic reference is cited first, and then the Geonic source from which the citation is drawn. The fact that these are Geonic citations is clear from the manuscript source itself, and is not always indicated explicitly. For cases in which the textual (rather than grammatical) reading of the Geonic text differs from that found in Talmudic manuscripts, no argument is being made that this is the "original" reading; the textual claims go no further than saying that a given Talmudic passage is cited in a specific textual witness in a particular form. Occasionally, I have noted my doubts about whether a particular word is original to the Talmudic text or represents a Geonic gloss. I have generally sought to cite only certain examples, and hence most of these cases are found in chapter 4, which deals with lengthier passages and Talmudic citations.

## 1.3 Note on Grammatical Terminology

Throughout this book I have employed the terminology current in grammatical literature on the Northwest Semitic languages, even though in some cases its appropriateness is subject to disagreement among scholars. For example, the terms "Perfect" and "Imperfect" are used throughout to describe the suffix and prefix tenses, even though these terms are historically drawn from the European grammatical tradition and do not accurately describe the function of these forms in RBA. The verbal stems (*binyanim*) have been referred to using the German notation system of G, D, C, Gt, etc., since the precise vocalization of these forms varies in the different Babylonian Aramaic manuscript sources and all the more so in the different Aramaic dialects. Hence to use, for example, a term such as *itpaᶜil* when referring to the Gt stem of Classical Syriac or Jewish Palestinian Aramaic is inappropriate, while it would be wholly correct for the RBA found in the best manuscripts.

# Toward a New Grammar of Rabbinic Babylonian Aramaic

## 2.1 Preface: The Need for a New Grammar

For many years now, the need for a new grammar of RBA has been one of the major desiderata of Aramaic studies. In this chapter, I aim to present a brief analysis of the current state of research, outlining both its accomplishments and its needs. I have sought to provide an assessment of the most significant publications in the field, indicating their strengths as well as their weaknesses. As in any discipline, research in this field has been cumulative, and hence my conclusions in this book are the outcome of this ongoing research. At the same time, fundamental differences in methodology have significantly influenced the conclusions reached by various scholars, and the need to clarify which methodology and sources are best suited to the task of describing RBA lies at the heart of this book.

## 2.2 Background

### 2.2.1 The Geonic Period

The first stages of the study of RBA are integrally connected to the spread of the Babylonian Talmud beyond the Aramaic-speaking world. While already in the Geonic period[1] a significant proportion of the urbanized Jewish population appears to have been Arabic-speaking, Aramaic remained the language of Jewish scholarship, and the leaders of the Jewish academies in Babylonia maintained a familiarity with Aramaic as a spoken language.[2] However, as study of the Talmud spread beyond the borders of Aramaic-speaking Jewry, it became increasingly necessary to explain rare words and terms, particularly the many lexemes describing the realia of Babylonian daily life. Accordingly, the earliest surviving linguistic analyses consist for the most part of glosses and commentaries that were intended to help the reader to understand words as they were used within a specific context. Many such lists are preserved in manuscripts of Geonic commentaries and glossaries on the

---

[1] For a definition of this period and an account of its literature, see Brody, *Geonim*.

[2] Evidence for the Geonim's acquaintance with spoken Aramaic was gathered by Epstein, *Grammar*, pp. 16–17. See further below.

Talmud or survive in later citations from such works. The breadth of the citations found, for example, in the medieval Talmudic dictionary הערוך by Nathan of Rome (ca. 1035–1106) implies that these glossaries once formed a considerable body of literature.[3]

The emphasis of the glossaries and commentaries is primarily lexical, and rarely do they deal explicitly or systematically with topics that we would regard as belonging to the field of "grammar." The grammatical analyses embedded in these glosses are generally tacit, and are expressed, for example, in the precise translation of conjugated forms. Among some of the later Geonic commentators (late tenth to early eleventh centuries) we occasionally find more explicit discussion of linguistic issues such as phonology or morphology. However, these still remain ad hoc explanations of individual forms, rather than systematic discussions of linguistic categories.

## 2.2.2 The Value of Geonic Sources

The importance of these early analyses lies in the fact that at the time they were written, Jewish Babylonian Aramaic dialects were still being spoken in the villages around Baghdad. This native-speaker familiarity makes a unique contribution to the discussion of topics such as the status of the pharyngeals, and en passant provides evidence for singular, plural, and diminutive forms not otherwise attested. The explicit testimony of R. Shemuel b. Ḥofni (d. 1034) regarding the vocalization of G participle forms such as נַחִית, with *patah* rather than *qamaṣ*,[4] confirms the authenticity of such forms in the Sassoon manuscript of *Halachot Pesuqot* and other early sources,[5] while his distinction between the forms אֵימָא "I shall say" and אִימָא "say (imper.)" provides important explicit support for the vocalization of MS **G1** of *Bava Mezia*.[6]

---

[3] The surviving material then known was gathered and published by B. M. Lewin in his monumental compendium, *Otzar Ha-gaonim*.

[4] The Gaon alludes to the Tiberian vowel markings rather than the Babylonian.

[5] On the importance of this manuscript, see §2.14.2.1.

[6] On this manuscript, see below, §2.7.1.    .

## 2.3 Modern Grammars

### 2.3.1 Luzzatto's *Elementi grammaticali*

It appears that the first systematic outline of RBA is found in the appendix to S. D. Luzzatto's 1865 *Elementi grammaticali del caldeo Biblico e del dialetto Talmudico babilonese*, which was subsequently translated into German (1873), English (1876) and Hebrew (1880). As Kutscher noted, this was a groundbreaking work, but was limited in scope and employed as its textual basis the inaccurate printed editions of the Talmud.[7] The linguistic treasures buried in Talmudic manuscripts were probably unavailable to Luzzatto, as were the best manuscripts of post-Talmudic (Geonic) RBA literature.[8] The rediscovery of the Cairo Geniza was many years off, and Firkovitch's collection was still being gathered. Nevertheless, Luzzatto's grammar provided a systematic outline of many of the dialect's basic forms.

Luzzatto's description is not without merit. For example, in §69 he mentions the form אשׁור "run (imper.)" (*Ber* 57b) and suggests that it is an apocopated imperative with umlaut. This incisive interpretation was accepted by Th. Nöldeke[9] and appears to be confirmed by my own findings.[10] Indeed, Nöldeke's assessment of Luzzatto's work was extremely positive, as generously expressed in the preface to his 1875 *Mandäische Grammatik* (p. v):

> Ich habe deshalb die verwandten Dialecte in ziemlich weitem Umfange zur Vergleichung herangezogen. Namentlich gilt dies von der mit dem Mandäischen sehr nahe verwandten Sprache des babylonischen Talmud's; ich hoffe immerhin einige beachtenswerthe Ergänzungen zu dem Buche des trefflichen LUZZATTO gegeben zu haben, einem Buche, dessen Verdienst viel grösser ist,

---

[7] Kutscher, "Review," p. 149 (reprinted in Kutscher, *Studies*, p. 227).

[8] Sussmann, "Talmud Fragments," has drawn attention to the remarkable lack of interest that early modern Talmud researchers showed in manuscript evidence. It was only with the publication of Rabbinovicz's *Variae lectiones in Mischnam et in Talmud Babylonicum* (1867–86) that manuscript material began to be considered seriously, if not systematically. Even if Luzzatto *had* consulted the manuscripts held in European libraries, it is unlikely that he would have been able to improve his work substantially, since the majority of those manuscripts stem from Europe and are linguistically unreliable. See below.

[9] Nöldeke, *MG*, p. 229 n. 1.

[10] See §3.4.3.3.

als es vielleicht dem oberflächlichen Beurtheiler scheinen mag, der sich, was ja heutzutage nicht schwer, ein bischen mit der Methode der neueren Sprachwissenschaft vertraut gemacht hat (vgl. die kürzlich im literar. Centralblatt erschienene unbillige Recension der deutschen Bearbeitung).

Based partially upon the material recorded by Luzzatto, Nöldeke was able to draw attention to numerous parallels between the dialect of the Talmud and Classical Mandaic, supplementing Luzzatto's findings with his own examples and observations.[11] In particular, Nöldeke's work made a considerable contribution to the diachronic explanation of the forms.

### 2.3.2 Three Monographs

G. Rülf's 1879 *Zur Lautlehre der aramäisch-talmudischen Dialecte. I. Die Kehllaute*, while containing some interesting examples, is limited by its comparisons between the Aramaic dialects of the Palestinian and Babylonian Talmuds. This comparison is particularly problematic given the textual status of the Palestinian Talmud, which is preserved in the printed editions (and in the later manuscripts) in a form strongly influenced by the Babylonian idiom which was more familiar to the scribes and copyists.

J. Rosenberg's *Das aramäische Verbum im babylonischen Talmud* was originally published as an article in the *Magazin für Wissenschaft des Judenthums*, and subsequently reissued as a monograph in 1888. The work is explicitly modeled on the description of verbal morphology found in Nöldeke's *Mandäische Grammatik*, to which it makes frequent cross-reference. Though it contains a more comprehensive description of the attested verbal forms of RBA than is found in Luzzatto's *Elementi grammaticali*, it is also solely dependent upon the printed editions of the Babylonian Talmud.

In 1895 A. Liebermann published his inaugural thesis, *Das Pronomen und das Adverbium des babylonisch-talmudischen Dialektes*. Unfortunately, Levias was accurate in his assessment that this is "a work incomplete and a mere compilation."[12] The study is essentially comparative, relating the RBA forms to those in other Aramaic dialects and Semitic languages;

---

[11] My late teacher, Prof. Jonas Greenfield, once told me that Nöldeke had reportedly studied Talmud with the then Chief Rabbi of Strasbourg. I do not know if there is a source confirming this information.

[12] Levias, *Grammar*, p. v.

however, it seems that the valuable comparisons are already to be found in Nöldeke's *Mandäische Grammatik*. Furthermore, a considerable proportion of the short volume also discusses the Hebrew elements of the Talmud, even though the author does not demonstrate any evidence for the linguistic influence of RBA on the Hebrew forms or vice versa.

### 2.3.3 Levias's Grammars

The editions of C. Levias's *Grammar*, which was first published in fascicles in the *American Journal of Semitic Languages and Literature* between 1897 and 1900, then republished as a single volume in 1900, and finally published in a completely revised Hebrew edition in 1930, remain the most comprehensive grammars of RBA available. As contemporary reviewers already noted, the value of these editions is reduced by the considerable amount of dubious material that they contain. Levias included a great number of questionable forms, which he vocalized according to uncertain principles.[13] These serious faults led Kutscher to give Levias's work a very negative assessment.[14]

Nevertheless, I think that Kutscher's overstated criticism of Levias's work has led to an unfair evaluation of his contribution to research. Already in his English edition Levias included important materials drawn from manuscripts, Geonic sources such as Harkavy's *Responsa*,[15] and from the Yemenite *Sefer Ha-maᶜasiyyot*. For example, Levias mentioned the phonetic spelling בדיאבא "ex post facto" from Harkavy's edition, and correctly analysed it as a phonetic spelling reflecting the elision of the ᶜ*ayin* and final *dalet*.[16] Similarly, he appears to have examined the Yemenite manuscripts in the Columbia University library, and on the basis of those manuscripts lists phonetic spellings such as איתביּדא "was done" (*Zev* 60a [**Col**]), איבי "it was asked" (*Zev* 6a bis, 14b [**Col**]) and others.[17] By employing these sources, Levias reintroduced non-European manuscript sources into the study of RBA.

---

[13] See for example my comments in §2.7.2.

[14] Kutscher, "Review," p. 150 (reprinted in Kutscher, *Studies*, p. 228). Kutscher was following, among others, Fraenkel, "Recension."

[15] Levias's decision to include this material was questioned by Fraenkel, "Recension," p. 93. However, subsequent advances in research would seem to suggest that this material was *more* valuable than the other sources he employed.

[16] Levias, *Grammar*, p. 21.

[17] Levias, *Grammar*, p. 17.

Furthermore, Levias distinguished between different phonetic processes (assimilation, dissimilation, and elision, which he curiously called "vanishing of consonants"), a linguistic sophistication which Epstein's *Grammar* lacks. Although Levias's grammar did not achieve the level of precision current in contemporary Semitic studies, to his credit he gathered a large amount of material from a wide array of sources, many of which had yet to be exploited in scholarly literature.

### 2.3.4 Margolis's Teaching Grammar

In 1910 M. Margolis's teaching grammar of Babylonian Aramaic appeared in the *Clavis Linguarum Semiticarum* series.[18] In assessing this work, Kutscher noted Margolis's philological expertise and experience with classical manuscripts, and accordingly expressed his disappointment that the grammar did not adequately address textual issues.[19] Perhaps Kutscher's expectations were too high for what was intended to be a teaching grammar. However, my own studies have indicated that Margolis occasionally edited his examples to accord with his preconceived grammatical notions.[20]

### 2.3.5 J. A. Montgomery's *Aramaic Incantation Texts*

In 1913, J. A. Montgomery published his groundbreaking volume, *Aramaic Incantation Texts from Nippur*. The editing of such texts was not a new phenomenon; they had been sporadically transcribed and printed since 1853.[21] However, Montgomery's edition was the first to contain a significant number of magic bowls, forty in all, of which thirty were writ-

---

[18] From the publication dates it appears to have been released simultaneously in German and English editions.

[19] Kutscher, "Review," p. 149 (reprinted in Kutscher, *Studies*, p. 227).

[20] See below, §5.7. A similar tendency may be seen in Malter's 1930 edition of the tractate *Taʿanit*, wherein he selected readings from the manuscripts according to his own grasp of RBA grammar. A manifest example of how such an approach may mislead research is Malter's selection of conjugated forms of the verb הו״י preceding a participle. In fact, RBA generally prefers the unconjugated הוה, e.g., כי הוה נפקין שבעא יומי דפיסחא "When the seven days of Passover would end" (*Pes* 30a [HPS 12:14]). See Kutscher, "Neutralization," p. 36 (observation attributed to Morag). Malter rejected a genuine RBA construction and followed the scribes of the later manuscripts in imposing the grammar of Rabbinic Hebrew onto RBA.

[21] Montgomery, *AIT*, pp. 16–22, summarizes the previous publication history.

ten in the Jewish script. The edition contained a comprehensive introduction, the texts in transcription and translation, and a running commentary. Handcopies of the texts appeared in lieu of photographs. Montgomery's transcriptions and translations do not always exhibit familiarity with the dialect, but as a first attempt to treat these texts as a corpus his efforts are commendable, and represent an advance over the work of his predecessors. In 1921 the great Talmudic scholar Jacob Epstein published a two-part study in which the texts were subjected to close scrutiny.[22] Epstein reread the texts on the basis of the handcopies[23] and made numerous lexical and grammatical comments.

## 2.3.6 J. N. Epstein's Contributions

Significant advances in Jewish Babylonian Aramaic lexicography and grammar are to be found in Epstein's articles. These studies, published primarily in English, Hebrew, and German between 1912 and 1922,[24] and from then on almost exclusively in Hebrew, reveal the author's vast knowledge of Rabbinic literature, Aramaic dialects, and the languages of the ancient Near East.[25] Epstein's interests were primarily philological

---

[22] Epstein, "Gloses."

[23] The handcopies are not always accurate. For example, based on the handcopy of **AIT** 14:6, Epstein, "Gloses," p. 47, suggested emending Montgomery's reading of הין to הדין. However, as already noted by Juusola, *Linguistic Peculiarities*, p. 115, the text reads ההין, as examination of a photograph confirms. ההין may be an intermediate form between standard Aramaic הדין and RBA האיי, reflecting the shift of fricative *ₔd* > *h* prior to its elision. I have discussed this issue in Morgenstern, "Non-Standard Spellings," though in that study I tended toward the assumption that we are dealing with a scribal error.

[24] A list of Epstein's articles in European languages may be found in his *Studies*, I, pp. 434–36. The volume contains Hebrew translations of the articles which also incorporate the author's own additions and corrections.

[25] Epstein's comments demonstrate an intimate knowledge of all the Aramaic dialects and familiarity with Arabic, Akkadian, Persian, and Greek. Cf. Müller-Kessler, "Die Stellung," p. 94 n. 24: "Aus den vorliegenden Einzeluntersuchungen Epsteins geht hervor, daß er zweifellos der bester und scharfsinnigste Kenner der ostaramäischen Dialekte war"; similarly, Sokoloff, *DJBA*, p. 16 n. 26, remarks: "The many contributions of J.N. Epstein toward the elucidation of the vocabulary of Jewish Babylonian Aramaic . . . overshadow the work of all other scholars."

rather than purely grammatical.[26] Nevertheless, his comments on grammatical phenomena are frequent and based upon a wide variety of sources. In particular, Epstein made extensive use of recently published manuscript sources, many of which were coming to light from the Cairo Geniza.[27] From Epstein's studies it becomes apparent that several linguistic traits preserved only in the best Rabbinic manuscripts are also reflected in the most ancient witnesses to the Babylonian Aramaic language, i.e., the magic bowl texts. Furthermore, Epstein often emphasized that these primary textual witnesses shared many features with other Eastern Aramaic dialects, especially with Mandaic.

Particularly important were Epstein's articles on post-Talmudic Aramaic sources: Geonic responsa, Anan's *Sepher HaMiṣwot*, and the *Sheʾiltot*.[28] These studies decisively proved that Aramaic remained a living language among the Geonim at least up to 1039, the year of Hai Gaon's death. This is indicated both by their explicit testimony to the living language, and by their use of a large number of authentic Aramaic words that are not found in the Talmud (and hence cannot be literary borrowings), but are attested in other Eastern Aramaic sources. Furthermore, Epstein demonstrated that the dialect of the Geonim differed from that in which the majority of the Talmudic tractates were composed, as may be discerned from several distinctive grammatical forms, particularly among the pronouns.

---

[26] It must be recalled that Epstein's primary contribution to scholarship was in the field of Talmudic studies.

[27] In particular, we may point to the following works which approximately correspond with Epstein's years of active research: L. Ginzberg's *Geonica II: Genizah Studies* (1909), in which fragments of 47 manuscripts were published, mostly containing Geonic works; S. Assaf's *Gaonic Responsa from Geniza MSS* (1928); L. Ginzberg's *Geniza Studies II* (1929); and B. M. Lewin's six volumes of *Ginze Kedem* (1922–44) and his aforementioned *Otzar Ha-gaonim* (1928–43). It is notable that these works concentrate primarily on post-Talmudic works, presumably because the texts were unknown and thus tended to attract more attention than Talmudic manuscripts, which were regarded as variants of already known materials. See Sussmann, "Talmud Fragments."

[28] Epstein, "Die Rechtsgutachten" (1912–13); "Notes I" on Anan (1914); and "Notes II" (1922) on *Sheʾiltot*.

## 2.3.7 Schlesinger's *Satzlehre*

In 1928 there appeared M. Schlesinger's *Satzlehre der aramäischen Sprache des babylonischen Talmuds*, which remains the only substantial syntactic description of RBA. Schlesinger's expertise in Talmudic literature is evident from the wide range of sources he cited, and this book has been justifiably regarded as an essential work on the subject.[29] While I agree with this generally positive assessment of Schlesinger's work, some aspects must now be reconsidered in light of both new textual evidence and new linguistic theories. In Chapter 5, I discuss in detail the structures of the direct object, and aim to demonstrate that the description found in Schlesinger's work does not match the findings in the best Rabbinic manuscripts.

Another example will be adduced here. Under the headings "ד-Sätze, deren ד' sich nicht auf das Prädikat des folgenden Satzes selbst bezieht (= deutsche Relativesätze), (a) ד' bezieht sich auf das Subjekt," Schlesinger lists the common Talmudic expression תניא דמסייעא לך (which he cites from the printed editions of *BM* 84a) and translates "Es gibt eine Baraitha, die dich unterstützt."[30] If I have understood Schlesinger's analysis correctly, he regarded תניא as a noun meaning "external teaching, *baraitha*," and the -ד here as a relative pronoun introducing a relative clause describing that noun. However, this is not possible: if תניא were a noun, then the verb of the relative clause would have to be m.s., whereas it is f.s.[31] In my opinion, תניא, a f.s. passive participle, is the predicate rather than the subject in this sentence, and means "[is] taught." What then is the subject? Two possibilities suggest themselves. First, it may be the independent relative clause דמסייעא לך "that which supports you," in which case we would have a simple cleft sentence: "That which supports you (דמסייעא לך) is taught (תניא)." Alternatively, the subject may be the following citation of Rabbinic teaching itself, in which case we would analyze "[XYZ citation], which supports you, is taught." The

---

[29] It is one of the few works to be warmly praised in Kutscher's "Review," even though he disagreed with some of Schlesinger's findings. See, for example, p. 169 n. 47 (reprinted in Kutscher, *Studies*, p. 247 n. 47).

[30] Schlesinger, *Satzlehre*, §133.

[31] So predominantly in the manuscripts, especially the better textual witnesses. In *Hul* 4a, MS **V**122, the form דמסייעא has been "emended" by a scribe who erased the final *ʾaleph*. The evidence is somewhat complicated by the tendency to drop the *ʿayin* or to append the *lamed*, or both. In one Geonic manuscript, we find מסייליה "It supports him" (**Geon** xxv i 15), which had been corrected by a second hand to מסייעליה.

widespread use of תניא to introduce citations from a taught source, wherein the subject is the citation itself, supports the latter analysis.[32]

The rise of Nazism in Europe and the destruction of European Jewry led to a lull in research into RBA, a field in which Jewish scholars have traditionally predominated. Only the American and Israeli centers of Jewish learning remained functional. In addition to sporadic publications by Epstein during this period, between 1934 and 1951 Cyrus Gordon published a series of editions of Aramaic magic bowls from various museums in the East and West.[33] For reasons which remain unclear, Gordon's many articles made little impact upon the study of RBA.[34]

## 2.4 A Turning Point

### 2.4.1 Epstein's *Grammar*

Well after the Second World War, research into RBA began to revive. In 1960, Epstein's *Grammar of Babylonian Aramaic* was posthumously published under the editorial guidance of E. Z. Melammed, and this remains the most up-to-date grammar of the dialect.[35] The book appears to be based upon notes that Epstein gathered for himself throughout his scholarly career and utilized for, among other things, teaching purposes. Following a brief historical/literary description of the dialect, the grammar includes a basic description of phonology, noting some of the most significant sound shifts, along with chapters on the pronouns, the morphology of verbs without object suffixes, noun patterns and declensions, and

---

[32] מתניתא, Rabbinic sources from the Mishna, and ברייתא, non-Mishnaic Tannaitic sources, are regarded as feminine singular nouns, and the feminine singular also serves as a neutral gender. See Wajsberg, "Principles," p. 341, and cf. Nöldeke, *SG*, §201.

[33] A list of these publications may be found in Juusola, *Linguistic Peculiarities*, pp. 256–57.

[34] Exceptional are the citations in Boyarin, "Reading Traditions," pp. 155–57.

[35] Other works published subsequently have dealt with more specific areas, such as verb morphology or noun patterns. Kara's *Yemenite Manuscripts* and my own unpublished dissertation do not deal with noun formation. Frank's *Grammar* is a didactic work aimed at students of the Talmud and is based on previously published materials, particularly Epstein's *Grammar* and Morag's *YT*. On Morag–Kara, *BAYTN*, which describes the Yemenite reading of the printed editions of the Talmud, see Breuer, "Yemenite Tradition," and Morgenstern, "Noun Patterns."

numerals. Finally, there are short chapters on prepositions, adverbs, conjunctions, and expressives.

Epstein's book is short yet rich. It contains a wide array of forms, both Talmudic and Geonic, selected from a wide array of manuscripts, early printed editions, and secondary sources, including the Aramaic magic texts. As noted above, Epstein was one of the pioneers of manuscript research into Rabbinic literature, blessed with an outstanding philological and grammatical sense, and had personally and laboriously gathered much of the material he cited. Epstein exploited his vast knowledge of Eastern Aramaic to provide comparative examples for many of the phenomena he described.

## 2.4.2 Kutscher's Review

However, the turning point in the study of RBA ultimately came with the publication of Kutscher's detailed review of Epstein's work. Kutscher, in accord with the principle he had practiced in his other works on Rabbinic philology, emphasized that linguistic work must be founded entirely on the systematic analysis of the most reliable textual witnesses, which must be treated as more than just a source of linguistic *curiosa*.[36] Moreover, Kutscher stressed the application of modern linguistic methods to the study of the dialect, and suggested that this could best be undertaken by a trained researcher.[37] In his detailed review, Kutscher examined numerous individual topics in RBA grammar, particularly relating to phonology and morphology, and attempted to identify manuscripts which may provide a reliable textual basis for further research.

Based on the limited number of sources then available in facsimile or transcription, Kutscher suggested that MS Sassoon of the Geonic legal collection *Halachot Pesuqot* (**HPS**) and MS Hamburg Hebr XIX (**H165**)

---

[36] Kutscher first stated his position with regard to Galilean Aramaic in 1950 and to the Hebrew of the Dead Sea Scrolls in 1959; see Kutscher, *SGA*, pp. 1–10, and *Isaiah Scroll*. He subsequently applied the same principles to Mishnaic Hebrew; see Kutscher, "Mishnaic Hebrew," first published in 1963.

[37] As I intimated above, Kutscher had a tendency to emphasize the weaknesses of the works he reviewed rather than their strengths, primarily as a means of directing future research to address what he regarded as the discipline's most pressing needs. Presumably, it is to this tendency that Müller-Kessler, "Die Stellung," p. 94 n. 24, refers: "Meines Erachtens wird die Grammatik Epsteins teilweise zu Unrecht von Kutscher 1962 kritisiert." I have found no specific cases wherein Epstein's opinion is to be preferred over Kutscher's.

of *Neziqin* were worthy of further research. For the first manuscript, he was forced to depend upon an inaccurate printed transcription published in 1950, while the latter manuscript had been published in facsimile in 1913. Kutscher was aware that the Hamburg MS was not actually a Babylonian manuscript, and that there were other, better manuscripts.[38] Nevertheless, he felt that the manuscript was worth mining for linguistic material. Kutscher alluded to two other manuscripts that may be of value to future research, MS Columbia of *Pesahim* and MS Paris of *Halachot Gedolot*.

Kutscher's review was a seminal work, both in terms of the attention to detail and of methodology. He rightly emphasized the necessity of finding the correct balance between descriptive and comparative linguistics: on the one hand, the researcher is obliged to describe the findings in the sources as they are; on the other hand, the restricted nature of the linguistic information that those sources provide (only sporadic marking of vocalization and gemination, unmarked stress, and historical spellings) demands a keen working knowledge of the comparative materials and their judicious application.

## 2.5 Another Approach—The Yemenite Reading Tradition

Kutscher's plea that future study of RBA be based solely upon the best manuscripts has been only partially implemented. In tandem, other avenues of research were being pursued. Of these, the most prominent was that of Shelomo Morag. Around the same time that Kutscher's seminal review was published, Morag published the first of his many articles on the Yemenite reading tradition of the Babylonian Talmud.[39] Morag's conclusions regarding the value of the Yemenite reading tradition were bold:

> Whereas the authenticity of the Yemenite oral tradition of post-Biblical Hebrew may be tested by comparison with vocalized Mss., the same is not true for the Yemenite tradition of the Aramaic of the Babylonian Talmud. Our opinion of the value of the latter must be based upon internal evidence only, in the absence of vocalized Mss. with which it could have been collated. Having examined the nature of this tradition as it stands, we may say that in many of its

---

[38] This rather opaque statement suggests that Kutscher did not regard MS H165 as belonging to the highest level of manuscript sources, an assessment that has been confirmed by subsequent study. See below, §2.9.3 and Chapter 5.

[39] The articles are Morag, "On the Yemenite Tradition" (1961) and "Vowel System" (1962); see also "Strong Verb" (1963).

features it would appear to constitute a genuine reflection of a Babylonian Aramaic dialect, as learned by Yemenite scholars, assiduous readers of the Talmud, who went to Babylonia for that purpose. [40]

The high esteem in which Morag held the Yemenite tradition is evident in all his subsequent work on RBA. The majority of his publications on the subject, published over a period of some thirty-five years, are dedicated to aspects of this tradition. Even in his works that deal with early manuscripts, Morag frequently cited comparative material from the Yemenite reading tradition. Since Morag and his students have been some of the most active researchers of RBA, and their publications account for a large proportion of the material written on the subject, Morag's decision to direct efforts into the study of the Yemenite oral and written traditions has greatly affected the development of research. I shall return to the issues raised by the Yemenite tradition below.

## 2.6 Manuscript Research

### 2.6.1 Morag's Manuscript Studies

Parallel to the investigation of the Yemenite reading tradition, research continued into the early manuscripts. In 1968, Morag published a fundamental study of RBA phonology based upon the hitherto-unknown vocalization of the Sassoon manuscript of *Halachot Pesuqot* (**HPS**).[41] As mentioned above, on the basis of an inaccurate printed transcription, Kutscher had concluded that this manuscript may serve as a primary source for the study of the dialect. However, it was Morag who examined the manuscript and discovered that for an undetermined reason, the last four or five lines of many leaves were vocalized with simple (early) Babylonian vocalization. Above we noted that the subsequent publication of R. Shemuel b. Ḥofni Gaon's *Introduction to the Talmud*, in which the author explicitly refers to issues of RBA phonology, has confirmed the accuracy of this manuscript's pointing, and thus supported Morag's assessment that it more accurately reflects the Babylonian phonology than **HGP**. Morag's study thus provided for the first time an accurate and reliable description of most of the issues relating to the vowel system of RBA.

---

[40] Morag, "Vowel System," pp. 219–20.
[41] Morag, "Phonology."

Morag's presentation of the data is almost comprehensive and generally accurate.[42] I have found only one significant omission: Morag does not explicitly mention the phenomenon of compensatory vowel change evidenced by forms such as מִיאוֹנִיךְ "from your ear" (*Hul* 132b [**HPS** 60:21]). Furthermore, some of this evidence may be interpreted in other ways; for example, I find Boyarin's explanation for the appearance of the *pataḥ* as a reflex of the historically long *$\bar{a}$ vowel (to be presented below) more convincing than Morag's. Nevertheless, Morag's description laid the groundwork for further research, and many of his findings have been confirmed by subsequent manuscript studies.

### 2.6.2 The Aramaic Verb in *Halachot Pesuqot*

Research into **HPS** continued with M. Ben-Asher's 1970 articles on its Aramaic verb morphology.[43] As Sokoloff immediately noted, Ben-Asher incorrectly parsed many of his examples and failed to distinguish between the different strata reflected in the work—Talmudic, Geonic, and document formularies—rendering his lists of limited value.[44] Furthermore, Ben-Asher relied upon the printed transcription of the Sassoon manuscript, which contains many transcription errors.[45] Nevertheless, on the basis of the material gathered by Ben-Asher, Malone was able to indicate some similarities between RBA and Mandaic, though on at least one occasion, Ben-Asher's reliance upon the inaccurate transcription led Malone astray.[46]

### 2.6.3 Geniza Studies

In 1973, Morag published another important manuscript study, this time based upon Geniza fragments. In addition to assorted notes on

---

[42] It appears that Morag recorded the vocalization he found while inspecting the original manuscript in a printed copy of the text. Collation of Morag's citations with the facsimile of the manuscript reveals very occasional errors in his transcriptions.

[43] Ben-Asher, "Conjugation."

[44] Sokoloff, "Aramaic Verb." Already with the publication of the second part of Ben-Asher's article, Kutscher appended a critique of those findings.

[45] See the preface to the 1971 reprint (between the Hebrew and English title pages), wherein it is explained that the original 1950 edition was produced during war time, when it had not been possible to send proof sheets to the editor.

[46] Malone, "Observations," and Morgenstern, "Non-Standard Spellings," p. 273.

orthography and phonology, most notably the shift *ə > i and *a > i,[47] Morag discussed the forms of participle plurals attested in a variety of Geniza fragments, particularly those of the III-*yod* verbs. This remains the most comprehensive discussion of the topic. In addition, he determined that the III-*yod* G participle is primarily of the form *miqṭā*, rather than the form *miqṭē* found in printed editions and other Aramaic dialects. Particularly important was his identification of the 1 m.s. G participle אמנא (rather than the printed אמינא) "I say" as characteristic of early manuscripts.[48] The survival of these early forms is also one of the identifying features of the early manuscript type.[49]

## 2.6.4 Boyarin's Contributions

Based partially on material in his unpublished 1972 M.A. thesis, "The Babylonian Aramaic Verb According to Codex Hamburg," Boyarin published a series of short, but incisive, notes on RBA.[50] Among his most important findings was the existence of verbal forms bearing an enclitic prepositional *lamed*. Subsequent research has uncovered further examples, including some in the Aramaic magic bowls.[51] In another article that appeared around the same time, Boyarin claimed that the encliticization of the prepositional *lamed* may explain the loss of final consonants in Babylonian Aramaic by the following process: first, the final consonant assimilated into the *lamed*, which was then separated from the verbal base.[52] Boyarin described the process as follows: (1) *ʾimar* ("I will say") > (2) *ʾimarlik* ("I will say to you") > (3) *ʾimalik* > (4) *ʾima* ("I will say"). This description is problematic in several ways. Quite apart from the vocalization of the preposition לך as *lik*, a reading not supported by the manuscript evidence (unless the 2 f.s. is intended), the intermediate form between stages 2 and 3, which Boyarin would presumably have regarded as *ʾimallik*, is missing. Furthermore, while this reconstruction may in

---

[47] The former shift is uncertain; see below, §3.4.2.2.1. The latter shift was also dealt with by Malone, "Observations," p. 163.

[48] On this form, see in detail below, §3.4.6.3.

[49] See the list below, §2.12.2.

[50] Boyarin, "Studies," and see following notes.

[51] See Boyarin, "Studies," p. 173; Friedman, "Early Manuscripts," p. 14; Kara, *Yemenite Manuscripts*, pp. 47–48 (on which see Boyarin, "Kara," p. 255); Morgenstern, "Geonic Responsa," p. 24. For examples in the magic bowls see Morgenstern, "Moussaieff Collection," p. 362.

[52] Boyarin, "Final Consonants."

theory explain the forms of some verbal roots exhibiting the apocopation of the word-final consonant, the phenomenon is not limited to verbal forms. Boyarin's explanation cannot account for forms such as אדא "Adam," which we find in the magic bowls, nor can it explain the loss of the *nun* in many pronominal forms.[53] Accordingly, it seems preferable to regard the loss of final consonants in this dialect as a phenomenon that is parallel to the assimilation of these consonants, but not caused by it. Both are caused by the weakening of the consonants in the pronunciation. The distribution of these phenomena in Mandaic, Syriac, and Neo-Aramaic differs from their distribution in RBA.

More convincing is Boyarin's important study of RBA phonology.[54] As mentioned above, based upon the vocalization of **HPS**, Morag had noted that in RBA we often find an *a* vowel for historical *$\bar{a}$, e.g., in positions wherein we would expect to find the *miqpaṣ pummā* sign we find the *miptaḥ pummā*. This is the case in both the vocalization of **HPS** and in the Yemenite reading tradition. Morag explained this as resulting from a conditioned shift of *$C\partial CV\#$ > $CaCV\#$ and ascribed the additional examples that do not fall into this category as resulting from analogy.[55] Boyarin accepted Morag's view that in Targum Onqelos we find the phonological distinction of *ä–ɔ* as reflexes of historical *$a$–*$\bar{a}$, but provided an alternative explanation of the distribution of these vowels in **HPS**. In Boyarin's opinion, in RBA both *$a$ and *$\bar{a}$ shifted to a single phoneme which had two allophones, [a] and [ɔ]. The distribution of these two allophones was determined by the phonetic environment in which the vowel appeared. The common reflex is [a], while the [ɔ] allophone (represented by the *miqpaṣ pummā* in the vocalization of **HPS**) was employed primarily in the vicinity of bilabials. Boyarin suggested that the Yemenite reading tradition artificially recreated the phonological distinction between the two vowels. "In my opinion," he wrote, "the most satisfactory explanation of this phenomenon is to assume interference between the liturgical reading tradition of the Targum and that of the Talmud."[56]

Overall, I find Boyarin's assessment compelling. The early vocalized sources appear to indicate that historical *$a$ and *$\bar{a}$ were both generally reflected in RBA as a non-rounded *a* vowel and that, contrary to Morag, who attempted to explain the occurrences of [a] as a reflex of *$\bar{a}$, it is the examples of [ɔ] that require explanation. Where I disagree with Boyarin's

---

[53] See below, §4.4.3 and §4.6.4 Further examples from the magic texts are presented in Morgenstern, "Non-Standard Spellings."

[54] Boyarin, "Reading Traditions;" "Low Vowel System."

[55] Morag, "Phonology," pp. 72–73 (reprinted in Morag, *Studies*, pp. 249–50).

[56] Boyarin, "Reading Traditions," p. 158.

final analysis is in his reconstruction of the array of vocalic phonemes. Boyarin reconstructs five: *i, e, a* ([a]~[ɔ]), *o* and *u*, whereas there is substantial evidence to suggest the existence of phonemic length distinctions between *a* and *ā*. There is also some evidence to suggest that phonemic distinctions may have existed between *e*/*ē* and *u*/*ū*.[57]

The study of RBA fell into a lull in the latter part of the 1970s, picking up again in the early 1980s. In 1980, S. Rybak presented his Yeshiva University thesis, "The Aramaic Dialect of Nedarim." This brief work is primarily an analysis of the textual sources that could be employed to produce a critical edition of the tractate, while much of the linguistic discussion is taken up with the presentation of the various theories regarding the unique idiom it employs. Regrettably, Rybak did not make greater use of his edition to elucidate the nature of this language. Most of the linguistic examples had been previously cited in the available literature, some already by Luzzatto.[58] A comprehensive study of the language of *Nedarim* and the other five tractates that were not studied in the Geonic academies is still a major desideratum, though Breuer's recent study of the language of *Karetot* represents a most significant contribution.[59]

### 2.6.5 Marcus's *Manual*

In 1981, Marcus's teaching grammar, *A Manual of Jewish Babylonian Aramaic*, was published. As Boyarin correctly assessed, while the work represents a laudable attempt to integrate the study of syntax into a teaching grammar of RBA, it is fundamentally flawed by taking as its textual base a corrupted *textus receptus* long after this had been demonstrated to be unreliable.[60] This is surprising, since even Margolis had attempted to integrate manuscript readings into his teaching manual. Furthermore, Marcus's discussions do not take into account the developments in the study of RBA. In particular, the important manuscript studies by Morag are not mentioned.

---

[57] For a discussion of evidence from the Geonic materials in light of other early manuscript sources, see Morgenstern, "Geonic Responsa," pp. 48–54. A detailed account of this issue will be presented in a future study.

[58] For example, the archaic form מקיימיתון (*Ned* 25a) preserving the final *nun*, discussed by Rybak on p. 88, is already mentioned by Luzzatto, *Elementi Grammaticali*, §70.

[59] Breuer, "Karetot."

[60] Boyarin, "Marcus."

## 2.7 Eastern Talmudic Manuscripts

### 2.7.1 Friedman's Study of *Bava Mezia* MS G1

The most significant publication of the early 1980s was a seminal article by Friedman, "Early Manuscripts, "which has unfortunately escaped the attention of many Aramaists. While undertaking a study of early manuscript sources for the Babylonian Talmud tractate *Bava Mezia*, Friedman reconstructed from fragments found in several libraries the remains of a substantial Geniza manuscript, which contained virtually all of the sixth chapter of the tractate, as well as parts of the seventh chapter. Friedman presents the    manuscript under the siglum ג1, and in this book I have referred to it as **G1** (for Geniza 1). The significance of this manuscript lies not only in the fact that it contains an early version of the textual tradition reflected in MS **H165**, but also that its language is of a type that until then was known primarily from Geonic manuscripts such as **HPS**. Friedman effectively demonstrated that many of the characteristics associated with the best Geonic sources (*plene* orthography, phonetic spellings) also appear in early Talmudic manuscripts.[61] Hence the manuscript's textual status (early eastern) rather than its genre/ provenance (Geonic) determines the nature of the language. Since Friedman's study, further Geniza fragments exhibiting these features have been identified.[62]

Friedman's article was not intended to be a comprehensive study of the manuscript's language, though his linguistic discussions are thorough and detailed. During my research I have systematically examined the contents of this manuscript, including those that do not appear in his critical edition of the sixth chapter of *Bava Mezia*,[63] and have cited from it widely in the studies in this volume.

---

[61] I have employed here the term "phonetic spellings" rather than the term "vulgar spellings" (כתיב עממי) employed by Friedman since the term "vulgar" ascribes a sociolinguistic dimension to these spellings that I do not believe they had. The fact that such spellings are to be found in the most accurate manuscripts emanating from the major centers of Jewish learning militates against such an interpretation.

[62] See below. As mentioned in n. 27, the publication history of the Geniza was such that it was primarily "lost" Geonic works that were published from Geniza manuscripts, giving the false impression that the unique language of these texts was somehow Geonic. In fact, in many cases, as Friedman showed, these were merely characteristics of early manuscript sources.

[63] Friedman, *Bava Meziᶜa Text*.

## 2.7.2 Y. Kara's Study of Yemenite Manuscripts

In 1982, Y. Kara completed his dissertation at the Hebrew University, "Babylonian Aramaic in the Yemenite Manuscripts of the Talmud: Orthography, Phonology and Morphology of the Verb." The dissertation was subsequently published in the ʿEdah ve-Lashon series.[64] Kara's study represents groundbreaking research into Babylonian Aramaic, though unfortunately its findings have not always been taken into account in recent scholarly publications.[65] For the first time, an important manuscript corpus, one that differs greatly from the European sources, was subject to detailed linguistic analysis. While the work did not deal with all aspects of the language, Kara's study was the first wide-ranging monograph to be based solely on manuscripts, and thus set a new standard for subsequent research. Furthermore, the dissertation deals with additional phenomena that relate to its main subject matter, and hence covers more topics than its title suggests. For example, the discussion of phonology does not rely solely upon material drawn from the verbal system but also cites examples of nouns and pronouns, while the section on verbal morphemes includes a list of the object pronouns. Occasionally, notes are included on issues relating to syntax, e.g., the structures of the direct object.[66] The examples are generally cited accurately and references are precise, such that the reader may check the material from which Kara draws his conclusions.

On the basis of the material he gathered, Kara was able to show that, as Kutscher and Friedman had suggested, the scope of phenomena such as apocopation of word-final phonemes was much more widespread in the eastern manuscripts than in the later European textual witnesses. Like Friedman's Geniza fragment of *Bava Mezia*, the Yemenite manuscripts retain early phonetic spellings that were often "corrected" in the western manuscripts and printed editions.[67] Numerous rare forms are

---

[64] Kara, *Yemenite Manuscripts*.

[65] Kara's work is not mentioned in valuable works, such as Juusola's *Linguistic Peculiarities* or Levene's *Corpus*. Similarly, Muraoka–Porten, *Grammar*, would have benefited from reference to this work rather than to Morag's *YT*.

[66] Kara, *Yemenite Manuscripts*, p. 323 n. 295. See further my discussion below, Chapter 5.

[67] Here a note of caution may be sounded: many of the unusual forms attested in the Yemenite manuscripts are occasionally found in the European witnesses. See, for example, the discussion of the form אמנא "I say" below, §3.4.6.3. Through the use of the Lieberman Institute's *Database of Talmudic Manuscripts*, it is now possible to locate such forms with relative ease.

preserved, for example תרנולא "cock" (*Yom* 20b [JTS1623]), akin to the form תארנאולא found in Mandaic and now also attested in the magic bowl texts.[68] Through comparisons with other Rabbinic Aramaic works, in particular Geonic writings, and his many cross-references to other scholarly studies, Kara provided an important and systematic discussion of many aspects of RBA phonology and morphology that often extends beyond the evidence of the Yemenite manuscripts. In this book, I have made frequent reference to Kara's work, and only rarely have I found significant omissions or analyses with which I disagree fundamentally.

Nevertheless, several aspects of the work require further consideration. First, we must bear in mind that all the Yemenite manuscripts are from a relatively late period; Kara determined that none of the manuscripts was copied earlier than the seventeenth century. While retaining a large number of rare forms that were lost in the European manuscript traditions (upon which the printed editions were later based), the Yemenite manuscripts are not free of late features and textual corruptions. Indeed, Kara dedicates a paragraph in his book to the subject. However, he does not discuss the degree to which outside textual traditions or other forms of Aramaic may have been influential in creating these corruptions. Recently, A. Amit has suggested that these manuscripts represent a mixed tradition, and that they show the influence of later Talmudic commentators.[69] Accordingly, while the Yemenite manuscripts are undoubtedly unique in preserving many phonetic spellings into a relatively late period, we must weigh their linguistic data against other early sources to assess the degree to which they retain RBA in its pristine form. In chapter 3, some of the aspects in which the Yemenite manuscripts differ from the early eastern text type will be discussed in great detail.

Furthermore, as Kara notes, not all of the Yemenite manuscripts are equally accurate. Kara regards the best manuscript to be MS J, which contains the tractates *Sanhedrin*, *Makkot*, and part of *Ta'anit*. One might have expected that, as the best source, this manuscript would have been cited most frequently in the lists of examples, since its examples would presumably be regarded as the most reliable. Kara preferred to cite a wide range of representative examples from different manuscripts, rather than to treat any one of his sources comprehensively.

It is therefore important to be aware that Kara's "Compendium of extant forms" (pp. 196–353) does not record all the examples found in the manuscripts, even those cited elsewhere in the volume. For example, in

---

[68] See Morgenstern, "Moussaeiff Collection," p. 363.
[69] Amit, "Yemenite Manuscripts."

his discussion on p. 98 of the shift of *$i$ > $a$ before the consonants החעי״ר,
Kara notes that in RBA this shift does not always occur, e.g., in the participle שמיענא "I hear" (*San* 7a [J]). However, this example is not listed on
pp. 204–5, where examples of the G 1 m.s. participles are adduced; indeed, none of the exceptions to the *$i$ > $a$ rule are cited in that list. Moreover, the list in the phonology section is incomplete, as Kara himself indicates.

Since the second half of Kara's work lists only attested *forms* and not
all attested *examples*, the reader is left uncertain regarding the frequency
of the various forms. Sometimes, it is precisely the rare forms that are the
most frequently cited. For example, on p. 161, in his discussion of the
3 f.s. perfect morpheme in the III-*yod* verbs, Kara notes that the classical
form קְטָת is relatively infrequent. However, in the list of examples on p.
281, Kara cites three examples of the קטת form, but only one of the form
קטאי, which is the form most common in RBA sources.

In this particular case, Kara explicitly states that the form קטת is rare,
and in principle, there is no reason to object to this method of listing examples.[70] However, in many cases Kara is less explicit, and the reader
cannot always discern from his list of examples the relative distribution
of each of the forms. For example, regarding the imperative morphemes
Kara states: "In Babylonian Aramaic, the imperative forms for m.s., f.s.
and m.pl. are similar to those current in Classical Aramaic. . . . In the imperative forms of the f.s. and m.pl. the final vowel sometimes drops."[71]
However, the latter two cases are very different. In the 2 f.s., the final *$ī$
vowel is regularly apocopated, and it is the examples preserving the vowel that are exceptional; in the m.pl., the vowel is generally preserved,
and the examples lacking the final vowel are few.[72]

The decision not to record all of the examples has occasionally led to
important evidence being omitted. For example, in *San* 94b, according to
the Yemenite MS J, we read: מהאי לא תסתפאי. אסתפאי מנבוכד נצר שנקרא
אריה "Do not fear this; fear Nebuchadnezzar, who is called a lion." The
verbs לא תסתפאי "do not fear" and אסתפאי "fear (imper.)" are respectively 2 f.s. imperfect and 2 f.s. imperative Gt forms of the root ספי״י. Kara
cites no examples for either of these categories, and Epstein similarly
omitted them from his *Grammar*. On the basis of the printed editions, the

---

[70] Such an approach was adopted, for example, by Bergsträsser, who in his Biblical Hebrew grammar cited predominantly forms that are exceptions to the rule.

[71] צורות הציווי לנוכח, לנוכחת ולנוכחים, בארמית הבבלית, דומות לאלה הנוהגות בארמית
הקלאסית . . . בצורות הציווי לנוכחת ולנוכחים נושלת, לעיתים, התנועה הסופית, Kara,
*Yemenite Manuscripts*, p. 152.

[72] See §3.4.3.3.

forms from *Sanhedrin* are cited in Rosenberg, *Das aramäische Verbum*, pp. 51–52, without vocalization as תסתפי and איסתפי, while in Levias, *Grammar*, p. 151, they are vocalized respectively תִּסְתָּפִי and אֶסְתָּפִי, with an unexplained *qamaṣ* after the *taw* and a final *ī* vowel which is contradicted by the *plene* spelling of the Yemenite manuscript. In Levias, *Diqduq*, pp. 187–88, the *qamaṣ* has been replaced by a *shewa*: אֶסְתְּפִי, תִּסְתְּפִי.

Can the *plene* spelling of the Yemenite manuscript be explained and regarded as providing new linguistic data previously unrecorded for our dialect? Let us begin with the imperfect form. In most of the dialects, we find examples based upon the pattern *tiqṭayn*. In Palestinian Aramaic, we find the *kethubba* formula תִּשְׁתְּבַיִין "you (f.s.) will be taken captive" (m. *Ket* 4:8 [MS Kaufmann]) and תחטיי "you will sin,"[73] while in TOJ we find תתנשׁין "you will forget" (Isa 54:4), with shift of *ayn* > *ān*.[74] In Classical Syriac, the form is ܐܠܗܝܢ with a shift of *ay* > *ē*.[75] The form is not recorded for Classical Mandaic.[76] תסתפאי would thus accord with the findings of other Aramaic dialects, being derived from an older form *tistap̄ayn* with the loss of the word-final *nun*. Evidence for the unapocopated form is widespread in the Aramaic magic bowls, e.g., תיתחזין "[do not] appear" (**AIT** 18:9), תידמין "[do not] appear" (**ZHS** 10:4).[77] We may also compare the D form found in a magic bowl formula, תשנאי "you (f.s.) will change" (**MS** 1927/11:5).

The imperative form is less well attested in the Aramaic dialects. In TOJ, we find אתדראָ "take rebuke" (Jer 6:8),[78] while in classical Syriac the form is ܐܠܗܝܢ.[79] Nöldeke records one example from Mandaic,

---

[73] Kutscher, *SGA*, p. 46.

[74] Dalman, *Grammatik*, §72.10 (p. 346); Garr, "Targum Onkelos," p. 717 n. 40; and cf. below, §4.5.4.4.

[75] Nöldeke, *SG*, §176.

[76] Macuch, *Handbook*, §226.γ.c. records examples such as **ti(ti)ksia** as "3f., 2m. & f." However, these examples appear to be drawn from Nöldeke's *MG*, wherein only masculine forms are recorded for the 2 s. A computer search of the Mandaic *Ginza* has not found this verb in 2 f.s.

[77] The example from Montgomery, *AIT* 18 is already noted in Juusola, *Linguistic Peculiarities*, p. 175; see also his discussion on pp. 188–89. Note that this evidence contradicts that of the Yemenite reading tradition, and accordingly, contra Juusola, I interpret these spellings as reflecting respectively *tiṯḥazayn* and *tiddammayn*.

[78] Dalman, *Grammatik*, p. 348, records a final *miqpaṣ pummā* vowel, which he suggests reading as a *mip̄taḥ pummā*. However, Dalman's suggested emendation is found in the manuscripts; see Sperber's edition, ad loc.

[79] Nöldeke, *SG*, §176.

ᶜtyklᵓy "werde zurückgehalten."[80] In all these dialects, the f.s. imperative endings are identical in all verbal stems; for example, Classical Syriac has the forms for G: ܙܘܽܟ, D ܙܶܟ, Dt ܐܶܙܕܟ, C: ܐܰܙܟ. Since in RBA, the f.s. imperative of the III-*yod* G is קטאי,[81] we may assume that the f.s. imperative of the Gt would be אי(ת)קטא. The example in the Yemenite manuscript is thus consistent both with the internal Babylonian Aramaic evidence and with the evidence of the other dialects.

As this example indicates, while Kara's lists are comprehensive, they are not exhaustive. My own experience is that one can only really identify the linguistically significant phenomena when all the available evidence is gathered. Accordingly, in my own work I have striven to collect as complete a set of data as possible. I have recorded representative examples rather than comprehensive listings only in those cases for which the evidence is so overwhelming that additional examples add nothing to the research, e.g., 3 m.s. G perfect forms such as כְּתַב.[82] By contrast, I record all forms of the 3 m.pl., כְּתַבוּ (very rarely also *plene* כתאבו), כְּתוּב, and apocopated כְּתַב, since only by recording all forms can we hope to assess the distribution of these forms, even if their attestation in the dialect has already been proven.

Kara dedicates considerable attention to the vocalized forms attested in the manuscripts, which are of benefit in understanding the history of the Yemenite pronunciation tradition. However, occasionally, this emphasis on the vocalized forms may be misleading. For example, in his lists of the G participle forms, Kara cites predominantly forms in which the long *ā* is not marked by a *mater lectionis*, i.e., קטיל rather than קאטיל. This would place the manuscripts closer to the orthographic practice of **HPS** than to the later Geonim, R. Sharrira and R. Hai, who preferred the *plene* spelling. (Neither group employs one of the spellings exclusively.) In fact, my impression of the manuscripts themselves is that the *plene* spellings are actually preferred, which explains the predominance of defective spellings amongst the vocalized forms: it is precisely those exceptional forms that required vocalization.[83] Clearly, not all vocalized forms

---

[80] Nöldeke, *MG*, §193.

[81] See in detail §3.4.3.2.

[82] The ideal situation would be to have at our disposal grammatically tagged databases in which all attested forms could be immediately recalled.

[83] The same phenomenon is found in partially vocalized Geonic manuscripts. For example, the G infinitive forms of I-ᵓ*aleph* verbs are generally spelled without the historical ᵓ*aleph*, e.g., למימר "to say" (*Ket* 85a [**HPS** 114:23]) or למיכליה "to eat it" (**HPS** 50:11). In the sporadically vocalized manuscripts, i.e., those in which vocalization is not a regular feature, I have found only two vocalized examples:

in sporadically vocalized manuscripts are necessarily exceptional in some way; however, by focusing predominantly on vocalized forms, the researcher is in danger of presenting a misleading picture of the norm, since unusual or "different" forms are more likely to be vocalized in these manuscripts than common ones.

Kara's analysis of the verb forms is generally sound, and I have found few errors.[84] Nevertheless, it does seem that on occasion, the contemporary Yemenite reading tradition has influenced his work. For example, he analyses the irregular and fossilized form איכפת as a Gt 3 m.s. perfect, in the face of evidence that it is a 3 f.s. from the root אכף, perhaps borrowed from another dialect.[85] Similarly, passive forms of I-*nun* roots which are presumably Ct are recorded as Gt, since in the Yemenite reading tradition they have merged with the latter category. For example, איתזק "he was harmed" (*Pes* 110a [JTS1623, 1608]) is read in the Yemenite tradition as אִיתְּזַק (*Pes* 110a ['Amr]) with a geminated *taw*, as though with the regressive assimilation of the *nun*. Morag noted that, in effect, the Yemenite reading tradition preserves *no* examples of the Ct in the I-*nun* category.[86] Kara's lists similarly contain none from the Yemenite manuscripts, even though such examples are found in the manuscripts.

The discussions do not always distinguish between the diachronic and synchronic aspects of the study. This is particularly marked in the section on phonology, wherein it is unclear what Kara regards as being the synchronic array of phonemes in RBA, while sound changes are in most cases recorded under the individual phoneme rather than as a specific phonetic process such as assimilation, dissimilation, metathesis or the like.[87] Boyarin already noted in his perceptive review that Kara's analysis leaves unanswered many issues in RBA phonology which have morphological implications, for example, the possible merging of historical III-ʿ*ayin* with historical III-ʾ*aleph*/*waw*/*yod* (this latter group had al-

---

למֵאכליה "to eat it" (**Hark** 190:33); למֹאימרֹה "to say it" (**TGAs28** i 4a 11). It is significant that both examples stray from the orthographic norms of the dialect. The scribes or copyists clearly felt that the forms were sufficiently unfamiliar to warrant vocalization, even though such vocalization is rare in both manuscripts. I have not included the examples from **HPS** and **HGP**, which contain vocalization of numerous words irrespective of their rareness or peculiar form.

[84] I have noted a few such errors in the following chapters.

[85] See Sokoloff, *DJBA*, p. 132 s.v. 1# אכף.

[86] Morag, *YT*, p. 188 and n. 25.

[87] Notable exceptions are the discussions of the "Loss of Final Consonants" (pp. 86–92) and "Dropping of Final Vowels" (p. 121).

ready merged in RBA).[88] Similarly, Kara's study does not clearly distinguish between what he regards as inherited features and "living" features of the dialect.

Nonetheless, Kara's book represents a major contribution to the study of RBA. He correctly identifies and explains numerous features that had not previously been recorded in the scholarly literature. For example, Kara noted that indirect object forms such as ניה ליה were sometimes affixed to the verb. As well as presenting examples from the Yemenite manuscripts, Kara also pointed to the form from **HPS**, הביניה לי "give it to me" (*Qid* 13a [**HPS** 167:2]).[89] Further study of the manuscript has revealed additional examples. In numerous cases, subsequent manuscript studies have confirmed Kara's findings.[90]

## 2.8 The Reliability of the Yemenite Reading Tradition

### 2.8.1 Kara's Studies

During his work on the Yemenite manuscripts, Kara considered the nature of the Yemenite reading tradition and its relationship to those manuscripts. In a lecture delivered in 1973, but published in 1980, Kara drew attention to the differences between the Yemenite reading tradition of the Talmud and his findings in the Yemenite manuscripts.[91] For example, while the reading tradition contains III-*yod* G participle forms such as קָטוּ, the *plene* orthography קאטו of the manuscripts clearly indicates an *a* vowel.[92] Kara convincingly ascribed these changes to the adoption within Yemen of the printed editions, wherein such *plene* spellings are extremely rare.[93] Kara's monograph similarly contains occasional notes regarding differences between the manuscripts and the reading tradition, though in that volume he did not systematically gather the examples or discuss their significance. I will return to this issue in the next chapter.

---

[88] Boyarin, "Kara." See further §3.3.1.1.2.

[89] Kara, *Yemenite Manuscripts*, p. 50.

[90] See below, §3.5.2.3.2.

[91] Kara, "Preservation."

[92] In my reconstruction of RBA phonology, an *ā* vowel.

[93] A notable exception is the form שאני *šāne* "it is different," which is regularly printed with the *ʾaleph*. It is not clear why this *plene* spelling survived while others were expunged.

## 2.8.2 Morag's *Babylonian Aramaic: The Yemenite Tradition*

The reliability of the Yemenite reading tradition is an essential issue because, to date, one of the most substantial academic publications on RBA remains S. Morag's 1988 volume, *Babylonian Aramaic: The Yemenite Tradition: Historical Aspects and Transmission, Phonology, the Verbal System*. Morag's authority has contributed to the popular impression that this work provides a reliable source for information about RBA of the Talmudic period. Morag himself concluded that "the Yemenite tradition may serve as an important source for the study and reconstruction of the Aramaic idiom of the Babylonian Talmud,"[94] and echoes of his methodology may be found in recent linguistic studies such as Juusola's *Linguistic Peculiarities in the Aramaic Magic Bowl Texts* and Muraoka and Porten's *Grammar of Egyptian Aramaic*.[95]

## 2.8.3 Doubts about the Yemenite Reading Tradition

Nevertheless, many questions remain concerning the value of the Yemenite tradition. In his 1992 review of Morag's volume, Kaufman cast some doubt on the reliability of the tradition. Kaufman's comments will be taken up in the next chapter. Kaufman was not alone in questioning the degree of this tradition's reliability. Based on S. Abramson's 1990 publication of surviving fragments of R. Shemuel b. Ḥofni Gaon's medieval treatise, *An Introduction to the Science of the Mishna and Talmud*,[96] M. Assis drew attention to the valuable and explicit linguistic testimony that the work contains.[97] In passing, Assis also noted that the Gaon's evidence often contradicts the Yemenite reading tradition.

## 2.9 Talmudic Manuscript Groups

## 2.9.1 The Significance of the Issue

One of the issues that has been clarified by both Friedman's and Kara's work is the importance of textual type. From the time that the Babylonian Talmud was committed to writing, it was transmitted and copied predominantly by scribes and copyists who were not speakers of Ara-

---

[94] Morag, *YT*, p. vii of English abstract.
[95] The latter publication is particularly emphatic about defending Morag's approach. See p. 371 of the second edition, especially the note on p. 140 n. 659.
[96] Abramson, **LPT**.
[97] Assis, "Linguistic Aspects."

maic. The accuracy of the manuscripts' transmission thus depended, among other things, upon these copyists' familiarity with the particularities of the Babylonian Aramaic idiom. In a process not entirely clear to us, different local recensions of the text emerged, in terms of both content and language. Occasionally, a single manuscript might even demonstrate a merger of different textual traditions, as Friedman indicated is the case with the Spanish MS of ʿAvoda Zara, JTS Rab15.[98]

## 2.9.2 Morag's Proposal

In a 1993 article, Morag attempted to address these issues by suggesting that the Talmud as preserved in the Yemenite tradition—both written and oral—more closely reflects the spoken and written language of Geonic Babylonia than the language in which other textual witnesses were written.[99] The details of Morag's proposal will be discussed in chapter 4, where I shall argue that this claim is not supported by the surviving textual evidence: the scribal practices that he regarded as unique to the Yemenite manuscripts are in fact common to early eastern manuscripts in general. However, what is significant is his suggestion that the differences between the various textual witnesses stem not from the process of transmission, but rather from the original encoding of the text in writing.

## 2.9.3 Friedman's Proposal

A prerequisite to determining the nature of textual transmission is identifying characteristic linguistic features of the manuscripts and gathering them into groups. Building upon his previous studies, Friedman has sought to trace the transmission history of the Talmudic text, initially, in a brief article dealing with two phenomena, and, subsequently, in a more comprehensive study.[100] Friedman suggested that the extant Talmudic manuscripts may be divided into groups according to a typology of their orthography. Friedman discerned four groups of manuscripts, Ashkenazic, Sephardic, Yemenite and "Mediterranean," each of which can be defined by certain orthographic features. The grouping of these manuscripts by type is an essential undertaking for understanding the transmission of the text and language of the Talmud in the Middle Ages. For our purposes, the issue is a critical one. Depending upon which group of

---

[98] Friedman, "Avodah Zara."
[99] Morag, "Oral Transmission."
[100] Friedman, "Typology."

manuscripts one chooses to study, the description of the grammar of RBA will differ significantly. It is not an exaggeration to claim that if we compare the language of the most accurate Geniza fragments to that of the printed editions of the Talmud we are dealing with two distinct "grammars."

Among Friedman's most important conclusions, we may highlight the following. First, he emphasized that the Spanish manuscript tradition was not, as had often been suggested, an accurate conduit for the Babylonian Talmud text, but shows clear indications of secondary linguistic editing. Furthermore, his investigations uncovered a fourth linguistic type, the "Mediterranean" text, which combines aspects of the various textual types, and appears to indicate a "Palestinian" role in the transmission of the Babylonian Talmud in Europe. Friedman also suggested that certain features common to the Mediterranean and Yemenite manuscripts might point to the preservation of authentic Babylonian forms that were edited out of the standardized Spanish tradition.[101]

Many points of Friedman's reasoning are compelling, particularly with regard to the more complete Talmudic manuscripts. However, Friedman's other publications and my own study of Geniza fragments and other early manuscript sources suggest that an important textual group remains unmentioned here: the Early Eastern Manuscripts (EEMss) of the type reflected in **HPS** and in several important Geniza manuscripts such as those that Friedman himself identified. The characteristics of this group will be discussed in greater detail below. I maintain that only this manuscript group reflects the Babylonian tradition of the Talmudic text before it underwent secondary editing in North Africa and was then transmitted to Europe (Spain and Ashkenaz).[102]

Furthermore, we must not rule out the possibility of mutual influence between the various textual traditions. In particular, recent research into the textual traditions of Yemen should militate against relying too much upon spellings common to the Yemenite and European traditions.[103] If these are also found in the EEMss group, then they may be regarded as authentic; otherwise, they may reflect influence of the European text upon the Yemenite manuscripts.

The use of synoptic editions often provides one of the most efficient methods of comparing the manuscript traditions and tracing their devel-

---

[101] Friedman, "Typology 2," p. 181.

[102] We may hypothesize that had a Babylonian Geniza been discovered, rather than the Cairo Geniza, we may have had many more manuscripts of this nature at our disposal.

[103] See particularly Amit, "Yemenite Manuscripts."

opment. Friedman was one of the pioneers of this type of Talmudic research, and has directed his students toward similar projects. These editions have the advantage of providing the reader with an immediate overview of all the textual sources for any given passage, and the linguistically trained reader can immediately identify significant forms and their development through the textual sources. On the basis of such editions, one can also follow any single textual witness and examine its linguistic consistency in comparison to other sources.[104]

## 2.9.4 The Language of Geonic Responsa

In my 2002 doctoral thesis on the language of the Geonic responsa preserved in early manuscript sources, I tried to establish the nature of the Aramaic language employed by the Geonim, both in their independent writings and in their Talmudic citations.[105] To this end, it was necessary to reread the manuscripts of the majority of early sources, not all of which had been published in accurate editions. Within the corpus of the responsa, it was possible to discern four registers that the Babylonian Geonim employed in their writing: the Talmudic idiom (in citations), an informal style employed for legal discourse, a formal style employed in legal pronouncements, and a highly formal style used only in the introductions of collections of responsa. In addition, Aramaic prayers and legal formularies employ their own archaic language.[106] These findings dispel some of the myths about the Geonic idiom that have entered scholarly literature, wherein certain grammatical forms have been declared "Geonic." Close examination of the Geonic sources reveals a more multifaceted and complex linguistic state in the Geonic period, showing considerable variation.

## 2.9.5 Ongoing Manuscript Research

Since completing that work, I have significantly widened my corpus to include the Sassoon manuscript of *Halachot Pesuqot* and additional early

---

[104] The advantages of synoptic editions have been outlined in Friedman, "Variant Readings."

[105] Morgenstern, "Geonic Responsa."

[106] The multileveled nature of Geonic language was already noted in several places in Sokoloff, "Aramaic Verb."

Talmudic sources.[107] All of this material has been analyzed and arranged according to grammatical categories and topics, with the intention that it may serve as the basis for an up-to-date and comprehensive grammar of Babylonian Aramaic based upon early manuscript sources. However, as mentioned, before such a grammar can be written, fundamental decisions must be made regarding the scope of the corpus and the nature of the manuscripts that it will include. In one way or another, the studies in this volume address these essential methodological questions.

## 2.10 Some Recent Publications

### 2.10.1 M. Sokoloff's *Dictionary of Jewish Babylonian Aramaic*

By far the most significant recent publication on the dialect is M. Sokoloff's *Dictionary of Jewish Babylonian Aramaic*. Sokoloff's reliance upon the best available textual witnesses and the scope of his corpus have enabled him to significantly advance the lexical study of RBA.[108] Furthermore, while not a systematic grammar, the material recorded on the basis of the best manuscripts may be exploited for this purpose. The appearance of this dictionary contributed considerably to the present work.

Nevertheless, the material in the dictionary may be exploited for grammatical purposes only when bearing the following issue in mind. The requirement that the dictionary include all the lexical material of available sources has sometimes forced Sokoloff to rely upon late sources which do not always reflect the dialect in its pristine state. I shall illustrate this point with a single example, though others could be adduced. For the plural of דוכתא "place," the early sources are unanimous in employing the forms דוכאתא (*dūḵātā* or *dukkātā*) or (rarely) דוכואתא (*dūḵəwātā* or *dukkəwātā*). These forms are duly recorded in the dictionary, but the dictionary also lists an alternative form, דוכתי.[109] However, this is found only in the secondary "Spanish" recension of R. Sharrira's Epistle, and reflects a medieval usage common in Rabbinic parlance from Rashi's commentary onward.[110] The form דוכתי would thus appear to belong to

---

[107] These sources are cited according to their published editions, though all have been examined in the original or in facsimiles.

[108] Not since Epstein's publications has such a momentous lexical study of Jewish Babylonian Aramaic appeared.

[109] Sokoloff, *DJBA*, p. 318 s.v. דוכתא.

[110] In the Lieberman database, I have found only four examples of דוכתי in the Talmudic textual witnesses. Two are from the early Soncino printed edition: *Shab* 152b (wherein the other textual witnesses read בדוכתיה "in his place") and *BM*

the medieval European level of this recension rather than to the original Babylonian Aramaic.[111] The grammarian wishing to draw material from the dictionary must be aware of the varying quality of the sources upon which the author was required to depend.[112] It is also possible that further manuscript discoveries and improved readings of the magic bowls will require the revision of several entries.[113]

## 2.11 Babylonian Aramaic Magic Texts

Almost entirely separate from the study of Talmudic sources, the past twenty years have seen a major upsurge in the publication of Aramaic magic bowls. As mentioned above, C. Gordon published numerous magic bowls in the first half of the twentieth century, while the postwar era saw only sporadic publications of new texts. Since the 1980s, however, there have appeared no fewer than six important books on this subject, which I shall briefly summarize here.

### 2.11.1 J. Naveh and S. Shaked's Corpora

The first is the 1985 volume by J. Naveh and S. Shaked, *Amulets and Magic Bowls*. This represented the first substantial corpus of such texts in almost twenty years,[114] and set a new standard for their publication. The volume was followed by a second volume, *Magic Spells and Formulae*, published in 1993.

---

101b (wherein the other textual witnesses read דוכתא). One example appears in MS O366 of *MQ* 16b (the other witnesses read דוכתא) and one MS M95 of *San* 92b (apparently a textual error for the place name רבתי, found in the other textual witnesses). None of these readings is a plural form.

[111] See Epstein, *Amoraim*, pp. 610–15, and, more recently, Brody, *Geonim*, pp. 21–22.

[112] Cf. also Friedman, "Akiva Legend," p. 93 n. 124, who notes the problems of presenting a text according to a single "best manuscript."

[113] Müller-Kessler, *ZHS*, includes numerous suggested corrections. I have suggested several others in my studies of the magic corpus.

[114] The previous book to be published, McCullough's *Incantation Bowls*, contained many errors.

## 2.11.2 H. Juusola's *Linguistic Peculiarities*

In 1999, H. Juusola published his Ph.D. dissertation, "Linguistic Peculiarities in the Aramaic Magic Bowl Texts." Juusola's corpus comprised the then-published materials, while his study covers various aspects of phonology and morphology, particularly regarding the pronouns and verbal suffixes. Juusola's discussions are often enlightening, and his work shows familiarity with some recent works on Babylonian Aramaic published in Hebrew. Particularly important is the attempt to integrate what was known of RBA with the evidence of the magic corpus.

Some aspects of Juusola's works require reconsideration in light of several factors. Juusola did not take full account of the most recent developments in the study of the Talmudic text and language. He mentions neither Friedman's article on the early manuscripts of *Bava Mezia* nor Kara's dissertation on the Yemenite manuscripts. By contrast, he often refers to Morag's volume on the Yemenite reading tradition of the Talmud. As a result, the discussions are occasionally based upon incomplete evidence from Talmudic manuscripts, or upon the assumption that the Yemenite reading tradition provides an accurate picture of the Aramaic of the Babylonian Talmud. Moreover, Juusola's corpus is restricted to then-published materials alone, and now needs to be updated in light of the dozens of magic bowls subsequently published.[115] More serious issues are raised by the question of the dialects employed by these texts, particularly in light of the observations by Müller-Kessler regarding the standard literary language current in Babylonia.[116]

## 2.11.3 J. B. Segal's *Catalogue*

The fourth book is J. B. Segal's *Catalogue of the Aramaic and Mandaic Incantation Bowls in the British Museum* (2000), which, theoretically, should have represented a major step forward in the study of incantation bowls, since the volume was intended to be a comprehensive edition of one of the major collections of these texts. Regrettably, the quality of the editions in the volume is on the whole very poor, and it appears that Segal lacked sufficient interest in or understanding of the material he was edit-

---

[115] Similarly Müller-Kessler, "Targum Onqelos," p. 187. However, Juusola's monograph is of greater value than Müller-Kessler credits.

[116] Müller-Kessler, "Targum Onqelos," passim.

ing.[117] Nonetheless, Segal's volume contains important photographs, and some of his readings are worthy of serious consideration.[118] Segal's edition of one text, 049A in his catalog, was preempted by an edition by Müller-Kessler and Kwasman, published under the thought-provoking title "A Unique Talmudic Aramaic Incantation Bowl."[119] According to these authors, this is the only Aramaic magic bowl published to date to be written in the dialect of the Babylonian Talmud.[120]

### 2.11.4 D. Levene's *Corpus*

Shortly after the appearance of Segal's *Catalogue*, D. Levene's *A Corpus of Magic Bowls: Incantation Texts in Jewish Aramaic from Late Antiquity* (2003) was published, containing some twenty new texts along with several parallels from the Schøyen collection. Levene's readings are generally accurate, though he did not always take into account the most up-to-date linguistic studies. In a recently published article, I have sought to advance the study of these texts by considering them in light of current research into Jewish Babylonian Aramaic.[121]

### 2.11.5 C. Müller-Kessler's *Zauberschalentexte*

The most recent volume of Aramaic magic texts is C. Müller-Kessler's *Die Zauberschalentexte in der Hilprecht-Sammlung, Jena, und weitere Nippur-Texte anderer Sammlungen* (2005). While most of the magic formulae in this collection have already been published on the basis of parallel bowls, Müller-Kessler takes the opportunity to correct the readings of her predecessors and to republish some of the previously known texts on the basis of her own collations. However, her tendency to emend the

---

[117] The book has been almost universally criticized by the reviewers. See, e.g., Müller-Kessler, "Die Zauberschalensammlung;" Ford, "Mandaic Incantation Bowls;" Morgenstern, "Segal."

[118] See my comments in Morgenstern, "BM 91767."

[119] I have reedited this text in my article "Magic Bowl," wherein a considerably different reading and interpretation is presented. See further Geller, "Tablets," pp. 57–61.

[120] Further unpublished bowls are written in a similar idiom. In particular, JNF 160, which Dr. James Ford is preparing for publication, is very close in its language to the Talmudic language as preserved in the EEMss.

[121] Morgenstern, "Moussaieff Collection."

transcriptions to accord with an assumed Urtext and overreaching "corrections" occasionally mar the work.[122]

## 2.11.6 Ongoing Research

Research continues into the Aramaic magic bowls. Hundreds of unedited bowls need to be published, while in many cases the published materials need to be collated and reedited. The particular challenges involved in publishing these texts, most notably the difficulties of the material reading, shape the nature of research in this field. The newly available sources permit a process of constant revision to the readings of previously published texts, particularly in places where those texts are either damaged or partially illegible. Nevertheless, as I have mentioned, a degree of caution must be sounded over emending the texts on the basis of parallels in order to make them conform to some ideal type—linguistic or textual, attested or imagined.

## 2.12 Characteristics of the Early Eastern Manuscripts

### 2.12.1 Identifying and Editing Talmud Manuscripts

Similarly, work on identifying and editing early Talmudic manuscripts continues. The forthcoming catalogue of Talmudic materials from the Cairo Geniza should significantly advance the manuscript study of RBA sources.[123] Meanwhile, other research projects are in progress, and it is to be hoped that these will further clarify the textual status of the remaining Talmudic and post-Talmudic sources, particularly as reflected in early manuscripts. The scope of this work is considerable. For example, Golinkin's facsimile edition of the surviving Geniza manuscripts of *Rosh Hashana* contains sixty-eight fragments drawn from some twenty-three manuscripts.[124] Similarly, Danzig lists twenty-two Geniza manuscripts of *Halachot Pesuqot*.[125] Shweka has identified around four hundred fragments of *Halachot Gedolot* surviving in the Geniza, of which about fifty percent are single sheets. In total, he estimates that the remains of about a hundred manuscripts of this work survive in the Geniza.[126]

---

[122] See my remarks in Morgenstern, "ZHS."

[123] The catalog is being prepared under the editorship of Prof. Yaᶜakov Sussmann.

[124] Golinkin, *Ginzei Rosh Hashana*. Prof. Sussmann informs me that he has since discovered more fragments.

[125] Danzig, *Introduction*, pp. 625–36.

[126] Shweka, "Studies," pp. 30–31.

In theory, all such sources may contribute to the study of the dialect. In practice, however, not all of these manuscripts are of equal value. Even within the corpus of the Geniza fragments, one finds typologically different texts ranging from the early eastern type, through Sephardic manuscripts, to later Ashkenazic manuscripts. My initial survey of the *Rosh Hashana* manuscripts suggested that number 5 in Golinkin's catalog stood out as particularly accurate. I subsequently discovered that in his unpublished doctoral thesis, Golinkin himself had noted this manuscript as particularly important on textual (rather than linguistic) grounds.[127] For this reason, synoptic editions are particularly helpful, since they allow the reader to peruse all the manuscript evidence for any given word or passage. My experience shows that through the use of synoptic editions, one can quickly identify the linguistically superior textual witnesses.

Above, reference has been made to some of the methodological issues involved in this study. Our identification of the most reliable manuscripts is based partially on the language, yet, at the same time, our description of the language depends entirely upon the corpus we choose to describe. The danger always exists that we are deluding ourselves with a circular argument: we define the best manuscripts on the basis of their language, but then determine the nature of Babylonian Aramaic on the basis of the manuscript corpus we have selected, rejecting manuscripts that do not accord to this ideal. While aware of this danger, I nevertheless believe that the initial groundwork has already been accomplished and that we now have sufficient criteria to make possible the identification of the best textual witnesses, at least in terms of language.[128] Many of these features are supported by the linguistic evidence of the magic bowls, which represent primary textual witnesses to Jewish Babylonian Aramaic, though not necessarily to RBA.[129] Other features are supported by internal evidence, i.e., their consistent use in the best textual witnesses.

---

[127] Golinkin, "*Rosh Hashana.*"

[128] On the distinction between linguistic accuracy and textual primacy, see Breuer, "Sabato," and see my comments in the introduction, above.

[129] Much of this material is discussed in Morgenstern, "Moussaieff Collection" and "Non-Standard Spellings."

## 2.12.2 Characteristics of the EEMss

Here I shall briefly describe the characteristics of the best manuscripts, as determined by previous researchers and by my own findings. Many of these topics will be discussed in greater detail later in this book. The purpose of gathering them together here is to give a wider perspective on the nature of the EEMss, and also to aid future researchers in identifying such sources:

### 2.12.2.1 Orthography and Phonology

Widespread use of phonetic orthography, characterized by:[130]

- *plene* spellings with medial *ʾaleph* for long *ā*, particularly to distinguish f.s. from f.pl. nouns, e.g., מתנאתא "prebends" and in 3 m.s. G participles of III-*yod*, e.g., קאנו "they acquire";[131]
- *plene* spellings with medial *yod* after prefixed prepositions ב, כ, ל and מ, e.g., לימחר "the next day," מישום "because of," כינחשא "like bronze";
- tendency of כיד "as" to be written as a separate word, e.g., כיד אמרי "as they say";[132]
- by contrast, non-final *ay* diphthong written with a single *yod*, e.g., ריחיהו "their scent";[133]
- non-historical spellings of the pharyngeals and laryngeals, apparently reflecting sound change, e.g., אקרה "he uprooted it," מהוזא "[the city] Maḥoza";[134]
- widespread apocopation of word-final vowels and of consonants בדלמנר״ית, e.g., דיאבא "ex post facto," שקי "he takes";[135]
- shift of final אי- (*āʾē*) to איי- (*āyē*), e.g., תנאיי "Tannaim";[136]

---

[130] The bibliographical references that follow are not exhaustive, nor do they necessarily credit the first researcher to discuss these phenomena. They are intended to direct the reader to sources wherein up-to-date discussions and more comprehensive bibliography may be found.

[131] Morgenstern, "Geonic Responsa," pp. 23, 27–31, with previous literature.

[132] Friedman, "Ancient Scroll," p. 28; Shremer, "Lishana Ahrina," p. 121; Lerner, "Sheeltot," p. 164.

[133] Kara, *Yemenite Manuscripts*, pp. 32–33; Morgenstern, "Geonic Responsa," p. 40.

[134] See in detail §§3.3.1, 4.4.1.

[135] §§4.4.3, 4.7.4.

[136] Breuer, "Karetot," p. 31; Morgenstern, "Noun Patterns," p. 76.

- appearance of anaptyctic vowels, e.g., למיקיבריה "to bury him," איפירעיה "I shall pay him";[137]
- assimilation of third radical *lamed* or *resh* to 1 m.s. pronoun in G participles, e.g., אזינא "I go";[138]
- preservation of short theme vowels before suffixed 1 c.pl., 3 pl. pronouns, e.g., קבילינהו "he accepted them";[139]
- occasional suffixing of prepositional *lamed* with pronoun to verbal stems, e.g., מסייליה "it supports him";[140]
- use of the numeral ארבעי "four" (f.s.);[141]
- use of the conditional particle או "if" rather than אי;[142]
- rare phonetic spellings such as בען "we require,"[143] יהכי "if so,"[144] etc. Verbal auxiliary קא is written as a separate word.

### 2.12.2.2 Grammatical Accuracy and Consistency

- Preservation of final ה- as 3 f.s. pronoun, particularly in verb forms such as תיסברה "Do you hold this opinion?" and גופה "itself";[145]
- agreement of masculine and feminine, particularly in cases of feminine plural;[146]
- preservation of the distinct 1 f.s. participle, and distinct f.pl. pronouns;[147]
- II-*waw/yod* C formed on pattern of I-*waw/yod*, hence always אותיב "he responded" מותיבי "they respond,"

---

[137] §3.3.2.

[138] §3.4.6.2.

[139] §3.5.2.5.

[140] Morgenstern, "Mandaic."

[141] §3.3.1.1.3.

[142] Friedman, "Early Manuscripts," p. 16; Morgenstern, "Geonic Responsa," p. 71.

[143] §3.3.1.1.2.

[144] Kara, *Yemenite Manuscripts*, p. 45; Shremer, "Lishana Aharina," p. 121; Morgenstern, "Geonic Responsa," p. 58; Breuer, "Karetot," p. 32.

[145] Wajsberg, "Principles," p. 339; Breuer, "Karetot," p. 30; and see in this book §4.6.3.1.

[146] Kutscher, "Review," p. 174 (reprinted in Kutscher, *Studies*, p. 252).

[147] Ibid.

rather than איתיב "he responded," מיתיבי "they respond";[148]

- use of הולכך "therefore" rather than הילכך[149] and of סופה
  "its end" rather than סיפא;[150]
- use of למיקטא rather than למיקטי in III-*yod* G infinitive,[151] and לאיתויי rather than לאתויי in C infinitive of
  את״י;[152]
- lack of confusion between *waw* and *yod;*
- accurate preservation of rare words and loan words.[153]

### 2.12.2.3 Preservation of Babylonian Hebrew Forms

The Babylonian tradition of both Biblical and Rabbinic Hebrew differs
from the Palestinian/Tiberian tradition. The better manuscripts preserve
Babylonian Hebrew in its more pristine form.[154] For example, the spelling אילא is characteristic of early Babylonian manuscripts in both Hebrew and Aramaic contexts.[155]

### 2.12.2.4 Syntax

- consistent use of verbal tenses;

---

[148] Friedman, "Early Manuscripts," p. 16; Shremer, "Lishana Aharina," p. 121;
Morgenstern, "Geonic Responsa," pp. 280–82.

[149] The earlier manuscripts appear to favor הולכך. See Kutscher, "Review," p. 176
(reprinted in Kutscher, *Studies*, p. 254). Breuer, "Karetot," p. 14, has proposed that
both forms may be regarded as original. Cf. also Breuer, *Hebrew*, pp. 91–92.

[150] Kutscher, "Review," p. 175 (reprinted in Kutscher, *Studies*, p. 253); Shremer,
"Lishana Aharina," p. 120; Friedman, "Typology 2," pp. 176–77. Contra Fried-
man, I have found little evidence for the form סיפא/סיפה with a *yod* in the EEMss.
In fact, I found only one example of סיפה "its end" (*San* 23b [**Hark** 33:35]) in the
EEMss. This manuscript, though generally accurate, contains sporadic North
African forms. See below, §2.14.3.2.

[151] Morag, "Geniza," pp. 70–73 (reprinted in Morag, *Studies*, pp. 303–6); Morgenstern, "Geonic Responsa," pp. 293–94, 301. Cf. Kara, *Yemenite Manuscripts*, pp.
181–82.

[152] See §4.4.5.4 and literature cited.

[153] See Morgenstern, "Noun Patterns," for numerous examples.

[154] See Morag, "Phonology," pp. 71–72 (reprinted in Morag, *Studies*, pp. 247–48).
A comprehensive list of Babylonian Hebrew forms may be found in Yeivin, *Babylonian Vocalization*.

[155] Yeivin, *Babylonian Vocalization*, pp. 1117–18.

- consistent patterns of direct objects.[156]

### 2.12.2.5 Vocalization

Some manuscripts are vocalized with the simple Babylonian vocalization. In the best manuscripts, the non-final historical *$\bar{a}$ is often reflected by the *mip̄taḥ pummā* sign, and has generally not shifted to [ɔ]. In addition to **HPS**, we may note the lengthy fragments published in **TGAs28** as Text I (Geonic), MS Bod. 2760/11–12, and the fragments of *Menaḥot* published by Chwat.[157] Since many of the manuscripts are unvocalized, or were vocalized at a late stage in the text's transmission history, this feature is not decisive.

### 2.12.2.6 Codicological Criteria

Once again, this cannot be the most important criterion for the selection of our textual basis, since later manuscripts written in a semiformal script sometimes contain a better text than earlier manuscripts written in a formal script. For example, the lengthy Geniza fragment identified by Friedman as containing a particularly accurate and typologically early copy of *Bava Mezia* (MS G1) was written on paper in a semiformal hand, and may perhaps be ascribed to the eleventh century. However, if it could be demonstrated, as is the case for **HPS**, that certain manuscripts were copied in Babylonia prior to the eleventh century and contain early Babylonian vocalization, this would strengthen their claim to having been copied by scribes familiar with both the text and language of the oral literature emanating from the Babylonian academies.[158]

### 2.12.2.7 Combination of *All* Features

It is essential to emphasize that the majority of these features are found in some measure in most manuscripts, particularly in Geniza fragments. The combination of *all* of these features and their consistent appearance throughout the text indicate manuscripts of rare accuracy. This point is stressed because sporadic *plene* spellings or apocopated forms alone are

---

[156] See chapter 5.

[157] Chwat, "Menahot." Vocalized words from this manuscript were cited in Morag, *Vocalised Manuscripts,* no. 10, from T-S F1(1).38.

[158] In Morgenstern, "Non-Standard Spellings," I have tried to show that the evidence of the Babylonian magic bowls authenticates many of the unique aspects of these manuscripts.

not sufficient to prove a manuscript linguistically accurate; the preservation of early features is a natural element of all textual transmission, and even the printed editions of the Talmud contain such forms. The manuscripts must be assessed according to the totality of their features, not according to occasional rare forms that are attested.

Moreover, while many of the EEMss contain Geonic works, as Friedman has shown, these features are not specifically Geonic. They also characterize Talmud manuscripts of the early eastern type. The identification of these features as Geonic results from the fact that they were first identified by modern research in Geonic works. Only later were Talmud manuscripts of this type identified and published.

## 2.13 The Early Eastern Manuscripts: An Example

To demonstrate the nature of the EEMss in contrast to the typologically later Spanish manuscripts and the standard printed editions of the Talmud, it is worth presenting readings of these witnesses side by side. Such a presentation immediately highlights the differences between these sources. I have selected a section from MS G1 of *Bava Mezia*; naturally, this section only represents some of the features I have mentioned above.

| MS **G1** | H165 | Printed Edition | Translation |
|---|---|---|---|
| ר׳ אלעזר בר ר׳ שמעון פגע ביה ההוא פַרְהָיגְבָאנָא [159] תפיס גנבי.דקא [160] | ר׳ אלעזר בר׳ שמעון אשכחיה ^להההוא^ פרה ג}{ }{נב} <בנ>א דמלכא. דהוה קא תפיס גנבי | רבי אלעזר ברבי שמעון אשכח לההוא פרהגונא דקא תפיס גנבי | R. El'azar son of R. Shim'on came upon a royal officer who [was] catching thieves. |
| אמל : היכי יכלת להו, לאו בחיתא מתילין? | אמ׳ ליה היכי יכלת להו לאו בחיותא מתילי? | אמר ליה : היכי יכלת להו, לאו כחיותא מתילי? | He said to him: "How do you overcome them? Aren't they likened to animals? |

---

[159] Accurate preservation of loan words. Cf. פְּרִיגְבָנָא (*BQ* 117a [**HGP** 18b:9]).

[160] קא written predominantly as separate word.

| | | | |
|---|---|---|---|
| בו תרמש דכתי [161] כל חיתו יער | | דכתיב בו תרמש כל חיתו יער | As it is written: 'wherein all the beasts of the forest do creep'" (Ps 104:20). |
| איכא דאמרי הכי ישרב אמיליה [162]: במסתר כאריה בסוכו וגו' | | איכא דאמרי מהאי קרא קאמר ליה : יארב במסתר כאריה בסוכו | There are those who say that he told him this: "He lies in wait like a lion in cover" (Ps 10:9). |
| | אמ' ליה. דיל' שקלת צדיקי ?ושבקת רשיעי | דלמא שקלת צדיקי ושבקת רשיעי? | (He said to him: "Perhaps you will take righteous people and leave the wicked?") |
| אמל' ומאי איבי? [163] הרמאנא [164] דמלכא הוא! | אמ' ליה. היכי אעביד | ומאי אעביד? הרמנא דמלכא הוא | "What should I do?—it's the king's command." |
| תא אמליה [165] אגמרך היכי תיבי | אמ' ליה. תא אגמרך היכי תעביד | אמר : תא אגמרך היכי תעביד | He said to him: "Come, I'll teach you how you should act." |
| שעי עול בארבעי [166] לחנותא | עול בארבע שעי קמיתא לחנותא דחמרא | עול בארבע שעי לחנותא | Go into the shop at the fourth hour. |

---

[161] Widespread apocopation of בדלמנר״ית.

[162] אמליה "he said to him" written as single word; enclitic ־ל mainly in EEMss.

[163] Highly phonetic spelling.

[164] *Plene* spelling of medial *ā* vowel.

[165] אמליה "he said to him" written as single word.

[166] Babylonian dialectal form of feminine digit "four."

| | | | |
|---|---|---|---|
| חזית איניש או <sup>167</sup> דקא שתי חמרא וקא מנמנים <sup>168</sup> עליהשאיל <sup>169</sup> | אי חזית איניש דקא שתי חמרא וקא מנמנם שאיל עליה | כי חזית איניש דקא שתי חמרא וקא נקיט כסא בידיה וקא מנמנם שאול עילויה | If you see someone who is drinking wine and dozing off, inquire about him. |
| | מאי עבדתיה. | | (What is his oc-cupation?) |
| או צורבא מרבנן הוא—מחמת גירסי[ה] <sup>170</sup> | אי צורבא מרבנן הוא—קדומי קדים לגרסיה. | אי צורבא מרבנן הוא וניים— אקדומי קדים לגרסיה | If he is a Rab-binic scholar—it is because of his toil. |
| | ואי פועל הוא. קדומי קדים לעבדתיה. | אי פועל הוא - קדים קא עביד עבידתיה | (If he is a labor-er—he has risen early for his work.) |
| או עיבידיתיה <sup>171</sup> בלילא הוא— רדודי רדיד. | אי עבדתיה בליליא—רדודי רדיד | ואי עבידתיה בליליא—רדודי רדיד | If his work is in the night—he had hammered [all night]. |
| ואילא—גנבא הוא, תיפסיה <sup>172</sup> | ואי לא—גנבא הוא ותפסיה | ואי לא—גנבא הוא, ותפסיה | "Otherwise, he is a thief, seize him!" |
| אזל עבד הכי והוה קא תפיס ואזי <sup>173</sup> | | | He went and did so, and went around catching. |
| מילתא אישתמעת בי מלכה, | אשתמע קלא בי מלכא | אישתמע מילתא בי מלכא | The matter was heard in the palace. |

---

<sup>167</sup> Use of או rather than אי for "if."

<sup>168</sup> *Plene* spelling of medial *i* vowel.

<sup>169</sup> Accurate reflection of Babylonian phonology, wherein short *\*i* remains [i].

<sup>170</sup> This passage appears as a marginal addition.

<sup>171</sup> Babylonian form of this noun, reflecting rules of ʿayin followed by a *shewa*. See Morgenstern, "Noun Patterns," p. 169.

<sup>172</sup> Distinction maintained between perfect qaṭl- and imperative qiṭl- base before enclitic object pronouns. See §3.4.3.5.

<sup>173</sup> Widespread apocopation of בדלמנרי״ת, especially in verbal forms.

| אמלהו מלכה | אמ' | אמרו | The king said to them: |
|---|---|---|---|
| קָרְיַאנַהּ דְאִיגַרתָא הוא ניהוי פרְנָאנקָא | קרינא דאיגרתא איהו ליהוי פרונקא | קרְיינא דאיגרתא איהו ליהוי פרונקא | "Let the one who makes the proclamation be the messenger!" |
| אתיוה לר' אלעזר בן ר' שמעון, והוה קא תפיס ואזי. | איתיוה לר' אלעזר בר' שמעון וקא תפיס גנבי | אתיוה לרבי אלעזר ברבי שמעון, וקא תפיס גנבי ואזיל | They brought R. Elʿazar son of R. Shimʿon, and he went about catching. |

Throughout this book, I have attempted to demonstrate that the manuscripts showing these features—the EEMss—preserve RBA in its most pristine form. In discussing these and other factors, I have drawn widely upon the evidence of the Aramaic magic bowls, which are effectively the only surviving epigraphic source for Jewish Babylonian Aramaic. I have sought to show, both here and elsewhere, that many of the linguistic features that characterize the EEMss are also found in the magic texts. Accordingly, these features, which were initially identified on the basis of internal criteria, can be authenticated by the external evidence of the magic corpus. This external evidence is important, since it indicates that these features are to be regarded as genuinely Babylonian; in the apparent absence of a large corpus of manuscripts stemming from Babylonia—most of our early witnesses appear to have been copied in North Africa—such confirmation is essential.[174]

## 2.14 Some Important Manuscripts

### 2.14.1 Introduction

A list of the sources employed in this study appears in the table of abbreviations, wherein bibliographical details of these manuscripts' publication are provided. Here I wish to note some of the most important manuscripts that I have employed, and rank them according to the criteria that I outlined above. Since no manuscript is without error, and since most of the early sources that we have were drawn from the Cairo Geniza, we must always take into account the possibility that the copyists had

---

[174] In contrast to most of the textual witnesses, **HPS** appears to have indeed been copied in Babylonia, as Glatzer, "Early Babylonian Manuscripts" demonstrated.

been influenced by other forms of Aramaic. I have listed these sources according to my own estimation of their quality.

## 2.14.2 Grade A EEMss

### 2.14.2.1 *Halachot Pesuqot Sassoon*[175] (HPS)

Three hundred and ten double-sided pages of twenty-one lines each containing the early Geonic legal compendium *Halachot Pesuqot* and a work dealing with blemished animals.[176] As mentioned above, this remarkable manuscript was already identified in 1962 by Kutscher as a primary source for RBA. Morag subsequently demonstrated that its vocalization provides one of the best sources for the vocalization of RBA, and Glazer has now shown on codicological grounds that it is indeed an early Babylonian manuscript, probably written in the tenth century. The manuscript is characterized by a remarkable degree of accuracy; it contains almost no grammatical errors. It has been studied and cited extensively in this volume.[177]

### 2.14.2.2 *Bava Mezia* MS G1

The discovery of this Talmudic fragment by Friedman proved that many so-called Geonic features were in fact characteristic of early manuscripts in general. The manuscript includes the text of *Bava Mezia* from fol. 70a to fol. 85b. Its language has been discussed extensively in Friedman, "Early Manuscripts," and substantial parts of it have been published in his volume, *Talmud Arukh, BT Bava Meziᶜa VI: Text.* The manuscript includes sporadic vocalization in Tiberian signs, though the phonology would appear to be Babylonian.

---

[175] The manuscript is now part of the Friedberg collection. I have retained the name Sassoon both since this is the name current in the research literature and in honor of Rabbi Sassoon, through whose endeavors the manuscript came to the knowledge of the research community.

[176] This work is not a part of *Halachot Pesuqot*, and has not been cited in this book.

[177] In my unpublished dissertation, which concentrated on Geonic responsa, I cited only the vocalized forms as comparative material. The inclusion of all the linguistic material from **HPS** has allowed me to supplement and refine many of my previous findings, and represents both a quantitative and qualitative difference between the two studies.

### 2.14.2.3 *Bava Qamma* MS G1

This unpublished manuscript contains extensive parts of the tractate *Bava Qamma* from fol. 79 to the end of the tractate. It is characterized by a high degree of textual accuracy and many phonetic spellings.

### 2.14.2.4 Ginsberg, *Geonica*, Text XXXVIII

The manuscript comprises fourteen sheets of paper, each double-sided, containing responsa of R. Natronai Gaon. The manuscript contains many rare Babylonian forms and Babylonian vocalization that strictly follows Babylonian phonology. The vocalization is often employed to interpret unusual defective spellings.

### 2.14.2.5 Assaf, *Geonic Responsa 1928*, Text I

Sixteen lengthy double-sided parchment sheets, containing two collections of early Geonic responsa. An additional fragment was published by Assaf in the same volume as text xxx. Assaf's edition of this manuscript is extremely inaccurate, and many of the manuscript's authentic features have been replaced by forms common in the printed editions of the Talmud.[178] Similarly, Assaf did not correctly identify the Babylonian vocalization and on occasion misinterpreted it.

## 2.14.3 Grade B EEMss

### 2.14.3.1. *Halachot Gedolot* Paris 1402

Sixty lengthy double-sized parchment sheets containing parts of this Geonic compendium. The manuscript is characterized by many phonetic spellings[179] but is most notable for containing extensive Babylonian vocalization of the complex type. Morag already noted that this vocalization is later and less accurate than that of **HPS**, and the same may be said of the text itself.[180] Nevertheless, the manuscript is an important textual witness of RBA.

---

[178] I have noted those cases wherein my reading differs from Assaf's.

[179] These have been collected in Shweka, "Studies," pp. 69–82.

[180] Morag, "Vocalisation," p. 94 (reprinted in Morag, *Studies*, p. 204). Cf. the assessment of Yeivin, *Babylonian Vocalization*, pp. 200–1.

### 2.14.3.2 Harkavy, *Responsen der Geonim*

This collection is in fact based upon four manuscripts containing Geonic responsa, and I have drawn upon examples from three of those manuscripts.[181] The majority of the volume is based upon the Firkovitch manuscript IIA32.1, which comprises 253 double-sided pages on paper, each containing about twenty-four lines, corresponding to pp. 1–259 of Harkavy's edition. The text includes occasional Tiberian and Babylonian vocalization. Most of the manuscript contains responsa by R. Sharrira Gaon and R. Hai Gaon, though several pages (corresponding to pp. 51–76 in Harkavy's edition) contain responsa of R. Yizḥak al-Fasi. These have not been included in the present study, but they provide an important reminder that, in spite of its great accuracy, this manuscript underwent compilation and editing in North Africa, and contains some secondary forms. Accordingly, it cannot be considered a Grade A manuscript. The second manuscript, Firkovitch IIA32.2, comprises 21 double-sided pages, some torn, containing responsa of R. ʿAmram, R. Semaḥ bar Ḥayyim, R. Saʿadia, and R. Naḥshon. This corresponds to pp. 260–69 of Harkavy's edition. Finally, MS Firkovitch IIA32.4 comprises 10 double-sided pages, containing responsa which are apparently all by R. Saʿadia Gaon.

## 2.15 Conclusion

In this chapter, we have considered the main developments in the study of Jewish Babylonian Aramaic. As noted, the first period of modern research was characterized by grammatical studies based primarily upon the printed editions of the Talmud, with only the most occasional reference to manuscript sources. The discovery of the Cairo Geniza and similar sources brought to light new material, some of which was exploited by Levias in his *Grammar*. The linguistic material preserved in these sources was more systematically exploited in Epstein's studies, as were the Aramaic magic bowls published by Montgomery. However, the turning point in Aramaic studies came with Kutscher's plea to base future research solely on the best manuscript sources. Subsequently, Morag, Friedman, and other scholars carried out important manuscript research based on early sources, while Kara's published dissertation contains a valuable description of the language of the Yemenite Talmudic manuscripts. More recently, I have studied the language of the Geonic respon-

---

[181] The fourth manuscript is very short, and it is only coincidental that it contains no material cited here.

sa and other manuscript sources, and compared these to the language of the magic texts, while Sokoloff has published his monumental dictionary.

As outlined above, the immediate needs of research are the publication of the magic bowls, and the identification and description of the best RBA sources. The present study concentrates primarily upon the second corpus, drawing upon the magic bowls as comparative material. I have used the term "sources" here advisedly because, as I have already indicated, in some publications much store has been put by the Yemenite reading tradition as a reliable fount of linguistic information. Similarly, the many unique features of the Yemenite Talmudic manuscripts have led researchers to regard them as being among the most reliable textual witnesses. In the next chapter, we shall consider the value of the Yemenite traditions—written and oral—for the study of RBA. Such a re-evaluation is critical, since the conclusions drawn from it will significantly affect the contents of a future grammar of the dialect.

# CHAPTER 3

# From Yemen to Babylonia in the Study of Jewish Babylonian Aramaic

## 3.1 Introduction

In the previous chapter, the considerable advances made in the study of Jewish Babylonian Aramaic (henceforth JBA) during the second half of the twentieth century were described. As mentioned, in 1960, J. N. Epstein's *Grammar* was posthumously published. This book, which, though small in size, contains a wealth of information, was based primarily on printed editions of the Babylonian Talmud. However, the author also wisely included a substantial amount of material drawn from more accurate sources, most notably, recently edited manuscripts of Geonic literature.

In his programmatic review of Epstein's *Grammar*, E. Y. Kutscher noted the positive and negative aspects of the work, while setting out the immediate desiderata of research into the dialect. Kutscher also attempted to identify manuscripts that might prove worthy of further study.[1] Kutscher himself did not return to the detailed study of RBA, and the challenge was taken up by Prof. Shelomo Morag, who, until his untimely death, was the leading authority on its grammar.

Thanks to Morag, today we know that one of the most important sources for the study of RBA is the Sassoon Manuscript of *Halachot Pesuqot* (**HPS**). Admittedly, Kutscher had already suggested, on the basis of an inaccurate transcription printed in the 1950s, that this manuscript might provide one of the primary sources for future grammatical study of RBA, but it was Morag who demonstrated the unique nature of the

---

[1] The number of sources readily available to Kutscher was limited, and accordingly, his selection has not been confirmed in its entirety. However, at least one of the manuscripts he noted as unique, the Sassoon manuscript *Halachot Pesuqot*, has been confirmed as an essential source for many aspects of the study of this dialect.

manuscript's vocalization, which provides a considerably more accurate reflection of RBA phonology than the later Paris Manuscript of *Halachot Gedolot* from which Epstein had drawn his vocalization. As noted in the previous chapter, Morag did not limit himself to the study of the Yemenite tradition alone.

However, it cannot be denied that at the heart of Morag's work on JBA lay his interest in the Yemenite reading tradition of the Babylonian Talmud. Through his enterprises, this tradition has become, in his words, "an important source for the study and reconstruction of the Aramaic idiom of the Babylonian Talmud."[2] From the 1960s until his untimely death in 1999, Morag published a series of articles in which he emphasized both the Babylonian source of this tradition and its unique nature compared to the reading traditions of other Jewish communities. Even when dealing with ancient and accurate sources such as **HPS**, material from the Yemenite reading tradition was always presented for comparison.

Morag acknowledged that the contemporary Yemenite reading tradition does not always entirely match the findings in the ancient manuscripts, but it is clear that in his opinion these differences were not significant, as he expressly stated: "Since the orally-transmitted forms of YBA disclose a large measure of agreement with those of the Sassoon MS of *Halakhot Pesuqoth*, we may infer that YBA also had its roots in Gaonic Babylonia, and that its structure had originally been that of a dialect spoken in the communities of the Gaonic period or of a reading-tradition of the Talmud used in these communities."[3] With these words, which appear in his detailed study *Aramaic in the Yemenite Tradition: The Language of the Babylonian Talmud*, Morag bestowed the seal of approval on

---

[2] Morag, *YT*, English abstract, p. vii. Morag's language in the Hebrew introduction, p. 37, is even stronger: מבחינת רקעה, עשויה אפוא מסורת תימן לשמש מקור עיקרי לשחזורה של מערכת הצורות של הארמית הבבלית "as regards its background, the Yemenite Tradition may serve as a primary source for the reconstruction of Babylonian Aramaic morphology."

[3] Morag, *YT*, English abstract, p. v. Again, the Hebrew formulation is somewhat stronger: ההתאמה הרבה שבין מסורת תימן של הארמית לבין הניקוד של כתב-יד זה של יהלכות פסוקותי מלמדת, שמסורת תימן משקפת בקווי הגייה ותצורה רבים שבה, מציאות לשונית שנהגה בבבל "The widespread agreement between the Yemenite tradition of Babylonian Aramaic and the vocalization in this manuscript of *Halachot Pesuqot* indicates that the Yemenite tradition reflects, in many of its phonological and morphological traits, a linguistic situation that was current in Babylonia" (ibid., p. 46). I have cited Morag's words at some length in order to reflect his opinion accurately.

the Yemenite tradition, relegating the differences between the findings in the manuscripts and the Yemenite oral tradition to the endnotes.[4] Thanks to Morag's efforts, and particularly to this book, the assumption that the Yemenite reading tradition reflects a Babylonian linguistic actuality has found great currency among both scholars and the general public.[5]

However, already in the 1970s the first doubts were expressed about the assumed high degree of conservatism of the Yemenite tradition of JBA. D. Boyarin raised the possibility that this tradition of Babylonian Aramaic had been influenced by the language of the Targumim (Onqelos/Jonathan), since it had reestablished the phonemic distinction between *qamaṣ* and *pataḥ*.[6] Y. Kara, Morag's student, emphasized that one cannot speak of "the Yemenite Tradition" as a monolithic entity, but must view it as a varied group of related traditions. Kara demonstrated that different editions of Talmudic works vocalized according to the "Yemenite tradition" contain many variants, and that these point to the existence of multiple traditions and to linguistic instability, even in the work of a single vocalizer.[7] As we mentioned in the previous chapter, Kara has also noted several aspects in which Yemenite manuscripts contradict the contemporary Yemenite reading tradition.[8]

In a review of Morag's volume on verbal morphology, S. Kaufman similarly cast doubt on the authenticity of this tradition. Kaufman warned of the circular nature of Morag's argument: the features of certain early manuscripts were determined to be authentic because they matched the Yemenite tradition, while the Yemenite tradition was authenticated by reference to early manuscripts. Moreover, as Kaufman noted, many of the distinctive features of **HPS** are not supported by the Yemenite tradition, a fact that led him to conclude: "In summary, this is an important book, but its premises are badly in need of systematic reex-

---

[4] Morag's book contains a brief appendix wherein he discusses some possible late influences.

[5] The book is cited as authoritative by Muraoka–Porten, *Grammar*; see particularly their sharp words in its defense on p. 371. Juusola, *Linguistic Peculiarities*, also refers to it often. The general reading public in Israel has been introduced to these ideas through Morag in his volume *YT* and through the Hebrew edition of Frank's grammar titled *Dayqa Nami*. The English reading public will find much material drawn from the Yemenite reading tradition in Frank's *Grammar*.

[6] Boyarin, "Reading Traditions." In the face of criticism by Morag, "Diphthongs," p. 337 n. 3, Boyarin subsequently somewhat retracted this critique, in my opinion unnecessarily. See Boyarin, "Talmudic Lexicon III," pp. 126–27.

[7] Kara, "Unity" and "Megilla."

[8] Kara, "Preservation."

amination."[9] Recently, Müller-Kessler has dismissed the Yemenite reading tradition as "secondary."[10]

Is it possible to reach a scholarly consensus regarding the value of the Yemenite oral tradition for reconstructing RBA? It must be said that its detractors have not stated their case well, but have generally been satisfied with apodictic pronunciations of their conclusions without providing supporting evidence. In his many publications, the late Prof. Morag presented his case clearly and in great detail. Researchers seeking to propose an alternative explanation of the evidence must similarly provide a balanced presentation of the linguistic evidence.

## 3.2 The Present Study

In the framework of my ongoing research into the grammar of Rabbinic Babylonian Aramaic on the basis of early manuscript sources I have often had recourse to the Yemenite reading tradition as recorded by Morag and Kara. In addition, I have frequently considered the older Yemenite manuscripts, with regard to both their alphabetic text and their vocalization. These comparisons have brought me to a conclusion radically different from Morag's: the more one studies the details, the more apparent become the differences between the modern Yemenite reading tradition and the grammar of Babylonian Aramaic as reflected in the earliest and most accurate manuscript sources (the EEMss). In contrast, the scope of the differences between the early Yemenite manuscripts and the other early manuscript sources is considerably smaller. That is not to say that every linguistic detail found in Yemenite manuscripts is confirmed by the early manuscript sources. My research suggests that the Yemenite manuscripts also represent a later stage in the transmission of the Talmud's language which, while characterized by a degree of conservatism not found in the later European manuscripts, does not fully preserve JBA in its pristine form.[11] However, as we shall see, the early manuscript sources and the Yemenite manuscripts frequently agree *against* the modern reading tradition. This is particularly true of the alphabetic text of the

---

[9] Kaufman, "Review," p. 544.

[10] Müller-Kessler, "Review of Muraoka–Porten," p. 286.

[11] The exaggerated claims for the unique nature of the Yemenite manuscripts will be discussed in chapter 4. However, they are exceptional in at least two areas: their widespread preservation of phonetic spellings, even into the seventeenth century, and in their general lack of the systematic editing found in the later European manuscripts and printed editions of the Talmud.

Yemenite manuscripts; the vocalization sometimes corresponds to the modern reading tradition, even if this contradicts the manuscript evidence itself.[12]

In my discussion here I have drawn my examples widely from the early eastern manuscripts, as that group is defined in chapter 2. Most of this material has not been previously presented in the relevant scholarly literature. For comparative material I have drawn widely upon the JBA magic bowls. The significance of this evidence lies more in its quality than its quantity. As the only epigraphic sources for JBA clearly written by native speakers at a time when it was the primary language of most (perhaps all) of the social strata of Babylonian Jewry, these texts hold a special place in JBA research.[13] However, since many of these texts are written in a literary dialect that differs from the Talmudic idiom, and since their writers may have spoken dialects that differed somewhat from those employed in Talmudic literature, it seems more methodologically sound to give preference to the evidence of the best Talmudic manuscripts. This can then be compared to these other JBA sources, which have the advantage of antiquity and proximity, qualities which most of the Talmudic manuscripts lack.

## 3.3 Phonology

### 3.3.1 Status of the Pharyngeals

Evidence for the loss of the pharyngeals is widespread in JBA, even in the printed editions of the Talmud.[14] For example, in the printed editions, the common word for "now" is always האידנא, never העידנא, even though the noun עידנא "time, age" from which it is derived is always spelled in the printed editions with an ʿ*ayin*.[15] The printed editions show a degree of systematization: certain lexemes tend to preserve the pharyngeals, while others consistently lose them. In the better manu-

---

[12] Here I deal only with the linguistic aspects of these manuscripts. Their value as textual witnesses to the original literary form of the Babylonian Talmud has recently been questioned by Amit, "Yemenite Manuscripts."

[13] On the social status of Aramaic and Persian in Sassanian Babylonia see Shaked, "Food." On the special value of the magic bowls see Morgenstern, "Moussaeiff Collection" and "Non-Standard Spellings."

[14] See already Nöldeke, *MG*, §57 n. 2.

[15] This spelling is also predominant in the manuscripts. Sokoloff, *DJBA*, p. 851 s.v. עידנא, lists one occurrence of this noun written with an ʾ*aleph*: באידן דבי מדרשא (*Hul* 86b [**Vat**122]). I have not found any others.

scripts, however, this distribution does not obtain, and free interchanges are attested, even within the same context.[16] Perhaps as a result of this confusing situation, the status of the pharyngeals has remained the object of some contention in the study of JBA. In this section I shall attempt to reconsider the evidence for the status of ʿayin and ḥet.

The most important theoretical discussion of these issues remains that by Boyarin. In his review of Kara's *Yemenite Manuscripts*, Boyarin attempted to distinguish between synchronic and diachronic aspects of the Aramaic language reflected in these manuscripts, an aspect in which Kara's analysis is weak. Boyarin suggested that the interchanges between forms preserving the pharyngeals and those indicating their loss may be explained in two different ways: (1) synchronically, i.e., the texts reflect different pronunciations within the spoken language for various possible phonetic reasons; (2) diachronically, i.e., the texts reflect different dialects, or an attempt "to preserve and reconstruct the pharyngeals in written sources of a dialect in which they no longer had any currency."[17]

On the basis of pseudocorrections found in the Yemenite manuscripts, e.g., cases in which ʿayin appears in non-historical positions, Boyarin favored the second explanation, placing particular emphasis on those examples indicating a morphological shift following the loss of a phonological distinction. Boyarin mentions several examples, not all of which occur in the Yemenite manuscripts.[18] Analysis of the data I have found in the EEMss, particularly the free interchanges between the historical and non-historical spellings, seems to confirm Boyarin's conclusions. Let us now consider each of the pharyngeals individually.

### 3.3.1.1 ʿAyin

Evidence for the weakening of the ʿayin is very widespread, and has often been noted in the relevant scholarly literature.[19]

### 3.3.1.1.1 Geonic Statements
Boyarin already noted the apparent contradiction between two Geonic statements regarding the status of the ʿayin. The first appears in a somewhat fragmentary manuscript. Although several words have been lost, the meaning can be understood.

---

[16] See below, §4.4.1.1

[17] Boyarin, "Review," p. 253 (my translation).

[18] See below, §3.3.1.1.2.

[19] See Luzzatto, *Elementi grammaticali*, §12; Nöldeke, *MG*, p. 50 n. 2.; and Levias, *Grammar*, pp. 9, 12, 17.

דעו כי עוכלא בלשון ארמי הוא פטיש... וכמו שיש בכל לשון שאומרין אלפין
במקום עינין ועינין במקום אלפין כן יש באנשי לשון ארמי כשם שאומ׳
**עכלא** כך אומ׳ **אכלא** ... וברור [הוא] בלשון ארמי והמלחים עכשו בבבל
שמות [ ]ה כליהן בלשון ארמי וקוראין למדוך שמכין בו את היתד **אכלא**
**ועכלא** וכו׳.

Know that עוכלא in Aramaic is a hammer... Just as in every language,[20] there are some who say ʾalephs for ʿayins and ʿayins for
ʾalephs, so among speakers of Aramaic,[21] just as they say *ʿakla* they
say *ʾakla*. [That is] clear in the Aramaic language, and the boatmen
now in Babylonia [...] their tools in the Aramaic language, the mal-
let with which they strike a peg *ʾakla* and *ʿakla*. (**TGAs28** xiv b 13–
22)

The interpretation of the second statement is less clear:

וקאמרינן **ערורה ארורה** חד לישנא הוא עינין אלפין ... בלשון ארמי שאין
עין הרבה מאי איריא ודקא ארי לה מאי קא ארי לה ארייה לגזיזיה וקם.

And we say *ʿarora* [or] *ʾarora*; it is one term, ʿayins and ʾalephs ...
in the Aramaic language, in which there are not many ʿayins, we
find מאי איריא and ודקא ארי לה, ארייה לגזיזיה וקם. (**Hark** 108:3–7)

The Gaon indicates that there is no difference between the two words,
one with an ʿayin and the other with an ʾaleph, and cites a series of examples to prove this. However, the interpretation of this passage depends
upon how we understand the syntactic role of the word הרבה. Boyarin
assumed it belonged with the second part of the sentence, i.e., מאי הרבה
איריא ודקא ארי לה מאי קא ארי לה ארייה לגזיזיה וקם, "many times [we
find] מאי איריא etc." Alternatively, it may be read as a modifier of אין,
i.e., שאין עין הרבה, "that there are not many ʿayins."[22]
    There is considerable evidence for the loss of ʿayin in the EEMss. Let
us begin with some of the more explicit statements by the Geonim on
this matter:

בפיקעא רגילין רבנן למימר **פיקא** לשון קל הוא מקום שניבקע בתחתוניות
שלאדם ...

---

[20] It is not certain to which languages the Gaon is alluding. The Geonim were
familiar with three spoken languages, Arabic, Aramaic and Persian.

[21] The expression אנשי לשון is here equivalent to أهل اللغة, i.e., native speakers.

[22] The text was also read this way by B. Levin; see **GK4**, p. 14 n. 1.

בפיקעא—the Rabbis are accustomed to saying **פיקא**, a "light" form.
It is the place that is split in a man's lower quarters [i.e., the anal
fissure].[23] (**Hark** 22:29–30)

ולאו הכין היא מילתא אלא הא פרישו ראשונים צימחי כגון **בועי** שהן
אבעבועות. דאמרן לישנא קלילא **בויי.**

And the matter is not so;[24] rather, the early authorities interpreted
[the word as meaning] "pustules," as in **בועי** which are boils. As we
say in a "light" form, **בויי**. (**Hark** 158:34–159:1)

In the same responsum by R. Hai Gaon, we find the interchange of two
forms, מן צולי (**Hark** 159:31) and מצולעי (**Hark** 159:32). The meaning of
this word is uncertain. Sokoloff has connected it to JBA צלא "leather,
skin," in which case the ʿayin of the form מצולעי would be a pseudocorrection based upon forms such as בויי wherein an historical ʿayin is
genuinely elided.

### 3.3.1.1.2 EEMs Evidence
After considering the explicit statements of the Babylonian Geonim, we
shall now turn to look at the implicit evidence of the forms attested in the
best manuscripts. The evidence will be divided into three categories: (1)
examples suggesting total elision of the ʿayin, in particular examples demonstrating *morphological* and not merely *phonological* change; (2) examples in which the ʿayin has shifted to ʾaleph; (3) examples of a non-
historical ʿayin.

### i. Total elision of the ʿayin.
The loss of the ʿayin is often complete and can cause morphological
change:

ולא **ניחזינהו** אינאשי ונירקו שלא יראו אותן אנשים ויברחו מהן.

"that people **should** not **see them** and flee." (*BQ* 79a [**Geon** xxviii
2b 6])

---

[23] This example is additionally enlightening in that the Hebrew gloss employs the
root בק״ע, presumably the historical root of both פיקעא and its variant פיקא.
[24] I.e., as the correspondents stated.

This citation from a Geonic responsum is accompanied by a translation, from which it is clear that וניֿרקו is a phonetic spelling for וניֿערקו, which is translated ויברחו "flee." The same Talmudic source appears in an accurate fragment of tractate *Bava Qamma*. Although the specific manuscript in question often employs a phonetic orthography and contains many phonetic spellings, this particular form appears in its historical spelling וניֿערקו (*BQ* 79a [**G1**]).[25] Further examples:

> כיון דמיקר אקרי להו "since they uproot them" (*BB* 94a [**TGAs28** i 3b 25]), from root עק״ר; מברא "a ferry" (*BQ* 117b [**HPS** 130:8]), from מרגופנא ;מעברא "cotton" (**Geon** xxxviii 2b 13]), derived from עמר גפנא, and translated צמר גפנים "wool of the vine" in the responsum;[26] מברתא "passageway [for strap]" (*Men* 35a [**TGAs28** v 3b 6]); ארא *ʾarā* "land" (*Qid* 26a [**TGAs28** ii a 27]) from ארעא *ʾarʿā; צבא ṣabbā "the dyer" (*Git* 52b [**HPS** 82:1]) from *צבעא ṣabbāʿā.[27]

As Boyarin noted, the clearest evidence for the loss of the pharyngeals in the spoken language comes from examples wherein the phonological shift has occasionally led to a systemic morphological change. Boyarin cited the example of איבלעאי[28] wherein the III-ʿ*ayin* root conjugates according to the pattern of the III-*yod* roots. I have found three clear examples of this phenomenon in the EEMss:

> דנפק משמרתו דיהויריב ולא **תבעיי**.

That the order of Yehoyariv went out and did not **demand** [the money]. (*BQ* 111a [**G1**])

The Hebrew word משמרת is f.s. and, accordingly, the verbs are in the 3 f.s. The form נפק demonstrates the apocopation of the 3 f.s. morpheme of the sound verb, while תבעיי, from the root תב״ע, has the -*ay* morpheme of the III-*yod* verbs, such as רמאי "she imposed" (*Shab* 156b [**Hark** 207:31]).

> שְׁמָעאִי אזל אחילתיה.

---

[25] I discuss the significance of such interchanges in chapter 4.

[26] See Sokoloff, *DJBA*, p. 879, s.v. מרגופנא, עמר גופנא.

[27] This example is discussed in greater detail in §4.4.1.1.

[28] I assume that the example is drawn from Epstein, *Grammar*, p. 51, who cites the reading איבלעאי "was inculcated" (*Ber* 24b [**M95**]).

**She heard**, went and redeemed it. (*Ket* 86a [**HGP** 44b:16])


The later Spanish manuscript MS **H165** contains a further example:
טבאי ארביה "may his ship sink!" (*BB* 153a [**H165**]), a reading supported
by the ʿAruch.[29]

ההיא חביתא **דפקעאי** לאורכה...והני מילי **דפקעאי** לאורכה

A certain barrel **split** along its length...and these words [apply]
when **it split** along its length (ʿ*AZ* 60b [**HGP** 56b:37–38])


In the II-ʿayin class we find מדייתי "they exude" (e.g., **TGAs28** xxv 2a 30)
from the secondary root דעת "to sweat"[30]. In the Yemenite manuscripts,
Kara found טיינו "they bear" (*RH* 23a [**JTS**108]) for טעני.[31] Further examples are found in other manuscripts.[32]

The elision of the ʿayin appears to lie behind some of the
morphological changes that have significantly affected two roots, בע"יי
and עב"ד. Forms of בע"יי in which the ʿayin has been apocopated are quite
common, e.g.:

*Perfect*:

   *3 m.s.:* איבי (*BQ* 99b [**G1**]), a phonetic spelling for איבעי.


---

[29] Sokoloff, *DJBA*, p. 494, s.v. טבי, טבע. This example was first noted by Kara,
*Yemenite Manuscripts*, p. 69; see especially n. 86. Epstein, *Grammar*, p. 59, noted
one possible example in roots ending with בדלמנר: אזלאי "I went" (*BB* 73b
[**H165**]), apparently a pseudo-historical spelling combining historical (אזלי(ת
with phonetic אזאי*.

[30] Sokoloff, *DJBA*, p. 323 s.v. דו"ית.

[31] Kara, *Yemenite Manuscripts*, p. 64. Kara's discussions would benefit from a
clearer distinction between phonological shift and morphological shift due to
phonological shift.

[32] Cf. also דו"ץ "to insert, stick in" (Sokoloff, *DJBA*, p. 320) from דע"ץ. I have not
found any examples of this root in the EEMss, but it is attested in the Yemenite
manuscripts and in Mandaic (ibid.), and there seems no reason to doubt its authenticity.

*3 f.s.:* איביא (*Nid* 69b [**TGAs28** i 5b 6]), a phonetic spelling for
איבעיא.[33] איבילהו (*ʿAZ* 22a [**GK4** 28:13]), a phonetic spelling for
איבעיא להו.

*Participles:*

G *m.s.:* באיי (*ʿAZ* 60b [**HGP** 56b:39]) for בעי. *f.s.:* בייא (*Pes* 113a
[**Hark** 99:36]). This form was apparently pronounced [*bāiyɔ:*], as
indicated by the vocalization in **HPS**: בֵּעִיּׅא (**HPS** 252:18) // בעִֺّא
(**HPS** 252:18). Gt *m.s.:* מיבי (*BQ* 85a [**G1**]) for מיבעי.

Particularly worthy of attention are the forms of the 1 c.pl. participle. In
most of the EEMss, the form בעינן, common in the printed editions of the
Talmud, is either non-existent or extremely rare. In its place, we generally find בענן or בנן. Kutscher already remarked upon the absence of בעינן
in the Hamburg manuscript of *Neziqin* (H165) which always employs
בענן, while Sabato has shown that even the earliest printed editions of the
Talmud consistently used בענן.[34] These findings are generally confirmed
by the EEMss. There are *no* examples of בעינן in **HPS**, and I have found
only one example in the four manuscripts published in Harkavy's collection of responsa. Even that single example appears in the question rather
than the responsum, and as I have demonstrated elsewhere, the language of the questions does not always reflect accurate Babylonian
usage.[35] Similarly, there are no examples in the important fragments such
as **TGAs28** i, **Geon** xxxviii, *BQ* [**G1**], *BM* [**G1**], *Bek* [**G1**]. In all these
sources, the regular form is בענן, with occasional examples of בנן, which
are sometimes vocalized:

בנן (*Suk* 7b [**HPS** 31:4]; **Geon** xxxviii 7b 17; **TGAs28** i 14a 8;[36]
**TGAs42** x 3a 1).

בְּנַן (*Nid* 22a [**G1**]; **Geon** xxxviii 7b 16).

In addition, I have found three examples of בעונן (**TGAs28** i 14a 7;[37]
**TGAs42** 9:24; 61:20).

---

[33] Assaf read איבעיא.

[34] Kutscher, "Review," p. 175 (reprinted in Kutscher, *Studies*, p. 253); Sabato, *Yemenite Manuscript*, p. 2 n. 44.

[35] See Morgenstern, "Geonic Responsa," pp. 7–9.

[36] In parallel copy published in **GS** i 11b 13: בענן.

[37] Assaf read בעינן.

A similar array of forms (including some with identical vocalization) is found in some of the Yemenite manuscripts.[38] In MS J, for example, we find only בענן, never בעינן.

I believe that all these forms can be explained by reference to the loss of the pharyngeal. *bāʿaynan > *bāaynan > bāanan.[39] According to this reconstruction, the spelling בען would be an historical spelling that attempted to reflect the original second radical which was no longer pronounced.

However, it seems that an alternative pronunciation of this form also existed, one in which the ʿayin survived either as a pharyngeal or as a glottal stop. This is evident in **HGP**, the primary eastern manuscript that preserves four such forms: בעינן (*BB* 142b [**HGP** 45a:12]; *San* 26b [**HGP** 39a:23,24]; *San* 27a [**HGP** 39a:33]). However, alongside these we find eight examples of בענן.[40]

We may summarize these findings in a table:

| Manuscript | בענן | בנן | בעונן | בעינן |
|---|---|---|---|---|
| HPS | 18 | 1 | | |
| BQ G1 | 5 | | | |
| Geon xxxviii | | 2 | | |
| TGAs28 i | 4 | 1 | 1 | |
| Hark | 12 | | | 1 |
| HGP | 8 | | | 4 |

Particularly common are forms of the root עב״ד with the loss of the ʿayin. Such forms are discernable especially in manuscripts written in the more phonetic orthography.

G:

**Perfect:** *3 m.s.:* אבא (*BQ* 99b [**G1**]; *Men* 109a [**G1**]).

---

[38] See the extensive discussion in Kara, *Yemenite Manuscripts*, p. 63.

[39] On the shift *ayn > an, see Morag, "Phonology," p. 75 n. 31 (reprinted in Morag, *Studies*, p. 252, n. 31); Dodi, "Grammar,"p. 138.

[40] The verb in question is not attested in the surviving pages of *BM* **G1**.

**Imperfect**: *1 c.s.:* איבי (*BM* 83b [**G1**]), אֵיבִי (*BM* 84a [**G1**]).[41] *2 m.s.:* תיבי (*BM* 83b [**G1**]). *3 m.s.:* ניבי (*Pes* 30b [**Geon** xxiv 2a 11]). *1 c.pl.:* ניבי (*RH* 34a [**HPS** 21:17];[42] *MQ* 25a [**HPS** 270:8]; *Shev* 41b [**HPS** 199:14, **HGP** 12a:32, vocalized נִיבֵּי]).

**Participle**: *3 m.s.:* אבי (*BQ* 102b [**G1**]; *ᶜAZ* 60b [**HGP** 56b:39]).[43] *1 m.s.:* אבינא (*BQ* 87a [**G1**]).

**INFINITIVE**: למֵיבַד (*BB* 35b [**HGP** 1b:22]).

Gt:

**Perfect**: *3 m.s.:* דיאבא (*Ber* 15a [**TS** NS 329.252];[44] *BB* 137a [**HGP** 46a:27]; *ᶜAZ* 33b [**HGP** 56a:10]; **Hark** 82:23; **TGAs28** v 5a 11).

Shemuel b. Hofni derives the form דיאבא from the G of עב״יד: דיאבא אן פעל ואדא פעל יענון אלפאעל בראי נפסה והו דאו עבד "*dyʾbʾ*—if he did or when he did, i.e., one who acted according to his own opinion, and this is דאו עבד" (**LPT** 50:21).[45]

In my opinion, there are several indications that even forms written with the *ᶜayin* were pronounced without it, and that the root had often shifted to the I-ʾaleph class. First, we find two examples with the *ᶜayin* written in the wrong place: ניבעי, נבעי (*BQ* 84b [**G1**]). The phonetic spelling is attested in the same context in the same manuscript: ניבי (*BQ* 84b [**G1**]).[46] Moreover, we find that, unusually, the 1 c.s. imperfect prefix is sometimes not written at all: עיביד "I shall do" (*BB* 4a [**T-S** AS 78.389]; *BB* 153a [**HPS** 187:5]). The best explanation for this unusual form would seem to be that this is a semi-historical spelling. The pronunciation was not [*ʾiᶜbid*], as we might have expected from the vocalization לִיעַבְּדוּ "let them make" (*Suk* 26a [**HPS** 39:19]), but rather [*ʾēḇi*], as indicated by the example אֵיבִי (*BM* 84a [**G1**]) cited above.[47] The weakening of the *ᶜayin* has

---

[41] On the vocalization, see my comments below.

[42] This may also be understood as 3 m.s.

[43] Several of these examples, with others from later manuscript sources, are recorded in Sokoloff, *DJBA*, p. 836 s.v. עבד.

[44] My attention was drawn to this example by Dr. Aharon Amit.

[45] **LPT** 50:21.

[46] I present these examples in full in §4.4.1.1.

[47] It is likely that this pronunciation also lies behind the spelling אעביד "I shall do" (*Git* 14a [**Hark** 273:25]; *Git* 25a [**Geon** xvii 3a 26]; *BM* 83b [**HGP** 6a:37]; *BB* 54a [**HGP** 3a:30]), which contracts the orthographic norms of the EEMss. In these manuscripts, the 1 c.s. prefix ʾi- is generally written plene, אי. Cf. also אעביד in

led to a pronunciation on the pattern of the I-ʾaleph roots such as אֵימָא "I shall say."[48]

The supposition that semi-historical orthography prevails in these cases would well explain the form נהרדעי "the Nahardeans" (BQ 40a [HPS 139:19; Hark 9:14]; BM 108a [HPS 141:12]). In the best of the EEMss, the gentilic plurals are formed using the place name with the addition -ʾāyē,[49] and hence we should expect to find the form *nəhardəʿāyē, נהרדעאיי. In fact, I have never found this spelling in the EEMss. Let us compare the findings of two long manuscripts, HPS and HGP:

| Spelling | HPS | HGP |
|---|---|---|
| נהרדאיי | 13 | 0 |
| נהרדאי | 1 | 1 |
| נהרדעי | 5 | 10 |
| נהרדעאי | 0 | 2 |

From the above table, it becomes clear that HPS greatly favors spellings in which the historical ʿayin is elided. Moreover, all five examples preserving the ʿayin are found within the space of four pages of the manuscript (pp. 139–42), while the other examples appear throughout the rest of the work. This may imply that the compiler of this legal collection drew upon a source favoring a spelling different from that used in his other sources. By contrast, in HGP only one example does not preserve the ʿayin at all.

We cannot simply say that the ʿayin was preserved in this linguistic tradition, such that נהרדעי was pronounced [nəhardəʿāy], with the loss of the final vowel, since this spelling of the gentilic plural morpheme is not supported by other gentilic forms in the manuscripts. I prefer to see this spelling as a reflection of the pronunciation [nəhardāʾī], with the older -āʾē

---

the Yemenite manuscripts (Suk 44b [O51, JTS218]; MQ 22b [Col]) and the discussion below, §3.4.2.1.

[48] On the vocalization with the e vowel, see below, §3.4.3.6.1.

[49] It is possible that this reflects an original *-āyē ending, but it is also possible that it is a reversion of *āyē > *āʾē > āyē. While this intermediate stage may appear unnecessary, there is some evidence that it occurred; the gentilic plural is generally written אי- in the Aramaic magic bowls and in the Babylonian tradition of Targum Onqelos, while in the EEMss, it is predominantly איי- See above, §2.12.2.1; Breuer, "Karetot," pp. 31–32, §2.2.2.1; Morgenstern, "Noun Patterns," p. 76.

gentilic plural morpheme reflected as -ā᾽ī. This morpheme is quite frequently attested in **HGP**, e.g., בַּתְרָאֵי "the latter ones" (*BQ* 115a [**HGP** 17b:28]) (**HPS** always בתראיי); פָּרְסָאֵי "Persians" (*BQ* 117a [**HGP** 18b:16]); קְבוֹרָאֵי "gravediggers" (*San* 26b [**HGP** 39a:25]).[50] The orthography with the ῾*ayin* would reflect an attempt to preserve the historical ῾*ayin* in the spelling, even though it had already been entirely elided in the pronunciation.

At the start of this discussion, I mentioned that the RBA word for "now" is derived from האיי + עידנא. The ῾*ayin* appears to have shifted to ᾽*aleph* and then been elided entirely: *hāyi᾽iddānā > hāyiddānā, spelled האידנא (*BQ* 117a [**G1**]), הידנא (**HPS** 214:3; **Geon** xvii 3a 22) or הידאנא (*Bes* 27a [**HPS** 5:11]).

The ῾*ayin* is regularly elided entirely in numerals formed by compounds of the number ten:

> **12:** *Masc.:* תְּרֵיסַר זוּזֵי "twelve *zuzin*" (*BM* 65a [**HGP** 27a:3]). תריסר ירחי "twelve months" (*Ket* 64a [**Hark** 36:10]) = תרי סר ירחי (ibid. [**HPS** 178:17]); תרי סר אלפי זוזי "twelve thousand *zuzin*" (*BQ* 104b [**HPS** 98:3]). *Fem.:* תרתי סרי שני "twelve years" (**Hark** 40:28).
>
> **13:** *Masc.:* תליסר כלדאי "thirteen astrologists" (*Shab* 156b [**Hark** 207:31]). *Fem.:* תליסרי שני "thirteen years" (*BB* 54a [**HGP** 3a:28]).
>
> **14:** *Masc.:* אַרְבְּסַר יוֹמֵי "fourteen days" (**HPS** 212:18).[51]
>
> **15:** *Masc.:* חמיסר "fifteen [days]" (**HPS** 17:4). *Fem.:* חמסרי "fifteen [years]" (**Hark** 40:34).
>
> **16:** *Masc.:* שיתסר גריוי "sixteen *griv*-measures" (*BQ* 106b [**HPS** 149:13]). *Fem.:* שיתסרי "sixteen [years]" (**Hark** 40:34).
>
> **17:** *Masc.:* שבסר "seventeen" (*Men* 68b [**HPS** 17:9]).
>
> **18:** *Masc.:* תמנסר יומי "eighteen days" (῾*Ara* 22a [**HPS** 188:21]).

The consistent loss of the ῾*ayin* in this position suggests that it was entirely lost in the pronunciation. In the EEMss I have found only two exam-

---

[50] The latter two examples were already noted by Shweka, "Studies." Regarding the gentilic ending of קבוראי, see Morgenstern, "Noun Patterns," p. 78.

[51] Sokoloff records both the forms אַרְבְּסַר and אַרְבֵּיסַר for the masculine, with אַרְבַּסְרֵי and אַרְבֵּיסְרֵי for the feminine. Further research into the early manuscripts is required to confirm the authenticity of these forms.

ples of these compound numerals preserving the *ʿayin* in the orthography: תרי **עסר** ירחי שתא "twelve months of the year" (*BM* 24b [**HGP** 22a:4]); תלת **עשר** אדריאתא תיבנא "thirteen sacks of straw" (*Ned* 25a [**Hark** 108:11]).

### ii. Shift from ʿayin to ʾaleph.

In numerous words, the *ʿayin* has apparently shifted to a glottal stop. Cited above are many examples of עב״ד perfects in which the initial *ʿayin* has become *ʾaleph*. Further cases are abundant, and I shall mention only a few representative examples here:[52] ארבא "boat" (*BB* 34b [**HPS** 137:16]); אקרה "he abrogated it" (*BM* 76b [**G1**]); דמיקר אקרי "that uproot" (*BB* 94a [**TGAs28** i 3b 25]); איביתא "a deed" (*BQ* 87b [**G1**]); מאיקבה "from the start" (*BQ* 103a [**HPS** 125:1]; *BQ* 106b [**HPS** 150:2, **HGP** 4a:37, vocalized מֵאִיקְּבָ֫ה]); באוביה "in his bosom" (**HPS** 53:5). In the case of the example קלפי טאבי בלאי "I received good blows" (*ʿAra* 22a [**HPS** 188:19]), we cannot know whether the verb was pronounced *bəlaʾi* or *bəlāi*, following the III-*yod* pattern, with the *ʾaleph* as a *mater lectionis*.

Extremely frequent is the use of the prefix א- (presumably *ʾa-* + gemination) instead of the preposition על.

### iii. Non-historical ʿayin

Examples of this phenomenon are very rare. The most widely discussed example is the form טיאעא "Arabic" which is apparently derived from Arabic طائى "member of Tayya tribe."[53] Examples of the spelling with *ʿayin* are found in the eastern manuscripts, e.g.: בר עדי טִיאעָא "Bar ʿAdi the Arab" (*ʿAZ* 33a [**HGP** 56a:3]), טִיאעִי (*BB* 36a [**HGP** 2a:6]), טיאעי (*ʿAZ* 11b [**HGP** 58b:19]), while examples of the form without the *ʿayin* are sporadically attested in such sources, e.g., זוזא דטיי "the Arabs' Zuz" (**Hark** 38:1).[54] Above I cited two other apparent examples: מצולעי "from skins" (**Hark** 159:32) and ניבעי, נבעי "let him do" (*BQ* 84b [**G1**]) for ניבי "let him do." One more example is found in the form בְּצִרִיפָא דְּעוֹרֹבְּנִי "in a hut of papyrus reeds" (*BM* 42a [**HGP** 23a:11]) which parallels צריפא דאורבני (*BM* 42a [**HPS** 126:14]) in the same citation in **HPS**. Since אורבנא

---

[52] Numerous examples were listed from the printed editions by Nöldeke, *MG*, §57 n. 2. A long list of examples is also found in Kara, *Yemenite Manuscripts*, pp. 62–69. See further §4.7.5.

[53] See Nöldeke, *MG*, p. 58 n. 2.

[54] See Kara, *Yemenite Manuscripts*, p. 67; Sokoloff, *DJBA*, s.v. טייעא, טיאעא, טייא.

is found in Syriac as ܐܘܒܠܐ,[55] the spelling with *ʿayin* is apparently a pseudocorrection, somehow connecting this word with the root ערי״ב.

### 3.3.1.1.3 Historical Depth

How deep are the roots of this phenomenon in JBA? Explicit evidence from the Talmudic period is not forthcoming within the Talmud itself. Accordingly, in theory, it might be possible to ascribe it to a later period, i.e., the period of the Talmud's encoding in writing. Nevertheless, I believe that there is considerable evidence to suggest that the *ʿayin* was lost at an early period, at least by the pre-Islamic period. Evidence is forthcoming from two sources: folk etymologies and contemporary Aramaic documents, namely the JBA magic bowls.

One important example of folk etymology is ביקתא—בי עקתא "hut— a place of trouble" (*Shab* 77b). This etymology, based upon the loss of the *ʿayin*, appears to have affected the spelling of the word in JBA; accordingly we find it spelled ביקתא, בעיקתא (**TGAs28** xxvii 3b 11) and perhaps ביקעתא (**TGAs42** 68:72, explaining ביקתא in 104a).[56] The folk etymology and pseudo-historical spellings would point to the loss of a distinction between the spellings with and without the *ʿayin*, implying that it was no longer pronounced.

The evidence of the Aramaic magic bowls is decisive. Juusola was able to list about a dozen examples of the loss of *ʿayin*, including one significant form demonstrating a shift of III-*ʿayin* to III-*yod*: אשבעיתי "I adjured" (Gordon 2:6), bearing the pronoun of the III-*yod* class.[57] Several more examples not included in Juusola's work can be adduced from the then-available sources. Furthermore, since the appearance of Juusola's work, numerous magic bowls have been published, some in dialects close to RBA. From these texts it has become clear that the loss of the pharyngeals was already widespread in the Talmudic period:

אכרנא "I detain them" (AIT 6: 6);[58] מתן ארבין ותמניא הדמין "two hundred and forty eight members" (Gordon 8:8); זבן ואידן "time

---

[55] Brockelmann, *LS*, p. 45 s.v. ܐܘܒܠܐ; Sokoloff, *DJBA*, p. 93 s.v. אורבנא, אורבאנא, עורבנא. Sokoloff regards this as an Aramaic loanword into Akkadian.

[56] The etymology of the word employed here metaphorically is uncertain; it may derive from ביקתא "house" or ביקעתא "valley," in which case the spelling with the *ʿayin* would be etymological.

[57] Juusola, *Linguistic Peculiarities*, p. 37. Juusola's hesitation regarding the accuracy of this reading has now proven unnecessary; see Morgenstern, "Mandaic."

[58] As Epstein noted, אכר is parallel to Syriac ܐܟܪ; see Epstein, "Gloses," p. 34 = Hebrew p. 334; see further Sokoloff, *DJBA*, 862 s.v. עכר, אכר.

and age" (BM 040A:11);[59] אאבדניכו "against your practitioner" (BM 049A:10), with prefixed א- for standard Aramaic על; cf. the parallel formula על עבדניהון (Gordon C:8);[60] שמנא "I hear" (M 145:1);[61] לבבא מיציתא דאסיפא "the middle gate of the vestibule" (MS 1927/13 verso) and לאיסקופתא במיציתא "for the threshold in the middle" (Schøyen 1927/20 verso), in both cases for מציעתא.[62]

In at least one case, the loss of the ʿayin appears to have caused morphological change. In Gordon's Bowl G, which is particularly rich in phonetic spellings, we find the expression מן ארבעי מיצעתא דביתיה "from the four parts of the house" (l. 12). The use of ארבעי as the feminine form of the numeral "four" characterizes the better manuscripts of RBA and corresponds to the form attested in Mandaic.[63] In fact, in the EEMss we *never* find the f.s. ארבע other than in the combination ארבע מאה "four hundred."[64] The evidence of the magic text indicates that ארבעי was an early form, but one which was not generally employed in the magic corpus.

### 3.3.1.1.4 The Status of the ʿayin in Written JBA Sources
There is widespread evidence for the weakening of the ʿayin in JBA. This evidence is manifold and varied in its nature, and may be summarized according to the following categories: (1) total elision of ʿayin; (2) loss of ʿayin indicated by morphological shift, even in cases in which it is preserved in the orthography; (3) shift of ʿayin to ʾaleph; (4) folk etymology pointing to the loss of ʿayin; (5) explicit testimony of later authorities; (6) comparative evidence from non-Rabbinic Jewish Aramaic sources; (7) the widespread loss of the ʿayin in many Eastern Aramaic dialects, including Classical Mandaic and many of the Northeastern Neo-Aramaic dialects. The cumulative force of this evidence, coupled with our knowledge of the neighboring Mandaic dialect, seems to indicate that the ʿayin had either shifted to ʾaleph in JBA, or been completely elided.

---

[59] For this reading see Morgenstern, "BM 91767," p. 18.

[60] See Morgenstern, "Magic Bowl," pp. 216–19.

[61] Levene, *Corpus*, p. 100.

[62] These texts are cited according to the preliminary report in Shaked, "Magic Bowls," p. 8.

[63] Epstein, *Grammar*, p. 125; Sokoloff, *DJBA*, p. 163 s.v. ארבעא. Cf. Nöldeke, *MG*, §§17 (end) and 151.

[64] In contrast to Mandaic ʾrbymʾ or ʾrbʾymʾ. See Nöldeke, *MG*, §152.

### 3.3.1.1.5 The Yemenite Reading Tradition

The Yemenite reading tradition follows the orthography of the printed editions. If the text is written with an ʿayin, then the reader will pronounce it with an ʿayin. Where it is written with an ʾaleph, the reader follows the printed text in reading with an ʾaleph.[65] It is unlikely that this pronunciation reflects the phonological realities of JBA.

### 3.3.1.2 Ḥet

Evidence for the status of the historical ḥet seems to imply that already in the fourth or fifth centuries ḥet and he were not distinguished, but appear either to have merged into the laryngeal he or to have been elided altogether.[66] As with the evidence for ʿayin, we shall consider here cases according to various categories.

### 3.3.1.2.1 EEMs Evidence

#### i. Total Elision of Ḥet

Epstein already connected JBA שׁודא דדיאני "judicial discretion" (e.g., **Hark** 111:14) to JPA שׁוחדא "discretion"[67] and cited the common JBA form תֻּותִי "under" (here cited according to BM 83b [G1]).[68] We note that the loss of the ḥet in the latter root has been lexicalized, as indicated by the denominative verb תתי״י "to lower."[69] Other examples are occasionally forthcoming in the early manuscripts, e.g., מיתפא "recovers" (BQ 85b [G1]) for מיתפח. Kara has noted that all three Yemenite manuscripts read צוצרתא "trumpet" (Suk 34a) for חצוצרתא.[70] Particularly significant is the form טלאפא "lentil [-shaped object]" (**Hark** 104:35),[71] since it may explain the story in the Babylonian Talmud, Ned 66b, of the Babylonian man who settled in the Land of Israel and married a local woman. A series of

---

[65] For examples of such forms from the printed editions, see below, §4.7.5.

[66] The evidence for this has been widely noted in the scholarly literature. See, for example, **Hark**, pp. 356, 368; Epstein, Grammar, p. 18; Epstein, Geonic Commentary, p. 122; Sasson, HPS, p. 28; Friedman, "Early Manuscripts," p. 17; Kara, Yemenite Manuscripts, pp. 58–62, 67–68; Boyarin, "Review," pp. 253–54; and Abramson, Inyanot, p. 194 n. 5. Cf. further Breuer, Hebrew, pp. 87–88, 103–5.

[67] See Epstein, Amoraim, p. 261; cf. Sokoloff, DJPA, p. 544 s.v. שׁחוד.

[68] The qamaṣ seems to represent a short [o] vowel, which may be an allophone of u in this manuscript.

[69] See Sokoloff, DJBA, p. 1239 s.v. תתי.

[70] Kara, Yemenite Manuscripts, p. 62. This form should be added to Sokoloff, DJBA, p. 479 s.v. חצוצרתא.

[71] This spelling should be added to Sokoloff, DJBA, p. 506 s.v. טלפחא, טלופחא.

misunderstandings occurred between the couple owing to differences between the Palestinian and Babylonian dialects. While the story is not to be taken as historical fact, Sperling has demonstrated that the story shows an awareness of genuine differences between the two dialects, though he assumed that the supposed interchange between טלפי "hooves" and "lentils" is not attested.[72] In fact, the manuscript evidence indicates that in JBA, the *ḥet* of טלפחא "lentil" was sometimes elided, which would have given its plural form a sound similar to טלפין "hooves" in JPA and Mishnaic Hebrew.[73]

### ii. Shift to He

Even in the printed editions of the Talmud, this phenomenon is very widespread, and in many cases the spelling with *he* is the only form of the word attested. For example, in all RBA sources the historical root חד״יר (< *ḥdr*) is written with a *he*.[74] Many further examples of *he* for historical *ḥet* are attested in the manuscripts.[75] In all of the following examples, the *he* appears in place of etymological *ḥet*. These examples are only a representative sample of the cases attested in the EEMss:

*Nouns*:

> הרואתא דדיקלא "palm branches" (**Geon** xxxviii 4b 11); הירגא דיומא "dust of a sunbeam" (*Yom* 20b [**Hark** 142:1]); מהוזא "Maḥoza [a town in Babylonia]" (*Pes* 5b [**HPS** 9:8]); *Pes* 30b [**HPS** 13:5]; *BM* 83a [**HPS** 114:12], *Nid* 67b [**HPS** 215:1], etc.); הושלא "barley groats" (*BB* 36a [**HPS** 138:14]);[76] למטרה "to take the trouble" (*BQ* 113b [**HPS** 133:20]); אהינא "unripe date" (*Suk* 35b [**HPS** 46:11]), Syriac ܐܚܝܢܐ;[77] הוהארי "bird-traps" (*MQ* 11a [**HPS** 277:13]), Akk. *huḥāru*.[78]

---

[72] Sperling, "Aramaic Spousal Misunderstandings," especially pp. 207–8.

[73] See Sokoloff, *DJPA*, p. 226 s.v. טלף. This noun is not attested in JBA. However, to Babylonian ears, the Mishnaic Hebrew form *ṭləfayim* (e.g., m. *Zev* 3:4) would have sounded like a pseudo-form for "two lentils." For this vocalization, see Yeivin, *Babylonian Vocalization*, p. 819.

[74] See further below, §4.7.5.

[75] Levias, *Grammar*, §§17 and 26; Epstein, *Grammar*, p. 18.

[76] This word is written חושלא in a parallel citation in **Hark** 144:17.

[77] Sokoloff, *DJBA*, p. 83 s.v אהינא.

[78] Sokoloff, *DJBA*, p. 86 s.v. הוהארא, אוחרא, אוהרא.

*Verbal* forms:

נהרתא "I snort" (*RH* 34b [**HPS** 23:3]); the *he* is very common in the verb חו״י "to show";[79] לאהויי (*Bes* 27a [**HPS** 5:10]); אהוי "showed" (*BQ* 100a [**TGAs28** ii b 10],[80] but in MS **G1**: ואחוי!); מהוו "they show" (**TGAs42** ii 1b 36).

### iii. Ḥet *for Historical* He

Interchanges in the other direction, i.e., *ḥet* for historical *he,* are also attested, e.g., חיזמי "prickly shrubs" (*Suk* 13a [**HPS** 33:10]), apparently derived from Persian *\*hēzam* (see *DJBA* 375). A common example in the EEMss is the root שה״י, which often appears as if from the root שח״י.[81]

### 3.3.1.2.2 Historical Depth

Several Talmudic statements appear to confirm the antiquity of this sound shift. The Talmud cites a ruling by Abayye (c. 280–338 CE) regarding the precise formulation of divorce deeds, which includes the following statement: ולא נכתוב לימחך דמשמע חוכא אלא למהך "And he must not write לימחך which means 'laughter' but rather למהך [to go]" (*Git* 85b, cited from **Hark** 129:32–33). The statement implies that the scribes were unable to distinguish aurally between the roots הו״ך and חו״ך, and were liable to interchange them. As noted, the shift of ח > ה is widely attested in the best manuscripts of JBA, and shifts in the other direction, while rare, are also attested.

The status of the *ḥet* in the JBA magic bowls is more difficult to assess, since the script of the magic bowls generally does not distinguish between the *ḥet* and the *he*, and employs the same grapheme for both.[82] Indeed, the scribes' failure to distinguish between these two letters may stem from the fact that the two consonants had in fact merged into a single phoneme. However, there is evidence for the total elision of the *ḥet* in two "false starts" in AMB 12b: ונ וחנק יתיה "and strangled him" (AMB 12b:8), and ולא אינ איחנוק ולא איקטול "I shall not strangle and shall not kill" (ibid. 12). The scribe who wrote this bowl apparently did not pronounce the *ḥet* in these forms and hence twice began to write the word before realizing that he had omitted the *ḥet*. The corrected version would seem to indicate that these spellings were regarded as substandard.

---

[79] Cf. Abramson, *Inyanot*, p. 194 n. 5

[80] My collation. Assaf read אחוי.

[81] On this root, see in detail §4.4.1.2.

[82] Juusola, *Linguistic Peculiarities*, p. 35 n. 44.

### 3.3.1.2.3 The Status of the *Ḥet* in Written JBA Sources

The total elision of the *ḥet* in numerous RBA forms and the widespread interchange with *he* indicate that *ḥet* ceased to be an independent phoneme in RBA but merged with *he*, which itself is occasionally elided. The assumption that *ḥet* merged with *he* finds wide support in the Aramaic magic bowls in the Jewish script.

### 3.3.1.2.4 The Yemenite Tradition

As in the case of the *ʿayin*, the Yemenite reading tradition generally follows the printed text. Words that are written in the printed text with a *he* are pronounced with a laryngeal *he*, while words written with a *ḥet* are pronounced with a pharyngeal *ḥet*. Since the printed editions are generally quite consistent regarding which lexemes employ which letter, there is little evidence for the much freer interchanges found in the best manuscripts.

## 3.3.2 Anaptyxis

### 3.3.2.1 Description of the Phenomenon

This phenomenon is quite frequently attested in the eastern manuscript tradition: when a consonant followed by a *shewa* follows a consonant closing a syllable, the unvocalized consonant is likely to receive an anaptyctic vowel: $VCC\partial CV > VCiCCV$.[83] In Mandaic, anaptyctic vowels are almost automatic in such circumstances.[84] In JBA, anaptyctic vowels are particularly common in imperfect forms with affixes such as plurals or verbs with pronominal object suffixes, and in G infinitive forms with object suffixes.

### 3.3.2.2 EEMs Evidence

In the EEMss, I have found the following examples:

---

[83] See Morag, "Geniza," pp. 65–66; Friedman, "Early Manuscripts," p. 25 and n. 94; and Lerner, "*Sheʾiltot*," p. 165; cf. Dodi, "Grammar," pp. 123–30. Boyarin, "Reading Traditions," p. 146, noted this as one of the features common to both JBA and the vocalization tradition of Targum Onqelos.

[84] Nöldeke, *MG*, §25. In Mandaic, we also find the additional vowel in Gt forms preserving the *taw*, e.g., *ʿtynsyb*. Such forms appear to be unattested in JBA, with the possible exception of I-*ʾaleph* roots.

*Imperfect*:

**1 c.s. + 3 m.s. obj.:** איגיזריה "I shall cut it down" (*BB* 33b [**HPS** 137:2]); איפירעיה "I shall pay him" (*BB* 5a [**HPS** 202:5]); אישיקליה להאיי דהבא "let me take this gold" (**TGAs28** i 10b 7).[85]

**2 f.s.** לא תידיחלי מינאי "don't be afraid of me" (*BM* 84b [**G1**]).

**3 m.s. + 1 c.s. obj.:** (לא) ליטירדן "he should not bother me" (*BB* 5b [**HPS** 202:5]). **+ 3 m. sing. obj.:** נשיבקיה "he would release it" (*Shev* 41a [**Geon** xxi 5b 13][86]). **+ 3 f.s. obj.:** נישיקלה "let him take it" (**Geon** xxxviii 8b 5); ונרימיה "let him cast it" (**Geon** xxxviii 8b 5); נישידייה "let him put it" (*BM* 80b [**G1**]).

**3 f.s. + 3 f.s. obj.:** תיקידמה "it will overtake it" (*San* 25a [**Hark** 182:15, 17]).

**2 m.pl. + 3 m.s. obj.:** לא תיקירעוה "do not tear it up" (*BB* 130b [**GK2** 19:12]).

**3 m.pl. without obj.:** ליכיתבון (**TGAs28** i 10b:21); נ[ני]כיתבון "they should write" (*Git* 40a [**Geon** viii 37b 19]);[87] וניכיתבו "and let them write" (*BQ* 103a [**GS** iv 1b 13]).[88] **+ 3 m.s. obj.:** דלא ניפיסלוה "that they should not render him unfit" (**TGAs28** iv 4a 15);[89] דלא נדיחקוה "that they should not trouble him" (*BM* 84b [**G1**]). **+ 3 f.s. obj.** לניסבוה "they should take her as a wife" (**HPS** 170:1).

**3 f.pl.** ניפיגען "they may encounter" (*BM* 84a [**G1**]).

*Infinitive*:

**+ 3 m.s. obj.:** למידירייה "to lift it" (**HPS** 115:1, 2); למיזיבניה "to buy it" (**HPS** 72:11, *BB* 88a [**HPS** 132:7], **Hark** 204:13); למיטירפיה "to seize it" (**GK1** 71:27); למיכיתביה "to write it" (**HPS** 99:12); ומימילחיה "and to salt it" (**TGAs28** iii 2a 2); למיפיסליה "to render him unfit" (Lerner, "*She'iltot*," 1b 10); למיקירעיה "to rip it" (**TGAs28** i 11a 7; **TGAs28** iii 2a 2); למיקיבׄריה "to bury him" (**HPS** 259: 20, 21); למיקיצייה "to cut it" (*Suk* 37b [**HPS** 48:2]); למישירייה

[85] So MS. Assaf read אישלקיה להאי דהבא.

[86] So MS. For דנשיבקיה Ginzberg read תשיבקיה.

[87] So MS. Ginzberg read דיכתבון, but the first part of the word is broken.

[88] The text here differs greatly from the editions of the Talmud found in other manuscripts.

[89] So MS. Assaf read: מיפסלה.

"to permit it" (**TGAs28** i 3b 27);[90] מישיקליה "to take it" (**Geon** xxvi b 13).

+ *3 f.s. obj.*: למיגימרה "to learn it" (**TGAs28** xvii 1b 4); למיזיבנה "to purchase it" (*Qid* 59a [**TGAs28** xvii 4a 8];[91] **HPS** 71:11); למישׁידֵיה "to cast it" (**HGP** 54a:36); למישׁירֵׁה "to permit it" (**HPS** 230:20); למיתיניה "to teach it" (**Hark** 34:16).

The vocalization of **HPS** indicates that the vowel was [i], presumably a short vowel. Furthermore, the appearance of this vowel before a *resh* demonstrates that the common Aramaic shift of \**i* > *a* before a *resh* is no longer productive. Theoretically, one could argue that the anaptyctic vowel was long and hence unaffected by the shift. However, it is unlikely that such a secondary vowel formed to break up a consonant cluser would be long, and there is additional evidence to suggest that the weakening of the *resh* led to a breakdown of the earlier phonological shift.[92]

### 3.3.2.3 Historical Depth

Montgomery already recognized that the form תישׁילטון "[do not] be empowered" found in AIT 6:10 contains a "new vowel" similar to that found in the parallel forms in Mandaic.[93] Other examples have now come to light: ניחידרון (or ניהידרון) "let them return" (Naveh and Shaked, MSF, 23:8), and יקירבון ביה "they may [not] touch him" (Levene, *Corpus*, M 112:4). The feature is thus shared by the language of the magic bowls, RBA, and Mandaic. It is also common in the Geniza fragments of Targum Onqelos and in Babylonian Hebrew.[94]

---

[90] So MS; Assaf read: למישׁרייה.

[91] So MS; Assaf read למיזבנה.

[92] See §2.7.2 and Morgenstern, "Non-Standard Spellings," pp. 259–60.

[93] Montgomery, *AIT*, p. 143, with reference to Nöldeke, *MG*, §25. On p. 30, Montgomery describes this form as "particularly characteristic of Mandaic" and states that the bowl's language "has other Mandaizing characteristics." These characteristics are in fact phonetic spellings found in other JBA sources written in the phonetic orthography; see Morgenstern, "Mandaic."

[94] For the Geniza fragments, see Dodi, "Grammar," pp. 123–30; for Babylonian Hebrew, see Yeivin, *Yiqtolennu*.

### 3.3.2.4 The Yemenite Manuscript Tradition

The Yemenite manuscripts contain several examples of this phenomenon, though in more limited measure.[95] Kara records around ten examples of imperfect forms, but only one infinitive form: למושעיה (*sic*) "to cover it" (*Suk* 51b [O51]).[96] However, in spite of its parallel למשעיה from JTS218, this may otherwise be interpreted as derived from root שו״ע, as the two roots interchange in this dialect.[97] I have found no others. Yet it is precisely in the infinitives that this phenomenon is most widely attested in the EEMss. The findings from the Yemenite manuscripts seem to imply that already at the time these manuscripts were copied, the preservation of such forms was diminishing in the Yemenite tradition.

### 3.3.2.5 The Yemenite Reading Tradition

In the Yemenite reading tradition, these vowels are completely absent, as they are in the printed editions of the Talmud. Consider the following examples, all mentioned above in §3.3.2.2:

אַגְדְּרֵיה "I shall remove [its dates]" (*BB* 33b [Morag, *YT*, p. 304], against printed איגדריה[98]); אַפְרְעֵיה "I shall pay him" (*BB* 5a [ʿAmr] against printed איפרעיה); תִּידְחֲלִין "you (f.s.) shall [not] fear" (*BM* 84b [Morag, *YT*, p. 130]); לִיטְרְדָן "he should [not] disturb me" (*BB* 5b [Morag, *YT*, p. 294]); לְשַׁדְיֵיה "let him put it" (*BM* 80b [ʿAmr]); תִּקְדְּמֵיה "it will overtake" (*San* 25a [Morag, *YT*, p. 304]); תִּקְרְעוּנַיה "[do not] tear it up" (*BB* 130b [Morag, *YT*, p. 296], against printed

---

[95] Kara, *Yemenite Manuscripts*, p. 119–20.

[96] The *waw* may be interpreted as a scribal error for *yod*. Alternatively, it could represent the shift *$^*$e/i > o/u* occasionally found in Yemenite sources. See Kara, *Yemenite Manuscripts*, pp. 110–15.

[97] See Sokoloff, *DJBA*, p. 1122 s.v. שעי, שוע. Such interchanges are not common in JBA but do occur in the roots לטי״י/לוי״ט (Sokoloff, *DJBA*, p. 620) and כפי״י/כפי״ף/כוי״ף (Sokoloff, *DJBA*, pp. 594, 596. For the infinitive forms of the II-*waw/yod* class bearing pronominal suffix, see n. 298 below and the literature cited there.

[98] The Yemenite reading follows the printed edition, in which the manuscripts' גזי״ר has been replaced by a questionable Aramaic root, גד״ר (see Sokoloff, *DJBA*, p. 262, s.v. 2#גדר, and bibliography *ad loc.*). Morag lists this as a C stem form. This vocalization could equally be interpreted as a G form.

(תקרעינייה);<sup>99</sup> לִידְחֲקוּהוּ "they [should not] trouble him" (*BM* 84b [Morag, *YT*, p. 295]).

For textual reasons, the Talmudic examples of the infinitive cited above are not found in the Yemenite reading tradition (the text on which they are based is not found in the printed edition). However, when we consider the examples from the sound verb with suffixed 3 m.s. object pronoun cited by Morag, it is clear that they do not preserve the anaptyctic vowel:<sup>100</sup>

לְמִיבְלְעֵיה "to enclose him" (*Shab* 30a); לְמִיעַבְּדֵיה "to make it" (*Meg* 26b); לְמִיקְטְלֵיה "to kill him" (*Git* 57b); לְמִיחְשְׁדֵיה "to suspect him" (*Bek* 29a).

As far as I have been able to ascertain, *no* examples with an anaptyctic vowel are attested in any of these categories in the Yemenite reading tradition.

### 3.3.2.6 Conclusions

There is widespread evidence from the EEMss for anaptyxis in the RBA verbal system. The phenomenon is common to Eastern Aramaic sources, being found also in JBA magic bowls, in Mandaic, and in the Babylonian vocalization of Targum Onqelos. It is also a feature of the Babylonian reading tradition of Hebrew. However, the Yemenite manuscripts seem to preserve this feature in reduced measure, and it is entirely lacking in the Yemenite reading tradition. Finally, I have not found any examples of the phenomenon in European manuscripts.

### 3.3.3 Prosthetic ʾaleph

Two roots having *šin* as the first radical appear to have a prosthetic ʾaleph in several verbal forms: שת״י "drink" and שת״ק "be silent."<sup>101</sup> Several examples of the root שת״ק "be silent" in the perfect are attested in our

---

<sup>99</sup> ʿAmr's edition reads תְּקרְעִינֵיה.
<sup>100</sup> All these examples are drawn from Morag, *YT*, p. 297.
<sup>101</sup> See Kara, *Yemenite Manuscripts*, p. 82. The forms of שת״י are discussed in Morgenstern, "Magic Bowl," pp. 214–15.

corpus. The verbs are cited here with grammatical prefixes as they appear in the text.

*With prosthetic ʾaleph:*

 *3 m.s.:* אישתיק "he was silent" (*Ber* 27a [**Geon** xxxii a 6]; *RH* 15b [**Hark** 121:12; *BM* 97a [**HPS** 113:18]); אשתיק "he was silent" (*RH* 15b [**Hark** 121:13]). *3 f.s.:* אישתיקת "she was silent" (*Qid* 12a [**HPS** 166:19]); ואשתיק "and she was silent" (*Ket* 69a [**HGP** 43a:32]).

*Without prosthetic ʾaleph:*

 *1 c.s.:* דשתיקי "that I was silent" (**Hark** 170:27). *2 m.s.:* שתיקת "you (m.s.) were silent" (**TGAs28** xvii 2a 1). *3 m.s.:* דשתיק "that he was silent" (**Hark** 121:19); ושתיק "and he was silent" (**HPS** 86:9; **Hark** 170:14); מדשתיק "from [the fact] that he was silent" (*BB* 138a [**Hark** 194:26]). *3 f.s.:* ושתיקא "and he was silent" (**HPS** 89:10). *3 pl.:* ושתיקו "and they were silent" (**TGAs42** 71:69).

From these examples, it is clear that the *ʾaleph* appears predominantly when the verb has no prefix. It therefore seems probable that we are dealing with a phonologically motivated prosthetic *ʾaleph,* and that all these examples are in the G form. By contrast, the Yemenite reading tradition regards the forms with the prosthetic *ʾaleph* as being in the Gt-stem, e.g., אִישְׁתִּיקוּ (Morag, *YT*, 126 n. 14), i.e., morphologically distinct from the G. On the basis of his findings from the Yemenite manuscripts of the Talmud, Kara hesitantly suggested that the two verbal stems interchange.[102] However, the examples he cited, אישתיק ... שתיק "he was silent … he was silent" (*RH* 15b [**JTS**218]), both appear in our corpus with the *ʾaleph.* It thus seems more likely that the two spellings represent variants of one morphological pattern, i.e., forms of the G-stem.

 Other factors speak against the historical reliability of the Yemenite reading. The assimilation of the *taw*-morpheme to the first radical consonant is extremely rare when that consonant is a sibilant and metathesis occurs, and it is not restricted to any particular verbal root.[103] The tiny number of exceptions wherein assimilation occurs is far outnumbered by the examples without assimilation. Accordingly, were אישתיק a Gt form we would also expect to find numerous examples of אישתתיק, given the

---

[102] Kara, *Yemenite Manuscripts*, p. 134.

[103] The few examples are discussed below, §4.4.5.2.2. In these cases, the unassimilated form is also attested. The phenomenon is also occasionally attested in Palestinian Aramaic. See Ben-Ḥayyim, "Word Studies," pp. 207–8; Bar-Asher, "Vatican 32," pp. 145–46.

frequency with which the verb appears. However, there appear to be no recorded examples of the Gt preserving the *taw*-morpheme. Moreover, there is considerable evidence for the imperfect of the G form.[104]

## 3.4 Verbal Morphology

### 3.4.1 The Perfect

In this section we shall consider various aspects of the morphology of the perfect. The following discussions do not generally apply to III-*yod* roots except in cases where the forms of this category match those of the sound verb.

#### 3.4.1.1 The 1 c.s. and f.s. Forms

#### 3.4.1.1.1 Background

The 1 c.s. and 3 f.s. forms vary greatly from dialect to dialect, and the forms in JBA remain somewhat uncertain. On the basis of the *plene* spellings of the G *paᶜil* forms (e.g., שתיקי "I was silent" [**Hark** 170:27]) and the D, קבילי "I received" (*BQ* 62b [**HPS** 133:9]), Kutscher suggested that in JBA, as in the Babylonian vocalization of Targum Onqelos, the perfect forms were derived from the 3 m.s. forms, with penultimate stress, e.g., *\*kə'tabit > kə'tabi* (כְּתַבִי), *\*kə'tabat > kə'tabā* (כְּתַבָא).[105] In contrast, Morag claimed that the vocalization of **HPS** distinguishes between two forms of the 3 f.s. perfect: one preserving the final *taw*, קְטַלַת, which conjugates "like Targumic Aramaic," and another, without the final *taw*, קטלָא.[106] Subsequently, Kara provided additional vocalized examples from the Yemenite manuscripts, as well as a further example from **HPS**.[107] When Morag addressed this issue once again in his comprehensive work on the Yemenite reading tradition, he noted that the Yemenite reading tradition demonstrates a complementary distribution between the forms bearing or lacking the final *taw* in both 1 c.s. and 3 f.s. forms:

---

[104] Sokoloff, *DJBA*, p. 1186, s.v. שת״ק. Examples are found in the Yemenite manuscripts and the Geniza fragments, e.g., לישתוק "let it be silent" (*Zev* 10a [**Col**]; *San* 15b [T-S NS 329.772]).

[105] Kutscher, "Review," pp. 163–65, 168–69 (reprinted in Kutscher, *Studies*, pp. 241–43, 246–47).

[106] Morag, "Vocalisation," p. 92 (reprinted in Morag, *Studies*, p. 201).

[107] Kara, *Yemenite Manuscripts*, pp. 138–39.

| | With final *taw*: | Without final *taw*: |
|---|---|---|
| **1 c.s:** | קְטָלִית | קְטָלִי |
| **3 f.s:** | קְטָלַת | קָטְלָא |

In this later study, Morag even went so far to claim that the verbal base *qaṭal-* does not represent genuine Eastern Aramaic, but was "apparently brought over to the Yemenite tradition from Targumic Aramaic."[108]

### 3.4.1.1.2 Evidence against Morag's Proposal

Morag's view may be challenged on several grounds. First of all, Morag assumes that there is a clear distinction between the language of the Talmud and the reading tradition of Targum Onqelos, as though the Babylonian language had no influence over the vocalization of the Targum. However, it has long been known that there are several points of contact between JBA and the language of Targum Onqelos.[109] It should be emphasized that in the case of the Talmudic corpus, this is not a result of external influence of the Targum language on JBA; if anything, it seems that the phonology of Targum Onqelos has been influenced by the Babylonian idiom.[110]

Secondly, there is no support for the assumption that the conjugation of all perfect forms of the G-stem on the basis of the 3 m.s. is a non-Eastern Aramaic form. As Morag himself noted, this morphological pattern is also unattested in the Western Aramaic dialects.[111] The vocalization traditions of these dialects concord with Classical Syriac and Mandaic in distinguishing between 1 c.s. and 3 f.s. forms, which are based upon *qVṭl-*, and other verbal forms, which are based upon *qaṭVl-*. The conjugation of the G perfect on the basis of the 3 m.s. cannot therefore be taken as a non-Eastern Aramaic form but must be regarded as an isogloss shared by the Babylonian vocalizers of Targum Onqelos/Jonathan and some vocalization traditions of JBA. Since, as we have seen, this pattern is unique to these Jewish Babylonian linguistic traditions, there is no

---

[108] Morag, *YT*, p. 128. Elsewhere Morag rejected the influence of Onqelos on the vocalization of these forms, declaring the explanation too simplistic. See Morag, "Oral Transmission," p. 341.

[109] Boyarin, "Reading Traditions," p. 146.

[110] I shall address this issue in a future study. Meanwhile, cf. Boyarin "Reading Traditions," p. 146, and Müller-Kessler, "Targum Onqelos," where a different perspective is presented.

[111] Morag, *YT*, p. 128 n. 26.

compelling reason to reject it as a result of secondary, outside influence.[112]

### 3.4.1.1.3 EEMs Evidence

The evidence of the vocalization found in the EEMss appears to support Kutscher's proposal that the G perfect in RBA shares with Targum Onqelos/Jonathan a conjugation based upon the 3 m.s.

Let us begin with the 1 c.s. All the manuscript evidence points to the form קְטַלִי:

וַאֲמַרִי, וְאָמְרִי "I said" (Morag, *Vocalised Manuscripts*, no. 3); נְטַרִי "I guarded" (ibid., no. 84); אֲמַרִי "I said." זְבַנִי "I bought" (Friedman, "Early Manuscripts," p. 25);[113] אֲמַרִי "I said" (*BB* 26a [**TGAs28** xxxii 5b 15]).[114]

The evidence for the 3 f.s. is less conclusive, but nevertheless there are grounds for casting doubt on Morag's supposition that קַטְלָא perfects are attested in the manuscripts. The two examples that Morag believed he had found in **HPS**, מכי נֹפְקָא "from when she leaves" (**HPS** 238:17) and עד דבֹּגְרֹה "until she matures" (**HPS** 238:17) are to be interpreted on contextual grounds as participle forms relating to potential cases in the future. They were clearly regarded as such by the translator of *Hilchot Re'u*, who rendered these examples משעה שתצא "from the time that she will leave" (**HR** 114:15), and עד שתבגור "until she will mature" (ibid.), respectively.

The example of קַטְלָא that Kara cited may similarly be interpreted as a participle.[115] The text reads: ואילו איתתא דְּיַלְדָא זכר ונקבא יֹתבֹא ארבסר יומי ... והיכא דיליד חד ולבתר כמה יומי הדר יֹלידֹא אחרינא ... ואילו איתתא דאֹפֹילֹת... "Whereas a woman who **gives/gave** birth to a boy and a girl sits for fourteen days. If she gave birth to one and after a few days gave birth to the other... Whereas a woman who aborted..." (**HPS** 212:18–20). Kara assumed on the basis of the parallel verbs דיליד and יֹלידֹא, both meaning "(who) gave birth," and דאֹפֹילֹת "who aborted," that the verb

---

[112] In later western transmissions of Targum Onqelos/Jonathan, the Babylonian vocalization was rendered into Tiberian vocalization, sometimes with minor phonological changes. However, these texts do not constitute independent evidence for this vocalization pattern in Aramaic dialects outside Babylonia, since they are clearly based upon the Babylonian model.

[113] פְּשַׁעִי "I was negligent," cited by Friedman, "Early Manuscripts," p. 25, is inconclusive. On this vocalization, see Friedman, ibid., n. 92.

[114] Printed by Assaf without vocalization.

[115] Kara, *Yemenite Manuscripts*, p. 138 n. 31.

דְּיָלְדָא must be translated as a perfect "who gave birth." While this may have been the original intent of the author of this legal formulation,[116] it is not impossible that the vocalizer understood the form דְּיָלְדָא as a participle, particularly in light of other examples wherein similar laws are formulated using a participle, e.g.: ואילו איתתא **דמפלא** דמות חיויא...לידה הויא ויהבינן לה ימי טמאה וימי טהרה "Whereas a woman who aborts the likeness of a snake … it is a birth, and we give her the days of impurity and the days of purity" (**HPS** 218:11–13).

By contrast, as Morag already noted, **HGP** vocalizes נְפַקָא "[What] resulted?"[117] Regarding the forms preserving the final *taw*, as Morag noted **HPS** contains one certain example נְפַקָת "it went out" (**HPS** 307:19). Since we have not found any clear evidence in these manuscripts of secondary linguistic borrowing from the Targum, it seems most likely that these forms are original to JBA, and that the admittedly meager evidence in favor of the form קְטַלָא should not be dismissed on the grounds of the later Yemenite tradition.

### 3.4.1.1.4 Conclusion

The Yemenite oral tradition differentiates between the verbal base of forms preserving the final consonant of the suffixed morpheme, *qəṭal-*, and the base of forms in which the final consonant has been apocopated, *qaṭl-*. We have seen that this distinction is not supported by the early manuscript evidence, which, on the contrary, seems to indicate that the verbal base remained *qəṭal-* or *qəṭil-*, whether the suffixed subject morpheme was apocopated or not.

We may suggest that the reading method attested in the Yemenite reading tradition has influenced by the homographs קטלי *qāṭlī* (G participle 3 m.pl.) and קטלא *qāṭlā* (G participle 3 f.s.). The vocalization of the participles was brought over into the perfect forms when the two spellings were identical, i.e., when the final *taw*-morpheme of the perfect was elided:

---

[116] **HPS** is not an authograph.

[117] Morag recorded this example as appearing in **HGP** 6a:34; however, this reference seems to be mistaken. The form appears twice in this manuscript in a citation from *BM* 68a [**HGP** 27b:20, 21].

| Tense Spelling | Perfect | Participle |
|---|---|---|
| קטלי | 1 c.s. | 3 m.pl. |
| קטלא | 3 f.s. | 3 f.s. |

### 3.4.1.2 1 c.s. Apocopated Forms

#### 3.4.1.2.1 EEMs Evidence

Twice in his writings Kutscher alluded to the existence of 1 c.s. perfect forms in **HPS** identical to those of 3 m.s., but cited no examples.[118] I have found the following examples, three in **HPS**, one in *BM* **G1**:

אין **חטף** ודידי **חטף.**

Yes, **I snatched** [it], but **I snatched** that which was my own. (*BB* 33b [**HPS** 137:8,9])

אין **שקל** ודידי **שקל.**

Yes, **I took** [it], but **I took** that which was my own. (*Qid* 13b [**HPS** 167:3])[119]

ההוא גברא דאוגר ליה חמארא לחבריה. אמליה לא תיזי באורחא דנהר
פקוד דאיכא מיא ; זיל באורחא דנרש דליכא מיא. אתא אמ״ל: אין באורחא
דנהר פקוד **אזל** ומיהו לא הוה איכא מיא ומית חמארא. אמי׳ רבה מה לי
לשקר? אובעי אמ״ל באורחא דנרש **אזל.**

A certain man rented out a donkey to his companion, and said to him: "Don't go via Nehar Peqod, where there is water; go via Narash, where there is no water." He came and said to him: "Yes, **I went** via Nehar Peqod, but there was no water and the donkey died." Rava said: "Why lie? If he wants he could say "**I went** via Narash."'" (*BM* 81b [**G1**])

---

[118] Kutscher, "Review," p. 170 (reprinted in Kutscher, *Studies*, p. 248); "Neutralisation," pp. 37–38. Kutscher stated explicitly that he had found examples but had not recorded their references.

[119] This is translated in the medieval Hebrew translation of *Halachot Pesuqot*, *Hilchot Reʾu* (p. 82): לקחתי ושל עצמי לקחתי.

אזל חד מיניהו מסרה לפהרגבנא דמלכא. אמר אביי. יכיל למימר. אין. **מסר** ודילי **מסר**.

One of them went and handed it over to the royal guard. Abbaye says: "He can claim, 'Yes, I handed it over, and it was mine that I handed over.'" (*BQ* 117a [**HPS** 129:16–17])[120]

In all of these examples, the context requires the 1 c.s., and in the other textual witnesses we find the קטלי form. It is interesting that all of these examples appear in the context of a statement of partial admission.

We may assume that the development here is similar to that of the doubly apocopated form of the 3 f.s., i.e., *ʾa'marit̲ > *ʾa'mari > ʾa'mar.[121]

### 3.4.1.2.2 The Yemenite Tradition

Kara noted the existence of the apocopated forms in the Yemenite manuscripts, such as אמר רב פפא או לא **נסיב** כהינתא לא **איעתר**. אמר רב כהנא או לא **נסיב** כהינתא לא גלאי "R. Pappa said: 'Had I not **married** a priest's daughter I **would** not **have grown rich'**; R. Kahana said: 'Had I not **married** a priest's daughter I would not have emigrated'" (*Pes* 49a [JTS1623, Col]). However, as he noted, in the one apparent instance in which this form has survived in the printed editions of the Talmud, **אנא איקלע** לסורא "I happened to come to Sura" (*Pes* 117b) the verb is corrected in ʿAmr's edition to אֲקַלַעִי.[122] Accordingly, this rare form is completely lost in the Yemenite reading tradition.

### 3.4.1.3 1 c.s., 2 c.s., 3 f.s. with Object Suffixes: Background

The manuscript evidence appears to suggest that the 1 c.s., 2 c.s., and 3 f.s. verbs bearing pronominal object suffixes share very similar structure. From the orthography and attested vocalized forms, it emerges that the 1 c.s. qa'ṭali(t̲) becomes qaṭalt-, while 3 f.s. qa'ṭala(t̲) becomes qaṭalt-, perhaps with a fricative inflectional *taw* as in Classical Syriac. Accordingly, as in Classical Mandaic, wherein the form *lgʾtth* may be "I took him," "you took him," or "she took him,"[123] in RBA we find identical

---

[120] The same form, מסר, also appears in the citation of this text in **HGP** 18b:9–10.

[121] For the 3 f.s. see Kutscher, "Review," p. 168 (reprinted in Kutscher, *Studies*, p. 246).

[122] Kara, *Yemenite Manuscripts*, p. 143.

[123] Nöldeke, *MG*, §200.

spellings for all three forms. In the following example, we find both the
1 c.s. and 2 m.s.:

ההוא דאמ' ליה לחבריה: מאי בעית בהא ארעא? אמי ליה: מיפלניא **זבנתה**
דזבנה מינך. אמ' ליה. ולא קא מודית דארעא דידי היא ואת מיני לא **זבנתה**.

A certain man said to his companion: What's your business with
this land? He replied: **I bought it** from X who bought it from you.
He replied: Aren't you admitting that the land is mine and that **you
didn't buy it** from me? (*BB* 30a-b [**HPS** 135:7–9])

Evidence for the 2 f.s. is extremely rare, but I have found the following
example:

לא יהבתיה "you did not give it" (*Ket* 85a [**HGP** 44a:18]).

For the 3 f.s. I have found several examples:

טרקתיה "it stung him" (*Ket* 50a [**Hark** 158:21]); שמעתיה "she heard
him" (*BM* 84b [**G1**]); ילדתיה "she gave birth to him" (*Yev* 80b [**Geon**
xx 1b 27]); תבעתיה "she sued him" (*BM* 17a [**HPS** 118:14]); שקלתיה
"she took him" (**TGAs42** vi 1b 3).

The examples gathered by Kara, e.g., שקלתיה "she took it" (*San* 21a [**J**])[124]
and גרעתה "it reduced it" (*Suk* 6b [**JTS**218]), appear to follow the same
pattern.[125]

### 3.4.1.4 1 c.s. Forms
Here we shall concentrate on the 1 c.s. forms, for which the evidence of
the early manuscripts differs from that of the Yemenite reading tradition.

### 3.4.1.4.1 EEMs Evidence
All the examples from the older manuscripts are written without a *yod*
between the third radical and the suffixed pronoun, i.e., קטלת- and not
קטלית-. The consistently defective spellings accord with the vocalized
form פְּרַעְתָּךְ "I paid you" (*Shev* 41b [**HPS** 199:19]) and the evidence of the
other Aramaic dialects in suggesting, as noted above, that when the ob-

---

[124] Kara, *Yemenite Manuscripts*, p. 317.
[125] An exception is קדימתיה "it preceeded it" (*Tan* 23a [**J**]), which is probably a G
form of the *paᶜil* pattern, hence *qadimteh* or *qᵊdimteh*. See Sokoloff, *DJBA*, p. 984
s.v. קדי, קדם.

ject pronoun is suffixed to the verbal base, the *i* vowel is not found between the root and the 1 c.s. morpheme. The rule is valid in all the examples I have gathered. The following are the Talmudic examples drawn from the EEMss. The post-Talmudic examples found in the EEmss are no different.

G

+ **2 m.s.:** גזלתך "I robbed you" (*BM* 16a [**Hark** 160:30]); פְּרַעְתָּך "I paid you" (*BB* 32b [**HGP** 1a:19]).

+ **3 m.s.:** דְּזַבַּנְתֵּיה "which I bought" (*BB* 36a [**HGP** 1a:34]); חטפתיה "I snatched it" (*BB* 34a [**HPS** 137:11]); מסרתיה "I handed it over" (*BQ* 98b [**G1**]); מְסֹרְתֵּיה "I handed it over" (*BM* 42b [**HGP** 23a:22]); דִּפְרַעְתֵּיה "which I paid him" (*BB* 32b [**HGP** 1a:18]).

+ **3 f.s.:** אכלתה "I used it" (*BB* 33b [**Hark** 168:24]); אמרתה "I stated it" (*Ket* 63b [**HGP** 42b:37]; *BB* 65a [**HPS** 147:2]); זבנתה "I bought it" (*BB* 30b [**HPS** 135:9,11]; *BB* 33b [**HPS** 137: 5, **Hark** 168:24]). זְבַנְתָּה *BB* 31a ([**HGP** 1a:30]); פרעתה "I paid her"(*BM* 17a [**HPS** 118:15]); שמעתה "I heard it" *ʿAra* 22a [**HPS** 189:10]).

+ **3 m.pl.:** גזרתינהו "I would chop them" (*BQ* 81b [**G1**]).

### 3.4.1.4.2 The Yemenite Manuscript Tradition
As with the 3 f.s. forms, the evidence for the 1 c.s. form from the Yemenite manuscripts of the Talmud matches the form found in the EEMss. Hence שבקתך "I have left you" (*Suk* 48b [**JTS**108]), שמעתה "I heard it" (*Meg* 29a [**Col**]),[126] and אמרתה "I stated it" (*Pes* 60b [**JTS**1623]).[127] Moreover, Kara notes that the form אמריתה, common in the printed editions, is *never found in the Yemenite manuscripts*.[128]

### 3.4.1.4.3 The Yemenite Reading Tradition
The evidence from the EEMss and the Yemenite manuscripts render suspect the examples found in the Yemenite reading tradition of קַטְלִית-, i.e., אֲמַרִיתַהּ (*Ber* 45b [Morag, *YT*, p. 293], printed text: אמריתא) and שַׁמְעִיתַהּ (*Git* 26b [ibid.], printed text: שמעיתא). These would appear to be readings influenced by the corrupt printed editions of the Talmud.

---

126 Kara, *Yemenite Manuscripts*, p. 328.
127 Ibid.
128 Ibid., n. 305.

### 3.4.1.4.4 Conclusion

The unanimous evidence of the EEMss and the Yemenite manuscripts, as well as comparative evidence from other Aramaic dialects, imply that the in the sound verbs, the form of the 1 c.s. G perfect to which pronominal suffixes were attached was qəṭalt-.[129] The examples formed on the basis of the forms qaṭliṯ- found in the Yemenite reading tradition are not supported by the historical evidence and represent the influence of the printed editions on the Yemenite reading tradition.

### 3.4.1.5 1 c.pl.

### 3.4.1.5.1 EEMs Evidence

While the Standard Aramaic morpheme -nā is often (though not exclusively) used in Geonic writings and in legal deeds, there is little evidence for its use in the Talmudic sections preserved in early manuscripts.[130] Instead, these manuscripts generally employ the morpheme -nan when the verb does not bear a pronominal object suffix. The following represent Talmudic examples attested in early manuscripts:[131]

G:

> חתמנן "we signed" (Giṭ 52b [**HPS** 81:20]); טרַחנן "we took the trouble" (BM 76a [**G1**]);[132] סמכנן "we relied" (BB 128b [**HPS** 93:7]). עבדנן "we did" (BM 76a [**G1**]); פתחנן "we opened" (BQ 112b [**HPS** 123:7]); שלחנן "we sent" (BQ 112b [**HPS** 123:7]; Shev 48a [**HPS** 198:3]).

C:

> אַשכחנָן "we found" (Shev 48a [**HGP** 14a:26]); אשכחן "we found" (Shev 48a [**HPS** 198:3]).

---

[129] We may assume that the a vowel following the middle radical is the original stem vowel. However, since no examples of paʿil or paʿul verbs are attested, and the one vocalized example from **HPS** is from a III-ʿayin root, this supposition remains to be proven.

[130] For the single example, seè below.

[131] I have excluded III-yod verbs, for which the suffixed morphemes differ.

[132] The vocalization is in the manuscript. See Friedman, "Early Manuscripts," p. 31, who recognized the significance of this example and its vocalization to the discussion at hand.

In addition, in only two roots do we find a form with a single *nun*:[133]

אמרן "we said" (*Pes* 6a [**HPS** 10:6]; *RH* 34b [**HPS** 23:3]; *RH* 35a
[**HPS** 26:14]; *BQ* 8b [**HPS** 82:19]; *Yev* 41b [**HPS** 230:2]; *Git* 42b [**HPS**
83:2,4,6]; *BQ* 112b [**HPS** 124:12]; *BQ* 113a [**HPS** 124:13,15]); אשכחן
"we found" (*Qid* 27b [**HPS** 197:5]; *Qid* 28a [**HPS** 197:8]).

In only one case have I found the *-nā* morpheme employed in Talmudic
material: אמרנא ליה "we said to him" (*Ned* 91a [**HPS** 176:10]).

The simplest explanation for this variety of forms seems to be that
the *-nan* morpheme developed on the basis of the pronoun אנן. The single occurrence of the morpheme *-nā* may be due to classical or dialectal
influence (it occurs in tractate *Nedarim*), but another possible explanation
is that the final *nun* has been assimilated into the *lamed* of the preposition
ליה.[134] It remains unclear why the roots אמ״ר and שכ״ח take the *-n* morpheme. Whatever the reason, the fact remains that in the overwhelming
majority of cases, Talmudic Aramaic employs the pronominal suffix *-nan*.

Very occasionally in the EEMss we find perfect forms with the subj.
suffix ין-: איצטריכינן "we needed" (**TGAs42** 70:25), אסיקינן "we concluded" (**Hark** 128:34), אסקינן "we concluded" (**Hark** 163:10, **GS** x 2b 6),
and אכרזינן "we announced" (*San* 26b [**HGP** 39a:23]). This morpheme
presumably arose by analogy to the 1 m.pl. participle forms such as
סֻמְכִינָן "we rely" (**HPS** 207:21), though it is unclear if this morpheme of
the perfect is *-inan* or follows the participle morpheme *-innan* in having a
geminated first *nun*.

In either case, these forms are extremely rare in the oldest manuscripts, and there appear to be no examples in the very best textual witnesses such as **HPS**, *BQ* **G1** and *BM* **G1**. It is possible that the confusion
of the perfect *-nan* and participle *-innan* endings is a phenomenon that
originated with the non-native copyists, rather than in the spoken language, and that it already affected some of the early manuscripts. Given
the wide prevalence of the participle forms—the Talmud "speaks" primarily with the 1 m.pl. participles "we do such and such"—the participle
morpheme gradually pushed out the genuine perfect morpheme *-nan*.

---

[133] In the III-*yod* verbs, we find also תנן "we have taught" (e.g., *Suk* 35b [**HPS**
46:11], *BB* 71a [**HPS** 148:9] and אתן "we have come" (e.g., *Pes* 36a [**HPS** 13:16];
*MQ* 13a [**HPS** 280:4]; *Hul* 104a [**G1**], always spelled defectively in the best manuscripts). It is not always possible to know if forms such as תנינן (*Shev* 41b [**HPS**
199:11]) are perfects or participles.

[134] See Morgenstern, "Mandaic."

### 3.4.1.5.2 Historical Depth

Examples of the 1 c.pl. perfect are rare in the magic bowls. Juusola includes only one example of the perfect -nā.[135] Recently published texts contain at least one more example: אנחנא לא ידענא "we did not know" (M142:5).[136] However, of greater significance than these forms preserving the historical morpheme are those that appear in a text from the British Museum with the morpheme -nan: סליקנן לאיגרא אמרן "we went up to the roof, we said."[137] סליקנן cannot be interpreted as a participle form, which would be סלקינן.

### 3.4.1.5.3 The Yemenite Manuscripts

According to Kara, the "classical" morpheme -nā is very common in the Yemenite manuscripts. However, there is also widespread representation of forms with the -nan morpheme, such as קבילנן "we received" (Suk 14b [O51, JTS218]).[138] The Yemenite manuscripts also show a wider distribution of the morpheme -n, which appears there in roots other than אמ״ר and שכ״ח: שכיבן "we lay" (San 7a [J]).[139]

### 3.4.1.5.4 The Yemenite Reading Tradition

What is the situation in the Yemenite reading tradition? In the sound verb, Morag found but a single example of the morpheme -nan: שְׁכֵיבַן "we lay" (San 7a [Morag, YT, p. 127]). Even this example appears in only some traditions and, interestingly, is a reading against the orthography of the printed edition, שכיבן, a reading which, as we have seen, is supported by the Yemenite manuscript of this tractate. Further examples are found in the I-yod class, יְהֵיבַן "we gave" (BB 73b [Morag, YT, p. 200]), and the II-waw/yod class (Morag, YT, p. 212): דַּשַׁן "we ignored" (Ket 62a), מֵיתַן "we died" (Ber 31a), and קַמַן "we arose" (Git 57b), a reading

---

[135] Juusola, Linguistic Peculiarities, p. 161.

[136] Levene, Corpus, p. 93.

[137] The significance of these examples was recognized by Juusola, Linguistic Peculiarities, p. 161, who drew from a preliminary publication by Gordon, but was unable to confirm their authenticity on the basis of photographs. A photograph is now found in Segal's Catalogue, pl. 36 (text 036A:6); the material readings are certain.

[138] Kara, Yemenite Manuscripts, p. 147. Kara rightly regarded these examples as sufficient to dispel Kutscher's doubts regarding the authenticity of this form, as expressed in Kutscher, "Review," p. 165 (Studies, p. 243).

[139] Kara, Yemenite Manuscripts, p. 147. The example אוקימן "we established" (Pes 11a [JTS1623]) that Kara cites appears only in a marginal addition, and is moreover written או קימן over two lines.

against the orthography of the printed edition (קמינן) which some authorities read קָמִינָּ.[140] When we consider the examples from the other
verbal classes and stems, it becomes clear that by far the most common
morphemes are נא- -nā[141] and ינן- -innan.[142]

### 3.4.1.5.5 Conclusions

Whereas in the accurate manuscripts the -nan morpheme is predominant
in the 1 c.pl., in the Yemenite reading tradition, which generally follows
the printed text, it is a minority form. Instead, the Yemenite reading tradition overwhelmingly favors the -nā or -innan morphemes. It thus seems
likely that the Yemenite reading tradition does not present us with an
accurate reflection of the 1 c.pl. perfect morphemes employed in the
Aramaic idiom of the Talmud. Whereas in the earliest manuscripts the
-nan morpheme is predominant, with the exception of very specific roots
which employ an -an morpheme, it is represented only as a secondary
form in the Yemenite reading tradition; by contrast, the -in(n)an morpheme, which is not attested for the perfect in the very best manuscripts
and is very rare in other early manuscripts, becomes widespread in the
Yemenite reading tradition, reflecting its common appearance in the
printed editions.

It is worth reiterating that although -nā is the more classical form,
this fact does not argue for its primacy in the Talmudic tradition. On the
contrary, as we have seen, its use is rare in Talmudic manuscripts and in
citations from the Talmud in later Geonic literature. This distinction between the language of the Talmud on the one hand and the language of
Biblical Aramaic, Targum Onqelos and later Geonic writings on the other
hand, is characteristic of the better manuscripts. It is possible that the
more widespread use of the -nā morpheme in the later manuscripts and
the printed editions resulted from secondary influence from these
sources on the manuscript tradition.

### 3.4.1.6 1 c.pl. with Object Suffix

### 3.4.1.6.1 Introduction

There is an even greater divergence between the Yemenite tradition and
the early manuscripts as regards 1 c.pl. verbs bearing object suffixes.

---

[140] It appears that Morag himself was uncertain regarding this latter reading. He
listed it both as a perfect form and as a 3 pl. participle. See Morag, *YT*, p. 212.

[141] The transcription follows the phonology of the Yemenite reading tradition.

[142] Cf. the examples of נא- -nå and ינן- -innan cited by Morag, *YT*, pp. 141, 147,
158, 164, 173, 177, 180, 193, 200, 206, 227, 246.

### 3.4.1.6.2 EEMs Evidence

In general, the early manuscripts demonstrate the following rule: the 1 c.pl. morpheme is shortened to -n-, and the pronouns are affixed as if to a verb ending in a consonant. This is clearly demonstrated by the fact that the 3 m.s. object pronoun is יה- *eh* rather than ה- *-h* or הי- *-hi*, the postvocalic allomorphs. JBA thus differs in this respect from the language of Targum Onqelos. Contrast, for example, גמרניה "we have learned it" (*BQ* 91a [**G1**]) with אתיבנֹהי "we have returned it" (TO Gen 44:8).[143] I have found only one exception to this rule, which appears in a deed formula cited in *Halachot Pesuqot*: ואנחנא הוא דאחרניהי "it is we who delayed it" (**HPS** 99:13). However, the language of this deed is archaic and does not reflect the standard Talmudic or Geonic idiom.

I have found the following examples in the early manuscripts:

G:

+ *3 m.s.:* גמרניה "we have learned it" (*BQ* 91a [**G1**]); שבקניה "we abandoned it" (**Geon** xxxviii 7b 20).

+ *3 f.s.:* אמרנה "we said it" (**GK1** 71:15,16); בדקנה "we checked it" (**Hark** 41:25); שאילנה "we asked it" (**Hark** 107:9); שבקנה "we abandoned it" (**TGAs28** i 5b 1); תנינה "we taught it" (*MQ* 8b [**HPS** 275:11]; *Ket* 81a [**HPS** 229:2]; *BQ* 88b [**G1**] and many other examples); דחינה "we rejected it" (**Hark** 46:20).

D:

+ *2 f.s.:* סליקניך "we would remove you [your claim]" (*Ket* 69a [**HGP** 43a:31]).

+ *3 m.s.:* חייבניה "we have obligated him" (**Hark** 278:5, 8).

+ *3 f.s.:* פרישנה "we have explained it" (**Hark** 43:4; **Hark** 118:32; **Hark** 167:13; **TGAs28** xvii 2a 11); תריצנה "we explained it" (**Hark** 81:12; **Hark** 155:24; **TGAs42** x 3a 13); סיענה "we supported it" (**Hark** 93:6).

C:

+ *2 m.s.:* אפסדנך "we caused you loss" (*BQ* 89a [**G1**]).

+ *3 m.s.:* אחזיקניה "we have given its rights" (**Hark** 277:7).

---

[143] The same is true of the 2 m.s. morpheme -*t*, which, in contrast to the practice in Targum Onqelos, does not take the -*hi* pronoun. See §3.5.1.2.1.

+ *3 f.s.:* אוקימנה "we have established it" (*BQ* 116b [**HPS** 129:2];
**Hark** 178:9, and many others); אשכחנה "we found it" (**Hark** 41:3);
אסיקנה "we concluded it" (**Hark** 225:33).

+ *3 m.pl.:* אדכריננון "we mentioned them" (**Hark** 45:9); vocalized example: יְהַבְנָהוּ "we gave them" (*BM* 70a [**G1**]).[144]

I have found only two examples which conform to neither the Babylonian Talmudic form nor the earlier classical form: (לא) גרסיניה מעולם
"we have never studied it" (**Hark** 133:32) and שאיליניה "we asked him"
(**Hark** 277:16). Both examples appear in MS Firk IIA32.1, which is overall
very reliable but also contains some later elements.[145]

### 3.4.1.6.3 The Yemenite Manuscripts
The examples recorded by Kara appear to match the findings of the
EEMss, e.g., שכחנה "we have forgotten it" (*Pes* 106b [**JTS**1623, **Col**]),
קטלנה "we killed her" (*Pes* 50a [**JTS**1623, **Col**]),[146] בטילניה "we would
have annulled it" (*Tan* 8b [**J**]),[147] and others. Exceptional would appear to
be אוקמינה "we established it" (*Yom* 33b, 80a [**JTS**1623]).[148]

### 3.4.1.6.4 The Yemenite Reading Tradition
When we compare this evidence to the Yemenite reading tradition, a
very different picture emerges. While forms according with the older
manuscript tradition are attested, such as קְרַעֲנֵיהּ "we ripped it" (*BB* 169a
[Morag, *YT*, p. 294]) and כְּתַבְנֵיהּ "we wrote it" (*BB* 171b [Morag, *YT*, p.
294]), these are in the minority. Regarding קְרַעֲנֵיהּ, Morag notes that some
authorities read קַרְעִינֵיהּ, in other words they emend the ancient form, in
this case preserved in the printed editions, in favor of a secondary form
which has little textual support in the oldest manuscripts.

In this category too, the fact that the Yemenite reading tradition is
based upon the printed editions of the Talmud has led to the creation of
questionable forms that appear to arise from textual errors:[149] קַבְּלִינָךְ (*Pes*

---

[144] Friedman, "Early Manuscripts," p. 26.

[145] See §2.14.3.2.

[146] Kara, *Yemenite Manuscripts*, p. 318.

[147] Ibid., p. 323.

[148] JTS217 reads אוקינוה, showing assimilation of the *mem* but also an unexpected
*waw*.

[149] The verb שַׁקְלִינָהוּ (*Tan* 22a [Morag, *YT*, p. 294]), which Morag interpreted as a
1 c.s. perfect + 3 m.pl. obj., is better interpreted in the context as a 3 m.pl. perfect +
3 m.pl. obj. suffix, "they took them."

89b [Morag, *YT*, p. 300]). The word appears four times on this page. The two Yemenite manuscripts predominantly read קבֵּילָנָךְ, and once *in one manuscript*, קבלינך.[150] Also consider: אַקְדִּישִׁינְהוּ "we sanctified them" (*ʿAZ* 52b [Morag, *YT*, p. 304]), against the grammatically correct Talmudic orthography אקדישננהו;[151] אַחֲתִינֵיהּ "we brought him down" (*BB* 31b [Morag, *YT*, p. 310]); אַסְקִינֵיהּ "we brought him up" (*Ket* 26b [Morag, *YT*, p. 311]); אוֹתְבִינֵיהּ "we sat him down" (*San* 20a [Morag, *YT*, p. 313]).

### 3.4.1.6.5 Conclusion
The EEMss almost exclusively employ the simple -נ- -*n*- inflectional morpheme before affixed object pronouns. The situation generally obtains in the Yemenite manuscripts as well. By contrast, the Yemenite reading tradition often employs a form -*inn*-, which does not appear to be original, but influenced by the printed editions.

## 3.4.2 Imperfect

### 3.4.2.1 1 c.s. Morpheme
#### 3.4.2.1.1 EEMs Evidence
In all verbal stems with the exception of the C, the 1 c.s. morpheme would appear to be *ʾi*-. We have one vocalized example from **HPS**, דָאִיהוֹי (HPS 235:21), and the vowel is frequently indicated by a *yod*:[152]

G:

איבדוק "I shall test" (*Yev* 65a [**HPS** 156:16, **Geon** xvii 2a 23]); איזבון "Shall I buy . . .?" (*BM* 108a [**HPS** 141:13, **HGP** 6a:7]; *BB* 30b [**HPS** 135:19); אִיטְרֹח "I shall take the trouble" (*BM* 67b [**HGP** 27b:4]); איטרח "I shall take the trouble" (*BM* 108b [**HPS** 142:19, **HGP** 6a:26]; **Hark** 171:28); איסוב "I shall marry" (*Yev* 65a [**HPS** 156:16]); איפוק "I shall go out" (**HPS** 177:13); אִיתֵּן "I shall give" (*BM* 51a [**HGP** 24b:1]); איפלוג "I shall divide" (**Hark** 171:28*); איפסוד "I shall lose" (*Ket* 94b [**HGP** 31b:2]); אישקול "I shall take" (*BQ* 103a [**HPS**

---

[150] For details see Kara, *Yemenite Manuscripts*, p. 323 and n. 296.

[151] So in Vilna ed. Morag reports the printed orthography as being אקדישיננהו, but I have not found this spelling in any of the printed editions that I have consulted. The manuscripts (**JTS15** and **P1337**) contain a textual (not merely grammatical) variant: אקדשונהו "*they* sanctified them."

[152] I have cited only forms relevant to our discussion here, i.e., forms wherein the Yemenite tradition is attested and differs from the findings in EEMss. Examples of the D are cited in the next section.

72:14]); אֵיקְנִי "I shall acquire" (*Qid* 26a [**HPS** 95:18, **TGAs28** ii a 28, 29]).

**With obj.:** *2 m.s.:* אֵיפְטְרָךְ "I shall release you" (*BQ* 99b [**G1**]). *3 m.s.:* אִיגַזְרֵיה "I shall cut it down" (*BB* 33b [**HPS** 137:2]); אֵיפִירְעֵיה "I shall pay him" (*BB* 5a [**HPS** 202:5]); אֵיקְטְלֵיה "I shall cut it down" (*Shev* 46a [**HPS** 125:8]); אִישִׁיקְלֵיה "let me take it" (**TGAs28** i 10b 7); אֵישְׁקְלֵיה "Should I take it?" (*Ket* 100b [**HPS** 191:15]); אִיתְבְּעֵיה "I shall sue him" (*BM* 51a [**HGP** 24b:1]). *3 m.s.:* אֵיפְרַעִינוֹן "I shall pay them" (**HPS** 119:18).

**Gt:**

אִישְׁתְּבִיק "I shall be divorced" (**HPS** 156:1).

**Dt:**

אִיבְּזִי "I shall be disgraced" (*Qid* 50a [**GS** ii 10b 19, 20]).

**Poᶜel:**

אִיסּוּבַר "I shall support" (**HPS** 257:3).

Examples without *yod* are rare, and note the vocalization:
**G:**

אַגְזְרֵיה "I shall cut it down" (*BB* 33b [**HGP** 1a:34]).

### 3.4.2.1.2 The Yemenite Manuscripts
Similar findings arise from the Yemenite manuscripts, though the number of examples is limited. The following examples are gleaned from various chapters of Kara's study; the list is not exhaustive:

**G:**

אֵיהֲדַר "I shall return" (*Meg* 29a [**Col**]); אֵיפְתַּח "I shall open" (*Zev* 5a [**Col**]); אֵיפְשׁוֹט "I shall strip" (*Zev* 96b [**Col**]); אֵיפּוּק "I shall go out" (*Pes* 38b [**JTS**1623]); אֵיסַּק "I shall go up" (*MQ* 22a [**Col**]); אֵימְנִי "I shall count" (*San* 39a [**J**]). **With obj.:** *3 m.s.:* אֵישְׁקְלֵיה "I shall take it" (*San* 64a [**J**]); אֵילוּטְיה "I shall curse him" (*San* 105b [**J**]); אִידְיְחֵיה "I shall push him aside" (*Yom* 87b [**JTS**1623]); אֵיתְנְיֵיה "I shall teach it" (*San* 80b [**J**]). *3 f.s.:* אֵידְרְשַׁהּ "I may teach it" (*San* 102b [**J**]).

In addition, some examples with defective orthography are found.[153]

---

[153] For the examples of אעביד see above, §3.3.1.1.2 and n. 47.

G:

אזכי "I shall merit" (*MQ* 22a [**Col**]). **With obj.:** אגמרה "I shall learn it" (*MQ* 22a [**Col**]).

As we have seen, such spellings are occasionally found in some of the EEMss and are often paralleled by *plene* spellings. The evidence of both the orthography and the vocalization appears to point clearly to *ʾi-*.

### 3.4.2.1.3 The Yemenite Reading Tradition
By contrast, the Yemenite reading tradition consistently pronounces the morpheme *ʾa-* in all of the categories for which I have brought examples above, even when the printed edition has preserved grammatically un-corrupted forms, e.g., איבדוק "I shall test" (*Yev* 65a [**HPS** 156:16]) but ac-cording to *YT* אַבְדוֹק (*Yev* 65a [Morag, *YT*, p. 129], against printed איבדוק). This is clearly a later Yemenite phenomenon, as the EEMss and the spellings with a *yod* in the Yemenite manuscripts indicate. It is there-fore not the case that the *qere-kethib* phenomenon "reveals the text of the Talmud in a form that is earlier than the printed text."[154] In this case, the printed text has often preserved the more authentically Babylonian form.

### 3.4.2.2 Prefixes of D Stem
### 3.4.2.2.1 EEMs Evidence
Morag demonstrated that in the Geniza manuscripts, a *yod* frequently appears after the prefixed morphemes of the D where we would expect to find a *shewa*.[155] Morag found examples such as לא תירבי "she will not raise" (*BM* 71a [**TS** F1(1).57 1a]) and לא נישכשך (*ʿAZ* 57b [**TS** F1(2).93]) "he should not dabble [his hands]." Morag noted that this phenomenon is also attested in **HPS** and in the MS H165 of *Neziqin*. My research con-firms his findings regarding the imperfect D-stem:

*1 c.s.:* אינטר "I shall guard" (*BM* 81b [**G1**]); אישלים "I shall pay" (*BQ* 100a [**TGAs28** ii b 11]); איצלי (*Ber* 30a [**Geon** xxxii b 29]). **With obj.: + 3 m.s.:** איסלקיה "I may remove him" (*Git* 52b [**HPS** 82:4, **Hark** 79:20]).

*2 m.s.:* תִּינטר "you will guard" (*BM* 81 [**G1**]).[156]

---

[154] Morag, *YT*, p. 76.
[155] Morag, "Geniza," pp. 64–65.
[156] Tiberian vocalization in original.

*3 m.s.:* ליבריך "let him bless" (**HPS** 48:9; **Hark** 30:21); לִיבָּרֵיךְ let him bless" (**HPS** 309:20); ניבריך "let him bless" (*Men* 43a? [**Geon** xxxviii 7a 9]); נימחי "let him protest" (*BM* 39a [**HPS** 109:2]); ליעכיב "let it prevent" (*BM* 79b [**G1**]); נִצְרֵיף "let him join" (**HPS** 209:20); ניקביל "let him receive" (*BB* 94a [**TGAs28** i 3b 25]);[157] לישלים "let him pay" (*BM* 83a [**G1**]; *BB* 34a [**HPS** 137:9]); ניתתי "let him go low" (*BB* 167a [**HPS** 100:14]). **With obj.: + *3 m.s.:*** ניזבניה "he should sell it" (**TGAs28** i 10a 26); לישיליה "let him ask him" (*ᶜAZ* 9a [**Hark** 20:14, 21:2, 4, 8, 12]). **+ *3 f.s.:*** ניגרשה "let him divorce her" (*BB* 174b [**HPS** 75:7]). **+ *3 m.pl.*** ליחייבינון "let him declare them liable" (**HPS** 240:15); ליפרשינון "may he explain them" (**GS** vi 1b 11).

*3 f.s.:* תיזבי "let her sell" (*BQ* 89a [**G1**]).[158] **With obj.: + *3 m.s.:*** תיזבניה "let her sell it" (*BQ* 89a,b [**G1**]); לא תיסיעיה "it will not support him" (**TGAs28** v 4b 15).

*1 c.pl.:* ניזבין "let us sell" (*BM* 105a [**HPS** 93:12]).

*3 m.pl.:* לישלמו "let them pay" (*BM* 83a [**HPS** 114:21]).

From Morag's examples and from mine, it is clear that the *i* vowel is attested not only after 3 m., but also after the other prefixed morphemes. Morag regarded this as a phonological phenomenon, i.e., the shift of the *shewa* to an *i* vowel. However, beyond this category I have found no clear cases in the EEMss of such an unconditioned shift of the *shewa* to a full vowel, and accordingly, I prefer to see this as a case of morphological analogy to the subject prefixes of the other verbal stems.[159]

### 3.4.2.2.2 Historical Depth

Not many cases of this form are forthcoming in the published magic bowls. However, there are a few certain examples, e.g., אישדר "I shall

---

[157] Assaf read ניקבל

[158] = תיזבין with apocopation of final *nun*.

[159] There are even sporadic examples of the *i* vowel in the C prefixes, e.g., אי משכיר קא באעי לאפוקי לשוכר דקא מיתבעי ליה ביתא, נודעיה שלשים יום מיקמי **דליפקיה** "if the landlord wishes to remove the tenant because he needs the house, he should inform him thirty days before **he removes him**" (**HPS** 107:19–20). However, these may reflect the shift of *\*a > i* in closed syllables. See Morag, "Geniza," p. 65 (reprinted in Morag, *Studies*, p. 298); Malone, "Observations," p. 163; Kara, *Yemenite Manuscripts*, pp. 104–5; Morgenstern, "Moussaieff Collection," p. 354.

send" (BM 040A:6),[160] איסאיב "I shall defile" (M164:10),[161] and תיבדרון "you will scatter" (M131:2).

### 3.4.2.2.3 The Yemenite Manuscripts
The Yemenite manuscripts conform to the general tendency of the earlier manuscripts and often (but not always) employ the *yod* in these cases:

> *1 c.s.:* אישלים "I shall pay" (*Yom* 85a [JTS218]); איקיים "I shall fulfill" (*Tan* 21a [J]).[162] **With obj.:** *+ 3 m.s:* איפיסיה "I shall convince him" (*Yom* 87a [JTS1623]). *+ 3 f.s.:* איקבלה "I shall accept it" (*Pes* 48a [Col]).

> *2 m.s.:* תיכפר "you shall atone" (*Zev* 6a [Col]).

> *1 c.pl.:* ניבריך "let us bless" (*Pes* 103b [JTS1623]).

### 3.4.2.2.4 The Yemenite Reading Tradition
This stands in contrast to the *Sanʕa* tradition, wherein only the 3 m. morpheme is vocalized with the *i* vowel, while the others are vocalized with a *shewa*, as in the following representative examples:[163]

> *1 m.s.:* אֲקַבֵּל "I shall receive" (*Ber* 28a). **With obj.:** *+ 3 m.s:* אֲנַשְׁקֵיה "let me kiss him" (*Git* 57b, against printed edition אינשקיה).

> *2 m.s.:* תְּשַׁפֵּץ "[if] you repair" (*Yev* 63a). **With obj.:** *+ 1 c.s:* לָא תְּצַעֲרַן "don't trouble me" (*Ber* 13b).

> *3 f.s.:* תְּשַׁמֵּשׁ "let her serve" (*Shab* 110a).

> *1 c.pl.:* וְתַקֵּין "let us enact" (*Hor* 13b). **With obj.:** *+ 3 m.s:* וְקַבְּלֵיה "let us take it" (*Tan* 8b).

---

[160] See Morgenstern, "BM 91767," p. 6. J. N. Ford informs me that another example appears in an unpublished bowl from the Chaya collection: ניבטלון "they will annul" (Chaya 99:7).

[161] Published in Levene, "Moussaeiff 164." Correct transcription on p. 62 to match the commentary on p. 65.

[162] Kara, *Yemenite Manuscripts*, pp. 213, 264. Cf. further אִיבַקֵּי "I shall search" (*Git* 56a [MGD 626:29]), according to MS JUNL 4º188 of the *Midrash HaGadol*. See Morgenstern, "Risqué Pun," p. 885.

[163] All these examples from Morag, *YT*, p. 148 (sound verb), pp. 300–1 (sound verb with object pronoun).

*Contrasting with*:

> *3 m.s.:* לִיזַמֵּר "let him sing" (*San* 7a).[164] **With obj.:** + *3 m.s:* לְבַטְּלֵיה "he should annul it" (*Git* 32a).

> *3 m.pl.:* לִיתַקְּנוּ "Should they enact . . .?"(*Git* 49b against printed edition ליתקני). **With obj.:** + *3 m.s:* לִיבַדְּרוּהּ "let them scatter it" (*Git* 56b, against printed edition ליבדרי).

The Yemenite tradition thus creates a phonemic distinction between 3 m.s. and 1 c.pl. forms, e.g., נְקַבֵּיל "it will receive" (*BB* 4a [Morag, *YT*, p. 148]) but נְקַבֵּל "shall we receive . . .?" (*Bes* 5b [ʿAmr]).

### 3.4.2.2.5 Conclusion
The early manuscript evidence shows no distinction between the vowel of the 1st and 2nd person pronominal prefixes of the D and those of the 3rd person. The Yemenite reading tradition has created a secondary phonemic distinction which is not supported by the earlier evidence.

### 3.4.2.3 2 f.s. of III-*yod* Gt

In the opening chapter we saw how the Yemenite MS **J** accurately preserves the authentic pattern of two rare verb forms: לא תסתפאי "do not fear" (*San* 94b [J]) and אסתפאי "fear" (ibid). Comparative material was cited to demonstrate that the *ay* ending is reflected in other Aramaic dialects. However, the *Sanʿa* tradition reads תִּיסתַּפִי (*San* 94b [Morag, *YT*, p. 264]) and אִיסתַּפִי (ibid. [ibid., p. 265]).

### 3.4.3 Imperatives

### 3.4.3.1 F.s. Morpheme

### 3.4.3.1.1 Manuscript Evidence
Kutscher seems to have been the first scholar to have recorded examples of the 2 f.s. imperative lacking the final vowel, as in Syriac and Mandaic, and wondered if perhaps such forms were also attested for the masculine plural.[165] Kara adduced an additional example of the 2 f.s. with no final vowel from **HPS**, as well as several examples from the Yemenite manuscripts and from the printed editions. As noted in §2.7.2, although Kara states that "in the imperative forms of the 2 f.s. and 2 m.pl. the final

---

[164] So Morag, *YT*, p. 148; ʿAmr vocalized לִיזַמֵּר.
[165] Kutscher, "Review," p. 169 (reprinted in Kutscher, *Studies*, p. 247).

vowel sometimes drops," in all but one of his examples of the 2 f.s. examples the final *i* vowel has been apocopated. The exception will be discussed below.[166]

I have found additional examples of the f.s. from the EEMss: אישתבע לי "take an oath for me" (**HPS** 182:8), זיל "go" (*BM* 84a [**G1**]), and, preserving the final vowel, איעכבי לי "wait for me" (**HPS** 156:12). I would tentatively suggest that the preposition לי may have been affixed to the verb, producing a pronunciation *ʾiʾʾakkaʾḇīlī*, and that the *ī* vowel was preserved since it was no longer in a final, unstressed position. This would also explain the one exception that Kara lists, הבי לי עצה "give me advice" (*San* 109b [**J**]). However, אישתבע is also followed by a *lamed*, yet the final vowel has been apocopated.[167]

### 3.4.3.1.2 The Yemenite Reading Tradition
The Yemenite reading tradition follows the printed edition, which has generally reintroduced the distinction between masculine and feminine imperative forms. Hence זִילִי "go" (*BM* 84a [ʿAmr]), עֲבִידִי "do [it]" (*San* 67b [ʿAmr]). Only in those rare cases that the printed edition preserves the apocopated form does it occur in the Yemenite tradition, e.g., קוּם "get up" (*Shab* 110b [Morag, *YT*, p. 215]).[168] As far as I have been able to ascertain, there are no examples wherein the Yemenite reading tradition employs an apocopated form against the classical form of the printed text, even though the apocopated form is by far the most common form in the manuscripts.

### 3.4.3.2 F.s. Morpheme of III-*yod* Roots
### 3.4.3.2.1 The EEMss and The Yemenite Manuscripts
In chapter 2 we briefly noted that the f.s. imperative morpheme of the III-*yod* verbs appears to be אי-. On the basis of Classical Syriac, we may assume that this is to be vocalized -*āy*.[169] Few examples are attested in the EEMss: דראי "lift up" (*Ket* 60a [**Hark** 99:17]), הואי "be" (**HPS** 156:15),

---

[166] Kara, *Yemenite Manuscripts*, p. 152. The example טאטי "sweep" (Meg 18a [**Col**]) which he lists under II-ʾ*aleph* roots is better regarded with Sokoloff, *DJBA*, p. 492, as a quadraliteral root, טאטיי.

[167] On the enclyticization of the prepositional *lamed*, see Morgenstern, "Mandaic."

[168] Kara, *Yemenite Manuscripts*, p. 153.

[169] See §2.7.2.

חזאי "see" (*BM* 84b **[G1]**). The Yemenite manuscripts include one form: חדאי "rejoice" (*Pes* 68b **[JTS**1623, **Col]**).[170]

### 3.4.3.2.2 Magic Texts

Juusola noted the form אישתאי "drink" in AMB 7:8.[171] The "Onqelos" form is now attested in Aramaic magic texts formulated in that linguistic type, e.g., (קדחי ופוקי ועירוקי) וגלה "(break away, leave, flee) and be exiled" (ZHS 12:5).[172] Compare forms such as וַחֲזָא "and see" (f.s.) (TJ Jer 2:19).[173]

### 3.4.3.2.3 The Yemenite Reading Tradition

In the Yemenite reading tradition, these f.s. imperatives follow the pattern of the m.s. However, the evidence of the Talmudic manuscripts does not support this reading.[174] אִיתְּלִי "ignite" (*Shab* 26a), even if it is to be interpreted with Morag as G, is not a reading supported by the best manuscripts (MS **O** איתלאי); this would presumably be an imperative (see §3.4.2.3 above).[175]

### 3.4.3.3 M.pl. Morpheme

### 3.4.3.3.1 Manuscript Evidence

The distribution of the apocopated m.pl. imperative differs from that of the f.s., in that in this case, the majority of the examples preserve the final vowel, and it is the apocopated forms that are the minority. Kara also identified examples in the Yemenite manuscripts, while Morag recorded two cases from the Yemenite tradition, both based on the apocopated forms in the printed editions: עַטוּף "wrap yourselves" (*MQ* 28b [Morag, *YT*, p. 131]) and הְדּוּר "do again" (*Git* 68b [ibid.]).

---

[170] Kara, *Yemenite Manuscripts*, pp. 167, 284. The example אית 'Bring' (*Tan* 25a [J]) that Kara cites remains unique.

[171] Juusola, *Linguistic Peculiarities*, p. 193.

[172] Contra Müller-Kessler, *ZHS*, p. 63 the correct reading of the final verb is וגלה rather than וגלח "shave." See Morgenstern, "ZHS," pp. 285–86.

[173] Dalman, *Grammatik*, p. 348.

[174] The following examples are drawn from Morag, *YT*, p. 257. Contra Morag, ibid., the form בְּעִי "request" (*Tan* 25a), which he lists as f.s., should be understood from its Talmudic context as m.s. The form בְּקִי "investigate" (*BM* 84b [Morag, *YT*, p. 257]) is surprising, since the root verb בק"י conjugates in the D in the earlier Yemenite tradition. See n. 162 above.

[175] See Morgenstern, "Risqué Pun."

Following Luzzatto, Nöldeke alluded to the existence of an infixed *ū* for the m. pl. imperative caused by vowel mutation (umlaut).[176] Such an infix is common in the perfect, and has been discussed in some detail in the relevant literature. There is some indication that it might also have existed for the imperfect.[177] I have found four examples in the EEMss that show this morpheme: אמלהו **זול** שימוה בעבדא "He said to them: '**Go** [and] evaluate him as a slave'" (*BQ* 84a [**G1**]);[178] cf. singular זיל "go" (e.g., *Git* 34a [**HPS** 92:9]). דאמיʼ להו לשהדי **איזול אטמור** וכתובו ליה "He says to the witnesses, '**Go** [and] **hide** and write for him'" (*Git* 33b [**HGP** 2a:32]). יהוב מתנאתא לכהנתא "**Give** the prebends to the priests' daughters" (*Hul* 131b [bis; **HPS** 58:10, 61:11]).[179]

### 3.4.3.4 F.pl. Morpheme
#### 3.4.3.4.1 Early Manuscripts
The f.pl. morpheme appears to be -*an* or -*ān*. Although not yet attested in the EEMss, in the better manuscripts, including the Yemenite *Midrash Hagadol*, this form is written ן without a *yod*, e.g., בידקן "inspect" (*Git* 68b [**MHE** 773:9]).[180]

#### 3.4.3.4.2 The Yemenite Reading Tradition
The Yemenite reading tradition of the Talmud employs an -*īn* morpheme for the f.pl. imperative: קְטוֹלִין "kill" (*Shab* 12a [Morag, *YT*, p. 131]). However, this form is found only in the printed editions of *Shab* 12a and finds no support in the manuscripts.[181] The difference between the

---

[176] Luzzatto, *Elementi grammaticali*, §69; Nöldeke, *MG*, § 173 n. 1.

[177] For the perfect, see Kutscher, "Review" pp. 165–67 (reprinted in Kutscher, *Studies*, pp. 243–45). Boyarin, "Studies," p. 175, demonstrated that the vocalization of **HPS** dispels Kutscher's doubts regarding the quality of the vowel. See further Friedman, "Early Manuscripts," p. 24, and Kara, *Yemenite Manuscripts*, pp. 144–45. The evidence for the imperfect is less forthcoming, but Shetreet, "Aramaic Verb," p. 20, as drawn attention to the example ניפלוג (*BM* 45a [**Fl8** and other witnesses]) "let them disagree," which appears in parallel with the plural participle אדמיפלגי "as long as they disagree."

[178] This reading is also supported by MS H165. For the broader context see §4.5.3.

[179] This reading, and its interpretation as an imperative, is supported by the Hebrew translation in *Hilchot Reʾu*: תנו מתנות לכוהנות (**HR** 34:12–13).

[180] The Yemenite reading tradition of the Talmud follows the printed text and reads בִּידְקוּ "inspect" (*Git* 68b [ʿAmr]).

[181] It is true that classical Syriac has a f.pl. imperative form ܩܛܘܠܝܢ, as already noted by Epstein, *Grammar*, p. 38, but this does not appear to be the genuine form

printed text and the manuscripts is all the more telling when we consider
the wider context in which the verb קטולין appears. While the printed
editions read אמר להו רב נחמן לבנתיה: **קטולין** ואשמעינן לי קלא דסנוותי
"(Rav Nahman said to his daughters:) '**Kill** and let me hear (?) the voice
of my enemies'," the eleventh-century Friedberg fragment reads **קטלינהי**
ואשמע לי קלא דסנוותאי "**Kill them** and let me hear the voice of my enemies" (*Shab* 12a).[182] The reading of the printed editions is not even supported by the Ashkenazi manuscripts: MS V127 reads קטלן ואשמעי ליה,
while MS Munich reads קטלן ואשמע.[183]

According to the Friedberg manuscript, the second verb אשמע bears
the expected -*ān* morpheme, while the verb קטלינהי would appear to
have no suffix at all. A similar form — in the imperfect, not imperative —
seems to occur in ננטרן "let them protect me" (*Ber* 23b [O23]), wherein
the f.pl. morpheme likewise seems to be elided before the object suffix.
Perhaps the f.pl. morpheme is lost through haplology.

### 3.4.3.5 G Imperative with Pronominal Suffixes

#### 3.4.3.5.1 EEMs Evidence

In the printed editions of the Talmud, the spellings קטליה and קטלוה are
often employed for both 3 m. perfect with pronominal object suffix and
2 m. imperative bearing the same suffixes. For example, the unvocalized
spelling שקליה may be interpreted as "he took it" (3 m.s. perf.) or "take
it" (2 m.s. imper.). Similarly, שבקוה may be read either "they left him"
(3 m.pl. perf.) or "leave him" (2 m.pl. imper.).

However, the spellings (*plene* or defective) of the many examples and
occasional vocalized forms indicate that EEMss generally distinguished
between the two forms: the base of the perfect was pronounced *qatl-*

---

in Babylonian Aramaic; the similarity would seem to be coincidental. He is followed by Morag, ibid.

[182] A photographic reproduction of this page appears in a 2005 catalog advertis-
ing the Friedberg Genizah Project. According to the catalog, the fragment may be
of North African origin.

[183] MS O23 reads: קטלינהו ואשמען לי קלא דסנואתי. The reading קטלינהו was already mentioned by Levias, Grammar, §220, but he apparently did not interpret
it correctly. Furthermore, he was incorrect in stating that this is the only surviving example of the f.pl. imperative, as Epstein, *Grammar*, p. 38, already recognized.

while the imperative was based on *qiṭl-*,[184] as in the following representative examples. I have included examples from III-*yod* roots, which conjugate like the strong verb in these cases.

*3 m.s.*

**Vocalized forms:**

+ *3 m.s. obj:* וְאַנְסֵיהּ "and he compelled him" (**HPS** 310:18); טַרְקָהּ "it bit her" (**HPS** 307:21); לְהַבֵּיהּ "he gave it" ([**HPS** 203:19]).

+ *3 f.s. obj:* שַׁחְטָהּ "he slaughtered it" (**HPS** 307:19).

**Unvocalized forms:**

+ *2 f.s. obj:* נסביך "he married you" (**HPS** 156:14).

+ *3 m.s. obj:* אכליה "he used it" (**Hark** 36:16); גזליה "he stole it" (*Suk* 31a [**HPS** 42:2]; **HPS** 127:4; **TGAs28** ii b 9); זרקיה "he threw it" (**TGAs28** i 7b 16); חזייה "he saw him/it" (*Bes* 27a [**HPS** 5:11]; *BB* 167a [**HPS** 100:9]; *Naz* 59a [**HPS** 220:9]); חטפיה "he snatched it" (*BB* 33b [**HPS** 137:8]); טרפיה "he seized it" (**HPS** 77:15); טרקיה "it stung him" (*Hag* 5a [**Hark** 158:21]); כבשיה "he suppressed it" (*BB* 35b [**TGAs28** xvii 1a 6]); כפריה "he denied it" (*BM* 17a [**HPS** 118:12]; **HPS** 127:4; **Hark** 161:29, etc.); כפתיה "he tied him" (*BB* 167a [**HPS** 100:10,13,21]); כתביה "he wrote it" (**Geon** xxvi b 17); מחייה "he struck him" (*BQ* 98a [**G1**]); מסריה "he handed him over" (*Yev* 46a [**GS** xvii 1a 11]); משכיה "he took possession of it" (*BQ* 103a [**HPS** 72:17]); נכתיה "it harmed him" (*Git* 67b [**Hark** 123:1]); נקטיה "it took hold of him" (*Git* 70b [**GS** xvi 1b 2]); עבדיה "he made it" (*BQ* 66b [**Geon** xxviii 1b 25]); פטריה "he released him" (*BQ* 117a [**HPS** 129:10]); פרעיה "he paid him" (*BM* 77b [**G1**]; *BB* 174a [**HPS** 74:3, **HPS** 104:11], etc.); קטליה "he chopped it down" (*Shev* 46a [**HPS** 125:9]); קנייה "he acquired it" (*Yev* 66b [**TGAs28** iv 3b 30]); לא שבקיה "he did not permit him" (*Git* 52a [**HPS** 80:19]); שדייה "he cast it" (*BQ* 116a [**G1**]); שמטיה "he tore it out" (*BQ* 117a [**HPS** 129:19]); שמעיה "he heard it" (*Ket* 54a [**Hark** 205:22]); שקליה "he took it" (**Hark** 102:16); תבעיה "he demanded of him" (**Hark** 277:15).

+ *3 f.s. obj.:* אמרה "he said it" (*Ket* 40b [**Hark** 123:17]; *BQ* 88b [**G1**]; *BM* 16b [**Hark** 178:6]); אסרה "he bound her" (*Qid* 13b [**HPS**

---

[184] I am assuming that the *shewa* was not pronounced, as it is never represented in the vocalized examples. The loss of the vocalized *shewa* is common in JBA in this position. See Morag, "Phonology," p. 74 (reprinted in Morag, *Studies*, p. 251).

164:17]); בזעה "he ripped it" (**HPS** 213:8); בעייה "he required it" (*BB* 88a [**HPS** 132:9]); זבנה "he sold it" (*BB* 30a [**HPS** 135:8]; *BB* 36a [**HPS** 139:11]); זרעה "he sowed it" (*BM* 107b [**TGAs28** iv 5b 13]); טרפה "he seized it" (*Ket* 91b [**HPS** 77:19]); יהבה "he gave it" (*BM* 16a [**Hark** 160:35]); כתבה "he wrote it" (**HPS** 96:3); מסרה "he passed it over" (*BQ* 117a [**HPS** 129:16]); משחה "he measured it" (*BB* 106b [**HPS** 149:13]); נסבה "he married her" (**TGAs28** iv 2b 25); סברה "he deduced it" (*BB* 89a [**HPS** 154:12]); אקרה "he uprooted it" (*BM* 76b [**G1**]);[185] פטרה "he released her" (**TGAs28** i 13b 24=**GS** i 11a 21); שבקה "he released her" (**HPS** 231:11); שלחה "he sent it" (*Qid* 12b [**HPS** 170:11]; *BM* 106a [**TGAs28** iv 5b 14]); שמעה "he heard it" (*Ket* 40b [**Hark** 123:16]); שקלה "he took it" (*Git* 17a [**Hark** 144:25]); שתיה "he drank it" (*BM* 43b [**HPS** 128:7]); תברה "he broke it" (*BM* 43b [**HPS** 128:7]); תברה "he broke it" (*BM* 83a [**G1**]).

## 3 m.pl.
### Vocalized forms:
+ **3 m.s. obj.:** חֲזיֹוה "they saw him" (*MQ* 4a [**HPS** 274:17]); עֲקרֹוה "they uprooted it" (*Shev* 45a [**HGP** 13a:30]); שָׁדיֹוה "they cast it" (*Shev* 45a [**HGP** 13a:31]); שְׁלחוה "they sent it" (*Shev* 48a [**HGP** 14a:24]); שְׁקלֹוהִי "they took him" (**HPS** 259:20).

### Unvocalized forms:
+ **2 m.s. obj.:** קדמוך "they preceded you" (*BB* 167a [**HPS** 100:19]).

+ **3 m.s. obj.:**[186] אמדוה "they evaluated him" (*Yom* 84b [**HPS** 29:6]); אנסוהי "they compelled him" (*BQ* 117a [**HPS** 129:9]) // אנסוה "they compelled him" (*BQ* 117a [**HPS** 129:12]);[187] גזלוה "they robbed him" (*BQ* 103a [**HPS** 72:16]); זבנוה "they sold it" (*BQ* 89a [**G1**]); חבשוה "they imprisoned him" (*BQ* 59b [**HGP** 16a:19]); חזיוהי "they saw him" (**Hark** 277:22); חזיוה "they saw him" (*BM* 101a [**HGP** 6b:32]); כתבוהי "they wrote it" (**HPS** 99:12); משכוה "they took possession of it" (*Git* 52a [**HPS** 81:8]); פרטוהי "they released him" (**Hark** 47:35; **Hark** 164:5); פרסוהי "they spread it" (*Yev* 66b [**TGAs28** iv 3b 30] = פרסוה [**HPS** 159:6]); שבקוה "they forsook/released him" (*BQ* 59b [**HGP** 16a:21]; **Hark** 33:36); קטלוה "they killed him" (*BM*

---

[185] Phonetic spelling for עקרה.

[186] These forms are cited at length as they are also relevant to the discussion below, §3.5.1.2.

[187] On this interchange, see §4.6.2.

78b [**G1**]); קנייה "they acquired it" (**TGAs28** iv 4a 3); קנסוה "they
fined him" (**Hark** 35:26); רמיוה "they imposed it" (*BB* 8a [**Hark**
265:12]); שטפוה "they washed it away" (*BM* 91b [**G1**]); שמעוה "they
heard him" (**Hark** 35:22); שקלוהי "they took it" (*Yev* 66b [**TGAs28**
iv 3b 30] = שקלוה [**HPS** 159:6]); שריוהי "they permitted him" (**Hark**
31:32); תברוה "they broke it" (*BM* 83a [**HPS** 114:21]); תבעוה "they
sued him" (*Ket* 85a [**HGP** 44a:18]; *San* 29b [**HPS** 120:14]); תפסוה
"they seized him" (*BM* 83b [**G1**]).

+ *2 f.s. obj.:* אמרוה "they said it" (*BM* 119a [**HGP** 7b:23]; **Hark**
169:14); בעיוה "they asked it" (**Hark** 205:30); חזיוה "they saw her"
(**Hark** 107:10); סברוה "they deduced it" (*BQ* 57b [**HPS** 115:16]; *BQ*
89b [**G1**]); פשטוה "they explained it" (**Hark** 205:30); קנסוה "they
fined her" (*Yev* 41a [**HPS** 229:16]); שדיוה "they imposed it" (*Shev*
43b [**HPS** 201:13]); שקלוה "they took it" (*BQ* 93a [**HGP** 16b:2]; *Shev*
43b [**HPS** 201:13]; **TGAs28** ii a 9); תניוה "they taught it" (**Hark**
103:33,34).

I have found only one form that does not comply with this rule: ניסבה
"he married her" (**HPS** 226:15; **HGP** 37a:3; **TGAs28** i 9a 17). A vocalized
example is found: דְנִיסּבֵֿה "he married her" (**HPS** 230:18), and this leaves
no doubt as to the quality of the vowel. Examples are also found in the
Yemenite manuscripts.[188] Malone had connected such forms in **HPS** to
the similar shift of *$*a > i$ in these forms in Mandaic.[189] However, since the
phenomenon appears to be restricted in the EEMss to this root alone, I
prefer to see it as assimilation of the *a* vowel to the sibilant.

In contrast to these examples, we find numerous examples of the
imperative formed on the base *qiṭl-*, though imperative forms are overall
rare in the manuscripts.

*M.s.:*
**Vocalized forms:**
+ *1 c.s. obj.:* פִירעַֿן "pay me" (*Shev* 41b [**HPS** 199:18]).

+ *3 m.s. obj.:* חיזיֵה "see it" (*Pes* 20a [**Geon** xv 2b 8]); תֵיפסֵיה "seize
him" (*BM* 83b [**G1**]).

**Unvocalized forms:**
+ *1 c.s. obj.:* גירשן "divorce me" (**HPS** 178:14); פיטרן "release me"
(**HPS** 156:14); פירען "pay me" (*Shev* 42a [**Hark** 115:1]).

---

[188] Kara, *Yemenite Manuscripts*, pp. 104, 332.
[189] Malone, "Observations," p. 163.

+ *3 m.s. obj.*: איכליה "eat it" (**HPS** 50:9); חישביה "count it" (**Hark** 169:31); שירקיה "plaster it" (*BQ* 81b [**G1**]); קיניה "acquire it" (**HPS** 96:7).

+ *3 f.s. obj.*: איפכה "reverse it" (*BQ* 84b [**G1**]); בידקה "test her" (*Ket* 60a [**Hark** 99:15]).

M.pl.:

+ *3 m.s. obj.*: תיפסוה "seize him" (*BM* 83b [**G1**]).

+ *3 f.s. obj.*: כיתבוה "write it" (*BB* 172a [**HPS** 103:20,21]).[190]

### 3.4.3.5.2 The Yemenite Manuscripts
Similar forms are found in the Yemenite MSS:[191]

M.s:

+ *1 c.s. obj.*: ניסבן "marry me" (*San* 22a [**J**]);[192] שיבקן "allow me" (*San* 38b [**J**]).[193]

+ *3 m.s. obj.*: זיבניה "buy it" (*Meg* 26b [**Col**]); שידייה "throw it" (*Yom* 33b [**JTS218**]).

+ *3 f.s. obj.*: שיקלה "remove it" (*Suk* 10b [**JTS218**]).

M.pl.:

+ *3 m.s. obj.*: קיליוה "burn it" (*Yom* 69b [**JTS218**]).

These are not the only spellings of the imperative attested in either the EEMss or the Yemenite MSS. Even in the most accurate manuscripts we find spellings such as זבנה "buy it" (*BB* 169b [**HPS** 103:17]) or שקליה

---

[190] It is very likely that כיתבו (*BB* 172a [**HPS** 104:1]) is to be interpreted as an imperative form in which the final pronominal suffix -*h* has been apocopated. ʿAmr vocalized the printed text כְּתֻבוּ, but also recorded the marginal correction כְּתוּבוּ.

[191] These examples are all drawn from Kara, *Yemenite Manuscripts*, passim. They are also mentioned on p. 104, in a discussion of the shift *a > i.

[192] Kara, *Yemenite Mansucripts*, p. 332, records this as 2 f.s. imperative + 2 m.s. obj., clearly a printing error. The correct interpretation is provided on p. 104. The Yemenite reading tradition here follows the printed edition and reads נִיסְבָן (*San* 22a [ʿAmr]).

[193] The Yemenite reading tradition here follows the printed text edition and reads שָׁבקֵיה.

"take it" (BQ 98a [G1]). However, in light of the vocalized examples cited above, and given the predominance of examples with the *yod* in a variety of accurate manuscript sources, it seems likely that the *i* vowel was also employed in these forms. The examples lacking a *yod* are to be regarded as defective spellings.[194] Defective spellings of short *i* commonly interchange with *plene* ones.[195]

### 3.4.3.5.3 The Yemenite Reading Tradition

In the Yemenite tradition, all of these forms are vocalized with an *a* vowel, even in cases wherein the printed edition has a *yod*. The following are representative examples. Preference has been given to examples wherein the manuscripts contain spellings with a *yod*, but the current Yemenite tradition reads with an *a* vowel:[196]

*M.s.:*

+ *1 c.s. obj.:* פְּרַעִין "pay me"(*Shev* 41b [Morag, *YT*, p. 296]).[197]

+ *3 m.s obj.:* אַכְלֵיה "eat it" (*Ber* 35a [Morag, *YT*, p. 296]); זַבְנֵיה "buy it" (*Meg* 26b [ʿAmr]); שָׁרְקֵיה "plaster it" (*BQ* 81b [Morag, *YT*, p. 296], against printed orthography שירקיה; שַׁדְיֵיה "throw it" (*Yom* 33b [ʿAmr]).

+ *3 f.s. obj.:* בַּדְקַה "test her" (*Ket* 60b [Morag, *YT*, p. 296]).

*M.pl.:*

+ *3 m.s. obj.:* תַּפְסוּהוּ "seize him" (*BM* 83b [Morag, *YT*, p. 296]).[198]

While the orthography of the Yemenite MSS often supports the vocalization and *plene* spellings found in the EEMss, the vocalized forms support the current Yemenite pronunciation. Hence we find the vocalized examples שַׁקְלֵיה "take it" (*Meg* 28a [Col]), שבקַה "leave her" (*Meg* 12b [Col]), and קַטְלַה "kill her" (*Meg* 12b [Col]).

---

[194] Accordingly, contra Kara, *Yemenite Manuscripts*, p.104, I do not regard the examples in the Yemenite MSS as sporadic shifts from *a > i.

[195] See examples below, §4.3.3.

[196] I have not cited here examples in which the forms in the printed text belong to a grammatical category different from those in the manuscripts; some of those examples were mentioned in the footnotes above.

[197] Morag notes that some authorities read פְּרַע. On פְּרַעִין see below.

[198] In R. ʿAmr's edition this verb is vocalized תַּפְשׂוּהוּ, while Morag's other examples are vocalized by ʿAmr with a *pataḥ*. On the object suffix *-hu*, see below.

#### 3.4.3.5.4 Conclusion

There is ample evidence that in RBA, the forms of G imperatives to which pronominal suffixes were attached were *qiṭl-/qiṭlū-*, while the perfects were formed on the basis of *qaṭl-/qaṭlū-*.[199] In the case of the root נס״ב "to marry," this distinction was occasionally lost by the shift of *\*a* > *i_s.* in closed syllables, but judging from the defective/*plene* spellings and occasional vocalized forms, it seems that it is generally maintained in the EEMss, in the orthography of the Yemenite manuscripts, and even in the printed editions of the Talmud. By contrast, it is lost in the Yemenite reading tradition, wherein the imperatives have merged into the perfects. The earliest evidence for this merger within that tradition is to be found in sporadically vocalized forms in the Yemenite manuscripts.

#### 3.4.3.6 Imperative of I-*ʔaleph* Roots

#### 3.4.3.6.1 Geonic and EEMs Evidence

M. Assis drew attention to the significance of R. Shemuel b. Ḥofni Gaon's statement regarding the vocalization of the homographs אימא "I shall say" (e.g., *Yom* 78a [**HPS** 29:21]) and אימא "say" (e.g., *BB* 32b [**HPS** 191:2]):

אימא בנקטתין תחת אלאלף אקול אימא בנקטה ואחדה תחת אלאלף קול.

אִימָא with two points under the *ʔaleph*, "I [shall] say." אִימָא with one point under the *ʔaleph*, "say" (**LPT** 146:21)[200]

The statement indicates, as Assis noted, that the Gaon distinguished between two realizations of this spelling, a 1 c.s. imperfect אֵימָא "I shall say" and a m.s. imperative אִימָא "say."[201] In the surviving manuscript of this work, only the imperative form is vocalized. Friedman noted that this vocalization is attested in MS **G1** of *Bava Mezia*: אובעית אִימָא "if you want, say" (*BM* 70b [**G1**]).[202]

---

[199] This does not include the object suffixes of 3 m.pl., 3 f.pl. and perhaps 1 c.s. See below.

[200] The long vowel in the Arabic imperative form קול is common in medieval Judeo-Arabic, in contrast to Classical Arabic قُل; see Blau, *Grammar*, §102.

[201] Assis, "Linguistic Aspects," p. 41.

[202] Friedman, "Brief Notes," p. 50.

### 3.4.3.6.2 The Yemenite Reading Tradition

This distinction is found neither in the Yemenite oral tradition nor in the Yemenite manuscripts.[203] In the Yemenite tradition, both forms are pronounced אֵימָא (imperfect: *Yom* 78a ['Amr]; imperative: *Pes* 3b [Morag, *YT*, p. 165]). It should be noted, however, that **HGP** already vocalizes the imperative with the *ṣere*.

## 3.4.4 Participle

### 3.4.4.1 M.pl. Morpheme

### 3.4.4.1.1 EEMs Evidence

Morag, following a reference from Epstein, noted that the vocalization of **HPS** distinguishes between the m.pl. morpheme of participles, which are vocalized with an *ī* vowel, and those of the nouns, which are vocalized with an *ē* vowel.[204] In **HPS**, the distinction appears to be maintained in all cases. Collation on the basis of the facsimile edition indicates that there are no examples with the participle vocalized with the *e* vowel, and that the two forms that Morag listed as such are clearly vocalized with *i*. Epstein convincingly explained the distinction as resulting from the different origin of the two morphemes: while the participle morpheme is an apocopated form of the old absolute morpheme -*īn*, the noun morpheme is an apocopated and contracted form of old determined morpheme -*ayyā*.

Further support for the suggestion that the two morphemes remained distinct may be found in the fact that while in the participles the -*īn* morpheme is used interchangeably with the apocopated form in all syntactic positions, this is never the case with the nouns.[205] The -*īn* morpheme is only employed for nouns in very specific cases when the earlier Aramaic absolute is retained, e.g.:

> 1. In frozen forms such as זימנין "times, sometimes," e.g., זמנין סגיאן אמרתה קמיה דרב "many times I stated it before Rav" (*BB* 65a [**HPS** 147:2]).

---

[203] The single vocalized example of the imperative listed by Kara, *Yemenite Manuscripts*, p. 95 (and in the index) as אֵימְ in fact reads אֵימָ (*San* 84b [J]).

[204] Epstein, *Grammar*, p. 40; Morag, "Vocalisation," p. 91 (reprinted in Morag, *Studies*, p. 199); and Morag, "Phonology," p. 78 (reprinted in Morag, *Studies*, p. 255).

[205] These interchanges are discussed in §4.5.4.1.

2. It is retained occasionally following numerals, e.g., ארבעה חולקין "four parts" (**HPS** 84:12); תלת שנין "two years" (*Git* 58b [**TGAs28** ii a 11]; **Hark** 119:32); עשר שנין "ten years" (**HPS** 155:15; **HPS** 177:1, 8, 13); תרתין נשין אחואתא "two women, sisters" (**HPS** 245:14); בעשרין גברין "with twenty men" (**Geon** xiii 2b 20); תלתין יומין "thirty days" (*MQ* 28b [**Hark** 189:34]; *BB* 6b [**Hark** 170:16]). This is not a firm rule; accordingly we find both תרין דארי "two generations" (**HPS** 224:21) and ארבעה דארין "four generations" (**HPS** 225:2).

The absolute form is similarly preserved in this position in Classical Syriac.[206]

### 3.4.4.1.2 Loss of Distinction

Morag noted that the distinction between the historical noun endings was partially lost in **HGP**. While the participles retain their final *ī* vowel, this has also sometimes spread to the nouns, e.g., זוּזִי "zuzim."[207] This distinction is lost entirely in the Yemenite tradition, wherein both the participles and the nouns take the morphemes *-e* or *-īn*, depending on whether the plural morpheme is -ֵי or -ִין in the printed text being read; for example, עָבְדִין "they make" (*Ned* 50a [Morag, *YT*, p. 132]) but עָבְדֵי "they [can] do" (*Yom* 19b [Morag, *YT*, p. 133]).

### 3.4.4.2 III-*yod* Plural

Kara aptly noted that there is a difference between the form of the 3 m.pl. participle of the III-*yod* verbs found in the Yemenite manuscripts and that found in the Yemenite reading tradition.[208] In the manuscripts, the form is almost always written with *plene* orthography, e.g., קאנו "they acquire," while the contemporary Yemenite pronunciation is קָנוּ, i.e., identical with the perfect.[209] From the evidence Kara has gathered, it also

---

[206] Nöldeke, *SG*, §202D.

[207] Morag, "Vocalisation," p. 91 (reprinted in Morag, *Studies*, pp. 199–200). This is one of many categories in which the vocalization of **HPS** is more conservative (and accurate) than that of **HGP**.

[208] Kara, "Preservation," pp. 177–79.

[209] In the Yemenite reading tradition, the III-*yod* G perfect 3 m.pl. morpheme is *-u*, a reading confirmed by the vocalization in **HPS**: בְּנוּ "they built" (*MQ* 12a [**HPS**

emerges that even the vocalization of MS Columbia, which often contains later Yemenite elements, preserves the early reading, e.g.: דָּאמוּ "they are similar" (*Meg* 26b [**Col**]). The *plene* spelling of the Yemenite manuscripts is confirmed by numerous examples in the EEMss, e.g., דאלי "they draw" (*Git* 74b [**Hark** 17:8]), קאנו "they acquire" (**Hark** 102:19), קארו "they call" (*San* 29b [**HPS** 120:13]), and ראמו "they place" (*Ket* 8a [**HPS** 172:2]). The vocalized forms in **HPS** similarly record the full vowel after the first radical: מְלוֹ "they are completed" (**HPS** 306:21) and קָארוֹ "they call" (*Suk* 30b [**HPS** 41:21]). Kara's proposal that the confusion arose in the Yemenite tradition following the adoption of the printed editions in Yemen is most likely correct.

## 3.4.5 Participle with Suffixed Subject Pronoun

Like the other Eastern Aramaic dialects, JBA employs forms of the participles with enclitic subject pronouns. The bases of these forms are the standard Aramaic participles, to which the pronouns are affixed with occasional minor changes to the verbal base or pronoun. In this section, we shall examine these forms as they appear in the EEMss, in the Yemenite manuscripts, and in the Yemenite reading tradition.

### 3.4.5.1 1 m.s.—Vowel of First Radical in G

#### 3.4.5.1.1 EEMs Evidence

The 1 m.s. participle is formed on the basis of m.s. participles and the enclitic subject pronoun -*nā*, hence *qāṭilnā*, *maqaṭṭilna*, *maqṭilnā*, etc. In the G active form, evidence for the high vowel (*i* or *e*) is ample, e.g., סמיכנא "I rely" (*BQ* 100a [**G1**, **TGAs28** ii b 11]),[210] but the first vowel is less frequently indicated with a *mater lectionis*. Nevertheless, there is some evidence for *ā*, both examples in *plene* orthography,

> כאתיבנא "I shall write" (**Hark** 165:32); שאביקנא "I leave" (**HPS** 88:15); סאמיכנא "I rely" (*BQ* 113b [**HPS** 134:5]),[211]

---

280:18]); בעו "they asked" (*MQ* 12a [**HPS** 278:17]); דיחזו "that they saw" (*Yev* 107b [**HPS** 235:12]).

[210] On the different reflexes of *ā* and and *i* in **HPS** and **HGP**, see Morag, "Vocalisation."

[211] The form עאבידנא "I am making" (*Pes* 30b [**HPS** 12:21]) represents an additional example; however, I do not regard this example as conclusive, given the presence of the *ʿayin* and the occasional examples found in the manuscripts of

and vocalized examples,

לְהִיבְּנָא "I shall give" (**HPS** 67:18);[212] תְּפִּיסִנָא "I shall seize" (*Ket* 85a [**HGP** 44a:18]); אָכִילְנָא "I shall eat" (*BM* 67b [**HGP** 27a:32]); שִׁיּמְנָא "I shall assess" (ibid.).

The same pattern emerges from II-*waw*/*yod* verbs: צאייתנא "I hear" (*BQ* 113a [**HGP** 17a:19]), which probably represents the pronunciation *ṣāyeṯnā*.

### 3.4.5.1.2 The Yemenite Manuscripts
The Yemenite manuscripts similarly appear to prefer the defective orthography for the first vowel, hence the vocalization cannot be derived from the *plene* spelling. However, Kara records a vocalized example: יְכֵילְנָא "I am able" (*Meg* 16a [**Col**]).[213] In the II-*waw*/*yod* category we find קאיימנא "I stand" (*MQ* 18a [**Col**]; *San* 7a [**J**]),[214] and with assimilation of final radical, קאיינא "I stand" (*Suk* 42b [**O**51], *San* 91a [**J**]).[215]

### 3.4.5.1.3 The Yemenite Reading Tradition
In contrast, the modern Yemenite tradition reads these forms with a *shewa*, e.g., יְהֵיבְנָא (*Ber* 5b [Morag, *YT*, p. 134]), שְׁקֵילְנָא (*Tan* 24a [Morag, *YT*, p. 134], against printed orthography שקלינא).

It would appear that in the modern reading tradition the vocalization of these participle forms has been influenced by the forms of the perfect, wherein the first radical is vocalized with a *shewa*.[216] The defective orthography may have encouraged such an analogy. It should be noted, however, that the Yemenite tradition is correct in emending forms of the enclitic pronoun from ‑ינא (‑*inā* or ‑*ena*?) to ‑נָא (‑*nā*, realized in the Yemenite tradition as [‑nå]), as the form ‑ינא is not attested in the EEMss or in other early sources.[217]

---

combined historical and phonetic spellings, e.g., כדמעאינת "when you consider" (**GK** I 71:12). The example סאמיכנא found in **HPS** is mentioned by Kara, *Yemenite Manuscripts*, p. 175 n. 204.

[212] The vocalized forms were cited by Morag in "Vocalisation," p. 92 (reprinted in Morag, *Studies*, p. 201). The verb יהיבנא in **HPS** 67:18 is vocalized with an *i*, contra Morag, "Vocalisation," p. 92 (reprinted in Morag, *Studies*, p. 201).

[213] Kara, *Yemenite Manuscripts*, p. 204.

[214] The first example is drawn from ibid., p. 262.

[215] Ibid., p. 89. On such examples see below.

[216] So already Morag, "Vocalisation," p. 92 (reprinted in Morag, *Studies*, p. 202).

[217] Naturally, this does not include the III-*yod* roots, wherein the *yod* marks the vocalic reflex of the historical root consonant. The complete absence of the ‑ינא

### 3.4.6.2  1 m.s.—Assimilation of Third Radical[218]

The weakening of *dalet* (fricative), *lamed, mem, nun,* and *resh* in JBA is a widely attested phenomenon, and will not be discussed at length here.[219] My comments will be limited to the assimilation of the third radical to the enclitic subject pronoun in 1 m.s. participle forms. I have divided the discussion into two parts: forms of the root אמ״ר, on the one hand, and forms of other roots, on the other, though, as I shall argue below, I regard all these examples as resulting from the same linguistic phenomena.

### 3.4.6.2.1 EEMs Evidence

Even in this EEMss, this phenomenon is only attested sporadically. I have found the following examples.[220]

> קָאֵינָא *qāʾennā* from קאימנא *\*qāʾimnā* "I stand" (*Ket* 69a [**HGP** 43a:29]); קטינא *qāṭinnā* from קטילנא *\*qāṭilnā* "I shall kill" (*Sheʾil-tot*[221]); אבינא *ʾāḇinnā* from עבידנא *\*ʿāḇidnā* "I perform" (*BQ* 87a [**G1**]).

---

enclitic on verbal stems ending in consonants in the EEMss confirms Epstein's opinion that "all the forms with the pronoun -ינא are dubious and result from scribal errors" (Epstein, *Grammar*, p. 40). Contra Sabar, *Homilies*, p. 240 n. 1, the existence of such an enclitic pronoun in some Neo-Aramaic dialects does not prove their use in JBA.

[218] Parts of this discussion have appeared previously in my article, "Non-Standard Spellings."

[219] The historical depth of this phenomenon in the magic corpus is demonstrated in Morgenstern, "Non-Standard Spellings."

[220] It is feasible that the sporadic spellings in the early textual witnesses reflect only a small portion of the examples found in the spoken language, and that in many cases the final radical is preserved in writing owing to the overriding tendency to preserve historical spellings. The reconstructed transliterations provided here follow the phonology of **HPS**, with the exception of the citation from **HGP**.

[221] See Lerner, "*Sheʾiltot*," p. 165, and the literature cited in n. 27. Contra Lerner, I regard these forms as reflecting assimilation rather than elision. Such an interpretation was already suggested by Boyarin, "Final Consonants," p. 104, though curiously he transcribed the form שקינא from the magic bowls *šāqina* without a geminated *nun*.

### 3.4.6.2.2 Historical Depth

The assimilation of the final radical into the -nā morpheme is found in several magic texts:

ואזינא (AIT 6:6) from ואזילנא *ʾāzilnā* "and I go;"[222] קינא (M145:1) and קאינא (MS 2053/159) from קאימנא *qāʾimnā* "I stand." [223]

### 3.4.6.2.3 The Yemenite Manuscripts

Kara lists several examples of the forms lacking the final radical under the heading "Conjugation of verbs in which the third radical has dropped":[224]

קאיינא "I stand" (*Suk* 44b [O51]); קיינא "I stand" (*Zev* 18b [Col]); מוקינא *mawqinnā* "I establish" (*Pes* 90a [O51]).[225]

### 3.4.6.2.4 The Yemenite Reading Tradition

Since no such examples survive in the printed editions (with the possible exception of אמינא; see infra), no such examples are preserved in the Yemenite reading tradition.

### 3.4.6.3 The Evidence for אמנא and אמינא

### 3.4.6.3.1 Introduction

By far the most common example of the loss of the third radical in the 1 c.s. participle is אמנא which, as Morag demonstrated, is the form generally employed in Geniza manuscripts of RBA instead of the printed editions' אמינא.[226] Subsequent research has proven his assessment to be correct. The earliest and most accurate sources of RBA almost exclusively

---

[222] This text contains many phonetic spellings.

[223] Morgenstern, "Moussaieff Collection," p. 358.

[224] נטיית הפעלים שלהי״פ שלהם נשלה; Kara, *Yemenite Manuscripts*, p. 309. The examples of the 1 c.s. participle are listed on p. 311 (G) and p. 312 (C).

[225] The Talmudic reference in Kara, *Yemenite Manuscripts*, p. 312, should be corrected accordingly.

[226] Morag, "Geniza," p. 74 (reprinted in Morag, *Studies*, p. 74). It appears that Epstein did not correctly analyze the form, as evidenced by his note "אמינא = אמנא" in Epstein, "Notes II," p. 326 n. 37 (reprinted in Hebrew in Epstein, *Studies* I, p. 101, with additional material). For an alternative view to Morag's explanation, see below.

read אמנא; indeed, the presence of this form is one of the most instantly recognizable distinguishing features of the EEMss group. Examples are numerous, and the following are but a few representative references:

אמנא (ʿEruv 40b [**Geon** xxxviii 6b 14]; RH 5a [**GS** xiv 1a 6]; Suk 16b [**HPS** 31:11]; Bes 10a [**Hark** 121:16]; Ket 40b [**Hark** 123:20]; Yev 17b [**TGAs28** iv 1b 12, 14]; Git 62b [**TGAs28** iv 5a 9] [227]; BQ 84a [**G1**]; BM 42b [**HPS** 127:1]; BM 64b [**Hark** 167:33]; Git 70b [**Geon** xxv a 1]; Men 42a [**Geon** xxxviii 8a 5,7]).

In addition, the early manuscripts contain several examples of the form most commonly found in the later manuscripts and in the printed editions of the Talmud:

אמינא (BQ 102a [**G1**] // אמנא BQ 102a [**G1**]; BB 6a [**Hark** 154:24]; BB 130b [**Hark** 175:26=**GK2** 19:12]; **Hark** 164:18).

Morag proposed several possible explanations for these two forms and their relative distribution. The first is that אמינא represents the morphological shift of אמ"ר to אמ"י, while אמנא, which he transcribed ʾåmanå, shows the loss (rather than assimilation) of the final *resh*. Morag even suggested that אמינא might have been the earlier form, from which אמנא was derived through vowel harmony. Morag also suggested that the two forms may have been dialectal variants.[228] However, Morag's reconstruction is not supported by the evidence.

First, we must clarify the pronunciation of אמנא. From the vocalizations found in **HGP**, it is clear that אמנא was not merely an alternative spelling of אמינא, but was pronounced differently. Although none of the five examples of אמינא in this manuscript is vocalized, thirteen of the fifteen examples of אמנא are, and in these, the *mem* is always vocalized with an *a* vowel, usually אָמְנָא.[229] However, in contrast to Morag's proposed vocalization, there is some evidence in the manuscripts for the gemination of the *nun*. In one case, we find the form הֲוָה אֲמַנָא, wherein

---

[227] Assaf read in all places אמינא.

[228] Morag, "Geniza," p. 74 (reprinted in Morag, *Studies*, p. 307).

[229] The vocalized forms are: Yev 100a [**HGP** 15a:33]; BQ 84a [**HGP** 20b:9, 11; Shev 41b [**HGP** 12a:28]; BQ 87 [**HGP** 20b:19]; BM 42a [**HGP** 23a:18]; BM 64b [**HGP** 26b:17]; BM 72a [**HGP** 2a: 29]; BB 32a [**HGP** 1a:12]; BB 41a [**HGP** 2a:37]; BB 41b [**HGP** 2b:16]; BB 170b [**HGP** 1b:19]).

the gemination is clearly marked.[230] In another example, from the important Geniza 1 fragment of *Bava Mezia*, the vocalization קָאמְנָא is attested. This manuscript only employs the *ḥatap̄-pataḥ* for short *a* vowels in syllables closed by gemination, e.g., לְדַבֵּר, מְשַׁנֵּי, מִפַּלִיג.

In the EEMss, we find the many examples of אמנא listed above, and in the magic corpus אמנה ליה "I (m.s.) say to him" (**MS** 2053/159:9)[231] reflecting *ʾāmannā* < *\*ʾāmarnā*, but by contrast, we also find ואמרנא להו "I (f.s.) say to them" (BM 049A:6), reflecting *ʾāmrānā*. Similarly, we find דאמריתון "that you say" (M142:5)[232] or אמריתו "you say" (AMB 13:19), but never forms in which the third radical is reflected by a *yod* such as **\*\*אמיאנא** *\*\*ʾamyānā* "I (f.s.) say," as we find in צבִיאֹנָא "I desire" (*Yev* 107b [**HPS** 235:17, document formula]). I therefore strongly doubt that the "loss" of the third radical in these examples of אמנא is to be regarded as resulting from a widespread morphological shift. It is better seen as a phonological phenomenon, sporadically attested in other roots but common in אמ״ר, resulting from the weakening of certain consonants which is sometimes reflected in their elision, other times in their assimilation.[233]

If I am correct in suggesting that the form אמנא is, contra Morag, the earlier one, how are we to explain אמינא which is virtually the sole form of the 1 m.s. participle of אמ״ר attested in the standard printed editions?[234] Since אמינא is now attested in an Aramaic magic bowl, and is so widespread in such a wide variety of sources (including very rare examples in **HPS**, **BQ G1** and **TGAs28** i, three excellent manuscripts), it must represent a dialectal form, perhaps indeed reflecting the morphological analogy of אמ״ר to אמ״י as Morag suggested.[235] However, אמינא is certainly not the typologically earlier form, nor can it be said to be derived from אמנא.

### 3.4.6.3.2 The Yemenite Tradition

Kara records only one example of אמנא from the Yemenite manuscripts: אמנא (*Yom* 62b [JTS1623]). I have found several other examples: אמנא (*Yom* 64b [JTS1623]; *Yom* 79b [JTS1623]; *Yom* 87b [JTS1623]; *Suk* 17a

---

[230] Morag, *Vocalised Manuscripts*, no. 121.

[231] Levene, *Corpus*, p. 100.

[232] Levene, *Corpus*, p. 93.

[233] I have discussed the various manifestations of consonant weakening in my article "Non-Standard Spellings."

[234] I have found one example of אמרנא in the Vilna edition (*BM* 85b), but none of אמנא.

[235] See my article "Non-Standard Spellings," pp. 266–68.

[JTS218]; *RH* 14a [JTS218]; *Tan* 22a [J]; *Tan* 23b [J]). In preserving sporadic examples of אמנא, these Yemenite Talmud manuscripts are thus no different from the European manuscripts, in which we similarly find occasional survivals of אמנא.[236] By contrast, MS J contains no examples of אמנא in the text of Sanhedrin or Makkot, nor have I found any in other Yemenite manuscripts.[237] In all of these, the form אמינא is consistently and frequently employed. Kara notes two examples in which this form is vocalized: אֲמֵינָא (*San* 60b [J]) and אמינא (*Suk* 17a [O51]).

The Yemenite reading tradition is entirely dependent upon the printed versions of the Talmud, and accordingly, preserves only the late form אֲמֵינָא (see Morag, *YT*, p. 167).

### 3.4.6.3.3 Conclusion

The form of the 1 m.s. participle of אמ״ר common in the earliest and most accurate textual witnesses, and supported by valuable evidence from the Aramaic magic bowls, was consistently pushed out of the textual tradition of Rabbinic Babylonian Aramaic. While occurrences of אמינא are absent from, or rare in, the best early textual witnesses, it becomes the dominant form in later sources, including most European manuscripts. In the standard printed editions of the Talmud, אמינא is the *only* form attested. From the evidence of manuscripts such as **HGP**, it would seem that already at an early stage, אמנא was being replaced with אמינא; similarly, the old form אמנא has barely survived in the Yemenite textual tradition, and it is entirely lost in the Yemenite reading tradition.

### 3.4.6.4 1 f.s.

### 3.4.6.4.1 EEMs Evidence

The EEMss contain several examples of a distinct 1 f.s. participle, formed on the basis of the f.s. participles with the enclitic pronoun: G active: *qāṭlānā*, D: *məqaṭṭəlānā*, C: *maqṭəlānā*. We also have evidence for a 1 f.s. G passive participle from the III-*yod* class: *qaṭlānā*. The existence of a 1 f.s. participle distinct from the 1 m.s. form may be clearly discerned in those cases wherein the *ā* vowel is marked with a *mater lectionis*:

---

[236] Examples in the manuscripts: **M6** (*Yoma*); **G3** (*Beṣa*); **M141** (*Yevamot*); **V487** (*Nedarim*); **H165** (*BQ, BM, BB*); **V140** (*Shevuʿot*); **V122** (*Ḥullin*); **F7** (*Bekhorot*). Several of these manuscripts are regarded as late and not particularly reliable textual witnesses; nevertheless, they occasionally preserve unusual or rare forms.

[237] Similarly, I have not found any examples of אמנא in the *Midrash HaGadol*, though it is possible that such forms are attested in the better manuscripts.

*Active participle:* הוה סלקאנא ומעיינָא ביה "I would go up and look at him" (*BM* 84b [**G1**]);[238] ידעאנא "I know" (*San* 31a [**GS** vi 1b 17]); מקבלאנא "I receive" (**HPS** 156:13);[239] מצׄעׄראׄא "I shall trouble [him]" (*Ket* 63b [**HGP** 43a:1]); בעיאנא "I want" (**HPS** 177:13,16); רעיאנא "I want" (*Yev* 107b [**HPS** 235:16, document formula]); צׄבׄיאׄא "I desire" (*Yev* 107b [**HPS** 235:16, document formula]); מונקאנא "I shall nurse" (**HPS** 174:20).

*Passive participle:* חזיאנא "I am fitting" (*Ned* 90b [**HPS** 176:9]).

Several examples of the 1 f.s. participle are written in defective orthography: לא נחתנא "I shall not go down" (**Geon** xvii 3a 8) and שקלנא "I shall take" (**TGAs28** iv 3b 11). Although, in theory, these forms could be read as the m.s. *qāṭilnā*, almost all the examples of the active m.s. recorded from the EEMss are written with a *yod*, e.g., דרישנא "I (m.s.) shall interpret" (*Suk* 34b [**HPS** 45:10]), except when the third radical prompts the partial assimilation of the short *i*, e.g., טרחנא "I (m.s.) shall take the trouble" (*BM* 87a [**G1**]).[240] In the III-*yod* category, I have found several 1 f.s. examples that are indistinguishable from the m.s. in their orthography: בעינא "I desire" (*Ket* 83b, vocalized בׇעׅינׇא [**HGP** 43a:1]; *BB* 151a [**HPS** 186:6]; **HPS** 156:1; **TGAs28** iv 3b 25). The evidence of the vocalization of **HGP** would suggest that the vocalizer no longer recognized the distinction when it was not reflected in the orthography. However, as we have noted before (§2.6.1), this vocalization is not as accurate as the orthography itself, and is often not in keeping with Babylonian phonology.

In the EEMss, we find one clear example of the m.s. form employed instead of the f.s.: משלימנא "I (f.s.) shall hand him over" (**HPS** 175:1).[241] The copyist may have been misled by the form משלימנא "I (m.s.) shall hand him over" (**HPS** 174:21) that appeared in the previous line.[242] However, since the same reading is found in **HGP** 42b:6, it may simply represent an early example of the neutralization of the distinction between the two categories. Perhaps both codices drew upon a single

---

[238] The significance of these examples was first noted by Friedman, "Early Manuscripts," p. 26 and n. 99.

[239] This example and the following מונקאנא were noted by Kara, *Yemenite Manuscripts*, p. 158 n. 123.

[240] So far I have found one exception: אזלנא "I shall go" (*Shev* 48b [**HGP** 14b:5]).

[241] Noted already by Kara, *Yemenite Manuscripts*, p. 158 n. 123.

[242] Contra Sokoloff, *DJBA*, p. 648 s.v. מוניקתא, the verb here is to be interpreted as "hand over," not "pay."

source, in which the distinction between the 1 m.s. and 1 f.s. participles had been lost.

### 3.4.6.4.2 The Yemenite Manuscripts

Kara recorded two examples of the 1 f.s. participle from the Yemenite manuscripts. The first, מהדרנא "I shall respond" (*San* 39a [J]), may reflect *mahdərānā* or *mahdarnā*, i.e., either a distinct 1 f.s. form or a form identical to the 1 m.s. The second example, מצילנא "I shall save" (*San* 109b [J]), is identical to the masculine form.[243] An additional ambiguous example, overlooked by Kara, is ידענא "I (f.s.) know" (*San* 31a [J]), which as noted above (§3.4.6.4.1) appears in a Geonic responsum in *plene* spelling.

### 3.4.6.4.3 The Yemenite Reading Tradition

The loss of the 1 f.s. participle appears to be complete in the Yemenite reading tradition, as becomes clear when we compare the Talmudic examples cited above with their contemporary Yemenite readings: יְדַעְנָא "I know" (*San* 31a ['Amr]), מצַעֲרָנָא "I shall trouble [him]" (*Ket* 63b ['Amr]), חְזֵינָא "I am fitting" (*Ned* 90b ['Amr]), and in the lengthy citation from a document formula, לָא רְעֵינָא בָּךְ וְלָא צְבֵינָא בָּךְ "I (f.s.) do not want you and I (f.s.) do not desire you" (*Yev* 107b [Morag, *YT*, p. 261]).

The loss of this form in the Yemenite tradition may be due to a combination of factors: the adoption of the printed edition, on the one hand, and the metanalysis of the *plene* spellings, on the other. I have found at least one example of metanalysis in the Yemenite *Midrash HaGadol*: משכח אנא "I (f.s.) will find" (*Git* 59a [**MHD** 626:29]).[244]

### 3.4.6.5 G 2 m.s.

### 3.4.6.5.1 EEMs Evidence

As in the 1 m.s., so in the 2 m.s. forms the evidence points to the fact that the first radical was vocalized with *ā*, since we find occasional *plene* spellings: יאכלת "you are able" (**Hark** 84:27; **GK1** 71:24), שאמעת "you hear" (**Hark** 161:35 bis), and שאקלת וטארית "you shall negotiate" (**Hark** 168:18). The vocalization of the other root consonants is uncertain. As Morag already noted, **HPS** contains several vocalized 2 m.s. forms, of which some are certainly participles:

---

[243] Kara, *Yemenite Manuscripts*, p. 158 n. 123.
[244] See Morgenstern, "Risqué Pun," p. 886.

אָמֹרְתֹּ "you say" (*MQ* 11a [**HPS** 277:20]);[245] סֹבַֿרְתֹּ (*MQ* 4a [**HPS** 274:19]).[246]

To these examples we may add:

וּפֹטֹרְתֹּ "you release" (*Hul* 132b [**HPS** 60:19]).

In **HGP** I have found:

קָא אָמֹרֹת "you say" (*Ket* 79a [**HGP** 44a:1]); פֹּרֹעֹת "you pay" (*Shev* 41b [**HGP** 12a:24]).

Morag also suggested at one point that examples with a *shewa* following the first radical found in **HPS** might be participle forms.[247] However, it is possible that he subsequently revised his position, as he did not cite any such examples from **HPS** in his discussion of Yemenite forms employing the enclitic pronoun.[248]

The manuscript evidence is divided regarding the vocalization of the enclitic suffix. The certain examples from **HPS** are in roots wherein the third radical is a *resh* or *ḥet*, and accordingly, the preceding vowel in any case shifts from *i* to *a*: \**sāvir* > \**sāvar* + \**ʾatt* > *sāvartt*, \**ʾāmir* > \**ʾāmar* + \**ʾatt* > *ʾāmartt* אָמֹרְתֹּ. The final *shewa* may reflect the pronunciation of the geminated *taw* of the pronoun. The same process appears to be reflected in vocalized forms such as מֹזֹבֹנֹתֹּ (*BM* 82a [**HGP** 2a:28]). I am unable to read the vocalization of the word in **HGP** 36:22.

Other examples seem to reflect a different process of development. From both the vocalized forms and the defective spellings in the EEMss it emerges that the *i* vowel was never orthographically represented after the second radical in these cases. Contrast the following examples:

---

[245] The vocalization in Morag, "Phonology," p. 69 (reprinted in Morag, *Studies*, 246) is slightly misplaced; in the original, the two *a* vowels are clearly written to follow the *ʾaleph* and *mem*.

[246] The expression מי סברת is translated by R. Shemuel ben Ḥofni as אתטין "do you think?" See **LPT** 157:30.

[247] It is not clear to which examples Morag was referring in "Phonology," p. 69 n. 15 (reprinted in Morag, *Studies*, p. 246 n. 15).

[248] See Morag, *YT*, pp. 43–44, 134–35.

| | M.s. participle | M.s. participle + enclitic pronoun. |
|---|---|---|
| G | זבין "buys" (*Qid* 26a [**HPS** 95:18]) <br><br> כאתיב "writes" (**Hark** 105:16) <br><br> סאמיך "depends" (**Hark** 93:31) <br><br> שאקיל "takes" (**Hark** 278:3) | זבנת "you buy" (*BB* 103a [**G1**]). <br><br> כתבת "you write" (*BQ* 103a [**GS** iv 1b 6]) <br><br> סמכת "you depend" (*BQ* 100a [**G1**]) <br><br> שאקלת "you negotiate"[249] (**Hark** 168:18) |
| D | מזבין "sells" (*BQ* 119a [**G1**]) <br> מסליק "removes" (**HPS** 78:2) <br><br> מתריץ "explains" (**Hark** 33:34) | מזבנת "you sell" (*BQ* 88b [**G1**]) <br> מסלקת "you remove" (**Hark** 196:8) <br><br> מתרצת "you explain" (**TGAs42** ii 1b 26)[250] |
| C[251] | מפיק "takes out" (*BQ* 172a [**HPS** 104:13] <br> מוקים "establishes" (**Hark** 115:26) | מפקת "you let out" (*Shev* 31b [**HPS** 193:16]) <br> מוקמת "you establish" (*BM* 79a [**G1**]) |

The consistent *defectiva* orthography found in the 2 m.s. participles, demonstrated here by these representative examples, seems to imply that at least in the case of participle forms with an *i* vowel in the final closed syllable, this vowel shifted when the enclitic pronoun was affixed. The simplest explanation, partially confirmed by pairs such as יאכיל "he can" (**Hark** 44:27) contrasting with יכלת "you prevail" (*BM* 83b [**G1**]), is that the affixing of the enclitic pronoun in the form -*att* caused the historically short *i* vowel to be reduced to a *shewa* in what is now an open syllable.[252] It would be difficult to explain how this vowel shifted to *a*, as we found in vocalized forms from **HPS** from etymologically III-pharyngeal roots. However, it does not seem that we can claim that we are dealing with a situation of complementary distribution, i.e., *CāCiC* + *ʾatt* > *CāCCatt* while *CāCaC* + *ʾatt* > *CāCaCt*, since we also find the vocalized form דקא

---

[249] In the idiom שאקלת וטארית.

[250] Assaf read מתרצית

[251] I have not found any examples of the strong verb in which the third radical is not a pharyngeal or *resh*.

[252] So in Classical Syriac and Classical Mandaic. See Nöldeke, *SG*, §64A and *MG*, §175, respectively.

אמרת "that you say" (*BM* 76a [**G1**]), wherein the opening vowel of the enclitic pronoun has been preserved: *ʾāmar + ʾatt > ʾām(a)ratt.

### 3.4.6.5.2 The Yemenite Reading Tradition

Further evidence must be garnered from early manuscripts before the precise shape and development of these forms can be determined. However, there is little support for three aspects of the Yemenite reading tradition:

1. The *shewa* after the first radical, e.g., שְׁמַעַתּ "you hear" (*Ned* 3b [Morag, *YT*, p. 135]). As we have seen, in the EEMss this verb is written *plene* with an *ʾaleph*: שאמעת "you hear" (**Hark** 161:35 bis).
2. The preservation of the *i* or *e* vowel after the second radical. e.g., טְעֵימתּ "you shall taste" (*Ned* 22b [Morag, *YT*, p. 135]). As we have seen, in the EEMss these forms are *always* written defectively.[253]
3. There is no evidence to support readings such as מְזַבְּנֵית (*BM* 72a [Morag, *YT*, p. 150]), employed by some authorities. This reading is plainly influenced by the erroneous Talmudic orthography, which has no basis in the early manuscript traditions.

### 3.4.6.5.3 Conclusion

Several aspects of the Yemenite reading tradition appear to be secondary developments that are contradicted by the orthography or vocalization of the EEMss. It seems that Morag himself regarded these as specifically Yemenite phenomena.[254] Further sources need to be identified and studied before we may reach more definitive conclusions about the original form in JBA.

### 3.4.6.6 III-*yod*

### 3.4.6.6.1 EEMs Evidence

Unlike the sound verb, the vocalization of the III-*yod* verbs is well attested. By combining the *plene* spellings with the vocalized examples, we can establish that this form conjugated on the pattern *qāṭet*, as demonstrated by the following representative examples:

---

[253] There is some evidence for the *plene* spelling in the Yemenite manuscripts, though its interpretation may be debated. The one vocalized form that Kara cites, שְׁלֵיפתְּ "you draw" (*Tan* 24b) appears in the apodosis of a conditional clause and hence may be in the perfect.

[254] Cf. references in n. 248 above.

באעית "you want" (*BB* 33b [**HPS** 137:5]); דאמית "you are like" (*BB* 168a [**HPS** 102:9]); חאזית "you see" (**TGAs28** xvii 1b 15); (שאקלת) וטארית "you negotiate" (**Hark** 168: 18); מאטית "you arrive" (**GK1** 71:15); קאנית "you acquire" (**Hark** 35:17); קארית "you read" (**TGAs28** vi a 3); ראמית "you cast" (**TGAs28** 1 3b 14); תאנית "you teach" (*BQ* 98b [**G1**]; *BB* 65a [**HPS** 147:3]).

In **HPS** we find a vocalized example שָׁרֵית "you permit" (**HPS** 2:20). Again, there is no indication whether the enclitic pronoun was pronounced with a plosive or fricative *taw*.

Surprisingly, no examples in *plene* orthography are found in **HGP**. There is some evidence to suggest that the scribe of this manuscript pronounced the participles like the perfects, e.g., בָּעִית "[What] do you want?" (*BB* 30a [**HGP** 2b:12]), though it is possible that he understood this form as perfect "[What] did you want?"

### 3.4.6.6.2 The Yemenite Manuscripts

The Yemenite manuscripts contain similar *plene* spellings: באכית "you are crying" (*Tan* 25a [**J**]), ראמית "you set" (*Tan* 14b [**J**]; *San* 6a [**J**]), שארית "you permit" (*MQ* 16b [**Col**]), and two vocalized forms: דָּרֵית "you carry" (*Meg* 28a [**Col**]) and מַצֵית "are you able?" (*San* 23b [**J**]).[255]

### 3.4.6.6.3 The Yemenite Reading Tradition

The contemporary Yemenite pronunciation of these forms always places a *shewa* after the first radical, e.g., קַבְּכֵית "you are crying" (*Tan* 25a [ᶜAmr]), בְּעֵית "you want" (*BB* 33b [ᶜAmr]), דְּרֵית "you carry" (*Meg* 28a [Morag, *YT*, p. 261]), רְמֵית "you cast" (*San* 6a [ᶜAmr]), and תְּנֵית "you teach" (*BQ* 98b [ᶜAmr]). The enclitic morpheme is always fricative; hence these forms have merged entirely with the perfects.

### 3.4.6.7 2 m.pl.

### 3.4.6.7.1 EEMs Evidence

The 2 m.pl. participle form is based upon the m.pl. participles to which a pronoun is affixed. In Talmudic sources, this pronoun is overwhelmingly based upon the apocopated pronoun אתו, while Geonic sources prefer a pronoun based upon the typologically older אתון.[256]

---

[255] Many of these examples are cited by Kara, *Yemenite Manuscripts*, p. 287.

[256] See Epstein, *Grammar*, p. 21; Friedman, "Three Studies," pp. 63–64; Juusola, *Linguistic Peculiarities*, pp. 75–76; and Morgenstern, "Geonic Responsa," p. 163.

G:

**Short pronoun:** *Active*: אמריתו "you say" (*MQ* 28b [**Hark** 189:34]); אתיתו "are you coming" (*Mak* 6a [**Hark** 19:30]); דיקיתו "you are precise" (*BQ* 98b [**G1**]); חזיתו "you see" (*BB* 130b [**Hark** 175:25]); ידעיתו "you know" (*BB* 172a [**HPS** 103:20]); יתביתו "you sit" (*BB* 172a [**HPS** 103:20]); כתביתו "you write" (*BB* 172a [**HPS** 103:20]); ענשיתו "you punish" (*Men* 41a [**Hark** 190:5]).

**Long pronoun:** *Active:* אמריתון "you say" (**Hark** 157:1; **Hark** 170:27); אתיתון "are you coming" (**Hark** 115:28); חישיתון "you are concerned" (**Hark** 98:26); ידעיתון "you know" (**Hark** 113:16). *Passive*: צריכיתון "you need" (**Hark** 98:24).

Gt:

**Short pronoun:** מיסתפיתו "you fear" (*Ber* 62a [**GS** iv 2b 8]).

D:

**Short pronoun:** *Active*: מחנפיתו "you show favor" (*Ket* 84b [**HPS** 78:14]); מתניתו "you teach" (*Yev* 18b [**TGAs28** iv 1b 25]).[257] *Passive*: מקרביתו "you are close" (*BB* 65a [**HPS** 147:11]).
**Long pronoun:** *Active*: מתניתון "you teach" (*Ket* 40b [**Hark** 123:18]); מקבליתון "you receive" (**Hark** 101:21).

Dt:

**Short pronoun:** מיחיביתו "you are required" (*Pes* 5b [**HPS** 9:8]).

Since all these forms are based upon pronouns which have a geminated *taw* (ʾattun and ʾattu)[258] we would expect to find that the *taw* of this morpheme is geminated.[259] Evidence for this is forthcoming in one early manuscript source: דמקַדְּמיתו ומחשליתו "that you will come early and stay late" (*BM* 83a [**G1**]).[260] See also בְּעֵיִיתו (*San* 6b [**HGP** 36a:13]).

---

[257] Assaf read מתניתון.

[258] A vocalized example of אתו appears in **HGP**, but the form was misprinted in Epstein, *Grammar*, p. 21. The word as it appears in the manuscript is אַתֽו (*BQ* 62a [**HGP** 16a:29]).

[259] So already Kara, *Yemenite Manuscripts*, p. 160 n. 132, who also noted the following example.

[260] See Friedman, "Early Manuscripts," p. 102 and n. 93.

### 3.4.6.7.2 The Yemenite Tradition

In contrast, in both the sporadic vocalizations in the Yemenite manuscripts and the Yemenite reading tradition the *taw* is *rafe*. Examples from the manuscripts include זַקְפִּיתֹ "you plant" (*San* 30b [J]) and מוֹתְבִיתֹי "you seat" (*San* 37a [J]).[261] An example from the reading tradition is אֲמְרִיתוּן "you say" (*Ned* 25a [Morag, *YT*, p. 135]).

### 3.4.6.7.3 Comparative Material

Since vocalization in the EEMss is rare and the orthography does not distinguish between fricative and plosive pronunciations, it is worth considering the evidence of the other Eastern Aramaic dialects that also join enclitic subject pronouns to participles. In almost all of these dialects, the enclitic pronoun is pronounced with the plosive *taw*, as it is in Eastern Neo-Aramaic.[262] In light of this, the fricative pronunciation should be regarded as a Yemenite innovation. We may suggest that this innovation arose by analogy to the 2 m.pl. perfect morpheme of the III-*yod* verbs, e.g., דְּמִיתוּ (*Tan* 14b [Morag, *YT*, p. 255]).

## 3.4.7 I-ʾaleph Verbs in Gt

### 3.4.7.1 Background

Morag placed great value upon the phenomenon of *qere-kethib* in the Yemenite reading of the Talmud. "The oral tradition is stronger than the written text, and in the deviations from the written text the Yemenite tradition reveals features of the ancient text of the Talmud that were widespread in Yemen."[263] However, as we have seen above, it is not always clear that the systematic emendations that the reading tradition presents are an accurate reflection of the RBA of the Talmud.

A clear illustration of this phenomenon may be found in the Gt forms of the I-ʾaleph verbs. The Yemenite tradition distinguishes between forms of the root אמ"ר and those of other roots. For the root אמ"ר, the ʾaleph is retained as a glottal stop even against the orthography of the printed editions, i.e., איתמר is read אֶתְאֲמַר "it was said" (passim).[264] In contrast, in the root אנ"ס the first ʾaleph is assimilated into the *taw* and the form is read, in accordance with the spelling, אֶתְּנִיס "he was com-

---

[261] Kara, *Yemenite Manuscripts*, p. 160.

[262] For classical Syriac, see Nöldeke, *SG*, §64. The information on Eastern Neo-Aramaic is based upon oral communication from Dr. Hezy Mutzafi.

[263] Morag, *YT*, p. 63 (my translation.)

[264] Morag, *Kethib-Qere*, p. 43 and *YT*, p. 169.

pelled" (*Ned* 27a [Morag, *YT*, p. 169]). As mentioned, the *ʾaleph* seems to have been assimilated to the preceding *taw*, which is always preserved in these instances.

### 3.4.7.2 EEMs Evidence

Evidence for this assimilation is to be found in the EEMss in vocalized forms דְמִיתְגַ֫ר "who is hired" (*BM* 76a [**G1**]), לְאִיתְגַ֫וֹרִי "to be hired" (ibid.). However, the EEMss show no evidence for the distinction between the verb אמ״ר and other I-*ʾaleph* verbs. On the contrary, forms of אמ״ר preserving the first *ʾaleph* are extremely rare. The following are a wide selection of representative examples:

*Perfect*:

> *3 m.s.*: איתמר (*Ber* 51a [**HPS** 291:13]; *Shab* 129a [**HPS** 1:17]); *ᶜAZ* 73b [**HPS** 11:15]; *Suk* 19a [**HPS** 35:8]; *Suk* 36b [**HPS** 46:17]; *Suk* 46a [**HPS** 38:20]; *Yev* 10b [**HPS** 226:16]; *Yev* 35b [**HPS** 227:4]; *Yev* 66a [**HPS** 158:15]; *Qid* 79a [**HPS** 170:6]; *BQ* 81b [**G1**]; *BQ* 86a [**G1**]; *BQ* 88a [**G1**]; *BQ* 115a [**HPS** 130:17]; *BQ* 117b [**G1**]; *BM* 29a [**HPS** 115:4]; *BM* 101a [**HPS** 109:17]; *BB* 64b [**HPS** 146:21]; *BB* 65a [**HPS** 147:7, 9]; *BB* 75a [**HPS** 152:6]; *BB* 106a [**HPS** 149:5]; *BB* 106b [**HPS** 149:20]; *BB* 107a [**HPS** 150:7]; *Shev* 47a [**HPS** 195:9]; *Shev* 48b [**HPS** 198:12]; **HPS** 169:4; **HPS** 204:7). *3 f.s.*: איתמרא (*Hul* 141a [**TGAs28** i 2a 7]; **Hark** 33:34; **Hark** 220:26; **Geon** ix a 13). *3 m.pl.*: איתמרו (**Hark** 158:14).

*Participle*:

> *3 m.s.*: מיתמר (**HPS** 294:16; **Hark** 103:33=Weiss, Fragments iii 4a 6). *3 f.s.*: מִיתֹמֹרָא (*BB* 39a [**HGP** 37b:17]). *3 m.pl.*: מִיתֹמֹרִי (*BM* 67b [**HGP** 27a:38]); מיתמרי **Hark** 189:22).

In fact, none of the EEMss that I have examined contain forms preserving the *ʾaleph*.

### 3.4.7.3 The Yemenite Manuscripts

Kara notes that the spelling preserving the root *ʾaleph* is common in the Yemenite manuscripts.[265] However, a computer search of the manuscript of *Sanhedrin*, which is regarded as being the most accurate of the Yemenite manuscripts, reveals forty examples of איתמר, but only one of אתאמר

---

[265] Kara, *Yemenite Manuscripts*, p. 229 n. 97.

(*San* 6a, 3 f.s.). Similarly, although Kara cited an example of איתאמר from a Geonic commentary, it is an exception rather than the rule.

### 3.4.7.4 Comparative Material

Forms of I-ʾ*aleph* roots wherein the ʾ*aleph* has been elided are already attested in the Dead Sea Scrolls, e.g., מתגר "rewarded" (1QapGen 20:10). One example has been recorded in the Geniza fragments of Targum Onqelos (אתשד), though in that dialect the ʾ*aleph* is generally preserved.[266] In Mandaic, the ʾ*aleph* of the I-ʾ*aleph* roots is regularly assimilated in the Gt stem, e.g., ʿ*tbyd* "it was done." (When the second radical is vocalized with *shewa*, we find an anaptyctic vowel after the *taw*: ʿ*tybd*ʾ*t* "it was done.")[267] In classical Syriac, the ʾ*aleph* is generally elided but not assimilated, e.g., ܡܬܐܟܠ "is eaten," but in one root the assimilation occurs: ܡܬܐܚܕ "is held."[268]

### 3.4.7.5 Conclusion

Weighing all this evidence, it seems likely that the genuine Babylonian form did not retain the ʾ*aleph*. The single example that has been recorded so far from Geonic literature and the single example in MS Jerusalem of *Sanhedrin* may be regarded as historical spellings or the influence of other Aramaic dialects. Certainly, the accurate manuscripts do not support this reading, and the evidence of MS Jerusalem implies that it was not the original reading even in the Yemenite manuscript tradition.

### 3.5 Pronouns

### 3.5.1 Object Pronouns

In RBA, the affixing of pronominal objects is obligatory, with the exception of those governed by a participle. In addition, proleptic object pronouns are quite common when the direct object is a substantive.[269] Accordingly, most of the affixed object pronouns are quite well attested in Babylonian Aramaic literature.[270] Several differences emerge from the

---

[266] Dodi, "I-ʾ*aleph*," p. 34.

[267] Nöldeke, *MG*, §180.

[268] Nöldeke, *SG*, §147C.

[269] See chapter 5 "The Direct Object."

[270] Exceptions are the 2 f. and 2 m.pl. forms.

comparison of the EEMss with the Yemenite manuscripts and the Yemenite reading tradition.

A general characteristic of the suffixed object pronouns is that they are formed on the same basis for all tenses. For some of the pronouns there are postconsonantal and postvocalic allomorphs. When pronouns are affixed to the infinitives of the derived stems (*qaṭṭawle*, *ʾaqṭawle*, etc.), the final -*e* vowel is lost, and the postconsonantal allomorphs are used.[271]

### 3.5.1.1 1 c.s.

#### 3.5.1.1.1 EEMs Evidence

In the EEMss the postconsonantal form this pronoun is -*an* (possibly sometimes -*ān*)[272] with a postvocalic allomorph -*n*:

*Perfect:*

> 2 *m.s.:* אפסידתן "you have caused me loss" (*BQ* 116a [**G1**]); אודעתָּן "you informed me" (*BM* 101b [**HGP** 7a:7]); אוניתן "you have cheated me" (*BB* 84a [**HPS** 152:15, 18]).

> 3 *m.s.:* פַּטְרָן "he released me" (*Hul* 132b [**HPS** 60:20]); מטיאן "it reached me" (**TGAs28** xvii 1b 11); אקפן "he surrounded me" (*ʿAZ* 58a [**HGP** 56b:10]); אודען "he informed me" (**Hark** 155:21).

*Imperfect:*

> 2 *m.s.:* תיפרען "you shall pay me" (*Shev* 41b [**HPS** 199:4,6]).

> 3 *m.s.:* לא ליטירדן "he will not bother me" (*BB* 5b [**HPS** 202:5]).

*Imperative:*

> *m.s.:* גירשן "divorce me" (**HPS** 178:14); פיטרן "release me" (**HPS** 156:14); פירען "pay me" (*Shev* 42a [**Hark** 115:1]); פִּירעָן "pay me" (*Shev* 41b [**HPS** 199:18]); אסקן "raise me up" (**Hark** 208:5);[273] אוקמן "stand me up" (*Ber* 30a [**Geon** xxxii b 29]); אשקיאן "give me to drink" (*Qid* 9a [**HPS** 166:11]; *BM* 97a [**HPS** 113:9]).

> *f.s.:* אגניין "lay me down" (*BM* 84b [**G1**]).

---

[271] The cause of the vowel's loss is uncertain, and its explanation would require a more certain understanding of the origin of the -*e*. Cf. Nöldeke, *MG*, §122.

[272] An indication of such a reading might be found in the plene spelling of אשקיאן "give me to drink" (*Qid* 9a [**HPS** 166:11]; *BM* 97a [**HPS** 113:9]).

[273] Harkavy erroneously read אסקו.

*Infinitive:*

לאודוען "to inform me" (*BM* 101b [**HPS** 108:7]).

### 3.5.1.1.2 The Yemenite Manuscripts

The same forms are employed in the Yemenite manuscripts, e.g.:

*Perfect:*

**2 m.s.:** קבילתן "you have received me" (*Pes* 89b [**JTS**1623, **Col**]); קבסתן "you have caused me to vomit" (*San* 55a [**J**]); **3 m.s.:** אודען "he informed me" (*Tan* 24a [**J**]); לא ברכון "they did not bless me" (*MQ* 9b [**Col**]).

*Imperfect:*

**3 m.s.:** ניברכן מר "May my master bless me" (*Tan* 5b [**J**]).[274]

*Imperative:*

**m.s.:** ניסבן "marry me" (*San* 22a [**J**]); שיבקן "allow me" (*San* 38b [**J**]).

### 3.5.1.1.3 The Yemenite Reading Tradition

In addition to the forms found in the earlier manuscripts, the Yemenite reading tradition contains a number of strange forms for which no support may be found in older sources:

1.　כִּי פְּרַעתִּין פַּרעִין לִי "When you pay me, pay me [before PN and PN]" (*Shev* 41b [Morag, *YT* p. 296, ʿAmr]). ʿAmr proposed an alternative reading: כִּי פְרַעת לִי לָא תִּפרַע אֶלָא "[Whe]n you pay me, do not pay me except [before PN and PN]" Similarly: כִּי פְרַעת לִי פַּרעִין לִי בְּאַפֵּי בֵּי תְּרֵי "When you pay me, pay me before two people" (*Shev* 41b [Morag, *YT* p. 296, ʿAmr]), for which ʿAmr proposes the alternative reading פַּרעַן בְּאַפֵּי ". . . pay me before . . . ." In both these cases, ʿAmr's alternative reading is preferable.

2.　Above (§3.4.3.5) we discussed the nature of the vowel after the *pe*. The object pronoun *-in* is similarly suspect. This very example is attested in a vocalized example from **HPS**, wherein the object is *-an*.

3.　לא תְסָייעִי "let it not support me" (*BM* 31a [Morag, *YT*, p. 316]). This form of the pronoun is not supported by any

---

Kara, *Yemenite Manuscripts*, p. 324, records this as 2 m.s. imperfect, but it is a 3 m.s. form of respectful address.

further examples of the imperfect nor by the manuscripts. MS H165, for example, reads תסייען, i.e., with the expected grammatical form.[275] The alternative Yemenite reading, תְּסַיְּעִי (Morag, *YT*, p. 316 n. 32) is similarly not supported and cannot be regarded as a better reading.

4. אַשְׁקִין "give (m.pl.) me to drink" (*San* 67b [Morag, *YT*, p. 329]). From the conjugation pattern of the III-*yod* roots in this dialect, one would expect אשקיון (vocalize: אַשְׁקְיוּן), which is indeed the form of this example as attested in the Yemenite manuscript of the tractate.[276]

5. לְמִקְטְלִי "to kill me" (*Meg* 16a [Morag, *YT*, p. 297]). This is a form influenced by the language of Targum Onqelos/Jonathan, in which the infinitive takes the possessive suffixes of the m.s. and f.s./pl. nouns rather than the object suffixes affixed to the verbs, e.g., בְּמִקְטְלִי (*TO Exod* 12:13).[277]

## 3.5.1.2 3 m.s.

### 3.5.1.2.1 EEMs Evidence

The distribution of the 3 m.s. object pronouns in JBA is determined by the following condition. If the verbal base ends in a consonant, then the pronoun יֵה- *-eh* is employed. If it ends in a vowel, then the יְהִי- *-hi* or its apocopated form ה- *-h* is employed.[278] In the latter category we find a few rare examples of an allomorph in which the *he* has been elided after a long *ū* vowel, and the pronoun is י-, perhaps pronounced *-y*. The pronoun *-hi* tends to appear more in Geonic materials, but even in the Geonic works there is a marked preference for the shorter forms in Talmudic citations.

As noted above in our discussion of the 1 c.pl. perfect morphemes (§3.4.1.6), some verbal bases that in Targum Onqelos are treated as ending in vowels and take the postvocalic object suffixes conjugate in RBA as consonant-final forms. The 1 c.pl. forms have been discussed above. The same is the case for the 2 m.s., wherein we may contrast RBA בטילתיה

---

[275] Similarly MSS **F**, **V115**, and **V116–117**.

[276] Kara, *Yemenite Manuscripts*, p. 349.

[277] Dalman, *Grammatik*, p. 378; Dodi, "Grammar," p. 417. In TOJ, the pronoun affixed to verbs is ני-, e.g., פְּקָדְנִי (TO Deut 10:5); see Dalman, *Grammatik*, p. 362; Dodi, "Grammar," p. 404.

[278] For a possible *-ø* morpheme, which may nevertheless alter the shape of the verbal base, see the discussion of the verb כיתבו (*BB* 172a [**HPS** 104:1]), above, n. 190.

"you annulled it" (**Hark** 167:15) with TOJ בָּחַרְתִּהִי "you chose him" (*Deut* 33:8).[279] Similarly, the m.s. imperative, which in TOJ curiously takes the postvocalic prefix, e.g., קָדִּישֹהִי "sanctify it" (*Exod* 19:23)[280] here takes postconsonantal forms, as we have seen above, e.g., שירקיה "plaster it" (*BQ* 81b [**G1**]).

While the *-ūn* plural morpheme is occasionally employed in RBA imperfects, the *-ū* morpheme is generally employed before object pronouns, to which the postvocalic allomorph is generally affixed. The following example demonstrates this phenomenon nicely:

בעל הבית גופיה ניחא ליה כהיכי דְּלִיתְּגְרוּן ליה פועלין אדרבה שכיר ניחא
ליה כהיכי דְּלִיגְרוּה

[This ruling] suits the householder himself: so that workers **be hired** for him. On the contrary! It suits the hired laborer: so that **they will hire him**" (*Shev* 45a [**HGP** 13a:32–33]).

Forms with the paragogic *nun*, such as are common in TOJ, e.g., תֵּלְקְטוֹנֵיה "you (m.pl.) shall gather it" (TO *Exod* 16:26),[281] are rare in the EEMss and appear exclusively in archaic usages such as legal formulary, e.g., לפרעונֵיה "let them pay him" (**HPS** 88:15, a will formulary for a mortally ill man).

The postconsonantal form is widely attested in all textual traditions and does not require further clarification or exemplification. It is the postvocalic forms that show considerable variation between the early and late sources.

The following examples illustrate the forms attested in the EEMss. 3 m.pl. G forms have been cited above, §3.4.3.5.1, and are not repeated here.

*Perfect*
**3 m.pl.**

> **D and quadriliterals:** גנדרוה "they pushed him forward" (**HPS** 231:7); הימנוהי "they believed him" (**Hark** 268:14, 15); זבנוה "they sold it" (*BQ* 103a [**HPS** 72:13]); חיבוהי "they required of him" (**Hark** 31:32); סלקוה "they removed him" (**TGAs28** i 9b 11); פייסוה "they persuaded him" (*BM* 77a [**G1**]); קבלוה "they took it" (**TGAs28** i 11a 12]); עסיוה "they compelled him" (*'Ara* 21b [**Hark**

279 Dodi, "Grammar," p. 404.

280 Dalman, *Grammatik*, p. 375; cf. Muraoka–Porten, *Grammar*, §38d, f.

281 Dalman, *Grammatik*, p. 373.

139:11, 166:2, etc.]); רציוה "they appeased him" (ʿAra 21b [**Hark** 263:32]); שויוה "they made it/him" (*BM* 45a [**Hark** 47:15]; **Hark** 136:9; **Geon** viii 36a 19; **TGAs28** iv 3b 27); פרשוהי "they interpreted it" (**Hark** 118:11); קירבוהי "they brought him forth" (**Hark** 276:17); שויוהי "they appointed him" (**TGAs28** iv 4a 3); שחררוהי "they released him" (**TGAs28** iv 3b 28); שמתוה "they excommunicated him" (ʿAra 22a [**HPS** 189:15]).

C: אתיוה "they brought him" (*BQ* 84b [**G1**]; **TGAs28** i 13b 18=**GS** i 11a 13);[282] אהדרוהי "they answered him" (**Hark** 82:20);[283] אגמרוה "they taught him" (*BB* 31a [**HPS** 136:13]; **Hark** 168:27); אודעוה "they informed him" (*BQ* 102b [**GS** iv 1a 10]); אכשרוה "they declared fit" (*Yev* 80b [**Geon** xx 1b 27]); אצרכוה "they required of him" (**Hark** 85:30); אצרכוהי "they required of him" (**HPS** 169:7); אוקמוה "they established him" (**Hark** 203:21); אשכחוה "they found him" (*BQ* 59b [**HGP** 16a:17]; **HPS** 120:3); אחזקוהי "they held him" (**Gil** i a 27); אחשבוה "they reckoned it" (**TGAs28** i 4a 14); אטרחוהי "they troubled him" (**HPS** 50:1); אֹטרֹחוֹה "they [did not] trouble him" (*BM* 42a [**HGP** 23a:8]); אטרחוה "they troubled him" (**Geon** xxxi a 23; **Geon** xxxviii 9b 9[284]); אֵמטיוֹהִֹ "they brought him" (**HPS** 259:20).

*Imperfect:*
**2 m.pl.:**
　　G: תקריוה "you should call him" (ʿAZ 60a [**HGP** 56b:30]);[285] תיקירעוה "tear it" (*BB* 130b [**GK2** 19:12, 14]).

**3 m.pl.:**
　　G: לא נדיחקוה "they should not trouble him" (*BM* 84b [**G1**]); נידינוה "should they judge it?" (*BM* 42a [**HPS** 126:18]); לידינוה "should they judge it?" (*BB* 34a [**HPS** 137:9]); לא ניקריוה "they should not call him" (*BM* 15b [**Hark** 160:26, 29]).

　　C: נתיוהי "let them bring it" (**TGAs28** i 8a 24).[286]

---

[282] On this form see §4.4.5.4.

[283] Harkavy read אהדרוהו.

[284] Ginsberg read אטריחוה.

[285] This passage occurs only in manuscripts; it has been censored from the printed editions.

[286] This is a C 3 m.pl. imperfect of the root אתי״י with a 3 m.s. suffixed object pronoun. Assaf read נתינה. The correct reading is found in Lewin, *Otzar Ha-gaonim*

*Imperative:*
**Pl.:**

> *G:* See above, §3.4.3.5.1 Also: שימוה "evaluate him" (*BQ* 84a [**G1**]).

> *D:* זבנוהי "sell it" (**TGAs28** iv 3b 25); שויוה "make it" (*BB* 172a [**HPS** 104:3,7, **HPS** 202:10,14]).

> *C:* אחתוה "put it down" (*Git* 63b [**GS** xiv 2b 25]); אסבוה "lash him" (*Ket* 10a [**Geon** xviii 2a 7]).

*All* the above examples employ one of two pronominal object forms, *-hi* or the apocopated *-h*. In the EEMss, I have found two examples with an elided *he*: אגמרוי "they taught him" (**TGAs42** 101:4) and אותבוי "they answered him" (**Hark** 50:32). This rare form is supported by evidence from the Aramaic magic bowls, e.g., נקטוי "they grabbed him" (M163:23).[287] Similar forms are found in Mandaic and Classical Syriac.[288]

By contrast, I have found only a *single instance* of the form common in the printed editions, *-hū*: דסייעוהו (**Hark** 193:25). Since this form is so rare in the early manuscripts, is not attested in the Aramaic dialects, and cannot be justified on linguistic grounds, but can easily be explained as a graphic error owing to the similarity of the *waw* and *yod* in the Jewish script (possibly encouraged by the parallel Hebrew morpheme *-hu*), I would unhesitatingly regard it as a scribal error.

### 3.5.1.2.2 The Yemenite Manuscripts

The distribution of forms in the Yemenite manuscripts is similar, though not identical. Following consonants, we find the *-eh* morpheme, as we do in the EEMss. However, Kara records several examples of the *nun* ending on verbs with consonantal endings, e.g., לישקליניה "that he take it" (*Tan* 25a [**J**]) and ניקטלניה "it would kill him" (*San* 95a [**J**]).[289] These examples would appear to reflect the influence of the Targumic grammar on the Yemenite manuscripts, a process for which evidence may be forthcoming in examples such as ניקדמיה (*Pes* 59a [**Col**]) = ניקדמיניה "let it precede it"

---

*Git* p. 44 n. vii, but Levin did not understand the form and unnecessarily emended it.

[287] See my comments in Morgenstern, "Moussaieff Collection," p. 363 and next paragraph.

[288] Nöldeke, *MG*, §77 and *SG*, §65, respectively.

[289] Kara, *Yemenite Manuscripts*, p. 187 (correct orthography there). Here we must exclude examples such as יספדוניה (*MQ* 28b [**Col**]), which as Kara notes (p. 320 n. 288), appear in older dirge formulae, and represent citations from a different dialect or register (as also indicated by the *yod* prefix).

(ibid. [JTS1623]).[290] In the EEMss, I have found no such use of the connecting *nun* for this category.

Following vowels, the overwhelming majority of the examples take the simple -*h* morpheme. Kara does not record any examples of the -*hi* morpheme. This matches our findings for the EEMss, wherein the -*hi* morpheme is primarily Geonic and is only rarely found in Talmudic citations in Geonic sources. I have found one example of the -*y* pronoun: דלא תספדוי "do not eulogize him" (*San* 46b [J]), and others were adduced by Levias from the *Sefer Ha-Ma'asiyyot*.[291]

Kara also notes three examples of the -*hu* pronoun, of which two appear in the same verb in the same context: אמדוהו "they evaluated him" (*Mak* 22b bis [J]).[292] However, examination of the wider context suggests that this is either a Hebrew verb integrated into the Aramaic discussion, or a result of secondary influence of the Hebrew on the Aramaic caused by later copyists. The examples are found in a Talmudic discussion, *m. Mak* 3:11, which is cited according to the version found in MS J:

מתניתין: אין אומדין אותו אלא לְמַכות הראויות להשתלש. **אמדוהו** לקבל
ארבעים; לקה מקצת, אמרו: אין יכול לקבל ארבעים. פטור. **אמדוהו** לקבל
שמונה-עשרה; משלקה אמרו: יכול הוא לקבל ארבעים. פטור. עבר עבירה
שיש בה שני לאוים. אמדוהו אומד אחד. לוקה ופטור. אם לאו. לוקה
ומתרפא וחוזר ולוקה.

גמ': לקה אין לא לקה לא. ורמינהי. **אמדוהו** לקבל ארבעים. חזרו ואמרו.
אינו יכול לקבל ארבעים. פטור. **אמדוהו** לקבל שמנה-עשרה. משלקה אמרו.
יכול לקבל ארבעים. פטור. אמ' רב ששת. לא קשיא. הא **דאמדוהו** ליומיה
הא **דאמדוהו** למחר וליומחרא.

It is taught in the Mishna: they only assess him for a number of lashes that is divisible by three. If **they assessed him** to receive forty, he received some and they said "He can't receive forty," he is exempted. If **they assessed him** to receiving eighteen, and after he was flogged they said "He is capable of receiving forty," he is exempted. If he committed a transgression which offended against two prohibitions, and they made one estimate [for both]; he is

---

[290] Kara, *Yemenite Manuscripts*, p. 187.

[291] Levias, *Grammar*, p. 173, nn. 3, 4.

[292] Kara, *Yemenite Manuscripts*, p. 187 (with erroneous Talmudic page-reference).

flogged and is exempted; if not, he is flogged, allowed to recover, and then flogged again.

Talmud: If he was flogged, yes [he is exempt], but if he was not flogged, no? But juxtapose them:[293] "If **they assessed him** as capable of receiving forty, and they changed their mind and said, "He cannot receive forty," he is exempt. If **they assessed him** as capable of receiving eighteen, and after he was flogged they said, "He is capable of receiving forty," he is exempt. R. Sheshet says: "It is not a problem. This [speaks of] when **they assessed him** for the same day; that [speaks of] when **they assessed him** for the next day or some other day."

Kara's third example is intriguing: יוֹמָא חַד אִינְּשׁוּהוּ לְסַנְדְּלֵי אַגַּבֵּהּ "they forgot the sandals on its back" (*Tan* 24a [J]).[294] However, from the context it emerges that, contra Kara, the object pronoun here is 3 m.pl. It will be discussed below, §3.5.2.7.2.

In summary, the Yemenite manuscripts contain several features that concur with the findings of the EEMss, and some features that seem to be the result of external influences: 1. the use of the connecting *nun*, particularly after verbal forms ending in a consonant; 2. the use of the pronominal form -*hu*, which in the context may be regarded as a Hebraism.

### 3.5.1.2.3 The Yemenite Reading Tradition
An entirely different distribution of grammatical forms emerges from the Yemenite reading tradition. First, following the printed editions, there are numerous examples of the connecting *nun*, e.g., אֲסַלְּקִינֵּיהּ "may I remove him" (*Git* 52b [Morag, *YT*, p. 300, against printed איסלקיניה]), but in EEMss איסלקיה "may I remove him" (*Git* 52b [**HPS** 82:4, **Hark** 79:20]), אַפְּקִינֵּיהּ "take it out" (*BB* 46a [Morag, *YT*, p. 311]), and נִיתְּבִינֵּיהּ "let him give it" (*Git* 29b [Morag, *YT*, p. 312]).[295]

---

[293] I.e., compare these two teachings, and you will see there is a contradiction.

[294] The Tiberian vocalization is in the original manuscript.

[295] Morag, *YT*, p. 317, records as an example of the 3 m.s. perfect אוֹתְּבִינֵּיהּ "he responded to him" (*'Eruv* 30a), but this may be understood as 1 c.pl. perfect "we responded to him." Furthermore, the Yemenite tradition does not appear to employ the paragogic *nun* in 3 m.s. + 3 m.s. pronoun, as evidenced by the marginal correction פַּטְרֵיהּ "he exempted him" (*BQ* 117a ['Amr], against printed פטריניה). 'Amr's proposed reading accords with the correct grammatical form found in the

However, it is in postvocalic forms that the most striking difference exists. Following the corrupt printed edition, the Yemenite reading tradition contains dozens of examples of the suffix -*hu*, which is virtually nonexistent in the earlier manuscripts. In Morag's study alone I have counted forty examples.

The difference becomes particularly apparent when we compare these examples with the same examples as preserved in EEMss or the Yemenite manuscripts:

*Perfect:*

G : קַטְלוּהוּ "they killed him" (*San* 96b [Morag, *YT*, p. 293]) but in MS J קטלוה; חַזְיוּהוּ "they saw him" (*Tan* 25a [Morag, *YT*, p. 323]) but MS J חזיוה.

*D/quad:* בַּטְלוּהוּ "they annulled it" (*Tan* 18b [Morag, *YT*, p. 299]), but MS J ביטלוה;[296] הֵימְנוּהוּ "they [did not] believe him" (*Tan* 23a [Morag, *YT*, p. 331]), but MS J הימנוה; עַיְילוּהוּ "they brought him in" (*MQ* 17a [Morag, *YT*, p. 320]), but MS **Col** עיילוה; קִיבְּלוּהוּ "they accepted him" (*San* 6a [Morag, *YT*, p. 299]) but MS J קבלוה.

*C:* אַשְׁכְּחוּהוּ "they found him" (*Tan* 23a [Morag, *YT*, p. 303]), but in MS J אשכחוה.

*Imperfect*

*G:* לֵיגְרוּהוּ "that them hire him" (*BM* 112b [Morag, *YT*, p. 306]), but in the parallel passage from *Shev* 45a cited in **HGP** 13a:33 ליגרוה; לִיכַהְיוּהוּ "let them blind it" (*San* 27a [Morag, *YT*, p. 329]), but **Hark** 183:3 ליכחייה "let him blind it;"[297] לִיסְמְכוּהוּ "they would ordain him" (*Tan* 3a [Morag, *YT*, p. 295]), but in MS J ליסמכוה; לְדַחְקוּהוּ "they [should not] trouble him" (*BM* 84b [Morag, p. 295]), but MS **G1** נדיחקוה; לִיפְסְלוּהוּ "let them declare unfit" (*Mak* 2a [Morag, *YT*,

---

earlier manuscripts: see פטריה "he exempted him" (*BQ* 117a [**HPS** 129:10]). Similarly, Morag *YT*, p. 294, records the form לֵיתְבָּעֵינֵיהּ as an example of the 3 m.s. + 3 m.s. obj. pronoun. However, examination of the context reveals this to be a corrupt form of the 3 m.s. + 3 m.pl. pronoun: לֵיתְבָּעֵינֵיהּ ליורשים "let him sue the heirs" (*Yev* 42b). The proleptic suffix is employed here preceding a Hebrew noun, as described in §5.6.4.7.

[296] The verb שַׁדְּרוּהוּ (*Tan* 21a [Morag, *YT*, p. 299]) is omitted entirely in MS J and other textual witnesses.

[297] MS J contains the reading לכחול ליה לעיניה, an ancient textual variant also mentioned in **Hark** 183:3.

p. 295), but MS **J** ליפסליה "let it declare him unfit;" נִקְרִיוּהוּ "they should [not] call him" (*BM* 16a [Morag, *YT*, p. 324]), but **Hark** 160:26, 29: ניקריוה.

*Imperative:*

G: שַׁבקוּהוּ "let him be" (*Meg* 28a [Morag, *YT*, p. 296]), but MS **Col** שבקוה; שָׁדיוּהוּ "put it" (*Yom* 69b [Morag, *YT*, p. 324]), but MSS **JTS**1623 and **JTS**218 שדויה; תַּפשׂוּהוּ "seize him" (*BM* 83b [Morag, *YT*, 296]), but MS **G1** תיפסוה.

D: שַׁיְּימוּהוּ "assess him" (*BQ* 84a [Morag, *YT*, p. 317]), but MS **G1** שימוה.[298]

### 3.5.1.2.4 Conclusion
In summary, the evidence is clear. On all grounds—historical-linguistic, comparative-linguistic, and textual—the postvocalic 3 m.s. object suffix -*hu* in JBA in general and RBA in particular is to be regarded as a later accretion. The very rare examples found in earlier manuscripts presumably result from the misreading of a final *yod* as a final *waw*, and no such forms are found in the very best manuscripts such as **HPS**, BQ **G1**, BM **G1**, etc. As a common morpheme, the -*hu* suffix is a creation of the later European textual tradition, and finds no real support in the early manuscripts, be they North African Geniza fragments, the Babylonian **HPS**, or the Yemenite manuscripts.[299] In this case, the Yemenite reading tradition is entirely dependent upon the printed edition.

---

[298] Incidentally, we may note that since we find the infinitive מישימיה "to assess him" (*BQ* 84a [**G1**]), this verb is to be regarded as being in the G. The Yemenite tradition similarly vocalizes this latter form with a geminated *yod*, לְמִשָׁיְּימֵיה (*BQ* 84a [ʿAmr]). The vocalization of these forms with gemination is already found in the Yemenite manuscripts: לְמִידַּיְּינֵיה (*Meg* 14b [**Col**]); see Kara, *Yemenite Manuscripts*, p. 339. R. ʿAmr vocalized this latter verb לְמַדַּיְּינֵיה (*RH* 16a [ʿAmr]). For a discussion see Morgenstern, "Geonic Responsa," pp. 340–41.

[299] The doubts expressed by Muraoka–Porten, *Grammar*, p. 143 n. 670, about the origin of forms such as שָׁקְלוּה result from a mistaken evaluation of the Yemenite reading tradition. Similarly, the criticism of Müller-Kessler, found on p. 371 of their *Grammar*, is misplaced.

### 3.5.2.3 3 f.s.

The case of the 3 f.s. pronoun is more complicated, but here too I believe that the evidence of the manuscripts differs from that of the Yemenite oral tradition.

#### 3.5.2.3.1 EEMs Evidence

In the EEMss, the distribution of the 3 f.s. object pronouns follows the same pattern as the 3 m.s. If the verbal base ends in a consonant, then the pronoun הָ- *ah* is employed.[300] If it ends in a vowel, the allomorph ה- *-h* is employed. I have found no examples with the connecting *nun*. The post-vocalic allomorph is presumably an apocopated form of the הָא *-hā* morpheme that appears in the postvocalic position in Targum Onqelos. The question remains whether the older unapocopated morpheme has survived in RBA.

Let us begin with a survey of the forms attested in the EEMss:

*Perfect*:

> **2 m.pl.:** *G:* תניתוה "you taught it" (*Yev* 93b [**HPS** 254:14]; *BM* 101b [**HPS** 108:14]).

> **3 m.pl.:** *G:* See examples cited above, §3.4.3.5.1. *D and quad:* אגרוה "they rented it out" (**TGAs28** ii a 10); סלקוה "they dismissed it/her" (**GK4** 28:15); פרקוה "they explained it" (**TGAs42** 9:5); קיבלוה "they [did not] accept it" (**Geon** iv 3b 24); תרגמוה "they explained it" (**Hark** 117:4);[301] תרצוה "they explained it" (**GS** vi 2b 5).

> *C:* אהדרוה "they sent it back" (*BQ* 88b [**G1**]); אזמנוה "they summoned her" (*RH* 31b [**HGP** 15a:34]); אנסבוה "they gave her in marriage" (**Geon** xxvi b 21); אצרכוה "they required her" (*Git* 78b [**TGAs28** i vii 2 28]); אוקמוה "they established it" (**Hark** 136:35; **Geon** xxviii 1b 16); אשפלוה "they carried it downstream" (*BB* 99b [**Hark** 152:5]); אקשיוה "they questioned it" (**TGAs42** 9:5).

*Imperfect*:

> **3 m.pl.:** *G:* ליניסבוה "they will marry her" (**HPS** 170:1); ליפטרוה "let them send her away" (**Hark** 206:2); ניפיסלוה "they should [not] render her unfit" (**TGAs28** iv 4a 15).[302]

---

[300] There are also several examples of the 3 m.s. pronoun יה- *-eh* used for the 3 f.s. On this phenomenon, see §4.6.3.2.

[301] Harkavy read תרגומוה.

[302] Assaf read מיפסלה.

*Imperative*:

**M.pl:** *G:* כיתבוה "write it" (*BB* 172a [**HPS** 103:20,21]); תפסוה "seize it" (*BB* 34b [**HPS** 137:17]); אפקוה "release it" (*BB* 34b [**HPS** 137:19]).

In the EEMss, I have found only one certain example of the הא- pronoun: אתיוהא "they brought it" (**Hark** 108:1).[303]

How are we to interpret these data? The overwhelming majority of examples in the EEMss demonstrate only the ה- pronoun. Since a surviving final *ā* vowel is always written with a *mater lectionis* in JBA, I conclude that this spelling reflects the form *-h* rather than *-hā*. This interpretation is supported by the vocalized form דְשַׁוְיוֹה "they made her" (**HPS** 254:20). Whether the single attested example of הא- represents a genuine RBA form or influence of the Targum on the copyists remains to be determined.

### 3.5.2.3.2 The Yemenite Manuscripts
In contrast, in the Yemenite manuscripts we find several examples of the typologically older pronoun preserving the word-final *ā*, either in the orthography or in the vocalization. Kara has listed the following examples, and I have found no others:[304]

אשכחוה שפוהא דובשא ואוקמוהא "they established it" (*San* 60a [**J**]); אוקמוהא "They found her, daubed her with honey, and placed her on the rampart of the city wall. The hornets came and ate her" (*San* 109b [**J**]); עברו-הא "they intercalated it" (*RH* 6b [**JTS218**], as two words); כבשוה "they conquered it" (*Tan* 21a [**J**]); גַּיְירוּהָ "they [did not] convert her" (*San* 99b [**J**]).

However, in contrast to these there are many employing the simple ה- pronoun, e.g.:[305]

סברוה "they regarded it" (*Pes* 54a [**JTS1623, Col**]); שמעוה "they heard her" (*Meg* 18a [**Col**]); קלטוה "they retained it" (*Zev* 120a [**Col**]);[306] אקריבתוה

---

[303] Another example is found in a Geniza fragment of *Halachot Gedolot*, Antonin 494, containing a citation from ʿ*Ara* 21b: סיירוהא ניהלי "inspect it for me." I have not examined the entire manuscript and cannot comment on its overall linguistic status. On this passage, see below, §5.9. The sentence וקידשוהא אימה או אחיה "and her mother or brother betrothed her" (**HPS** 237:9) is in Hebrew.

[304] Kara, *Yemenite Manuscripts*, p. 188.

[305] These examples are collected primarily from Kara, *Yemenite Manuscripts*, pp. 317–52.

ופסלתוה "you have sacrificed it and rendered it unfit" (*Zev* 101a [**Col**]); אזמנוה "they summoned her" (*RH* 31b [**JTS**1608]); אסרוה "they forbade it" (*Pes* 7a [**JTS**1623]); אמרוה "they recited it" (*San* 69a [**J**], *Zev* 45b [**Col**], etc.); סיימוה "they [did not] clearly specify it" (*MQ* 12b [**Col**]).

Kara also lists occasional examples with the paragogic *nun*.[307] However, the expression דליעברינה לך "that he should impregnate her for you" (*San* 109b [**J**]), is correctly parsed by him elsewhere as a phonetic spelling for דליעבריה ניהלך.[308] The support he brings for such forms may be supplemented by additional examples: אהדרנה להו "return it to them" (*BB* 33a [**HPS** 191:7]) = אהדרה ניהליהו "return it to them" (ibid. [**H**165]);[309] דזבנינה לי "who sold it to me" (*BB* 33b [**HPS** 137:2]) = דזבניה ניהלי "who sold it to me" (ibid. [**H**165]); שדייניה לה "he threw it to her" (*Qid* 52b [**HPS** 167:7]).

The rarity of the -*hā* pronoun in the EEMss in contrast to its more frequent appearance in the Yemenite manuscripts arouses the suspicion that the Yemenite tradition applied the Targumic reading -*hā* to the Talmudic spelling ‎-ה at a period before these manuscripts were copied (perhaps under the influence of the Hebrew pronoun ‎ָה-, which is regularly written defectively).

### 3.5.2.3.3 The Yemenite Reading Tradition
The modern Yemenite reading tradition is consistent in pronouncing the postvocalic ‎-ה pronoun of the printed editions –*hɔ*, the same pronunciation accorded to the Targumic form ‎ָהא-, e.g., קַבְעוּהָ "they established it" (*Ber* 9b [Morag, *YT*, p. 293]); אַקְרֵיבְתּוּהָ וּפְסַלְתּוּהָ "you have sacrificed it and rendered it unfit" (*Zev* 101a [Morag, *YT*, p. 294]); לִתְבְּעוּהָ "that they sue her" (*Yev* 65a [Morag, *YT*,p. 295]), etc.

---

[306] The reference in Kara, *Yemenite Manuscripts*, p. 318, should be corrected accordingly.

[307] Kara, *Yemenite Manuscripts*, p. 188.

[308] Ibid., p. 50. The ‎-יה pronoun is again employed for a 3 f.s. object. Cf. §4.6.3.2.

[309] The example from **HPS** seems to imply that the form ניהליהו found in MS Hamburg, with the *ay* diphthong following the *lamed*, may be secondary. The compound forms of ‎-ניהל are composed of the base ‎ניה- followed by the preposition ‎-ל with suffixes. Since the forms of ‎-ל not preceded by ‎-ניה do not take the diphthong (hence להו rather than ליהו), we would also expect this to be the case for forms of ‎-ניהל. Cf. further שקליה יהביה ניהלהו "he took it (and) gave it to them" (*BQ* 117b [**HGP** 18b:27]) with שקליה ויהביה ניהליהו (ibid. [**H**165]; the reading שקליה was corrected from שקלוה). Further study of this issue is needed.

### 3.5.2.3.3 Conclusion

The consistent orthography of the EEMss coupled with rare vocalized forms indicates that the postvocalic allomorph of the 3 f.s. object pronoun is -h, in contrast to TOJ's -hā. I have found only one exception to this rule. The Yemenite Talmud manuscripts appear to show increased influence of the Targumic idiom on the language of the Talmud: it has penetrated some examples in the orthography, and others in the vocalization. When we consider the reading tradition, the Targumic forms have entirely superseded the Talmudic forms.

### 3.5.2.4 1 c.pl.

While our discussion has followed the traditional grammatical order, before we can clarify the 1 c.pl. forms and the nature of their attachment to the verbal stems it is preferable to clarify the grammar of the 3 pl. pronouns, by which they appear to have been influenced. Accordingly, the 1 c.pl. forms will be considered below in §3.5.2.8.

### 3.5.2.5 3 pl. — Non-III-*yod* forms

#### 3.5.2.5.1 EEMs Evidence

There are several forms of the 3 pl. in the EEMss, formed from two primary bases: the older Aramaic pronoun אִינּוּן, and the Babylonian dialectal form אִינְּהוּ. The vocalization of these forms may be reconstructed both on historical grounds and on the basis of vocalized forms such as אִילֵינְהוּ "he brought them in" (**HPS** 279:18).

When the pronouns are attached to a verbal form ending in a consonant, the *ʾaleph* is usually elided and the pronouns take the form of -innun or -innəhu, respectively.[310] When the verbal base ends in a vowel,

---

[310] Exceptions to this rule are a number of examples found in the writings of the later Geonim which preserve the *ʾaleph* after infinitive forms: למקטלאנן "to kill them" (**Hark** 190:30); מיקטלאנן "to kill them" (**Hark** 190:31); למיעקראנן "to uproot them" (**Hark** 30:24); לזבונאנן "to sell them" (**TGAs42** 61:20); נטוראנן "to guard them" (**Hark** 271:16); לחיובאנן "to declare them liable" (**Hark** 98:21); לסיועאנן "to support them" (**Hark** 193:6); לשלומאנן "to pay them" (**Hark** 36:6); לשוויאנן "to appoint them" (**GKI** 71:15, 72:1,3); להנפוקאנן "to extract them" (**Hark** 272:9); לאהדוראנן "to return them" (**Hark** 109:11); לאכשוראנן "to declare them fit" (**TGAs42** 61:30; **Gil** i a 24); אצולאנן "to save them" (**Hark** 190:33); לאעולאנן "to bring them in" (**Gil** i a 18); לאקנויאנן "to transfer their ownership" (**Hark** 116:34); cf. 3 f.pl. להימונאנין "to trust them" (**Hark** 1:21). Since none of

elision occurs at the juncture of the verbal base and the pronoun, and it is generally the final vowel of the verbal base that is preserved.

While the independent object pronouns found in other Aramaic dialects are not found in RBA, there is internal evidence to suggest that the fusion of the 3 pl. pronouns with the verbal base was a relatively late phenomenon. This is indicated by the fact that they do not reduce the short vowels to a *shewa*, as is the case with most of the other pronominal object suffixes.

Since short *a* vowels are not marked by a *mater lectionis*, in non-vocalized texts this phenomenon is discernable in the G-stem only in the *peᶜil*-based perfects and in imperfect or imperative forms.

## G
### Perfect:

> *3 m.pl. + 3 f.pl. obj.:* נסיבונין "they (m.pl.) married them (f.pl.)" (HPS 245:15). **Vocalized form:** כְּתַבִּינְהוֹ "he wrote them" (HGP 33b:12).

### Imperfect:

> *2 m.s. + 3 m.pl. obj.:* תישבוקינהו "leave them alone" (TGAs28 i 14b 16).
>
> *3 m.s.+ 3 m.pl. obj:* ליתיבנהו "let him give them" (HPS 97:10); נישחוטינהו "let him slaughter them" (HPS 61:18).

### Imperative:

> *m.s. + 3 m.pl. obj.:* שקולינהו "take them" (*BM* 101a [G1]).

## D:
### Perfect:

> *3 m.s. + 3 m.pl. obj.:* הימינינון "he believed them" (Hark 101:5); קבילינהו "he accepted them" (*Kar* 3a [G2]). **Vocalized forms:** חַיְּיבִינהו "he declared them liable" (*BM* 81a [G1]); שַׁדְּרִינהוֹ "he sent them" (*Ket* 85a [HGP 44a:11]); פַּרְעִינהוֹ "he sent them" (*Ket* 85a [HGP 44a:12]); בַּדְּרִינְהוֹ "he scattered them" (HGP 37a:17); קַבִּילְנהוֹ "he accepted them" (*BQ* 119a [HGP 19a:20]).
>
> *+ 3 f.pl. obj.:* זבינינהו "he sold them (f.pl.)" (*Ket* 91b [TGAs28 iv 5b 27]) = זבנינהי "he sold them (f.pl.)" (ibid. [HPS 77:18]).

---

these examples is vocalized, it cannot be determined whether this spelling is merely an orthographic variant or reflects a morphological difference.

*3 m.pl.: + 3 f.s. obj.:* חשיבונהי "they [did not] count them" (*BM* 107b [**HGP** 30b:35]); תקינונון "they enacted them" (**Hark** 103:9).

One example from the imperfect would appear to contradict this pattern: וּלְשֵׁחרּרִינהו "and he should free them" (**HGP** 36b:30). However, though this example is vocalized as an imperfect, from the context it is clear that it should be an infinitive. The complete context reads צריכין למיהדר ולשחררי`נהו לדידהו "And one needs to go back and free them themselves." Nevertheless, one could claim that since the vocalizer thought that this was an imperfect form, the vocalization reflects that form.

## C:
### Perfect:

*3 m.s. + 3 m.pl. obj:* אוקימנהו "he set them up" (**TGAs42** 61:19); אמשיכינון "he drew them" (**HPS** 216:9; **GK4** 98:18); ואפיקינהו "he removed them" (**Hark** 24:30); אקדישינהו "he sanctified them" (*BB* 88a [**HPS** 132:11]); אשהידינון "he brought them as witnesses" (**Hark** 35:24; **Hark** 111:28,29); דְּאֹפֵּיקֹנהֹו "it expressed them" (**HGP** 13b:3); אַשְׁלֵמֹנהֹו "he gave them over" (*BM* 42a [**HGP** 23a:15]; but אוֹתְּבֹּינֹהֹו "he put them" (*BM* 42a [**HGP** 23a:11]). *3 m.s. + 3 m.pl. obj: + 3 f.pl. obj:* אסיקיני-ן "he lit them up" (Lerner, "She²iltot," p. 185 l. 12).

### Imperfect:
*3 m.s. + 3 m.pl. obj.:* לימשיכינון "he should take them" (**HPS** 96:17).

Similar examples are found in the Yemenite manuscripts, e.g., אסמיכונהי "they gave them support" (*Suk* 28a [**O51**]);[311] אוקימנהו "set them up" (*San* 39a [**J**]).[312]

### 3.5.2.5.2 The Yemenite Reading Tradition
When we compare these findings to the Yemenite reading tradition, a different picture emerges. Let us begin by discussing the preservation of the stem vowel. Admittedly, for the G pa²il form Morag has recorded one example preserving the theme vowel, שָׁאֵֵילְינֵהו "he asked them" (°Eruv 53b [Morag, *YT*, p. 291]), and forms preserving the theme vowel are

---

[311] This is the correct reference, as cited by Kara, *Yemenite Manuscripts*, p. 326 (the reference in ibid., p. 116, should therefore be corrected accordingly). Kara interprets these forms as examples demonstrating a *ḥiriq* for a *shewa*. Since the short *²i* vowel was probably never reduced to a *shewa* in this case, I prefer to see it as a case wherein the original vowel is preserved.

[312] So in the MS, contra Kara, *Yemenite Manuscripts*, p. 340.

common (though not exclusive) in the imperfect, e.g., לִישְׁקוֹלִינְהוּ "let him take them" (Git 68b [Morag, YT, p. 295]). However, in the perfect forms of the D and C with the *i* theme vowel, we find only forms with the *shewa*, e.g., תַּרְצִנְהוּ "he set them straight" (Ber 61b [Morag, TY, p. 298]), אַפְּקִינְהוּ "he sent them out" (Hul 110a [Morag, YT, p. 310]), and אוֹתְבִינְהוּ "he sat them down" (Tan 21b, BM 42a [Morag, YT, p. 313]).

### 3.5.2.6 3 pl. — III-*yod* Forms
### 3.5.2.6.1 EEMs Evidence
Further evidence for the relatively late affixing of this pronoun may be found in the III-*yod* class. As we have seen, the III-*yod* class conjugates like the sound verb in 3 m. forms with suffixed object pronouns, in that the *yod* is consonantal, e.g., חזא "he saw" (BQ 113a [HPS 124:20]), but חזייה "he saw him" (Bes 27a [HPS 5:11]);[313] דיחזו "that they saw" (Yev 107b [HPS 235:17]), but חֲזיוּה "they saw him" (MQ 4a [HPS 274:17]). Similarly in the imperfect: לישדי "let him add" (ᶜAZ 9a [Hark 22:2]), but נישידייה "let him cast it" (BM 80b [G1]); ליקנו "let them acquire" (BM 148b [HPS 187:16]), but ניקריוה "they [should not] call him (BM 15b [Hark 260:26,29]). Such interchanges in the verbal base are not found when the object pronouns are 3 pl. Instead, the verbal forms to which 3 m.pl. object pronouns are affixed lack the final root *yod*, and are thus identical in form to the unsuffixed forms.

### G
**Perfect:**

> *3 m.s. + 3 m.pl.:* חזנהו "he saw them" (Tan 28b [GK5 52:12]); לואנהו "it accompanied them" (BQ 116a [G1]); קנאנון "he acquired them" (Hark 43:22); קנאנהו "he acquired them" (BQ 101a [G1]; BB 138a 9 [Hark 194:26]); קראנהו "he called them" (Hark 163:19); בְּדִשְׁרֵנהוּ "when he permitted them" (HPS 33:18); דִקְנֵנהוּ "that he acquired them" (HPS 41:18). + 3 f.pl.: בננין "he built them" (TGAs28 i 10b 19); תנאניּן "he taught them" (Hark 231:14).

> *3 m.pl. + 3 f.pl.:* תנוניּן "they taught them" (Hark 103:31, 32 = **Weiss**, Fragments, iii 4a l. 5).[314]

---

[313] Contrast BA בְּנָהִי "built it" (Ezra 5:11).

[314] This is the correct reading in both instances in the Kaufmann manuscript cited by Weiss. The transcription as printed is inaccurate.

**Imperfect:**

> *3 m.s.* + *3 m.pl.:* נקנינהו "let him acquire them" (*Ket* 79a [**Hark** 43:24]); נימנינהו "let him count them" (*Yom* 22b [**Hark** 156:31]).

What happens when the final vowel of the verb merges with the pronoun ʾinnəhu or ʾinnəhi? From the examples cited above, it is clear that usually, the vowel of the verbal base is preserved and the pronoun is shortened to an allomorph -nnəhu or -nnəhi. In the examples found in the EEMss, this is always the case in the sound verb with the plural morpheme -*ū

The situation regarding the III-*yod* verbs ending in a vowel requires some clarification, as it appears to vary greatly among the different sources. The vocalized forms and examples written with *plene* orthography make it clear that in the 3 m.s. perfect, the vowel linking the verbal base to the 3.pl. pronoun is ā, e.g., קנאנהו/דְקַנָּנהו, both of which reflect qənānnəhu or qənānhu. I have found only one clear exception to this pattern in the EEMss: תראינהו "he soaked them" (*BQ* 101a [**G1**]), perhaps to be read tərāʾinnəhu. The verb קלינהי "he parched them" (**HPS** 293:18) may be interpreted as a D form,[315] though if it is in the G, it would constitute another exception. The evidence from the magic bowls appears to support the hypothesis that the vowel of the unsuffixed verbal base is preserved. For example, in the magic bowl M 102:3 we read: כל מאן דעבדינון ושדרינון וקרנון "all who made them and sent them and recited them."[316] The *plene* spelling of the verbal bases ending in a consonant, דעבדינון ושדרינון, contrasts with the defective spelling of the form וקרנון.

However, in the EEMss we find the imperfect form ולא **ניחזינהו** אינאשי ונירקו "that the people **should** not **see them** and flee" (*BQ* 79a [**Geon** xxviii 2b 6]) = ניחזינהי "should see them" (ibid. [**G1**]). It seems that in this case, the vowel of the object pronoun -innəhu has superseded the final *ū vowel of the verbal base.

### 3.5.2.6.2 The Yemenite Manuscripts
The picture in the Yemenite manuscripts differs somewhat. In these manuscripts too we frequently find spellings that suggest that the pronouns were affixed to the verbal bases while preserving that base's final vowel. For the 3 m.s., Kara lists four examples, and I have found several others, e.g., חזנהו "he saw them" (*MQ* 18a [**Col**]; *San* 100a [**J**]) and קננהו "he acquired them" (*San* 72a [**J**]). For the 3 m.pl., Kara lists the form שרונהו

---

[315] Cf. Brockelmann, *LS*, p. 666 s.v. ܡܠܐ **pa**.

[316] See Morgenstern, "Moussaieff Collection," pp. 352–53.

"they untied them" (*San* 109a [J]).[317] We may add חזונהו "they saw them" (*Tan* 21a [J]) and מלונהו "they filled them" (*San* 109a [J]). However, Kara also cites several examples of the 3 m.s. with a linking -*i*- vowel, e.g., חזינהו "he saw them" (*Pes* 51a [JTS1623]),[318] and again קלינהו "he burnt them" (*San* 93a [J]).[319]

### 3.5.2.6.3 The Yemenite Reading Tradition

In the Yemenite reading tradition, forms with -*innhu* have almost entirely replaced those preserving the final vowel of the verbal bases. Let us begin with the sound verb. While forms such as קַטְלוּנְהוּ "they killed them" (*Tan* 21a [Morag, *YT*, p. 293], against printed קטלינהו) are indeed found, there are also many examples in which the Yemenite readers follow the printed edition in reading with an *i* vowel, e.g., שַׁקְלִינְהוּ "they took them" (*Tan* 22a [Morag, *YT*, p. 294]) and תַּקְנִינְהוּ "they enacted them" (*Ber* 33b [Morag, *YT*, p. 299]). This tendency toward losing the original base vowel is even more pronounced in the III-*yod* roots. In the 3 m.s., the vocalization is *always* with an *i* vowel, even when the orthography of the printed edition is defective, e.g., חֲזִינְהוּ "he saw them" (*Ber* 28a, *Pes* 51a [Morag, *YT*, p. 322]), תְּרִנְהוּ "he soaked them" (*BQ* 101a [ibid.]), and שְׁרִנְהוּ "he released them (*BB* 24a [ibid.]). No examples showing the older *ā* vowel survive. Similarly, while the reading tradition has numerous examples of the 3 pl. which preserve the plural morpheme, e.g., שְׁרוּנְהוּ (*Ber* 23a [Morag, *YT*, p. 323]), we also find many examples with an *i* vowel, e.g., חֲזִינְהוּ "they saw them" (*ᶜAZ* 17b [ibid.]), a form not found in the perfect in the EEMss.

While these forms have little support from the EEMss, the fact that the phenomenon is occasionally attested in those manuscripts means they cannot be dismissed out of hand as textual errors. We cannot rule out the possibility that these forms genuinely reflect JBA. However, it is clear that regarding the 3 m.s. of the III-*yod* forms, the Yemenite reading tradition gives us an inaccurate picture of the findings. The vocalized examples in **HPS** demonstrate that forms preserving the final *ā* vowel of the verbal root were found in RBA, and the orthography of the EEMss suggests that perhaps this is the *only* form attested in these manuscripts.

### 3.5.2.6.4 Conclusion

We have seen that the EEMss contain numerous examples of verb forms which demonstrate evidence for the relatively late affixing of the 3 pl.

---

[317] Kara, *Yemenite Manuscripts*, pp. 344.

[318] I have also found the identical form in the Yemenite MSS in *San* 95a [J].

[319] Kara, *Yemenite Manuscripts*, p. 343.

object suffixes to the verbal bases. This accords with the comparative Aramaic evidence, which demonstrates independent object pronouns for these forms.[320] In the EEMss, when the verbal base ends in a vowel, the 3 pl. object suffix is predominantly נהו- -n(n)əhu. The Yemenite manuscripts demonstrate that the use of this pronoun is in decline, and that the form -innəhu, originally suffixed only to verbal bases ending in consonants, is increasingly dominant in this position. In the Yemenite reading tradition, the -innəhu form has almost entirely superseded the -n(n)əhu allomorph.

### 3.5.2.7 3 pl. object suffix הי-/הו-?

#### 3.5.2.7.1 EEMs Evidence
In addition to the forms based on אינהו and אינהי, I have found occasional examples of object pronouns that appear to be based upon the possessive pronouns הו- and הי-, e.g., דבעי אסויהו "that he has to cure them" (BQ 86a [G1]) and דאנסוהי לכולהי ארעתא "that they seized all the lands" (BQ 116b [HPS 128:18 = HGP 18a:28]). It would be easy to dismiss these forms as textual errors but for the fact that the example from Bava Qamma is attested in two excellent manuscripts (and in a slightly corrupted form, דאנסוה לכולהו ארעאתא, in MS H165).

#### 3.5.2.7.2 The Yemenite Manuscripts
Kara cites two examples of the הו- form, but both are suspect.[321] It is unlikely that the pronoun in the expression כַּלְבָּא לֵיכְלִיהוּ לְשִׁירוּתֵיה "may a dog eat his meal" (Tan 11b [J]) is plural. The vocalization of the noun שֵׁירוּתֵיה speaks against this analysis, and it is better regarded as a f.s. object pronoun, perhaps corrupt.[322] The second example cited by Kara as ניהימניהו "they will trust them" (Pes 4b [JTS1623])[323] is written in the manuscript as two words: ניהי מניהו. However, as mentioned above, one certain example belonging to this category is אִינְשׁוּהוּ לְסַנדְלֵי "they forgot the sandals" (Tan 24a [J]).

---

[320] Cf. Muraoka–Porten, Grammar, §74h, and my comments in Morgenstern, "Review of Muraoka–Porten," p. 147.

[321] Kara, Yemenite Manuscripts, p. 189.

[322] MS O366 reads כלבא אכלה לשירותיה "a dog ate his meal" (Tan 11b), while the printed editions of the Talmud read ליכול כלבא לשירותיה (ibid.).

[323] The orthography ניהמניהו may be a printing error in Kara's lists on p. 189; the form as found in the manuscript is correctly transcribed by him on p. 331 and in the index.

### 3.5.2.7.3 The Yemenite Reading Tradition

Since this form is not attested in the printed editions, it is likewise not found in the Yemenite reading tradition.

### 3.5.2.8 Excursus: 1 c.pl.

Contrary to the 3 pl. forms, the evidence suggests that already at an early stage in the development of Aramaic the object pronouns of the 1 c.pl. were affixed to the verbal base. So, for example, in the Elephantine corpus we find החוין "he let us gloat" while in 3 pl. we always find the disjunctive pronouns.[324] Above, we noted that the relatively late conjunction is still discernable in the preservation of the short vowels in what are now open unstressed syllables.

There is some evidence to suggest that by analogy to the 3 pl. forms, the 1 c.pl. forms also have the appearance of being of relatively late conjunction. This is discernable through both the phenomena we noted above:

*i. The preservation of short vowels:*

I have found two examples in the Yemenite manuscripts: ליפרוקינן "may he rescue us" (*RH* 32b [**JTS**1608]; *San* 105a [**J**]).[325] Since this may be the only example of an *u*-stem imperfect verb ending in a consonant base with a 1 pl. suffix attested in RBA, it is not possible to say whether this was a widespread phenomenon in the dialect.[326]

*ii. III-yod verbs:*

As noted in §3.5.2.6.1, when object pronouns are affixed to the 3rd person forms of the III-*yod* verbs, the verbal base conjugates on the pattern of the sound verb, i.e., the *yod* becomes consonantal; however this does not happen when the pronouns are for the 3 pl. From the scanty manuscript evidence it appears that the pronouns for the 1 c.pl. follow the pattern of the 3 pl., as may be discerned from the example חזונן "they saw us" (**TGAs28** i 6a 21).[327] Another example appears in a Talmudic citation in *Midrash HaGadol:* אקרונן "they recited the verse to us" (*Ber* 56a [**MHG**

---

[324] Muraoka–Porten, *Grammar*, §38.

[325] The first occurrence is recorded by Kara, *Yemenite Manuscripts*, p. 319.

[326] The example ליטרדן cited by Levias, *Grammar*, p. 176 = Levias, *Diqduq*, p. 239, actually bears a 1 c. *singular* object suffix (see above, §3.5.1.1). Furthermore, the anaptyctic vowel in ליטירדן "he will not bother me" (*BB* 5b [**HPS** 202:5]) indicates that the *resh* was originally vocalized with a *shewa*.

[327] Assaf misread דחזו לן.

703:9, 13]). The Yemenite reading tradition of the Talmud follows the printed edition of the Talmud and reads אַקְרְיַן "he recited the verse to me" (*Ber* 56a [Morag, *YT*, p. 328]), even though the form taking the 1 c.s. object, אַקְרְיוּן "they recited the verse to me" (*Ber* 56a [Morag, *YT*, p. 328]), appears in the same context with a plural verbal base.[328] Additional research may reveal further examples.

## 3.6 Conclusion:
## The Place of the Yemenite Tradition in Research of JBA

In chapter 2, I emphasized that considerable differences exist between the grammar of the oldest and most accurate textual witnesses of Babylonian Rabbinic literature and those of the later manuscripts and printed editions. In practice, we are not dealing with a single grammar, but rather with a series of grammars, for example, the grammar of the early manuscripts, the grammar of the Yemenite manuscripts, the grammar of the Spanish manuscripts and the grammar of the printed editions. To these we may add the grammar of the Yemenite reading tradition. Each of these may be described as an independent stratum in the development of JBA as a literary idiom, and while there naturally exists a considerable degree of overlap between them, each is distinct.

However, as I have sought to demonstrate in this chapter, the later strata cannot be adduced as evidence for the JBA of the earlier period, i.e., the language as written by native users. Even within the Yemenite manuscripts, which have often been praised for their conservatism and preservation of ancient forms, we find numerous linguistic traits that distinguish them from the earliest manuscript sources available to us today, manuscripts that on both internal and external grounds have been proven to be accurate textual witnesses. This is all the more true when we compare the Yemenite reading tradition to the findings from the earliest manuscripts. The reading tradition has been influenced by numerous factors, the most important of which would appear to be the abandonment of the earlier Yemenite manuscript traditions in favor of the printed editions of the Talmud. Among the other influences we may note the predominance of Targum Onqelos, of the Tiberian tradition of Hebrew and Aramaic, and of internal analogies.

From my analysis, the Yemenite tradition of Babylonian emerges as a conservative but developing conduit of JBA. Since, as we have seen, the reading tradition of the recent generations often contradicts the earliest manuscripts, I cannot accept Morag's assessment that it can comprise one

---

[328] Morag reports that this latter form is read by some authorities as אַקְרוּנַן.

of the primary sources for the reconstruction of JBA. Similarly, the Yemenite manuscripts contain much that is important, but this too must be corroborated from other sources before being accepted.

There is no simple solution to many of the frustrating conundrums connected with the study of JBA. Nevertheless, I believe that through the patient and judicious study of the best textual witnesses (from both Rabbinic and epigraphic sources) and the integration of linguistic evidence from a variety of early sources, it is possible to arrive at a reasonable reconstruction of the main elements of JBA grammar, even if certain aspects remain unclear.

# CHAPTER 4

# Variant Forms in Jewish Babylonian Aramaic

## 4.1 Introduction

In chapter 2, we noted that one of the most complex issues in the study of Jewish Babylonian Aramaic is the multiplicity of forms in any given grammatical category. While the phenomenon of doublets is found in even the most conservative Semitic languages, such as classical Arabic,[1] JBA documents appear to contain a frustratingly free interchange between more conservative and less conservative forms, and such interchanges may be regarded as one of the most salient linguistic features of JBA literature.

In this chapter, we shall examine this phenomenon in detail, and to consider the various explanations that have been suggested for it. It is shown that no single explanation can account for all examples of the alternative grammatical forms. Particular attention is paid to examples which would appear to defy explanation. In some cases I have hesitatingly suggested a possible cause, though for many examples these explanations remain speculative. I have occasionally indicated avenues of research worthy of further consideration, wherein at least partial solutions for these conundrums may be found.

## 4.2 Definition of the Problem

It seems that we must distinguish here between several types of interchange between alternative grammatical forms:
1. Different forms of a single word that appear within a single context according to a particular textual witness.
2. Different forms of multiple words of the same grammatical category (e.g., 3 f.s. perfect) that appear within a single context according to a particular textual witness.
3. Different forms of a single word that appear within a single context according to different textual witnesses.

---

[1] See Blau, "Structure," p. 24, who noted several examples from classical Arabic, e.g., the *majzūm* forms of the geminates: يَمُدَّ/يَمْدُدَ.

4.  Different forms of multiple words of the same grammat-
    ical category that appear in different contexts according
    to a particular textual witness.
5.  Different forms of multiple words of the same grammat-
    ical category that appear in different contexts in different
    textual witnesses.

It is beneficial to distinguish between these categories since they may
relate to different possible explanations for the phenomenon. If we begin
with the last category, it may be suggested that the language of the different textual witnesses was encoded in different places or at different
times, and that therefore we may not be dealing with sporadic interchanges but with systematic differences resulting from alternative linguistic traditions (either going back to the original encoding or resulting
from the linguistic tendencies of the copyists).[2] For example, as mentioned above in Chapter 2, the early eastern textual witnesses primarily
employ the form אמנא *ʾāmannā* "I say," while the later manuscripts and
printed editions predominantly employ the form אמינא *ʾāmenā*. Since this
seems to cut across all contexts, this difference would belong to category
5.[3] Unfortunately, seldom can the differences be neatly and systematically ascribed to varying linguistic or copying traditions. More frequently,
the differences appear within a single textual witness, or even within a
single context.

The examples in this chapter primarily demonstrate the first two
phenomena, i.e., alternative grammatical forms appearing within a particular textual witness, either in identical words or in words of the same
category. Occasionally, I have cited examples of the third phenomenon,
i.e., of alternative grammatical forms employed for the same word in
parallel textual transmissions. This phenomenon is particularly striking
when, for example, the same passage from the Talmud is cited twice
within a Geonic work with differences in the grammatical forms.

---

[2] Recognition of the phenomenon of different linguistic traditions has considerably enhanced our understanding of the differences between variant forms of
Hebrew, even within the textual transmission of a single text such as the Bible or
the Mishna. Cf., for example, Ben-Ḥayyim, *Studies*, and Bar-Asher, "Traditions."

[3] As I have stated above, §3.4.6.3, the evidence appears to suggest that in this
case, the change originated during textual transmission, even though אמינא is
now attested in the Babylonian Aramaic magic texts.

## 4.3 Orthography

The most common interchanges are orthographic. Since the orthography of JBA was never entirely fixed, interchanges are extremely frequent, even within a single context of a single textual witness. The following are representative examples:

### 4.3.1 Use of ʾaleph as a Vowel Letter for Medial ā

#### 4.3.1.1 G Participle Forms

אמי ורדינאה הוה **בדיק** בכרי דבי נשיאה. ביומא טבא לא הוה **בדיק**. אמי׳
רבי אמי. שפיר עביד דלא **באדיק**. והא ר׳ אמי גופיה **דבדיק**.

Ammi of Wardin used to **inspect** the firstlings of the Nasi's house. On a festival he would not **inspect**. R. Ammi said: He acts properly in not **inspecting**. But R. Ammi himself **inspects**! (*Bes* 27a [**HPS** 5:7–8])

The participle form of the verb *bāḏiq* appears four times in this context, thrice with defective orthography and once with plene orthography, with no difference in meaning. Further examples:

דריש "[he] interprets" (**Hark** 102:26) // דאריש (**Hark** 102:29); יאדע "[he] knows" (**Hark** 21:37) // ידע (**Hark** 22:2); קארו "[they] read" (**Hark** 103:14) // קרו (**Hark** 103:16) // קארו (**Hark** 103:17).

#### 4.3.1.2 Nominal Forms

אבל **זמרא** דאסר מר עוקבא דברים שאינן כסדר הזה אלא נגינות שלאהבת
אדם לחברו ולשבח יפה ביפיו ולקלס גבור בגבורתו וכיוצא בזאת...
ודאמרינן רב הונא אסר **זמארא** רב חסדא זליזיל ביה...

But **the music** which Mar ʿUqba prohibited was not like these things, rather love songs between a man and his friend, or praising a beautiful man for his beauty, or to proclaim a brave man for his bravery, and the like... And when we say, "Rav Huna prohibited **music**, Rav Hisda despised it ...(*Sot* 48a)." (**Hark** 27:32–28:1)

אמור דאמרינן תלתה עדיפי לענין **אומדנא** דכמה דנפישי ידעי **באומדאנא** טפי.

You may say that we say [that] three are better for **assessing**, because the more numerous they are, the more they understand **assessing.** (**Hark** 33:8–9)

דאם מת אבי אשתו או קרוביה מקמי דמיתה היא, ונפלו לה נכסים דבית **נאשה**, והדר מיתה היא. בעלה יורשה. מיתה לה מיקמי בית **נשה**. הוה ליה בעל ראוי ולא יריָת.

If his wife's father or relatives died before she died, and she received property from her **family** home, and then she died, her husband inherits [from] her. If she dies before [the members of] her **family** home, he is [in the category of] the husband of [property] fit [for inheritance] who does not inherit. (**HPS** 85:18–20)

Cf. also: בית **נאשה** (**Hark** 35:29, 32, 35) // בית **נשה** (**Hark** 36:2).

איכא דניחא ליה **בחלא** ולא ניחא ליה בחמרא. בחמרא ולא ניחא ליה **בחאלא**.

Sometimes he is satisfied with **vinegar** and is not satisfied with wine; or with wine and is not satisfied with **vinegar.** (*BM* 84b [**HPS** 153:2–3])

ודקאמ' ליה לוי: אילו הוה כתיב לך שטר הוה אית ליה **קאלא.** אטו **קלא** בכתיבה תלי?

As for what Levi says to him, "Had he written you a deed, it would have **publicity** [lit., "would have had a voice"]." Is **publicity** [lit., "the voice"] dependent upon writing? (**Hark** 102:15–16)

שקלוה יתמי פרסוה **אמיתנא.** אמ' ראבא: קני[י]ה **מיתאנא.**

The orphans took it [and] spread it over the **dead man.** Rava declared: "The **dead man** acquired it." (*Yev* 66b [**HPS** 159:6])

Further examples may be found in proper nouns, e.g.:

רבינא (Hark 24:12), ראבינא (Hark **באטי** בר טובי (Hark 24:9) // בטי בר טובי
162:19) // רבינא (Hark 163:6).

These examples demonstrate that there is no determined linear order to
the occurrences to the *plene* and defective examples, and that either may
appear first. Additional examples:

**הידנא** "now" (**Geon** xvii 3a 22) // **והידאנא** (**Geon** xvii 3a 30).

Cf. in a Yemenite MS:

דעד **הידנא** לא אותיבניה "until now we did not seat him" (*MQ* 27a
[**Col**]) // דעד **האידנא** לא אוכילניה "until now we did not feed him"
(*MQ* 27a [**Col**]).

### 4.3.1.3 F.pl. Morpheme

The f.pl. morpheme –*ātā* is generally written with *plene* orthography, and
thus prevents the homographic representation of forms such as משכנתא
"mortgage" (*BM* 108b [**HPS** 142:10]) and משכנאתא "mortgages" (*BM*
110a [**HPS** 143:18]). An exception to this rule is noun forms for which the
plural form is always distinguishable from the singular, even when written defectively, e.g., ארעתא "lands" (e.g., *BM* 39a [**HPS** 109:3]), which
cannot be confused with ארעא "land" (e.g., *BB* 169b [**HPS** 103:16]). Nevertheless we occasionally find defective orthography in the first category,
i.e., plural forms that may be read as singulars, even in the best manuscripts:

לרב חיסדא דאמ': מקילין **בטענאתא** דחמירן; תבעינן ליה בטעני דקילן.
ודומה לדומה לא תבעינן ליה. **ובטענתא** דאית בהי ממשא נמי פתחינן ליה
פיתחא.

According to R. Hisda, who says "We are lenient regarding serious
**claims**, we sue him regarding lenient **claims**," we do not sue him
regarding secondary claims. And even in **claims** that have sub-
stance we find him a solution." (**TGAs28** i 1b 15–17)

### 4.3.1.4 Following *waw* or *yod*

In many early manuscripts, particularly in the writings of R. Sherira and
R. Hai, a long *ā* vowel following a *waw* or *yod* is generally marked with

an ʾaleph, apparently to prevent the reading of the waw or yod as a vowel marker.[4] Nevertheless, we find interchanges in this category:

אמ' רב חונא: הלכה כאחרים. אמי רב אשי : טעמיהו דאחירים לא ידעינן,
הלכה נימא **כואתיהו**! תניא. דיאני גולה אמרו. עושין שומא ביניהם
ומשלשין. אמי רב חונא. הלכה כדיאני גולה. אמי רב אשי. טעמיהו דדיאני
גולה לא ידעינן. הלכה נימא **כותיהו**!

> R. Huna says: "The *Halacha* follows the Others." R. Ashi says: "We
> don't know the reason of the Others, would we state the Halacha in
> **accordance with them**? It is taught: "The judges of the Exile said:
> We assess among them and divide into three." R. Huna says: "The
> Halacha follows the judges of the Exile." R. Ashi says: "We don't
> know the reason of the judges of the Exile, would we state the Ha-
> lacha **in accordance with them**?" (*BB* 107b [**HPS** 150:20–151:2])

## 4.3.2 Use of ʾaleph or he as a Vowel Letter for Final -ā[5]

In the overwhelming majority of examples of the noun marker (-ā), it is
written with an ʾaleph. In the early manuscripts, the number of exceptions to this rule is minimal.[6] However, there are several categories
wherein interchanges are occasionally found, even within a single context.

### 4.3.2.1 Feminine Singular Morpheme Attached to Participles

This may be written either with an ʾaleph or with a *he*, with no distinction:

**דתפיסא** לא מפקינן מינה דלא **תפיסה** לא יהבינן לה.

> If she has **seized** [property], we do not take it away from her, if she
> has not **seized** [property], we do not give [it] to her. (*Ket* 64a [**Hark**
> 139: 32])

---

[4] Cf. Morgenstern, "Noun Patterns."

[5] In **HPS** this vowel is generally marked with the *miqpaṣ pummā*, and apparently
realized as [ʾ].

[6] Kara, *Yemenite Manuscripts*, p. 40, notes that in his corpus the *he* is rare in this
category. The same situation obtains in the Geonic Responsa; see Morgenstern,
"Geonic Responsa," p. 32.

Cf. further קניא ליה "she **acquires** it" (**TGAs28** i 7b 18) // קניה ליה (**TGAs28** i 7b 20).

## 4.3.2.2 The Final Vowel of III-*yod* Roots

The 3 m.s. forms of III-*yod* verbs in the G are commonly written with an *'aleph*, e.g., קנא "he acquired" (**HPS** 77:2), but may occasionally be written with a *he*, e.g., קנה (*BB* 151b [**HPS** 88:10]).[7] In the early manuscripts, this phenomenon appears to be limited to roots found also in Hebrew and may thus be ascribed synchronically to the influence of Hebrew orthography upon Aramaic. An exception to this rule is the root הו"י, the forms of which are almost exclusively written with a *he*, apparently to maintain a distinction between הֲוָה (*həwā*) "it was" (**HPS** 268:21), and הוּא (*hū*) "he" (e.g., **HPS** 203:18).[8] In fact, I have found only one case employing the *'aleph*: דהוא ביה "that had in it" (*ʿAZ* 61b [**Geon** xxi 1b 9]).

Occasionally both spellings are found together in one context:

הני מילי היכא **דטעא** בעל הבית אבל **טעה** שליח...

These words [apply] where the householder **made a mistake**, but if the messenger **made a mistake**... (**GS** xv 1b 24–25)

## 4.3.2.3 Numerals

The morpheme of the masculine numerals 3–10 may be written with either an *'aleph* or a *he*. A single manuscript may employ both spellings, even within a single context:[9]

אמ' רב יהודה: דקימן **תלתה תלתא** אטירפי בחד קינא.

R. Yehuda says: When they exist with **three** leaves on each stem. (*Suk* 32b [**HPS** 43:15])

לאו פרעתך מאה קבי אפצי דהוה קימי **בשיתא שיתה**.

---

[7] Cf. Kara, *Yemenite Manuscripts*, p. 40; Morgenstern, "Geonic Responsa," p. 32.

[8] The vocalization of both these forms is found in the manuscript.

[9] On the spellings with a *he*, see Friedman, "Early Manuscripts," pp. 14–16, nn. 20*–21, and p. 49.

Did I not pay you a hundred qabs of gall nuts worth **six** [*zuzim*] apiece? (*Shev* 41b-42a [**HPS** 199:19–20])

### 4.3.2.4 Grammatical Particles

Certain words have a final *ā* vowel that may have originated in the OA article *ā* but is now no longer regarded as a noun marker. For example, וֹהֹשׁתֹא (**HPS** 41:19) "now" is apparently a contraction of הדא שעתא "this time."[10] However, since this word functions as an adverb, it does not follow the rules of nouns. Accordingly, the ending is occasionally written with a *he*. Two examples of this spelling occur in **HPS** in Talmudic passages: השתה (*MQ* 11a [**HPS** 277:19]; *Ket* 96b [**HPS** 184:3]). I have also found two examples in which the spellings are employed interchangeably:

ואשקינן **השתא** ומה שלמים שהן טעונין סמיכה ותנופות חזה ושוק אמרת ממונו בכור מיבעיא ... ואמרינן מאי קאמי למעוטי שלמים דאלמא אין ממון בעלים **השתה** ומה בכור אין קדושתו מרחם אחרת ממונו הוא שלמים מיבעיא.

And we ask the question: "**Now**, if regarding the peace offerings that require the laying on of hands and the waving of the breast and calf you say are wealth, a firstling is required;" and we say, "What is he saying? To exclude peace offerings." From which we learn that it is not the wealth of the owner. "**Now** if a firstling's holiness which not from another's womb is his wealth, peace offerings are also required." (*BQ* 12b ([**Hark** 162:34–163:7])

Cf. also: **השתא** "now" (**TGAs28** xvii 4a 13) // **השתה** (**TGAs28** xvii 4b 2)[11].

## 4.3.3. The Orthography of a Medial *i* in Closed Syllables

### 4.3.3.1 Non-final Closed Syllables

There is a tendency to mark such vowels with a *yod*, e.g., בישרא (**TGAs28** i 9b 24), though this is not a rule, e.g., in the same manuscript (though a

---

[10] Cf. Sokoloff, *DJBA*, p. 391 s.v. השתא. The entry does not contain examples written with a final *he*.

[11] Assaf mistakenly transcribed השתא.

different responsum) **בסרא** (ibid., 3b 9).[12] We also find such interchanges within the same context:

עביד איניש דפרע בגו **זימניה** ... לא עביד איניש דפרע בגו **זמניה**

One is likely to pay within his [allotted] **time**... one is not likely to pay within his [allotted] **time**. (*BB* 5a–b [HPS 202:4–9])

אבל חד זבן עדית וחד זבן בינונית. מבינונית **מישתלם**. מעידית לא **משתלם**.

But if one bought finest land and the other bought average land, **he is paid** from the average land; **he is** not **paid** from the finest land. (**HPS** 82:17–18)

### 4.3.3.2 Syllables Closed by Gemination

הכי נמי דכל אימת **דמיכסי** איניש גלימיה מחיב לברוכי. ורב יהודה, האיי
דלא מבריך אילא כל צפרא—שאני רב יהודה דאיניש צניעא הוא, ולא שארי
ליה לגלימיה מיניה כוליה דיומא. אבל כל אימת דשארי איניש גלימיה והדר
**מכסי** ליה. צריך לברוכי להתעטף בציצית.

Here too, whenever a person **covers himself** with his garment, he has to say the benediction. And regarding Rav Yehuda, the fact that he only says the benediction in the morning—Rav Yehuda is different, because he is a modest man, and does not take off his garment the entire day. But whenever a person takes off his garment and **covers himself** again, he has to say the benediction "To wrap oneself in fringes." (**Geon** xxxviii 7a 9–14)

This example indicates how difficult it is to distinguish between the D and Dt participles. While there is a general tendency to employ a *yod mater lectionis*, apparently in order to distinguish the former from the latter, there are several examples of defective orthography. These interchanges are common in Dt forms of the root חו״ב, e.g., מחייב (**Hark** 202:24), דמן דמחייב (**Hark** 202:26), contrasting with דמאן דמיחייב (**Hark** 202:27), דאיחייב (**Hark** 202:29). In **HPS**, we find the defective spelling is explicitly vocalized as a Dt form: מֻחִיבִין (**HPS** 56:18).

---

[12] On the interchange of *samek* and *śin*, see below, §4.3.4

*Additional examples:*

עזי "goats" (*BB* 36a [**HPS** 138:13]) // עיזי (*BB* 36a [**HPS** 138:16]).

ציפוראה "man of Sepphoris" (**Hark** 131:22) // צפוראה (**Hark** 131:28).

## 4.3.4 The Orthography of Historical *śin*

The historical *śin* appears to have completely merged with *samek*, and many lexemes with etymological *śin* are written in JBA with a *samek*, e.g., סיתוא "winter" (*Yom* 29a [**Hark** 12:22]). However, historical spellings are occasionally maintained in JBA,[13] and these may interchange freely with phonetic spellings.

> רב פפא זבן ארעא מיהההוא גברא. אמר ליה: כמה הויא? אמי' ליה: **עיסרין**
> גריוי. משחה אשכחה שיתסר גריוי. אתא לקמיה דאביי. אמי' ליה: סברת
> וקבילת. אמי' ליה: והא פחת שתות תנן! אמי' ליה: הני מילי היכא דלא קי לי
> בגוה; מר קי לי בגוה. והא **עשרי** אמר לי! דשויא **כעסרי** אמר לך.

> Rav Papa bought land from a certain person. He said to him: "How much is it?" He said "**Twenty** *griv*s." He measured it and found it contained sixteen *griv*s. He came before Abaye; he said: "You considered and accepted." [Rav Papa] said: "But didn't we teach: "Less than a sixth…"[14] He said: "This applies when one is not fully acquainted with it[15] [i.e., the property]; Sir is fully acquainted with it!" "But he told me '**Twenty**'." "He told you it was worth as much as **twenty**." (*BB* 106a-b [**HPS** 149:12–16])

In this story, we find within the space of a few lines three forms of the numeral twenty: עיסרין, עשרי and עסרי. The latter two also demonstrate the elision of the final *nun*. There is no apparent rule governing the use

---

[13] Historical spellings with *śin* are similarly found in early Syriac legal documents; see Brock, "New Syriac Documents," p. 261 n. 13 (comment on the form ܚܐܢܝ in Syriac P. Mesopotamia A l. 7).

[14] According to *m. BB* 7:3, a sale is valid as it stands if the difference between the size of actual property and the size declared by the seller amounts to no more than one sixth. Since the difference in this case was larger than one sixth, R. Papa demanded that he receive a rebate, as the Mishna stipulates.

[15] קי לי is a phonetic spelling for קים ליה; see below, §4.4.5.3. On this idiom, see Sokoloff, *DJBA*, p. 995b, and the discussion below.

of either spelling or form, and I have found no other examples of the apocopated forms of the numeral twenty.

*Additional examples:*

ואיתי ליה סמא לאסוקיה שפיר ואחוריה **לבישריה**. דצריך לאותובי ליה
סמא ואנקוטיה גונא **דבסריה.**

He brought him a medicine to heal it well, and it whitened his **skin**; so he needs to give him a medicine and to give him [back] the color of his **skin**. (*BQ* 85b **[G1]**)

דכי אמרין **לשהדי** כתבו גט לאשתו.

. . . that when they say to the **witnesses** "Give a deed of divorce to his wife." (**HPS** 204:14)

*which parallels:*

עד דאמרי **לסהדי** תנו גט, אין נותנין.

. . . until they say to the **witnesses**, "Give a deed of divorce," they do not give it. (**HPS** 204:16–17)


## 4.3.5 The Orthography of $\underline{b}$ or Shift *$b > w$?

JBA seldom demonstrates the shift of *bet* to *waw* in native Aramaic words,[16] and the phenomenon appears to be restricted to certain roots, and perhaps phonetically conditioned.[17] The interchange is particularly common in the root אב״ד "be lost, perish," for reasons that remain unclear.[18] It is similarly uncertain what phonetic reality this reflects, though the fact that these spellings are so rare would appear to suggest the

---

[16] Examples are attested in loanwords, e.g., גריוא ~ גריבא "*griv*" (a measure).

[17] The unconditioned shift of *$\underline{b} > w$, found in Neo-Aramaic dialects, is not attested.

[18] The shift is also shared with Mandaic. Perhaps in these dialects, which have lost the pharyngeal *ᶜayin*, a secondary shift occurred to distinguish between *ʾabad* "did" (historically עב״ד) and *ʾawad* "was lost, perished" (historically אב״ד). In JBA, the *dalet* of the first root is often elided. However, since the use of the root עב״ד is far more widespread than that of אב״ד, it is difficult to determine whether this is due to phonetic change arising from common use in the spoken language or is merely coincidental, being dependent upon the more widespread attestation of forms of the historical root עב״ד.

"soft" *bet* generally remained phonetically distinct from *waw*, and that this reflects a sporadic (though perhaps lexicalized) shift.

The reconstruction is further complicated by interchanges between the two spellings, either within one textual witness or between different textual witnesses. Let us begin with an example from a single witness, a responsum by R. Sharrira:

ואתא הרמאנא דשמיא במאי דלא הוה ידיע בההיא שעתא **ואבד** ההוא אשראי פטור הוא.

...And a heavenly order came regarding something that was not known at that time, and that outstanding credit **was lost**—then he is not liable. (**Hark** 99:31–32).

Further on in the same responsum, we read:

ואו זבין באשראי **ואוד** פטור.

If he bought on credit and it **was lost**, he is not liable. (**Hark** 100:10)

In the following example, we find the forms used interchangeably in two different transmissions of the same Talmudic passage, twice in a citation in *Halachot Pesuqot*, and once in a citation from *Halachot Gedolot*:

האיי מאן דאוזפיה לחבריה אלפא דזוזי ואחית ליה קתא דמגלא עליהו. **אוד** קתא דמגלא. **אוד** אלפא דזוזי.

A certain man loaned his friend a thousand *zuzim* and gave him the handle of a sickle [in surety] for them. The handle of the sickle **was lost**; the thousand *zuzim* **were lost**. (*Shev* 43b [**HPS** 200:19–20])

האיי מאן דאוזפיה אלפא דזוזי לחבריה ואנח ליה קתא דמגלא משכונא. **אבד** קתא דמגלא **אבד** אלפא דזוזי.

A certain man loaned his friend a thousand *zuzim* and gave him the handle of a sickle as a surety. The handle of the sickle **was lost**; the thousand *zuzim* **were lost**. (*Shev* 43b [**HGP** 13a:12–13])

The text is cited again one more time in **HPS** (115:6–7), in yet another spelling:

האיי מאן דאוזפיה אלפא דזוזי לחבריה ואחית ליה קתא דמגלא על(א)יהו.
**אואד** קתא דמגלא **אואד** אלפא דזוזי.

This spelling is somewhat surprising, since the *ʾaleph* is generally employed as a medial vowel letter for a long vowel. The exceptions to this rule are very few. We may possibly be dealing with secondary vowel lengthening resulting from stress.[19]

### 4.3.6 Summary

In this section, we have seen examples of variable spellings occurring in JBA sources. This widespread phenomenon is found even in the best manuscripts, even within a single context. While the best manuscripts are characterized by widespread use of *matres lectionis* and non-historical spellings (see further §2.12.2.1 and the next section), even these lack consistency and may contain alternative spellings side by side.

With the exception of the forms עיסרין *ʾisrīn* and עסרי~עשרי *ʾisrī*, which are morphological variants, I regard all the examples cited in this section to be free orthographic variants. In the next section, I shall consider examples that may represent phonetic variants.

### 4.4 Phonetic Process

As noted in chapter 3, already by the fourth or fifth century CE Babylonian Aramaic had undergone far-reaching phonological changes. It seems likely, however, that many of these changes were masked by historical orthography.[20] We also saw that while use of phonetic (non-historical) spellings is more widespread in the eastern manuscript tradition and appears there in a wider variety of forms than in other sources, the phenomenon is attested in *all* textual witnesses, even in the standard printed editions of the Babylonian Talmud. For example, sources contain forms like תיקו "let it stand" from the root קו"ם, and such forms were not replaced or "corrected" in any of the textual traditions.

Moreover, even in the best textual witnesses, it is generally only a minority of forms that are written with phonetic spelling, and these may interchange with historical spellings without any apparent condition. In

---

[19] I have found one additional example of this in the EEMss: פראסו "they spread" (*BM* 85a [**G1**]). The regular spelling מאן "who" may reflect the lengthening of the biliteral particle to the triliteral form. This phenomenon is paralleled in Arabic dialects; cf. Blau, *Grammar*, §8.

[20] See Morgenstern, "Non-Standard Spellings."

other words, the unusual phonetic spellings that distinguish the EEMss from later textual witnesses are generally not attested in *all* cases of any given form; even in the best textual witnesses, they frequently appear together with historical spellings.[21]

## 4.4.1 Weakening of the Pharyngeals

### 4.4.1.1 The Weakening of ʿ*ayin*

In chapter 3 above, we saw that ʿ*ayin* appears to have shifted to ʾ*aleph* in RBA, or to have been elided completely. We also noted the interchange found in a responsum of R. Hai Gaon between מן צולי (**Hark** 159:31) and מצולעי (**Hark** 159:32), though as mentioned there, the definition and etymology of this word are uncertain.[22] Here I shall present further examples wherein phonetic and historical (or pseudo-historical) spellings are found side by side.

> האיי מאן **דבעי** אהויי חתימות ידיה לא ניתתי במגילתא ונהוי דילמא משכח
> לה איניש ואזיל כתיב מלעיל מאי **דבאיי.**

A person who **wishes** to demonstrate his signature should go to the bottom of a scroll and demonstrate, lest somebody finds it and goes and writes above whatever he **wishes**. (*BB* 167a [**HPS** 100:13–15])

In this statement, the historical spelling דבעי and phonetic spelling דבאיי interchange. In the following example, the pseudo-historical spelling ניבעי appears alongside the phonetic spelling ניבי for historical נעביד "we should carry out."

> ועוד תשלומי כפל ותשלומי ארבעה וחמשה דקיצי **ניבעי** שליחותהו. אמרי:
> כי **עבדינן** שליחותהו בממונא; בקנסא לא קא **עבדינן** שליחותהו. אדם
> באדם דממונא הוא; **נבעי** שליחותיהו! אמרי: כי **עבדינן** שליחותהו במילתא
> דשכיחא. אדם באדם דלא שכיחא, לא **עבדינן** שלוחתהו. בושת נמי דשכיחא
> **ניבי** שלוחתיהו.

---

[21] See further §4.7.5 below.
[22] See §3.3.1.1.1. Note also the interchange of the preposition מן with the prefixed (assimilated) form -מ. On this phenomenon, see below, §4.4.5.1.

Moreover, in the case of double-payments and fourfold or fivefold payments, which are specified, **we should carry out** their commission! They say: When **we carry out** their commission it is in monetary matters; in matters of fines, **we** do not **carry out** their commission. [Injury of] man against man is a monetary matter; **we should carry out** their commission! They say: When **we carry out** their commission, it is in common matters. Man against man, which is not common—**we** do not **carry out** their commission. Degradation is also common—**we should carry out** their commission! (*BQ* 84b [**G1**])

Note that in the later Spanish manuscript **H165**, the text reads as follows:

ועוד תשלומי כפל ותשלומי ארבעה וחמשה דקיצי **נעביד** שליחות׳. אמרי : כי עבדינן שליחותיהו בממונא. בקנסא לא **עבדינן** שליחותיהו. אדם באדם דממונא הוא **נעביד** שליחותיהו. אמרי. כי **עבדינן** שליחותיהו. במלתא דשכיחא. אדם באדם דלא שכיחא. לא **עבדינן** שליחותיהו. בשת ופגם [23] נמי דשכיחא **נעביד** שליחותיהו.

We will often find a phonetic spelling in one textual transmission, paralleled by an historical spelling in another tradition, even when both manuscript sources are regarded as accurate witnesses, e.g., עמרם צבא "Amram the dyer" *Git* 52a [**HPS** 82:1]), a citation in a legal digest, parallels עמרם צבאעא (*Git* 52a [**Hark** 78:31]) in a citation of the same passage in a responsum.

#### 4.4.1.2 The Weakening of *ḥet*

In §3.3.1 we noted that *ḥet* and *he* appear to have merged already in the fourth or fifth century. The relative distribution of the two spellings appears to be on etymological grounds, though the manuscripts show numerous phonetic spellings reflecting the shift of * *ḥ* > *h*.

On several occasions, we find the interchange of the *he* and *ḥet* even within a single context. As mentioned above, a non-historical *ḥet* is frequently employed for the root שה״י "delay," but even this may interchange with the historical *he*.

---

[23] Added in manuscript.

ואי איכא קרובים או נמי שיאראתא דאזלי ואתו, נטרינן **ומשהינן** ליה עד
תרי סר ירחי שתא. כי הא דראבינא **שהייה** למארא דאהא בר סמא תרי סר
ירחי שתא עד דאזיל שליחא ואתי לבי הוזאיי.

But if there are relatives or caravans that go and return, we wait
and **postpone** it[24] up to twelve months of the year, as in the case
when Ravina **postponed it** for Master of Aha bar Samma twelve
months until the messenger should go to and come [from] Be-
Hozaye. (*BQ* 112b [**HPS** 124:4–7])

והיכא דהוה קא אכיל **לחמא** ואיצטריך לאיפנויי ואזל איפני והדר אתא
לגבי **נהמא.** שארי המוציא לחם מן הארץ מירישא והדר אכיל.

If he was eating **bread** and needed to relieve himself, and went and
relieved himself and once again came to his **bread**, he starts [the
blessing] "Who brings forth bread from the earth" from the beginning and then eats. (**HPS** 291:4–6)

In this example, the OA form לחמא occurs alongside the later JBA נהמא
in the same sentence.[25] On the interchange of *nun* and *lamed*, see §4.4.4.

## 4.4.2 Weakening of the Laryngeals

### 4.4.2.1 *He-ʾAleph* Interchange[26]

Interchanges of the roots הפ״ך and אפ״ך are attested within the Semitic
language family. In earlier Hebrew and Aramaic sources (most notably
the Sefire inscription) only the form with the *he* appears, while already in
the Proverbs of Ahiqar we find the root אפ״ך with an *ʾaleph*.[27] The Isaiah
scroll (1QIsaᵃ), which often subjects the text of Isaiah to linguistic updat-
ing, substitutes the nominal form מאפכה for MT's מהפכה, while in Tannaitic Hebrew we find אפ״ך employed in the technical sense of "to turn

---

[24] I.e., the issuing of a certain document.

[25] נהמא is also found in a magic bowl. See Morgenstern, "Magic Bowl," p. 209.

[26] See Morgenstern, "Non-Standard Spellings," pp. 251–3, wherein the evidence
of the Aramaic magic bowls is presented.

[27] For Biblical Hebrew, see **BDB**, p. 245ff s.v. הפך. The older Aramaic sources are
listed in Hoftijzer–Jongeling, *DNWSI*, p. 291.

the earth."[28] These later Hebrew uses may reflect Aramaic dialect forms. JPA employs both forms, even within the same idioms.[29] Classical Syriac appears to employ only מהפך, while Mandaic primarily employs *ʾpk* though the *Mandaic Dictionary* also lists *hpk* as an attested variant.[30] In JBA, we find both forms, used interchangeably:

איכא ביניהו **למיפך** שבועה. דאוריתא לא **הפכינן**. דרבנן **הפכינן**.

> They are divided on the transfer of oaths. Those from the Torah we do not transfer; those from the Rabbis we transfer. (*Shev* 41a [**HPS** 119:8])

The infinitive למיפך "to transfer" is spelled as though derived from the root אפי״ך, while the participle forms are derived from the root הפי״ך. By contrast, the same Talmudic source is cited or alluded to on several occasions in early manuscripts, always with the participle form אפכינן (**Hark** 202:19 bis, 21,[31] 203:8, 10; **Geon** xxi 5a 23 bis, 24).

There is further evidence to suggest that the *he* in such forms might represent no more than an historical spelling. Müller-Kessler has pointed out that the spellings הפיכה, אפיכא, היפיכה and איפיכא are all equally attested in Aramaic magic texts, and that all are passive participles indicating vowel assimilation, *\*ʾapīk-* > *\*ʾəpīk-* > *ʾipīk*. [32] However, the evidence of the Rabbinic corpus seems to imply that this phenomenon was restricted to I-*ʾaleph* roots, e.g., אימיר (**Hark** 33:3, 171:25)/אימירא "it is said" (**Hark** 33:14,15; 36:32, etc.) and איניס "compelled" (*BM* 77b [**G1**];[33] **Hark** 167:12; 178:16). I have found no other roots wherein a first radical *he* is followed by a *yod* in the *qal* passive participle. In light of the frequently attested form based on the root אפי״ך, and the infinitive form למיפך, it is possible that the forms הפכינן and היפיכה reflect an historical spelling, and that the *he* was not in fact pronounced.

---

[28] For the Isaiah scroll, see Kutscher, *Isaiah Scroll*, 251, while the Tannaitic sources are discussed in Moreshet, *Lexicon*, p. 104.

[29] See Sokoloff, *DJPA*, p. 71 s.v. אפך and p. 167 s.v. הפך.

[30] Drower–Macuch, *MD*, p. 151 s.v. **HPK**.

[31] So MS.

[32] Müller-Kessler, "Die Zauberschalensammlung," p. 119.

[33] Friedman, *Bava Meziᶜa Text*, p. 329.

## 4.4.2.2 Weakening of the ʔaleph in Juncture

The verbal auxiliary קא, which only precedes participles, is generally written as a separate particle in the earliest manuscript sources. I have not found any examples of the bound form in **HPS**, while in other manuscript sources, we occasionally find the auxiliary prefixed to the following word, e.g., קאסבר "he holds [the opinion]" (**Geon** xxi 2a 3), particularly in frequently used verbs. Such spellings are quite common in **HGP**. Very rarely in these manuscripts is the preformative written simply as a prefixed -ק, a spelling widespread in the printed editions, and even then it is restricted to very common phrases such as קסבר "he holds [the opinion]" (**Hark** 42:30; 44:35; **HGP** 4a:25). Once again we must emphasize that even these spellings are rare. A computer search of the text of the Vilna edition according to the version found in the Lieberman Institute database found 799 examples of קסבר in contrast to only 42 examples of קא סבר. **HGP** contains only one example of קסבר but 12 of קא סבר.

An exception to this rule is participle forms of the root אמ״ר preceded by קא. For example, **HGP** contains only three examples of קא written as a separate word before the root אמ״ר, as opposed to 91 with the prefix.[34]

Let us summarize these findings as a table, recalling that **HPS** contains *no examples* of the prefixed קא- .

| Source | Separate קא | Prefixed -ק |
|---|---|---|
| Talmud, Vilna ed. | 42 קא סבר | 798 קסבר |
| Talmud, Vilna ed. | 108 קא אמר וכו׳ | 2379 קאמי׳ וכו׳ |
| HGP | 12 קא סבר | 1 קסבר |
| HGP | 3 קא אמר וכו׳ | 91 קאמי׳ וכו׳ |
| HPS | Always | Ø |

In other words, while the printed edition shows a marked preference for the prefixed -ק, it is a minority form in the eastern manuscripts. An exception to this rule is the root אמ״ר.

In several cases, the two forms interchange, e.g.:

דילמא אתו עדים ואמרי כי **דקאמרא**.

---

[34] This includes abbreviated forms such as קאמ׳ or קאמ.

Lest witnesses will come and say as she says. (*Yev* 119b [**TGAs28** i 6a 10])

But later in the same responsum:

דילמא אתו עדים ואמרי כי **דקאאמרא.**

Lest witnesses will come and say as she says (*Yev* 119b [**TGAs28** i 6a 22]).

**דקאמרי** עדים ידעינן דלא הויא ליה ארעא להאי מעולם

That the witnesses say, "We know that this one never had any land." (*BB* 44b [**Hark** 92:37])

But further on in the same responsum:

**דקא אמרי** עדים וכו'

That the witnesses say, etc... (*BB* 44b [**Hark** 93:13])

Do these interchangeable spellings reflect different pronunciations? Why is קא frequently shorted to ק- prior to the root אמ"ר? Is this an orthographic difference, arising from an unwillingness to write the *ʾaleph* twice in succession? Such an orthographic convention does exist in JBA, namely in the nouns ending in *āʾā*, particularly common in gentilics, e.g., ארמאה "Aramaean" (**TGAs28** i 8a 20) and ordinals such as קדמאה "first," בתראה (**HPS** 203:17) "latter" (**HPS** 203:16, 17).[35] However, it seems more likely to me that the unusual distribution of forms for this verb arises from a combination of factors: on the one hand, the frequency of the root אמ"ר and, on the other, the weakening of the *ʾaleph* between two *ā* vowels.[36] In other words, forms such as קא אמר were in fact pronounced *qāmar*. Evidence for such a pronunciation may be found in the Yemenite manuscripts, e.g., וקמר רחמנא "the Merciful One says" (*Suk* 25a [**JTS**218]), paralleling a more historical spelling on MS **O51** קאמי (*Suk* 25a [**O51**]).[37]

Evidence for the weakening of initial *ʾaleph* may be found in JBA.[38] For example, the common expression או בעית אימא "if you wish, say"[39] is

---

[35] By contrast, Classical Syriac employs two *ʾalephs*, e.g., ܪܒܐ "great."

[36] This phenomenon is extremely common, e.g בתרא "latter" (**HPS** 230:18) < בתראה.

[37] Kara, *Yemenite Manuscripts*, p. 71.

[38] For the evidence of the Jewish Aramaic magic bowls, see Morgenstern, "Non-Standard Spellings," p. 254.

found written as a single word, e.g., ואיבעיתימא "if you wish, say" (**Hark** 42:33), ואו בעיתימא "if you wish, say" (**Hark** 42:37).[40] But these examples appear alongside the more frequent spelling preserving the initial *ʾaleph* או בעית אימי "if you wish, say" (**Hark** 42:29). Similarly, אלתר "immediately" (*BQ* 112b [**HPS** 123:21]) is derived from על אתר.

### 4.4.3 Elision/Assimilation of Third-Radical Consonants

In chapter 2, we noted that the widespread elision of word-final consonants is a salient feature of the EEMss, and this feature is also fairly well attested in the Jewish Aramaic magic bowls.[41] However, even in the best textual witnesses we find apparently free interchanges between the spellings showing elision and those that do not, e.g.:

קא **יהי** ליה "he **gives** him" (*BQ* 85b [**G1**]) // קא **יהיב** ליה (*BQ* 85b [**G1**]); "**I עבידנא** יומא טבא לרבנן. דאמנא לא מפקדנא וקא **אבינא** מצות **would practice** the festival according to Rabbis; for I said, 'I am not commanded, yet **I practice** the commandments'" (*BQ* 87a [**G1**]); דאמליה בעל הבית בארבעה **ואזא** אמלהו בתלתה "That the householder said to him for four, and he **went** [and] said to them for three" (*BM* 76a [**G1**]) // אמליה בעל הבית בארבעה **ואזל** אמלהו בתלתה (*BM* 76a [**G1**]); אמרו ליה לחד מיניהו **זיל** אפי לן "They said to one of them, '**Go** and bake for us'" (*BM* 81a [**G1**]) // ואמרו ליה לדידיה **זי** אפי לן (*BM* 81a [**G1**]); ניחא ליה **דניקום** בהימנותיה "It satisfies him **that he should maintain** his trustworthiness" (*BM* 15b [**Hark** 160:26, 28, 29]) // ניחא ליה **דניקו** בהימנותיה (*BM* 15b [**Hark** 161:2–3]); **כתי** ביה בי "**He writes** it in the court" (*Ket* 22a [**Hark** 82:26]) // **כתיב** ביה בי דינא (*Ket* 22a [**Hark** 82:31]).

In the above examples, the interchanges occur within a single context in a single textual witness. The interchange is paralleled in the Aramaic

---

[39] The verb אימא is imperative, and hence to be read *ʾima*. Shemuel b. Ḥofni glosses in Arabic אן שית קלת "if you wish, then you will say" (**LPT** 146:25.) For this vocalization, see §3.4.3.6.1.

[40] On the interchange of the particles או and אי "if" cf. Kara, *Yemenite Manuscripts*, pp. 44 n. 95, 46; Morgenstern, "Geonic Responsa," p. 71; and Breuer, "Karetot," p. 32.

[41] See Juusola, *Linguistic Peculiarities*, pp. 41–44, and Morgenstern, "Non-Standard Spellings," passim.

magic bowls, e.g., אבי קיניא "one who makes a purchase" (SD 34:11) //
אביד קיניא (l. 13).[42]

The same phenomenon is found when we compare two textual witnesses of the same Talmudic passage. Both are counted among the most
accurate linguistic sources of RBA.

| BQ 103a | |
|---|---|
| **MS G1** | **HPS 72:13–16** |
| רב כהנא יהב זוזי אכיתנא. | רב כהנא יהב זוזי אכיתנא. |
| לבסוף יקר כיתנא. | לבסוף יקר כיתנא. |
| זבניה ניהליה מרואתיה דכיתנא. | זבנוה ניה ליה מרואתיה דכיתנא. |
| אתא לקמיה דרב. | אתא לקמיה דרב. |
| אמ' ליה : מי **איזי שקו**[43] זוזי? | אמ' ליה : מאי **איזי אישקול** זוזי? |
| אמ' ליה. אי כי מזבני ליה אמרי. | אמ' ליה : אי כי קא מזבני ליה מעיקרה אמרו |
| דהאי כיתנא דכהנא הוא, | דהאיי כיתנא דכהנא הוא, |
| **זי שקו**. | **זיל שקול**. |
| ואילא לא **תשקו**. | ואילא. לא **תישקול**. |

R. Kahana gave money for [the purchase of] flax. Eventually flax
increased in price. The owners of the flax sold it for him. He[44] came
before Rav. He said to him: "Should **I go [and] take** the money?"
He said to him: "If when they sold them (originally)[45] they said:
'This flax belongs to Kahana,' then **go [and] take** it; otherwise, do
not **take it**."

---

[42] See Levene–Bhayro, "Bring to the Gates," p. 243. Both אבי and אביד are phonetic spellings for עביד "one who makes."

[43] This is best interpreted as a junctural phenomenon: ʾezi ʾišqu > ʾeziʾišqu >
ʾeziyišqu with the loss of the ʾaleph.

[44] Or "The matter."

[45] This form is found only. in the version in **HPS**, and may be a gloss.

### 4.4.4 *Nun-lamed* interchange

Already in the language of the magic bowls we find interchanges of *l* and *n*, even in native Aramaic verbal roots.[46] Such interchanges are common in the prefixed morphemes of the verbs, hence a form such as ליתין may mean "let him give" (**HPS** 231:16) or "let us give" (**HPS** 157:6).[47] R. Shemuel b. Ḥofni Gaon in his dictionary of Talmudic expressions translates the Aramaic expression **לימא** בהא קא מיפלגי with the Arabic ירידו בה פי הדה הם מכתלפין **נקול** אן הל "By this they mean, 'Should we say that they disagree regarding this?'"[48]

On some occasions, we find the two prefixes interchanging within a single sentence, e.g., וליקום ניגזר "Should we come [and] enact?" (**TGAs28** iv 2a 15). Similarly, there are several examples wherein the prefixes interchange when the same verb is repeated in a single context, apparently demonstrating that they are free variants. Consider this Talmudic citation with Geonic commentary:

אמרי נהרדאיי: האיי עיסקא פלגא מלוה ופלגא פיקדון. מאי טעמא? עבדו רבנן מילתא דניחא ליה למלוה וניחא ליה ללווה. ניחא ליה למלוה, דאי אמי' מר: **"נשוייה** לכוליה עיסקא הלואה", אסיר ליה למלוה למיכל רואחא, דהוה ליה רבית. אי אמי' מר: **"לישוייה** לכוליה פיקדון", אי מיתניס אי מיגניב, לית ליה לאשתלומי מלווה ולא מידי. הולכך שוויה רבנן פלגא מלוה.

*The Nehardeans say: This venture is half loan, half deposit. What is the reason? The Rabbis made a decision that satisfies both lender and borrower (BM 104b). It satisfies the lender, because if he had stated, "**Let us make** the whole deal a loan" then the lender would have been forbidden to enjoy the profit, which would have been interest. Had he said "Let us make the whole thing a deposit," had it been seized or stolen, he would not be able to be paid back anything from the borrower. Accordingly, the Rabbis made half of it a loan. (HPS 69:10–15)*

I have cited the passage at length because the repetitive structure leaves no doubt as to the fact that the verbs are equal in meaning. It also seems from the context that they are 1st person plural verbs, representing as it

---

[46] See Morgenstern, "Magic Bowl," pp. 219–20, and "Further Notes," on the interchange of the verbal roots חב"ל and חב"ן.

[47] So rendered in *Hilchot Reʾu*, a medieval Hebrew translation of *Halachot Pesuqot*: ונתן (**HR** 77:19).

[48] **LPT** 155:15.

were the expression of a legal position before the deciding counsel, hence "let **us** make." The final decision is reflected in the statement, "Accordingly, the Rabbis made" in the 3 m.pl.[49]

Further examples: מיקמי **דליתבעינהו** "before **he would sue them**" (*BB* 174a [**HPS** 74:4]) // מיקמי **דניתבעינהו** (*BB* 174b [**HPS** 74:11]); **ליחוש** "**let us be concerned**" (*Git* 70b [**GS** xvii 1b 1, 4]) // **וניחוש** (*Git* 70b [**GS** xvii 1b 8]); **ניכתוב** רחמנא "the Merciful One **should write**" (*BQ* 88a [**G1**]) // **ליכתוב** רחמנא (*BQ* 88a [**G1**]); אם כן **ליתני** "If so, **let him teach**" (*ʿAra* 21b [**Hark** 139:12]) // אם כן **ניתני** (*ʿAra* 21b [**Hark** 166:3]); היכי **נידיינוה** דיאני להאיי דינא "How can the judges **try** this case?" (*BM* 42a [**HPS** 126:18]) // היכי **לידיינוה** דיאני להאיי דינא (*BB* 33b [**HPS** 137:9]).[50]

## 4.4.5 Assimilation and Dissimilation

### 4.4.5.1 Assimilation of *nun* and *lamed*

In §4.4.1.1 we noted the interchange of מן צולי and מצולעי. Further examples of this interchange are attested, e.g., ומן קמי דלימטי גיטא לידה "and before the divorce deed reaches her hand" (**HPS** 203:2–3) // מיקמי דלימטי לידה (**HPS** 203:6).

In RBA, על is commonly fused with the following word, and through the loss of the pharyngeal and assimilation of the *lamed* is represented orthographically as -א.[51] In some cases, the historical form may appear alongside the non-historical form, apparently resulting from a different register.

רב פפא כי הוה ליה תריסר אלפי זוזי בי הוזאיי לא אקנינהו לרב שמואל בר אחא **על גב** קרקע סתם וסמך על חלק דארץ ישראל אלא הכין אקני ליה **אגב** אסיפא דביתיה.

R. Pappa, *when he* had 12000 zuzim in Bē Hozaye, did not transfer possession of them to R. Shemuʾel bar Aha **along with** undefined *land and rely upon a portion in the land of Israel. Rather, he transferred*

---

[49] Cf. the Hebrew translation נעשה "let us make" of **HR** 39:17, 18.

[50] In this case, it is parallel texts from within the Talmud (rather than the same Talmudic text) that are cited in different places in **HPS**.

[51] This form is already found in the Aramaic magic bowls. See Morgenstern, "Magic Bowl," p. 211, and Levene, "Corpus," pp. 40 (M101:12), p. 100 (M145:1 // MS 2053/159:1).

*possession to him thus:* **along with** the vestibule of his house. (**Hark** 93:14–17)

The entire passage is a commentary upon *BM* 46a; the Talmudic citation is presented here in roman font while the Geonic commentary is presented in italic lettering. In the Geonic addition, the more classical על גב "along with" is used, while the citation retains the Talmudic form אגב. This is one of several examples of the later Geonim's use of a more conservative, literary language in their own writing, while retaining the less conservative register of the Talmudic discourse in citations from the Talmud.[52]

## 4.4.5.2 Assimilation of the Gt and Dt Stem Morpheme

In JBA, the *taw*-morpheme of the *t*-stems is generally preserved in I-ʾ*aleph* roots, hollow verbs (or geminate verbs that have shifted to this category) and, usually, verbs in which the first root consonant is a metathesizing sibilant. In other cases, it is often assimilated into the first root radical, though this phenomenon, while very common, is not entirely consistent, at least not in the orthography.[53]

### 4.4.5.2.1 Sound Verbs

Interchanges between assimilated and unassimilated forms are found even in the same context. In the following example from *Halachot Pesuqot*, Talmudic material from *Yom* 73b is glossed with Geonic explanations (here underlined).

דתניא: **ומיתבעי** ליה לאיניש לאפסוקי בערב יום הכפורים <u>מיאדנהר</u>.
"ועניתם את נפשותיכם בתשיעה". יכול בתשעה ממש. תלמי-לומי "בערבי".
או "בערב" יכול משתחשך. תלמי-לומי "מיערבי". הא כיצד. מתחיל ומיתענה
מיבעוד יום. מיכן שמוסיפין מחול על קדש. ואין לי אילא בכניסתו דיבענן
אקדומי אפסוקי. ביציאתו מנין **דמיבעי לן אחורי עד דחשכא.** תלמי-לומי
"עד ערב".

---

[52] See in detail Morgenstern, "Geonic Responsa," pp. 11–17.

[53] See Rosenberg, *Das Aramäische Verbum*, p. 6. In the Geonic responsa, the *taw* is often preserved when the first radical is an etymological pharyngeal; see Morgenstern, "Geonic Responsa," pp. 134–35. Breuer, "Karetot," pp. 34–35, has shown that the *taw* is often preserved when the second radical is an etymological ʿ*ayin*. Could the phonological weakening of the middle radical have caused the II-ʿ*ayin* verbs to assimilate partially to the II-*waw-yod* class, wherein the *taw* is always preserved?

**And one must** cease [eating] on the eve of the Day of Atonement while it is still light, as it is written: "And you shall afflict your-selves on the ninth" (Lev 23:32). Could it really mean "on the ninth"? Scripture says "in the evening" (Lev 23:32). If it is "in the evening," could it be from when it gets dark? Scripture says "from the evening" (Lev 23:32). How can this be? One starts to fast while it is still [the previous] day. From this [we derive] that one may add from the profane to the holy. I only find here regarding its [the festival's] entrance, for which we have to cease preemptively. Regarding its exit, from where [do we learn] **that** we **must** require to wait until it gets dark? Scripture says "until the evening" (Lev 23:32). (**HPS** 27:5–10)

### 4.4.5.2.2 I-sibilant Verbs

As mentioned above, the preservation of the *taw*-morpheme is the rule when the first radical is a sibilant and metathesis occurs, e.g., אִישְׁתְּחִיט (**HPS** 308:20). In §3.3.3, we noted that rare examples of assimilation are found, e.g., איצריך "was required" (*Hul* 102a [T-S Misc 26.53]).[54] On one occasion we find an assimilated morpheme interchanging with an unassimilated one: לא **איסתים** גוליל "the rolling stone **was** not **closed**" (**HPS** 261:2), but only several words later, מעידנא **דאיסתתים** גולל "from the time that the rolling stone **was closed**" (**HPS** 261:4).

### 4.4.5.3 Partial Assimilation at Word Boundaries

It has long been noted that the apocopation of final consonants in JBA may sometimes result from the enclitic status of the prepositional *lamed*.[55] According to this theory, the final consonants assimilated to the *lamed* of the preposition, and then, by recutting, the *lamed* was separated from the verbal base, which now no longer bore its final consonant. Evidence for this process may be found, as mentioned, in the manuscript

---

[54] On this early manuscript, see Friedman, "Ancient Scroll," p. 42. אצרוכו "they were required" (*Ket* 97a [**Hark** 150:30]) is probably a copyist's error for אצריכו, unless the *\*i* vowel has been colored by the final *ū* vowel. On this phenomenon, see §3.4.3.3.1. Examples of assimilation of the *taw*-morpheme are also attested on rare occasions in the Aramaic magic bowls; see Morgenstern, "Non-Standard Spellings," p. 272; cf. Nöldeke, *MG*, §164.

[55] See Boyarin, "Final Consonants." As I noted in Chapter 1, Boyarin somewhat overstated his case, as not all losses can be accounted for in this way.

tradition, for example, קיל לה "she is acquainted with" (*Qid* 7b [**HPS** 165:5]) in place of historical קים לה.[56] Above, in §4.3.4, we saw an example of the spelling קי לי for historical קים ליה. The same Talmudic source is cited in **HGP**, where the spelling is קילּיה (*BB* 106b [**HGP** 4a:30]).[57]

Similarly, we find interchanges between various spellings:

> ועדאן לא פליגי אביי ו[רבא] אלא בטלית בלחוד וכיוצא בה מידעם דכל
> איניש **קיל ליה** ביה, דאביי סבר אפילו טלית דכל אדם **קים ליה** בגוה לא
> סמכינן אלא אתגר בכרכין עד כדי שיראה לתגר דשכיחין תגרין ובכפרים עד
> ערבי שבתות דאתו תגרים או דאזלין בני ההוא כפר להיכא דאיכא תגרים
> וקסבר סלע וטלית חד דינא אינון ורבא סבר מדעם דכל איניש **קים ליה** ביה
> בין בכפרים ובין בכרכים וכו׳...

There is still no disagreement between Abbaye and [Rava] except regarding a garment, or, similarly, something in which everyone **would be expert**;[58] for Abbaye holds that even regarding a garment, in which everyone **is expert**, we only depend upon the merchants from the towns. "Until he shows it to a merchant"—for merchants are frequent—"and in the villages: until the eve of Sabbath"—for the merchants come or the people of that village go to where there are merchants. He holds that a coin and a garment are one law; but Rava assumes that something in which everyone **is expert**, whether in a village or a town, etc. (**Hark** 44:31–45:1)[59]

For a possible explanation of this variation, see §4.4.6 below.

---

[56] On this idiom, see Sokoloff, *DJBA*, p. 995.

[57] Already cited in Sokoloff, *DJBA*, p. 995. An additional example appears in Morag, *Vocalised Manuscripts*, p. 50, no. 164.

[58] The Mishna (*BM* 4:3) declares that a buyer may go back on a fraudulent deal, and has as much time as it would take to show it to a merchant or a relative, i.e., an expert who would be able to determine the quality of the merchandise. Abbaye and Rava disagree as to whether this rule applies to simple items on which the buyer himself should be expert.

[59] Harkavy emended the form קיל ליה in his transcription, but, as was his custom, he noted this carefully in his footnotes.

## 4.4.5.4 Dissimilation

It appears that E.Y. Kutscher was the first scholar to question the claim of complementary distribution between C forms and D forms of את״י, and to claim that all of the transitive forms meaning "to bring" were in fact in the C.[60] Kutscher explained the lack of the *yod* following the *ʾaleph* in forms such as אתייה "he brought it" (e.g., **Hark** 272:28) and אתיוה "they brought him" (*BM* 84b [**G1**]) as resulting from dissimilation.[61] Boyarin refined Kutscher's explanation and proposed that the dissimilation occurs when the second (root) *yod* directly follows the *taw*.[62] Support for this distribution may now be found in two parallel Aramaic magic bowls. In one case, the client is male, and the verbal form used is מיתי "he brings" (Moussaieff 145:14), while in the parallel text the client is feminine, and accordingly we find the form מתיא "she brings" (Schøyen 2053/159:15).[63]

However, there is some variance in the application of these rules. For example, for the fixed expression "she brought forth two [pubic] hairs"[64] we find דאֵתאֵי שתי שערות (**HPS** 237:21), while in parallel rulings we read אי אֵיתאֵי שתי שערות (**HPS** 236:19, 239:21), והוא דאיתאי שתי שערות (**HPS** 239:1–2). This example would seem to suggest that dissimilation occurred not only when the *taw* was directly followed by a consonantal *yod*, but also when it was preceded and followed by *ay* diphthongs.[65]

Still more problematic are the variant forms מיתינן "we bring" (**HPS** 303:2) // מֵתִיֵּנָן (**HPS** 302:19).[66] Given that the diphthong *\*ay* is preserved

---

[60] The alternative position was that of Rosenthal, *Die Sprache*, and Drower–Macuch, *MD*, p. 42.

[61] Kutscher, "Hermopolis Papyri," p. 107 n. 21 (reprinted in Kutscher, *Studies*, p. 57 n. 21 [English section]).

[62] Boyarin, "Studies," p. 174.

[63] Levene, *Corpus*, p. 101.

[64] This is a sign of having reached maturity, with many legal implications, particularly in the field of marriage law.

[65] By analogy, the 3 f.s. perfect morphemes were employed in all the III-*yod* verbs regardless of their original theme vowel. Hence, instead of איתיאת (e.g., **HPS** 179:1) *ʾayʾtiyʾat* > איתיא (found only rarely, e.g., *Nid* 20b [**Vat** 113; Ashkenazi MS]) *ʾayʾtiyʾa*, we find אֵיתאֵי *ʾaytay* which employs the 3 f.s. morpheme -*ay*. The -*ay* morpheme is presumably derived from forms with an *a* theme-vowel by the process *\*baʾnayat* > *\*baʾnaya* > *baʾnay*, as proposed by Kutscher, "Review," p. 169 (reprinted in Kutscher, *Studies*, p. 247).

[66] The same vocalized form also appears in **HPS** 2:18, while unvocalized forms appear in *MQ* 27a [**HPS** 267:11], **HPS** 303:6, 8; 307:6.

in this manuscript's tradition, the first form may be read *maytinnan*, while the vocalization of the second suggests should be read *matyinnan*. The difference may arise because of the interchange of the 1 c.pl. morphemes in III-*yod* roots. See further below, §4.5.4.4. However, the fact that we also find the form מֵיתִיֵּין (*BM* 70a [**HGP** 25b:20]; *San* 29a [**HGP** 38a:34]) suggests that the final morpheme is not the determining factor, or that the dissimilation did not occur in all cases. The precise conditions for the distribution of these forms are even more difficult to determine since in the linguistic tradition of MS Paris of *Halachot Gedolot*, the diphthongs have been contracted, at least in the vocalizer's tradition.[67]

### 4.4.5.5. Anaptyxis

The consonant cluster *VCCəCV* shifts to *VCiCCV*, e.g., וניכיתבו "and let them write" (*BQ* 103a [**GS** iv 1b 1]), through the process \**wəniḵtəḇū* > *wənikitḇū*.[68] This phenomenon is similarly attested in the Aramaic magic bowls.[69]

Forms bearing the anaptyctic vowel are found alongside forms showing no evidence for it, e.g.:

> והכא תרגימו **תיקדמה** יונך ליון שאומרין אם יונך תקדום אתן לך כך ואם
> יוני תקדום תתן לי כך. ולמאן דאמ׳ **תיקידמה** יונך ליון מאי טעמי לא אמ׳
> ארא. מפני דרכי שלום בעלמא ולא גזל הוא. ולמאן דאמ׳ ארא מאי טעמי לא
> אמ׳ **תיקידמה** יונך ליון. אמי׳ לך כי האומרין אם תקדום ואם לא תדקום
> הינו משחק בקוביא. ומי שפרש מפריח יונים משום **תיקדמה** יונך ליון
> שנוטל זה מזה בלא משפט שלא גמר זה להקנותו.

Here they interpreted: "If your dove **overtakes** my dove," i.e., they say "If your dove will overtake [it] I will give you such-and-such and if my dove will overtake [it] you will give me such-and-such." According to one who says [the Mishna discusses the case of] "If your dove **overtakes** my dove," why did it not mention the decoy-bird? It is only a case of good manners, not of theft. According to one who says [the Mishna discusses the case of] the decoy-bird, why did he not say [it discusses the case of] "If your dove **over-takes** my dove?" He would say to you: "Those who say 'If it over-takes [it], if it doesn't overtake [it]' fall into the category of dice-

---

[67] Morag, "Vocalisation," p. 92 (reprinted in Morag, *Studies*, p. 200).

[68] I assume here that the *rap̄e* pronunciation of the *kap* and *bet* remained unchanged.

[69] See §3.3.2.

players." One who interprets the expression מפריח יונה [setting a dove to flight] as meaning "If your dove **overtakes** my dove," it is because one person takes from the other person illegally, because he never intended to transfer ownership. (**Hark** 182:14–19)

It is impossible to determine if we are dealing here with a phonological phenomenon or merely an orthographic one. It is feasible that all the above examples were pronounced *tiqidmah,* but that the second (anaptyctic) *i* vowel was not always represented in the orthography. Evidence of this phenomenon may be found in another manuscript wherein we find the form למשׁחטֶה "to slaughter it" (*BM* 85a [**G1**]).[70]

### 4.4.6 Analysis

Such a multiplicity of spellings in these various categories open to several different interpretations. It is possible that they reflect different phonological realities, representing different historical stages of the form's development, e.g., קים ליה *qīm leh,* קיל ליה *qīl leh,* קׂיליה *qīlleh*[71] and קי לי *qī le.* However, it is also possible that all the spellings reflect only one phonological reality, perhaps *qīlle* or *qīle,* and that the various orthographies are different attempts to reach a compromise between the historical and phonetic forms. The historical orthography may disguise the phonological realities.

## 4.5 Verbal morphology

### 4.5.1 Perfect

#### 4.5.1.1 3 f.s.

The morpheme of the 3 f.s. perfect in Aramaic is *\*at* ( > -*at̯*);[72] however, in RBA we frequently we find the apocopation of the final *t̯,* often accompanied by the rounding of the *\*a* vowel to [ɔ].[73] This unstressed final vowel was also sometimes apocopated, which caused the merger of the 3 f.s. perfect forms with those of the 3 m.s.: *\*qə'atlat > \*qə'tala* (> [*\*qə'talɔ*]) >

---

[70] So MS. The phenomenon was noted in Friedman, "Early Manuscripts," 25, but the orthography should be corrected there.

[71] Note that **HGP** marks short and long *i* vowels, and the long vowel sign is employed here.

[72] The morpheme of the III-*yod* verbs, -*āt̯,* is not discussed here.

[73] For this phenomenon, see Boyarin, "Studies," 173.

*qə'tal*.[74] Since it seems that [a] and [ɔ] are allophones, and that the [ɔ] allophone was not found in all traditions of RBA, the third stage is not essential to the development of the fourth.

In fact, three endings are attested in RBA, e.g., נְפֻֿקֶת *nə'paqat̲* "came out" (**HPS** 307:19), נְחִיתָֿא *nə'hita* "she went down" (**HPS** 59:20), and תפס *tə'p̄as* "she seized" (*Ket* 98a [**HPS** 160:1]), even alongside one another:

> וְאִילוֹֿ אִיתְּתָֿא דִּילֹדָא זְכר וְנֻקְֿבָֿה לֹתבָֿא אַרֹבֹסֹר יוֹֿמֹי טְמָֿאֹה דִּנֻקְֿבָֿה וִיוֹֿמֹי
> טְהֹרֹה דִּנֻקְֿבָֿה שֹׁתִין וְשֹׁיתָֿא. וְהֹיֹכָֿא דִּילִֿיד חד וּלְבָֿתֹֿר כְֿמָֿא יוֹֿמֹי הֹדֹר **יִלֹדָֿא**
> אָֿחֹדֹֿנָֿא לֹתבָֿא יְמֹי טְמָֿאֹה וִיְמֹי טְהֹרֹה לְשֹׁיֹנִֿי. וְאֹילוֹ אֹיתְּתָֿא דְֿ**אָֿפֹילֿת** שֹׁילֹיֹא
> בְֿעָֿלְֿמָֿא ...

Whereas a woman who gives birth to a male and female sits the fourteen days of impurity for the female and the days of purity for the female, sixty-six. If **she gave birth** to one and after a few days **she gave birth** to another, she sits the days of impurity and days of purity for the second. Whereas a woman who only **aborted** a placenta... (**HPS** 212:18–21)

In this passage, not only are all three forms employed together, but two are even employed with the same verbal form in the same sentence. The entire passage appears in a vocalized section of **HPS**, and the vocalization clearly indicates that the three morphemes were distinct in their pronunciation.

This phenomenon is quite common in the manuscript tradition. Cf. the following examples:

> אבל ההוא שבח דְ**אשבחת** ארעא מימילה לא מחייב יהודה למיהביה
> לשמעון. דאמרינן נהי הא הא תוספה שמעי' אוספה מן ממוניה וקא שקיל ליה
> השתא. אבל מאי דְ**אשבחא** ארעא נפשה אמי' ליה יהודה ארעאי דילי הוא
> **דאשבח**. והדר שמעי' על הדין לוי דקביל ליה אחרויות וגאבי מיניה עיקר

---

[74] This explanation was first proposed by Kutscher, "Review," pp. 168–69 (reprinted in Kutscher, *Studies*, pp. 246–47). Kutscher notes that the previous discussions of this phenomenon (Nöldeke, *MG*, p. 420 n. 3; Levias, *Diqduq*, p. 291; Schlesinger, *Satzlehre*, pp. 53ff.) had assumed it was a syntactic rather than phonological phenomenon. The existence of these forms has been confirmed by subsequent manuscript findings; see Kara, *Yemenite Manuscripts*, p. 142; Morgenstern, "Geonic Responsa," p. 139. I have now found many more examples in early manuscripts, and these will appear in my forthcoming grammar.

דמים וגאבי מיניה ההוא שבאחא ד**אשבחת** ארעא מימילה דהכין הוא דינא
דאחריות.

However, that improvement that the land **improved** by itself Yehuda does not need to give to Shimᶜon , as we say: "Granted, the
increase that Shimᶜon increased from his own money and is now
taking; but regarding that which the land itself **improved**, Yehuda
would say, 'It's my land that **improved**'." And Shimᶜon goes back
to that Levi who took upon himself the surety, and collects from
him the principal sum and also collects from him [the value of]
that improvement that the land **improved** by itself, because thus is
the law of sureties. (**Hark** 204:28–33)

אם איתה **דאפילא** לא מחזקא נפשה בעקראתא.

If she had really **aborted**, she would not ascribe to herself the reputation of the barren. (*Yev* 65b [**HPS** 177:21])

which parallels:

אילא **דאפיל** תלתה לא הוה מחזקא נפשה בניפלי.

Had she not **aborted** three [times], she would not ascribe to herself
the reputation of miscarriages. (*Yev* 65b [**HPS** 178:3])

וכי מיתזאנא מימקרקעי ולא מימטלטלי. ואי **תפס** מטלטלי. **תפסא** לה.
דאמ' ר' אלעזר : אלמנה שתפסה מטלטלין במזונותיה. מה שתפסה תפסה.
והני מילי והוא **דתפס** מיחיים דבעל. אבל **תפס** לאחר המיתה. לאו כל
כמינה. וכי קא אמרינן דוקא לימזוני. אבל לכתובה אפילו **תפסא** מיחיים
ולא כלום. כוליה כי היכין דכתיבא.

But when she is supported by land and not by movables, if she
**seized** movables, she has **seized**. *As R. Eliezer says: A widow who
seized movables for her support, whatever she seized, she seized* (*Ket* 96b).
These words apply when she **seized** during the husband's lifetime;
but if she **seized** after [his] death, she is not empowered to do so.
When we say so, it is specifically for maintenance. But for her

ketubba, even if **she seized** during his lifetime, it is nothing; it all
goes according to what is written. (**HPS** 183:18–184:2)

ומאי טעמא דלא סמך בעל אדיבורא דאשתו ד**שויא** שליח לקבלה.

And why did the husband not rely on his wife's word that **she had appointed** an emissary to receive it? (**TGAs28** iv 5a 21)

which parallels:

אבל הכא לא סמך בעל [א]מימרה דאשה ד**שיואת** שליח לקבלה.

But here the husband did not rely upon his wife's word that **she had appointed** an emissary to receive it. (ibid., 28)

Similarly these examples:

והיכא ד**עיילא** ליה בהמה או עבדי.

And if **she brought in** [to the marriage] for him a beast or slaves. (**HPS** 179:10–11)

which parallels:

והיכא דמיתן הנך אמהאתא ובהמה ד**עיילת** ליה.

If those maidservants and [the] beast **that she brought in** [to the marriage] for him died. (**HPS** 179:15–16)

הואיל וכד **נפקא** מיעיקרה **נפקת** בקלא דלא פסיק ובדבר מכוער.

Since when she initially **left**, she **left** through a rumor that does not cease and through a repulsive thing. (**HPS** 209:12–13)

והוא ד**שחייה** עשר שנין.

And that is in the case that **she waited** ten years. (**HPS** 177:17)

which parallels:

והיכא דלא **שהת** עשר שנין.

And if **she had** not **waited** ten years. (**HPS** 178:4)

## 4.5.1.2 3 m.pl.

In the 3 m.pl. perfect of all verb classes except III-*yod*, RBA employs three morphemes. One is the old Aramaic suffix *-ū, which appears to have remained unstressed in the strong verb and was perhaps realized as short *u* when standing in word-final position, e.g., שְׁלַחוּ "they sent" (*RH* 27a [**HPS** 24:18]).[75] The second is an infixed *u* or *ū* vowel, e.g., אֲמוּר "they sent" (*Yeb* 50b [**HPS** 255:17]). In the third form, the final vowel is apocopated, e.g., פַּשׁ "they remained" (**Hark** 273:22).[76] It is hard to determine specific conditions for the use of these various forms. A single root may be attested in all of them, ruling out a simple morphological explanation. For example, for עלל/עול "to enter" we find עיילו (**TGAs42** 61:30), עול (*Shev* 48b [**Hark** 110:29]), and עָיוֹל (*MQ* 12a [**HPS** 280:20]), all meaning "they entered."

The following examples are particularly striking. First, we find the same Talmudic passage, *BM* 110b, cited twice in the legal codex **HPS** *with varying grammatical forms.* The first occurrence is a reworked citation appearing in **HPS** 83:10–12: ויתמי ניתו ראיה ראיה ונישקלו. ואי איתו יתמי ראיה דאינהו **אשבחו**, מסלקינן להו בדמי "Let the orphans bring proof and collect; and if the orphans brought proof that it was they who **made the improvements** [of the land], we remove them [i.e., satisfy their claim] with the value." A lengthier reworked citation of *BM* 110b appears at **HPS** 144:9–12:[77]

הכי אמ' רבי יוחנן : על היתומים להביא ראיה. מאי טעמא? ארעא כיון דלגביאנא קימא כמאן דגביא דאמי. ויתמי ניתו ראיה ונישקלו. איתו יתמי ראיה דאינהו **אשבוח**. סבר רבי חנניה למימר. בארעא מסלקינן להו. ולא היא. בדמי מסלקינן להו.

---

[75] Evidence for the lack of stress may be found in the preservation of the short stem vowels in open syllable, e.g., שְׁלַחוּ (cited above), דְּדַחִילוּ "that they feared" (**HPS** 259:19) and דְּשְׁלִימוּ "that they were completed" (**HPS** 40:19). We may suppose that this *-ū morpheme was shortened to *-u* in unstressed word-final position since it is often elided. By contrast, in the III-*yod* class, it is never elided, implying that it remained stressed and, presumably, long.

[76] See Luzzatto, *Elementi grammaticali*, §69; Epstein, *Grammar*, p. 47, and n. 70; Kutscher, "Review," pp. 165–67 (reprinted in Kutscher, *Studies*, pp. 243–45); Boyarin, "Studies," p. 175; Friedman, "Early Manuscripts," p. 24; Kara, *Yemenite Manuscripts*, pp. 144–45; Morgenstern, "Geonic Responsa," pp. 142–143. Cf. the evidence of the magic bowls: Juusola, *Linguistic Peculiarities*, pp. 163–69; Morgenstern, "Magic Bowl," p. 215, and "Moussaieff Collection," pp. 357–58. In Morgenstern, "Non-Standard Spellings," §6.2, I discussed the evidence from the magic bowls for the apocopation of the imperative *-ū* morpheme, and its free interchange with the historical form.

[77] The citation has slightly shortened the Talmudic discussion as preserved in our textual witnesses, e.g., MS **H165**.

So said R. Yohanan: The orphans must bring proof. What is the reason? Since the land is collectable, it is as though it were already collected; hence the orphans must bring proof and take. The orphans brought proof that they had **made the improvements**. R. Hanina considered saying "We remove them [i.e., satisfy their claim] with land." But this is not so; we satisfy their claims with the value.

Cf. also the following example:

| Ket 84b | |
|---|---|
| HPS 78:14 | HPS 78:10 |
| **דון** דיאני כר׳ טרפון. | **דאנו** דיאני כרבי טרפון. |
| ואהדריה ריש לקיש לעובדא מיניה. | ואהדריה רבי שמעון בן לקיש לעובדא מיניהו. |

The judges **judged** according to R. Tarfon, and R. Shimʿon ben Laqish[78] reversed their decision.

| BB 172a | |
|---|---|
| HPS 202:9–12 | HPS 104:3–5 |
| אמר ראבא. האיי מאן דנקיט שטרא בר מאה | אמ׳ ראבא. האיי מן דנקיט שטרא בר מאה |
| ואמ׳. שוויה ניה לי תרי בני חמשין חמשין. | ואמ׳. שוויה ניה לי תרי בני חמשי חמשי |
| לא משיינן ניה ליה. | לא משגחינן ביה. |
| מאי טעמא. | מאי טעמא. |
| **עבדו** רבנן מילתא דניחא ליה ללווה וניחא ליה למלוה. | **עבוד** רבנן מילתא דניחא ליה ללווה וניחא ליה למלוה. |

Rava says: "A person who holds a deed of a hundred and says, change it into two of fifty each—we do not pay attention to him/we

---

[78] The free interchange between the two forms of this Amora's name, רבי שמעון בן לקיש and ריש לקיש is discussed by Wajsberg, "Taxonomy." The interchange is also found in a single context in MS Oxford of *Karetot*. See Breuer, "Karetot," p. 41.

do not change it for him."[79] Why? The rabbis **acted** in a way that satisfies the borrower and satisfies the lender.

בי תלתא **דנחית** ביתרי **ופלוג** ולא הוה אידך למיפלג בהדייהו הכי נמי דבטלה מחלוקת. אמ' ליה. התם מאיקבה אדעתא דבי תלתא **נחיתו**. הכא לאו אדעתא דבי תלתה **נחיתו**.

A group of three [partners] from whom two **went off and divided**, *and the other one was not there to divide with them*—so too the division is annulled. In that case, **they** originally **went off** at the will of the three; here, it was not at the will of the three that **they went off**. (*BB* 106b [**HPS** 150:1–3, with explanatory gloss, here in italics])

In this case, all three plural forms appear: נחיתו, נחית, and פלוג.

## 4.5.2 Imperfect

Elsewhere I have tried to prove that the Talmudic form of the masculine imperfect suffix is *-ū*, e.g., נישקלו "let them take" (*BM* 110b [**HPS** 83:11, 144:11]) or לישלמו "let them pay" (*BM* 83a [**HPS** 114:21]). By contrast, the Geonim occasionally employ forms with the suffix *-ūn*, e.g., ליכתבון "let them write" (**Hark** 102:13), alongside the Talmudic forms.[80] In the early manuscripts I have found no certain examples of נקטלון, i.e., the *nun* prefix morpheme used alongside the *-ūn* suffix.[81] I have found few exceptions to this rule. In Geonic citations of the Talmud, we occasionally find the long imperfect forms, e.g.: להוון "let them be" (*BM* 49b [**HPS** 127:17]), though such examples are rare.[82]

---

[79] There is no apparent reason for the interchange of these two verbs.

[80] When the Geonim employ the shorter forms, they use the *lamed-* and *nun-* prefixed forms without any apparent distinction.

[81] Morgenstern, "Geonic Responsa," pp. 148–49. One apparent exception cited there would appear to be נ]יכיתבון] "they should write" (*Git* 40a [**Geon** viii 37b 19]). However, further collation with the manuscript has revealed that the manuscript is torn, and that the reading of the first *nun* is uncertain.

[82] I have assumed here that the morpheme was vocalized *ūn*, rather than *ōn* found in III-*yod* verbs in BA and TOJ, since we find the vocalized form להוּן (**HPS** 30:17). However, one could feasibly argue that the same complementary distribution between the vowel of the word-final closed syllable ון- and that of the word-final open syllable ו- existed in these forms as is found in the suffixed pronouns,

On at least one occasion we find apparently unconditioned inter-change of the "Talmudic" and "Geonic" forms:

אמ׳ להו : לא **תימרו** ליה. אמי׳ רב זביד. הא קא אמי׳ להו : לא **תימרו** ליה. רב
פפא אמי׳ : לדיליה דלא **תימרון** ליה. לאחריני אימרו להו.

He said to them: "Don't **tell** him." R. Zabid says "Look, he says to them 'Don't **tell** him'"! R. Pappa said, "It's *him* **you should not tell**; as for the others, tell them!" (*BB* 39a [**HPS** 138:21–139:1])

Surprisingly, it is actually the longer forms that are consistently used in MS **H165**:

אמי׳ : לא **תאמרון** ליה לפלי׳. אמי׳ רב זביד. הא קאמי׳. לא **תאמרון** ליה לפלי׳.
אמי׳ רב פפא. לדידיה לא **תימרון** ליה. לאחריני אמרו.

By contrast, in **HGP** 2a:10–11, we find the same text cited with only the short forms:

אמ להו לא **תימרו** ליה אמי׳ ר׳ זביד הא קאמי׳ לא **תימרו** ליה ר׳ פפא
אמ לדידיה הנ[ו]א דלא **תימרו** ליה לאחריני אימר(ו)[ו] ליה.

### 4.5.3 Imperative

In §3.4.3.3, we noted the existence of an infixed -$\bar{u}$- morpheme for the 2 m.pl. imperative that parallels the corresponding infixed morpheme in the perfect (and perhaps imperfect). As in the case of the infixed mor-pheme in the perfect, this morpheme seems to occur in free interchange with the suffixed -$\bar{u}$ morpheme, as in the following example:

ההוא חמארא דיקטע ידא דינוקא. אתא לקמיה דרב פפא בר שמואל.
אמלהו : **זילו** שימו ליה ארבעה דברים.
אמי׳ ליה ראבה. והא חמשה האו!
אמליה : לבר מנזקיה קא אמנא.
אמיליה : והא[83] ושור אין משלמים אילא נזק!
אמלהו : **זילו** שימו ליה ניזקיה.
אמליה : והא בעבדא בעיי מישימיה!

---

e.g., לְהוֹן "them" (**HPS** 57:17; 224: 19) and לְהו֗ (**HPS** 33:19; 219:19), though in that case the original vowel was short. See further below, §4.6.4.

[83] In margins: חמור הוא. וחמור כשור.

אמ' להו : **זילו** שימוה בעבדא.

אמ' להו אבוה : הואיל ובעבדא הוא לא בעינא משום דזילא לי מילתא.

אמרי ליה : והא קא חיב את ליה לינוקא.

לכי גדיל מפייס ליה מדיליה.

ההוא תורא דאלס ידא דינוקא. אתא לקמיה ראבא.

אמלהו : **זול** שימוה בעבדא.

A certain donkey severed the hand of a child. [The matter] came before R. Pappa son of Shemuel. He said to them: **"Go** [and] assess him according to four criteria."[84] Rava said: "They are five!" He said to him: "I meant without his damage." He said to him: "But with an ox one pays only damage."[85] He said to them: **"Go** [and] assess him his damage." He said to him: "He[86] has to assess him as a slave." He said to them: **"Go** and assess him as a slave!" His [the boy's] father said to them: "Since it is as a slave, I don't want it, since it is a disgrace to me." They said to him: "Then you owe the child!" "When he grows up, I [lit., "he"] shall pay him from my [lit., "his"] own."[87]

A certain ox chewed the hand of a child. [The matter] came before Rava. He said: **Go** [and] assess him as a slave! (*BQ* 84a [**G1**])

It is possible that the interchange here results from the fact that the form זול belongs to a different story, and may have been drawn from another source. Alternatively, it might have the prosodic function of marking the end of the discourse unit. The distinction between the consistent use of זילו in the first story and the use of זול in the second is also maintained in MS H165. Further research is required to determine the prosodic role of variant forms in Babylonian Aramaic.[88]

---

[84] *M. BQ* 8:1 lists five criteria according to which a person who causes injury must pay the injured party.

[85] The marginal note adds: "It's a donkey. And [the law of] a donkey is like [the law of] an ox."

[86] I interpret the form בעיי here is a pseudo-historical spelling for *bāye*.

[87] Literally, "He shall pay him from his own"; the father refers to himself in the 3 m.s.

[88] The prosodic nature of pausal forms in Tiberian Hebrew has recently been studied in DeCaen, "Distribution," with previous bibliography. The pausal forms in the Babylonian-Yemenite tradition of Targum Onqelos are discussed in Dodi, "Pausal Forms," while the evidence of Rabbinic Hebrew is gathered in Bar-

### 4.5.4. Participles

#### 4.5.4.1 M. pl. Morpheme

The sporadic apocopation of the word-final *n* of the historical masculine plural morpheme -*īn* has led to the use of two alternative forms in this category, i.e., -*īn* and -*ī*.[89] Both are extremely common, with perhaps a slight preference for the historical form in Geonic literature in contrast to the apocopated form in the Talmud.[90] Occasionally, we find these forms interchanging even within a single context. Let us start with a Talmudic citation:

מה אחות אשה לא **תפסין** בה קידושי. אף כל העריות כלן לא **תפסי** בהי קידושי.

> Just as in the case of a wife's sister, the betrothal **is invalid**, so in the case of all the prohibited unions, the betrothal **is invalid**. (*Qid* 67b [**HPS** 224:5–6])

The same phenomenon is attested in the Geonic portions of *Halachot Pe-suqot*: ואף-על-גב **דמיגירי**, דכתי' בהון עד עולם "And even though **they convert**, for it is written of them 'forever' (Deut 23:4)" (**HPS** 224:17), אבל מצרי ואדומי כי **מיגירי** תרין דארי **אסירין** למיעל בקהל "But the Egyptian or the Edomite, if **they convert, they are forbidden** to enter the community for two generations."[91] But contrast: כותים כי **מיגירין** יין נסך לא משואן כי איתייה ברשותא דישראל ונגע ביה "Cutheans [Samaritans], if **they convert**, they do not render wine impure when it belongs to a Jew and he touched it." (**HPS** 225:3–4); ממזרי ונתיני אף על גב **דמיגירין** לא עיילין בקהל עד עולם "*Mamzers* and *nethins*, even though **they convert**, never enter the community" (**HPS** 225:4–5).

Similarly in a Geonic responsum, we find: וכל ברייתא **דפליגין** עלה בתלמוד "And any *baraitha* about which **they disagree** in the Talmud"

---

Asher, "Contextual and Pausal Forms," republished in French in Bar-Asher, *L'hébreu mishnique*, pp. 105–83.

[89] On this distinction, see §3.4.4.1.1.

[90] Cf. Morgenstern, "Geonic Responsa," pp. 153–56. Breuer, "Karetot," p. 10, has found that about one fifth of the participle forms in MS **O1** of *Karetot* employ the ין- plural.

[91] Note that the participle אסירין has the unapocopated form.

(**Geon** xxxviii 6b 5) contrasting with וכל מילתא דבמתניתין **פליגי בה** "And anything in the Mishna about which **they disagree**" (**Geon** xxxviii 6b 19).

It is not clear what conditions the use of either form. While from the examples cited above it may appear that the *nun* is preserved prior to a word beginning with an *ʿayin* (which might indicate that the other examples represent assimilation across word boundaries), it must be emphasized that the apocopated forms are also attested preceding an *ʿayin*, e.g., למימרא **דפליגי** עליה בחד אחא "That is to say that they disagree about it in the case of a single brother" (**HPS** 246:6–7).

### 4.5.4.2 1 m.s. Participle of אמ״ר

In §3.4.6.3, we saw that the older forms of the 1 c.s. G participle of אמ״ר are אמרנא *āmarnā* and (through assimilation) אמנא *āmannā*, and that the later form, אמינא, finds little support in the EEMss. However, in at least one example all three (!) forms appear side by side:

> **ואמרנא**. אי מהדרנא לה לארעא **ואמרנא** דאית לי זוזי. אמור רבנן. הבא
> ליפרע מיניכסי יתומים לא יפרע אילא בשבועה. אילא איכלה שיעור זוזי.
> דמיגו דאי בעינא **אמינא**. לקוחה בידי. כי **אמנא** דאית לי זוזי. מהימננא.

> I said [to myself]:[92] "If I return the land and **I say** that I have [a claim on] money, the Rabbis said: 'One who seeks recompense from orphans' property can only be repaid through an oath.' Instead, I shall use it [the land] to the value of the money. Because, since if I wanted to, **I can say** 'I bought it,' if **I say** that I have [a claim on] money, I will be believed." (*BB* 33a [**HPS** 191:3–6])

### 4.5.4.3 3 m.pl. Passive Participle of III–*yod*

The forms of the III-*yod* participle plural are numerous in the Aramaic dialects, and even within RBA we find a wide variety.[93] I have found one example of interchange between two alternative forms. In a responsum

---

[92] The participle of אמ״ר is often employed in narratives with a preterite meaning.

[93] The seminal discussion is that of Morag, "Geniza," pp. 68–70 (reprinted in Morag, *Studies*, pp. 301–3). See further Friedman, "Early Manuscripts," pp. 28–31; Kara, *Yemenite Manuscripts*, pp. 169–71; Morgenstern, "Geonic Responsa," pp. 176–79 and "Moussaieff Collection," p. 351.

of R. Natronai Gaon, containing a commentary on *Shab* 47a (here in italics), we find:[94]

> וכי תימ׳: *חזו* הני קרטין לעניים. ומי אמרינן הכין? *והתניא*. בגדי עניים
> לעניים ובגדי עשירים לעשירים. אבל בגדי עניים לעשירים לא. לעניין טמאה
> קאמרינן. בגד שיש בו ג׳ טפח׳ על ג׳ טפח׳ חזי לעש׳ ומיקרי בגדי עשירים.
> מטלות שאין בה אילא ג׳ אצבעות על ג׳ אצבעות אין ראויה אילא לעניים
> ומיקרי בגדי עניב. וקאמרינן: אבל בגדי עניים והן שלעשירים לא מקבלי
> טמאה. הכא נמי הני קרטין אף על גב *דחזיי לעניים* לגבי עשירים לא
> מטלטלינן.

And if you should say: These grains [of spice] **are fitting** for paupers. Do we say so? But is it not taught: "Paupers' clothes for paupers, rich men's clothes for rich men, but not paupers' clothes for rich men?" (*Shab* 47a) Regarding impurity, we say: "A garment that is three hand-breadths by three hand-breadths is fitting for rich men and is called rich men's clothing; a rag that is only three finger-widths by three-finger widths is only suitable for paupers and is called paupers' garments." And we say, "But paupers' garments belonging to rich men do not receive impurity." Here too, these grains—though they **are fitting** for paupers—regarding rich men we do not move them [on the Sabbath].' (**Geon** xxxviii 4a 13–20 = Brody, *Teshuvot*, p. 587, no. 425.)

In this case, it is possible that the statement at the end of the responsum, דחזיי לעניים "they are fitting for paupers" is not merely a Talmudic citation, but a complete reworking of the Talmudic source in Geonic language, and that accordingly, the "Talmudic" form דחזו "[that] are fitting"[95] has been replaced by a Geonic form דחזיי.[96] The "Talmudic" form is attested elsewhere in the EEMss, e.g., חזו "they are fitting" (*BQ* 97b

---

[94] The words of the Talmudic text have been presented in italics. The discussion revolves around items that it is permissible to move on the Sabbath, owing to some immediate utility that they have for the Sabbath day.

[95] According to HPS, the 3 m.s. active participle morpheme of the III-*yod* verbs is -*ū*, as in מְלוֹ "are completed" (**HPS** 306:21). קָארוֹ "they call it" (*Suk* 30b [**HPS** 41:21]). See above, §3.4.4.2. I assume that the passive participle is to be vocalized *ḥazū*, though there is some evidence to suggest that the penultimate stress may have caused the first vowel to be lengthened to *ā*, e.g., חאזיי "fitting" (e.g., **Hark** 48:23). See Morgenstern, "Geonic Responsa," pp. 74, 292.

[96] Cf. the detailed discussion of this phenomenon in Morgenstern, "Geonic Responsa," pp. 11–13.

[**G1**]),[97] while the latter form is found vocalized in a Geonic passage in **HPS**: דְּחָזִיֵי "that they are fitting" (**HPS** 230:19). The form חָזִיֵי would appear to be built upon analogy to the feminine passive participles, e.g., רְמִיָא "is incumbent" (*Shev* 41b [**HPS** 199:18]) and שָׁרִיָאן "are permitted" (**HPS** 224:17). I would cautiously suggest that the form חזיי may be regarded a Geonic form.

### 4.5.4.4 1 c.pl. Active Participle of III–*yod*

In the printed editions of the Talmud, the 1 c.pl. participles of the III-*yod* verbs always bear the ending -ינן, e.g., חזינן "we see." However, in the EEMss, the range of forms found in this category is wider. Alongside the forms attested in the printed editions, e.g., חזינן "we see" (*Ket* 85a [**HPS** 100:4]), we also find חזיינן (*Git* 58b [**TGAs28** ii a 5]),[98] חזנן (*BM* 108a [**HPS** 141:17, 21]), and שרונן "we permit" (*BQ* 113a [**HPS** 124:19]).[99] R. Sharrira and R. Hai Gaon employ the forms חזיינא "we see" (e.g., **Hark** 34:27, 51:8) and חזינא (**Hark** 47:23). In addition, we find the examples of בנן "we require," derived from בע"יי, which were discussed in §3.3.1.1.2.

It would appear that all of these forms were based upon the III-*yod* plural base *qāṭayn*[100] + pronoun *-nan* or *nā*.[101] The *ay* diphthong was quite unstable before the *nun*, and occasionally shifted to *ā* (realized as

---

[97] Cf. also the examples cited by Kara, *Yemenite Manuscripts*, p. 286, e.g., חזו "are fitting" (*Pes* 17b [**JTS**1628]). I suspect that in spite of the vocalization, forms such as סָנֵי "are hated" (*Meg* 25b [**Col**]) may be scribal errors for סנו. The existence of these forms must be proven on the basis of the EEMss. In any case, from the examples cited here and those found in the Yemenite manuscripts, it is clear that Müller-Kessler, "Targum Onqelos," p. 189, is incorrect in listing מחין as *the* Babylonian Talmudic Aramaic form of the 3 m.pl. passive participle of III-*yod*.

[98] Assaf erroneously read חזיינו.

[99] My reading according to the facsimile edition; Dr. Kara, in his transcription, which I received from the Academy of the Hebrew Language, read שרינן.

[100] As in בָּנַיִן "they are building" (Ezra 5:4). Cf. Morag, "Geniza," p. 70 (reprinted in Morag, *Studies*, p. 303), and see Kutscher, *SGA*, p. 43.

[101] Prof. Moshe Assis has suggested to me that the forms of the pronoun spelled -ננא may be vocalized *-nānā* < *\*(a)ʾnahnā*. If he is correct, then the spellings חזיינא and חזיננא would represent different forms, *hazaynnā* and *hazaynānā* respectively. In Morgenstern, "Geonic Responsa," p. 26, I interpreted spellings such as חזיננא as examples of digraphs on morpheme boundaries and hence regarded these as orthographic variants of *hazaynnā*. Such digraphs are found elsewhere, e.g., זביננא "I buy" (*BQ* 103a [**GS** iv 1b 5]).

[ā]~[ɔ:]).[102] The vocalization of these forms in MS **G1** of *Bava Mezia* implies that examples in defective orthography (חזנן) may have been pronounced with the *ā* ([ɔ]) vowel: מבקָן "we search" (*BM* 70a [**G1**]), מכלָן "we use up" (*BM* 79a [**G1**]), and may not have always been different from those forms written with a *waw*.[103] In contrast, forms with a *yod* must have been pronounced either with a high *i* or *e* vowel or with a diphthong *ay*. The vocalized form מדֹּמֵינָן "we compare" (**HPS** 11:19)[104] implies that the diphthong *\*ay* became *ē*, though we also find מֹלקֹינָן "we give lashes" (**HPS** 308:19), perhaps reflecting the shift *\*ay > ī*,[105] or possibly analogy to the sound verb, e.g., וּבֹדקֹינָן "we inspect" (**HPS** 239:19, 21). It is not certain if the evidence of the vocalized example מֹתיֵינָן "we bring" (**HPS** 302:10), discussed above in §4.4.5.4, can be brought to bear here, since this verb is irregular.

In several cases we find alternative forms appearing interchangeably:

אמ' רב פפא: האיי שטרא דיתמי דלא מיקרע קרעינן ליה ולא אגבויי **מגבינן**
ביה. אגבויי לא **מגבנן** ביה משום דרב ושמואל. מיקרע נמי לא קרעינן להו.
דיאנא דעבד כרבי אלעזר עבד.

R. Pappa says: "This document of orphans, we do not tear it up, nor do **we exact payment** on it." **We do** not **exact payment** on it because of Rav and Shemuel. We also do not tear it[106] up: a judge

---

[102] Cf. Morag, "Geniza," p. 70 (reprinted in Morag, *Studies*, p. 303) and "Phonology," p. 75 (reprinted in Morag, *Studies*, p. 252). Morag regarded this shift as occurring only before a final *nun*. However, the evidence of forms such as מונינין "brine" (**Hark** 184:24) < מֵי נוּנֵי, Syriac ܢܘܢܐ; Brockelmann, *LS*, p. 283), as well as the participle forms discussed here, imply that the shift was wider than Morag suggested.

[103] Cf. Friedman, "Early Manuscripts," pp. 26–30. My analysis of the data differs from that of Friedman, and I have presented it in greater detail in *Geonic Responsa*, pp. 50–51. In my opinion, the *qamaṣ* sign is employed in this manuscript to reflect the quality of a rounded vowel, [o], [ɔ], [o:], or [ɔ:] reflexes of historical *\*ā, \*u* and *\*aw*. These may have been phonologically distinct only in terms of vowel quantity. Cf. further Sharvit, "Lack of Contrast"; and Harviainen, "Karaite Bible Transcription."

[104] The *ē* and *a* vowels can also be discerned in the damaged form מדֹּמֵינָן "we compare" (**HPS** 11:21).

[105] See below, n. 107.

[106] We would expect ליה "it" rather than להו "them," and I have translated accordingly.

who acted according to R. Elazar acted legally. (*Shev* 48b [**HPS** 198:14–16])

Consider also the following example, wherein a citation from the Babylonian Talmud (*Qid* 65b) is discussed:

וקא אמרינן 'גובה כתובתה מן החבלה.' **ומקשינן** עלה: חבלה מטלטלי היא. ומפרקינן: הא מני? רבי מאיר היא, דאמ': מטלטלי משעבדי לכתבה. ואי סלקא דעתא כתובת אשה כבעל חוב משיינן לה, דכל מיניה **מגבנן** אפילו מגלימא דעל כתפיה, אמאי **מקשינן**: חבלה מטלטלי היא? הא קימי אינהו. אילא לאו שמע מינה: כי **מגבנן** כתובתה אפילו מיחיים, מימקרקעי **מגבנן** מימטלטלי לא **מגבנן**.

We say: "She collects her *ketubba* payment from the chattels" (*Qid* 65b). And **we challenge** this: the chattels are movables![107] Then we explain: Who[se opinion] is this? It is Rabbi Meir who says: movables are mortgaged to the *ketubba* (*Qid* 65a). And if one should think that we regard the wife's *ketubba* as a creditor, and **we exact payment** of everything from him including the garment from his shoulder, why **do we ask**: "The chattels are movables"? Don't they remain? Rather, learn from this: when we exact the *ketubba* payment, even during his lifetime, **we exact** it from real estate and **do not exact** it from movables. (**HPS** 161:13–19)

I have also found an example of interchange between different primary textual witnesses: משהנן "we delay" (*Ket* 64a [**HPS** 178:17]) // משהינן "we delay" (*Ket* 64a [**Hark** 36:9]).

## 4.6 Possessive and Object Pronouns

### 4.6.1 2 m.s.

The 2 m.s. pronoun suffixed to nouns may be written either ך- or יך-. According to the vocalizations of **HPS**, these were pronounced respectively

---

[107] This statement, חבלה מטלטלי היא, does not appear in our versions of the Talmud, but on the basis of both the documentation here and the ensuing Geonic discussion, it would appear that these words forms formed part of the editor's Talmudic text.

-*ak* and -*ik*,[108] irrespective of whether the base to which they were attached ended in a consonant, a vowel, or an historical diphthong, as the following examples illustrate: בְּנָךְ דִּידָךְ "your sons" (**HPS** 219:18); אָמְרִין תַּלְמִידָךְ "your students say" (*MQ* 24a [**HPS** 264:21]); בְּגֹוָיךְ "in your midst" (**HPS** 70:21); מֵאוּנָיךְ "from your ears" (*Hul* 132b [**HPS** 60:21]).[109]

The verbal object suffix is by rule ־ךְ, of which one vocalized form is attested in **HPS**, פְּרַעְתָּךְ "I paid you" (*Shev* 41b [**HPS** 199:19]), while the consistent defective spellings imply that this -*ak* morpheme was generally employed for the object suffix. However, sporadic examples of the ־יךְ morpheme are occasionally attested: הכא מצי אמ' ליה. האיי דלא **תבעתיך** "In this case he can say to him: 'The reason **I did** not **sue you** was …'" (**HPS** 74:13–14); **פרעתיך** כל דאית לך "**I paid you** all that you are owed" (**HPS** 116:12).

Although these examples are drawn from Geonic sections of **HPS**, the morpheme is also found in a lengthy Talmudic citation, alongside the example פְּרַעְתָּךְ that I cited above:

ההוא דאמ' ליה : פרע מאה זוזי דמסיקנא בך. אמ' ליה : **פרעתך** בפני פלוני ופלוני. אתו פלוני ופל'. אמרו : לא היו דברים מעולם. סבר רב ששת למימר : הוחזק כפרן. אמ' ליה ראבא : כל מילתא דלא רמיא עליה דאיניש לא דעתיה.

ההוא דאמ' ליה : פירען שית מאה זוזי דמסיקנא בך. אמ' ליה : לאו **פרעתך** מאה קבי אפצי דהוה קימי בשיתא שיתה. אתו שהדי אשהידו ביה דארבעה ארבעה הוה קימי. סבר רב ששת למימר : כל מילתא דלא רמיא עליה דאיניש לא דעתיה. אמ' ליה ראבא : כל קיצותא דתרעא מידכר דכירי אינשי.

---

[108] Or perhaps -*īk̲*. The ־יךְ form is presumably a reflex of historical -*ayk*, showing the unusual shift of \**ay* > *ī*. The same shift is found in the 1 c.s. pronoun ־ין, for which evidence is also found in HPS: מָתְנִיתִין "our teaching (Mishna)" (**HPS** 35:20 bis); מתניתין "our teaching (Mishna) (*BB* 47a [**HPS** 202:18]). Cf. Morgenstern, "Geonic Responsa," p. 73.

[109] See Epstein, *Grammar*, p. 122 (wherein the proposed vocalization is to be ignored); Kutscher, "Review," p. 160 (wherein the example בנך דידך is already cited without vocalization); Morgenstern, "Geonic Responsa," pp. 85–86, with a table showing the distribution of attested forms. Juusola, *Linguistic Pecularities*, pp. 83–85, has aptly noted the problem of determining whether one should read בישמיך or בישמוך in the opening formula of numerous magic bowls. The reading with a *waw* would reflect the pronunciation of the rounded *qamaṣ*. To this I would add that the formula could also be in Rabbinic Hebrew, wherein the possessive suffix is ־ךְ. Cf. Ben-Ḥayyim, *Studies*, pp. 22–39; Kutscher, "Mishnaic Hebrew," p. 264–66 (reprinted in Kutscher, *Studies*, pp. 91–93).

ההוא דאמ׳ ליה: פירען מאה זוזי דמסיקנא בך והא שטרא. אמי ליה: לאו
**פרעתיך.** אמי ליה: הנהו סיטראיי נינהו.

A certain [man] said: "Pay me the hundred *zuzim* that I claim from
you." He said to him: "**I paid you** before X and Y." X and Y came
and said: "This never happened!" R. Sheshet considered declaring:
"He's a proven liar." Rabba said to him: "Anything that is not incumbent upon a man he is not aware of."[110]

A certain [man] said: "Pay me the six hundred *zuzim* that I claim
from you." He said to him: "**Did I** not **pay you** a hundred qabs of
gallnuts, worth six apiece!?" Witnesses came and attested that that
they were worth four apiece. R. Sheshet considered declaring:
"Anything that is not incumbent upon a man he is not aware of."
Rabba said to him: "People remember the fixed market price."

A certain [man] said: "Pay me the hundred *zuz* that I claim from
you, and here is the deed!" He said to him: "**Did I** not **pay you**!?"
He said to him: "Those were aside from these." (*Shev* 41b–42a
[**HPS** 199:15–200:3])

The Aramaic context, the parallel structure of the narrative and the other
examples found in **HPS** suggest that פרעתיך is a genuine Aramaic form
rather than a Hebrew borrowing.[111] Interestingly, in the parallel citation
in **HGP**, the form פרעתיך is used in all three instances (**HGP** 12a:35, 37;
12b:2).[112] As far as I can ascertain, this use of the יך- morpheme as an ob-

---

[110] I understand לא דעתיה as equivalent to לא אדעתיה. Cf. Sokoloff, *DJBA*, p. 347.

[111] The roots תב״ע and פר״ע are also both employed in Rabbinic Hebrew, and
hence the Aramaic nature of these forms cannot be conclusively determined. An
example of the יך- pronoun attached to a uniquely Aramaic verb would be more
decisive. In several manuscripts, we find the form שדרתיך "I sent you" (e.g., *BM*
108a [**H165**]; *BB* 169b [**H165**]); the passage from *BB* also appears in **HPS**, but
there the reading is שויוך "they appointed you" (*BB* 169b [**HPS** 103:17]). The Lieberman Institute database records 36 instances of שדרתיך, and only one of שדרתך
(*Qid* 42b [Venice printed edition]). However, as we have seen in many cases, the
nature of the manuscript sources is more important than the number of occurrences of any particular form, and we may hope that examples of this form will
turn up in EEMs textual witnesses.

[112] It is noteworthy that we find even the Aramaic form פרעתך in what might have
been regarded a Hebrew context, i.e., before the expression בפני פלוני ופלוני containing the Hebrew בפני "before." The JBA form would be באפי.

ject pronoun has not be previously recorded in the grammatical literature, and further manuscript research is necessary to determine the range
of its distribution.

As noted above, the interchange of the ד- and די- morphemes is better attested in the possessive pronouns. I have found the following example of a free interchange in one context:

אמ' ליה. פשעת **בנפשך** ושקלת מינאי טפי. אמ ליה. קוץ לי מיקץ. אמיליה
פשעת **בנפשיך** וקארו לי שור המזיק.

> He can say to him: "You will be negligent **with yourself** and take
> more money from me." He can say to him: "Specify a sum!" He
> can say: "You will be negligent **with yourself** and they will call me
> a harmful ox." (*BQ* 85a **[G1]**)

It is possible that a different grammatical form here serves the prosodic
function of marking the last circuit in the repeated structure.

## 4.6.2 3 m.s.

As is the case with other parts of speech, pronouns are subject to the loss
of final unstressed phonemes. Accordingly there are many doublets
within this system as both historical and apocopated forms frequently
appear.[113]

In the case of the 3 m.s. pronoun appearing after vowels, both the
historical form -*hi* and the apocopated form -*h* are attested.[114] The two
may occasionally appear side by side:

ההוא **דאנסוהי** ואהוי אחמרא דרב מארי ורב פנחס בני רב האסא. אתא
לקמיה דרב אשי. פטריה. אמרו ליה רבנן לרב אשי: האיי כמי שנשא ונתן
ביד דאמי. אמ' להו: התם דאהוי מינפשיה. אבל האיי כיון דמינס **אנסוה**
מיעיקבה מיקלא קלייה.

---

113 For the possibility that the historical object morpheme may occasionally be
entirely elided see chapter 3, n. 190.

114 The form הו-, common in the printed editions, is non-existent in the Grade A
EEMss, and extremely rare in the Grade B EEMss, to the point of being almost
non-existent. The few attested examples are probably scribal errors. See above,
§3.5.1.2.

A certain [person] was **compelled** [lit., "they **compelled him**"] and showed them the wine of R. Mari and R. Pinhas sons of R. Hasa.[115] The matter came before R. Ashi. He exempted him. The Rabbis said to R. Ashi: "There is like [the case of] someone who personally took and gave!" He said to them: "That is a case where he showed of his own volition; but here, since they **compelled him**, it is as if he had already burnt it." (*BQ* 117a [**HPS** 129:9–12])

Parallel transmissions of a single Talmudic tradition may employ alternative grammatical forms. For example, שקלוהי יתמי פרסוהי "the orphans **took it** and **spread it**" (*Yev* 66b [**TGAs28** iv 3b 30]), cited here in a Geonic reponsum, is also cited in *Halachot Pesuqot* as שקלוה יתמי פרסוה (*Yev* 66b [**HPS** 159:6]). The responsum itself shows many such interchanges of the two forms within the space of a few lines: זבנוהי "**sell it**!" (**TGAs28** iv 3b 25), שחרורוהי "they **released it**" (l. 27), שויוה "they **made it**" (l. 27), but דשויוהי "that they **made it**" (**TGAs28** iv 4a 3).

The historical forms preserving the final *yod* cannot merely be dismissed as historical spellings in which the final *yod* was not pronounced and this for two reasons: (1) we find two vocalized forms in **HPS**: וּשְׁקלוֹהִי ... וְאַמטיוֹהִי "and they **took him** ... and **brought him**" (**HPS** 259:20); (2) the final vowel is reflected in examples in which the *he* has been elided, e.g., אותבוי "they **replied** to **him**" (**Hark** 50:32); אגמרוי "they **taught him**" (**TGAs42** 101:4). Such forms are also found in the Aramaic magic bowls.[116]

## 4.6.3 3 f.s.

### 4.6.3.1 Elision of Final *he*

The better manuscripts of RBA literature generally preserve the *he* of the affixed הָ- -*a* pronoun, which is attached to both nouns and verbs.[117] While in verbal forms the elision of the final *he* is generally unambiguous,[118] it is extremely difficult to distinguish nouns bearing the pro-

---

[115] The text here is abbreviated; the other textual witnesses indicate that the man was forced to help the brigands carry the wine.

[116] See above, §3.5.1.2.

[117] Wajsberg, "Criteria," p. 339.

[118] The exception is the loss of the suffixed morpheme *h* following the long vowel -*ū*, since in an unvocalized text, the only distinction between שקלו *šəʾqalū* "they took" (*Yev* 46a [**GS** xvii 1a 12]) and שקלוה *šaqlūh* "they took it" (*BQ* 93a [**HGP**

nominal suffix from those bearing the nominal marker -ā if the final *h* is lost. Theoretically, we could argue that the distinction would still be maintained between, for example, גַּבְרָא *gaḇrā* "[the] man/husband" and גַּבְרָא *gaḇra* "her husband" < גַּבְרַה \**gaḇrah*.[119] However, the vocalization of **HPS** suggests that such a distinction had been lost. While other manuscripts often employ the Babylonian *miptah pummā* or the Tiberian *patah* even for the final *ā*, **HPS** employs almost exclusively the *miqpaṣ pummā*. Particularly telling is the following example from **HPS**:

> וכי היכין דאסירא **לבעלה קדמאה** הם הכי אסירא **לגברה בתראה**. מִן גַּבְרָא
> קָדְמָאה דתנן כשם שאסורה לבעל כך אסורה לבועל. ונפקא מן גַּבְרָא
> קָדְמָאה בגיטא ומישתריא לעלמא ומן גַּבְרָא בתראה לא צריכא גיטא.

Just as she is forbidden to her first husband, so too she is forbidden to her subsequent husband. From the first husband—as we have taught: *Just as she is forbidden to the husband, so she is forbidden to the paramour* (*m. Soṭ* 5:1). And she leaves the first husband with a divorce deed and is permitted to all others. And from the second husband she does not require a divorce deed (**HPS** 203:15–18).

Since the vocalizer has clearly distinguished the pointing of לגַּבְרה "to her husband" from that of גַּבְרָא, we may argue that the latter form is to be translated "the husband." However, the context would appear to require the translation "her husband" in all cases, and so it was understood by the medieval translator of *Halachot Pesuqot* (*Hilchot Reu*):

> וכשם שאסורה **לבעלה** ראשון כך אסו' **לבעל'**[120] אחרון. דתנינן: "כשם
> שהיא אסור' לבעל כך אסורה לבועל" ויוצא מן **בעלה** אחרון[121] בגט ומותרת
> בעולם. ומן **בעלה** אחרון אינה צריכה גט.

Just as she is forbitten to her first husband, so she is forbitten to [her] subsequent husband, as we teach: 'Just as she is forbidden to the husband, so she is forbidden to the paramour." And she leaves the first husband with a divorce deed and is permitted to all oth-

---

16b:2]) is the *he*. Cf. the discussion of the form כיתבו (*BB* 172a [**HPS** 104:1]), probably an imperative < \**kiṯḇūh* "write it," in chapter 3, n. 190.

[119] This distinction exists in Neo-Mandaic, e.g., *bietā* "house" contrasts with *bieta* "her house." See Häberl, *Khorramshahr*, §2.3.2.

[120] The presence of the abbreviation mark clearly indicates that this Hebrew noun bore a possessive pronoun.

[121] So MS; read with **HPS** ראשון.

ers. And from the second husband she does not require a divorce deed" (**HR** 98:25–27).

In the Geonic responsa, there are no certain examples of the loss of the final *he* in these circumstances, while in the published chapters of R. Shemuel b. Ḥofni's *Introduction to the Talmud*, there are two examples that on the basis of their Arabic translation would appear to belong to this category:

איפכא מיסתברא עכסהא יט׳ין וקד יפסר צ׳יד דלך מעולם ויקאל עכסהא מפהום.

איפכא מיסתברא—"Its opposite is held [as correct]"; and it may be interpreted "The opposite of that is known"; and some say "Its opposite is understood." (**LPT** 146:13)[122]

מאי שנא רישא ומאי שנא סופה[123]—לם אפתרקא ותפסירה לם אכתלף חכם **אולהא** מן **אכרה** ותגייר.

מאי שנא רישא ומאי שנא סופה—why did the two differ? Its meaning is: why does the law of its first part diverge from (the law of) its latter part and vary? (**LPT** 156:16–17)

From these examples, it appears that we may understand the interchange in this passage from one of the best EEMss as resulting from the weakening of the final *he*:

תנא **סופא** לגלויי רישא. שלא תאמר: **ראשה** שידה תיבה ומגדל אבל עצים לא. תנא **סופה**. שדה תיבה ומגדל. מכלל **דראשה** עצים.

He taught **the** [i.e., its, the Mishna's] **latter clause** to explicate the opening clause. So you should not say: "**Its opening clause** [refers

---

[122] From this Arabic translation it emerges that the Gaon understood איפכא as a noun, since the subject of the verbs יט׳ין and מפהום must be עכס, which therefore cannot be a verb. This is in spite of the f.s. participle form מיסתברא, which does not agree with the m.s. איפכא. It is therefore likely that the interpretation presented in Sokoloff, *DJBA*, p. 156 s.v. אפך vb. *Pe* 2b, to the effect that the form איפכה is to be understood as a singular masculine imperative with an object pronoun, is preferable. (Contra Sokoloff vocalize אִיפַכַהּ; see above, §3.4.3.6.1.) However, for our purposes, what is important is that the Gaon clearly understood the form איפכא as bearing a 3 f.s. pronominal suffix.

[123] So MS; Abramson read סיפא.

to] a case, a box, or a cupboard, but not to timber" he taught **its lat-ter clause**: "A case, a box, or a cupboard," which implies that **its opening clause** [refers to] timber. (*BQ* 98b **[G1]**)

### 4.6.3.2 Interchange of ‫ה‬- and ‫יה‬-

Over thirty years ago Friedman drew attention to the use of the 3 m.s. pronoun ‫יה‬- in place of the 3 f.s. ‫ה‬- in Jewish Babylonian Aramaic.[124] Friedman's findings have subsequently been confirmed by further evidence from the EEMss and the magic bowls.[125] In the following Talmudic citation found in a Geonic responsum of R. Matityah, both forms appear interchangeably:

סמך עליה. **נסביה** לחומה ברתיה דאיסי בריה דרב יצחק בריה דרב יהודה.
**דנסבה** רחבה מפום-בדיתא ושכיב. רב יצחק בריה דראבה בר בר חנה
ושכיב. **ונסבה** אביי ושכיב.

He [Abbaye] relied upon him. He **married** Homa, daughter of Isi son of R. Yiṣḥak son of R. Yehuda, whom Rahba of Pum Bedita had **married**, and died; [and so too] R. Yiṣḥak son of Rava son of Bar-Hanna and died. Abayye **married** her and died. (*Yev* 64b **[TGAs28** iv 2b 24–26)[126]

### 4.6.4 3 m.pl.

RBA employs several forms of the 3 m.pl. possessive pronoun, which vary according to two main criteria.

1. Preservation or apocopation of the final *nun*, i.e., ‫הון‬- and ‫הו‬-. Morag established that the vocalization of **HPS** distinguishes between the vowel of the historical form -*hon* and that of the apocopated form, -*hu*.[127]

---

[124] Friedman, "Three Studies," pp. 64–69.

[125] Cf. Juusola, *Linguistic Peculiarities*, p. 89–92 (possessive pronoun). Morgenstern, "Geonic Responsa," p. 89 (possessive pronoun), pp. 108–9 (object pronouns).

[126] In the following line, Assaf transcribed והינו דקא אמרה ליה "and this is what she said to her"; however, in the manuscript the final word reads לה.

[127] Morag, "Phonology," pp. 80–81 (reprinted in Morag, *Studies*, pp. 258–59).

2. Use of connecting diphthong, i.e., וֹהֹ- -(ə)hu[128] and וֹהֹי-ֵ
   -ayhu. The diphthong originates in the "masculine"[129]
   plural construct morpheme -ay, and seems to be employed consistently in its historical value. However, in
   JBA it is also sometimes used with masculine singular
   nouns, e.g., ריחיהו "their scent" (Suk 13a [**HPS** 33:9]), or
   with nouns bearing the feminine morpheme, e.g.,
   עיבידתיהו "their work" (BM 97a [**HPS** 113:11]). Since the
   -ay- forms have spread into other categories, their distribution is quite wide in JBA, though not entirely unconditioned (see below).

Let us summarize these forms in a table:[130]

|                   | Lack of -ay- | Use of -ay-. |
|-------------------|--------------|--------------|
| Non-Apocopated    | הֹון-         | יהֹון-ֵ       |
| Apocopated        | הֹו-          | יהֹו-ֵ        |

**HPS** itself appears to use the two forms distinctly. In Talmudic citations,
nouns appear to take only the apocopated form, e.g., אבוהו "their father"
(BB 175a [**HPS** 75:12, 13]; Shev 48a [**HPS** 197:18]); אולמיהו "their strength"
(BB 88b [**HPS** 153:17]); see also the examples cited above. Prepositions
which never employ the -ay- diphthong, e.g., -ב and -ל, appear in both
forms, e.g., להו (e.g., Pes 5b [**HPS** 9:7]) and להון (BM 83a [**HPS** 114:18];
Shev 30b [**HPS** 192:17]). However, while in the Talmudic citations in **HPS**
the apocopated form appears over ninety times, I have found only the
two examples of להון mentioned. By contrast, the Geonic sections of **HPS**
contain some 25 examples of להו but over 35 examples of להון.[131]

In some textual witnesses the apocopated and non-apocopated forms
interchange freely. Consider the following example, wherein a citation
from Nid 45b is glossed with Geonic commentary:

---

[128] The shewa is employed when the base ends in a consonant, e.g., דידֹהֹו (**HPS**
57:17).

[129] Some nouns employing this morpheme are feminine, e.g., אימֵיהֹו "their
mother" (**HPS** 219:19, possibly a citation from an alternative version of Naz 57b).

[130] Cf. the findings presented in Morgenstern, "Geonic Responsa," pp. 91–92
(nouns), and pp. 95–100 passim (prepositions).

[131] Cf. Breuer, "Karetot," p. 9, and his statistics in Table 1.

רב ור' חנינא דאמרי **תרוייהון** תוך זמן כלפני זמן ואע״ג דאיתי שתי שערות
בתוך זמן קטן הוא ר' יוחנן ור' יהושע בן לוי דאמרי **תרוייהו** תוך זמן כלאחר
זמן ואו מיתי שתי שערות בתוך זמן גדול הוא וסימן אינון

Rav and R. Hanina, who **both** say: Within the period is like before
the period—even though he brought forth two [pubic] hairs, within the period he is a minor—R. Yohanan and R. Yehoshua son of
Levi, who **both** say: Within the period is like after the period—and
if he brings forth two [pubic] hairs during the period, he is an
adult, and they are a sign [of puberty]. (**Hark** 41:35–7)

Further examples:

ותרוייהו "And both of them" (**Hark** 120:19) // ותרוייהון "And both of
them" (**Hark** 120:20); כולהון "All of them" (**GS** vi 1a 8) // כולהו "All
of them" (**GS** xvi 1a 10).

In the following example, already cited above in our discussion of the
loss of the *ᶜayin* (§4.4.1.1), we find forms with the *-ay-* morpheme interchanging freely with forms without it:

ועוד תשלומי כפל ותשלומי ארבעה וחמשה דקיצי ניבעי **שליחותהו**. אמרי:
כי עבדינן **שליחותהו** בממונא. בקנסא לא קא עבדינן **שליחותהו**. אדם
באדם דממונא הוא נבעי **שליחותיהו**. אמרי: כי עבדינן **שליחותהו** במילתא
דשכיחא. אדם באדם דלא שכיחא לא עבדינן **שלוחתהו**. בושת נמי דשכיחא
ניבי **שלוחתיהו.**

Moreover, in the case of double-payments and fourfold or fivefold
payments, which are specified, we should carry out **their commission**! They say: When we carry out **their commission** it is in monetary matters; in matters of fines, we do not carry out **their commission**. [Injury of] man against man is a monetary matter; we should
carry out **their commission**! They say: When we carry out **their
commission**, it is in common matters. Man against man, which is
not common—we do not carry out **their commission**. Degradation
is also common—we should carry out **their commission**! (*BQ* 84b
[**G1**])

It is possible that the *-ay-* forms have been employed here with the prosodic function of marking the end of a discourse segment. If this is the
case, then the distinction has been lost in the later version found in H165
(cited above, §4.4.1.1), which consistently employs the *-ay-* forms. Further

research into the use of the *-ay-* forms in the best textual witnesses is required.

## 4.6.5 Demonstrative Pronouns

The standard Talmudic pronoun for proximate plurals is הני, while the typologically older form הלין is found sporadically in tractates *Nedarim, Nazir, Temura, Karetot,* and *Tamid*,[132] and in the writings of some Geonim.[133] It is quite frequent in *Halachot Pesuqot*, though only in the Geonic sections that are not citations from a Talmudic source.[134] However, even in the non-Talmudic elements of *Halachot Pesuqot*, by far the most common form is הני.[135]

In the following citation, both forms appear to be employed as free variants:

> אסוקי דהוה מסיק ביה מייקרה והשתא פרעיה. או נמי אמ' ליה: בחר לי
> **הני** זוזי. או נמי שדריה בשליחותא ואמ' ליה: זיל אמטי ליה לפלניא **הלין**
> זוזי.

He had initially owed him but now he paid him. Or he said to him: "Choose for me **these** *zuzim*." Or that he sent him on a commission and said to him: "Go and bring **these** *zuzim* to X." (**HPS** 120:5–7)

Breuer has shown that both forms are attested in the Aramaic of *Karetot*, though no examples survive in the same context.[136]

---

[132] On the unique nature of these tractates and their language, see Breuer, "Karetot," and the literature cited there. Surprisingly, the form הלין is *not* found in tractate *Maʿila*, wherein we find only הני.

[133] See Morgenstern, "Geonic Responsa," p. 121. Even in the responsa literature this form is rare, and appears to be restricted to the earlier Geonim. It is never found in the responsa of R. Sharrira or R. Hai Gaon.

[134] In these sections it appears a total of fourteen times in **HPS**.

[135] It appears around sixty-five times in such sections. The precise number is difficult to determine, since in the legal codices we occasionally find the expression הני מילי "these words [derive from or apply to]" inserted into a Talmudic discussion. See, for example, **HPS** 209:15, where the words are interpolated into a discussion drawn from *Yev* 25a. It is not clear whether this formula was found in the Talmudic *Vorlage*, or was inserted into *Halachot Pesuqot* as an explanatory gloss.

[136] Breuer, "Karetot," p. 9. According to Breuer, the use of הלין in this tractate is rare.

## 4.7 Explanation of the Phenomena

### 4.7.1 Introduction

The phenomena presented above are wide-ranging, and it is likely that more than one explanation is required in order to explain the diverse forms of linguistic variation found in JBA. Here I shall briefly summarize some of the main theories that have been presented by researchers and indicate the problems connected with them.

### 4.7.2 Chronological and Geographical Explanations

Following the medieval Talmudic commentators, who were already aware that tractate *Nedarim* is formulated in a different idiom, Luzzatto suggested that this unique phraseology (shared also with *Nazir*) was connected to the Palestinian dialect.[137] Luzzatto further noted that certain features, such as the use of דין rather than Talmudic האי, tend to appear in Palestinian contexts within the Babylonian Talmud.[138] It would appear from Luzzatto's comments that he regarded these non-standard elements as resulting from Palestinian influence on the language of the Babylonian Talmud.

In his English grammar of 1900, Levias suggested that "As might have been expected from the compilatory nature of the Talmud, its language is not uniform, but shows traces of various stages of development. Originally, the dialectical and chronological variations must have been quite marked. But in course of time these differences were smoothed down by later scholars, familiar forms and expressions being substituted for rare ones, and dialectical characteristics have thus largely been obliterated."[139] In other words, according to Levias, it is not the Talmud's linguistic variation that requires explanation, but rather the high degree of linguistic uniformity.

Moreover, Levias noted that "Traces of a more original character have been preserved in a few treatises containing laws of no practical application after the destruction of the Temple. Such treatises were not frequently studied in the schools and therefore were not subjected to the process of obliteration as much as other parts of the Talmud. Here belong, among others, Tāmîd, Meʿîlā, Temûrā, Nedārîm and Nāzîr."[140] In

---

[137] Luzzatto, *Elementi grammaticali*, §2.

[138] Ibid., §47.

[139] Levias, *Grammar*, p. 2.

[140] Ibid. I do not know why *Karetot* was omitted; it is included in the list in Levias's Hebrew *Diqduq*, p. 17, though in that list *Tamid* is curiously omitted.

this version of the *Grammar*, Levias suggested that the "language of the Gaonic literature shows the influence of the Targum."[141]

Levias later changed his opinion, perhaps under the influence of Epstein, who demonstrated in several places that the Aramaic language remained alive in the Geonic period.[142] Levias accepted Epstein's explanation that later Geonic works such as the *Sheʾiltot* reflect the language of Pumbedita, and on the basis of the similarities in language between the *Sheʾiltot* and these tractates, determined that they too reflect the language of Pumbeditha.[143] Epstein himself did not make this claim. Rather, he stated that they were composed in another academy and were not fully accepted in the academies of Sura and Pumbedita.[144] Epstein similarly believed that rather than preserving the ancient form of JBA, these tractates reflect "a different dialect that was spoken in a different place at a late time."[145] Epstein also noted that archaic survivals are found in citations from legal formularies.[146]

## 4.7.3 Register

So far we have seen that the explanations for the phenomenon of variant forms are twofold: chronological and dialectal.[147] In 1974, S. Friedman

---

[141] Ibid., p. 4.

[142] See especially Epstein, *Der Gaonäische Kommentar*, pp. 54–57 and "Notes II" passim; and above, §2.3.6.

[143] Levias, *Diqduq*, p. 18, following Epstein, "Sheeltot," p. 303. Epstein's comments were tacitly directed against Ginsberg's view, presented in *Geonica* I pp. 86–89, that the *Sheʾiltot* reflect a Palestinian idiom. See Brody, *Geonim*, p. 203.

[144] Epstein, *Grammar*, p. 15; Epstein, *Amoraim*, p. 54. Epstein suggested that Nedarim may have been edited in the academy of Mahoza; see *Amoraim*, pp. 69–70.

[145] דיאלקט אחר שנדבר במקום אחר בזמן מאוחר. Epstein, *Grammar*, p. 16.

[146] Ibid., p. 13.

[147] In a recent series of articles, E. Wajsberg has attempted to identify characteristics of both of these dimensions. See Wajsberg, "Early Amoraim" and "Palestinian Traditions." I have not always found his analysis convincing. In particular, I am not certain that the manuscript evidence he cites is always sufficiently reliable to allow the type of analysis he undertakes. For example, his analysis of the 1 c.s. perfect patterns קטלי and קטלית draws evidence from a variety of sources, including Spanish Mss (e.g., **H165**), Ashkenazi Mss (e.g., **M95**), and even printed editions. However, if we consider one example, זבנית "I bought" (*BM* 83a [**H165**, **F8**]), we find that though this reading is supported by several textual witnesses, the EEMs *BM* **G1** reads זבני (see Friedman, *Bava Meziʿa Text*, p. 408), and this

proposed another distinction: register. Friedman suggested that certain forms may be employed in formal contexts. Specifically, Friedman noted the use of the *yod* prefix instead of standard JBA *lamed* for 3 m.s. imperfect in prayers and dream interpretations, which may result more from genre than time or place. Similarly, he suggested that court proceedings may have been conducted and recorded in a formal register that preserved more archaic forms, for example אנת "you" (instead of standard JBA את). Friedman dubbed this register לשון טענות "the language of claims."[148]

However, all of these explanations imply a high degree of homogeneity within any one stratum of JBA. In other words, we would expect to find that any particular Talmudic or Geonic statement is consistent regarding the language it employs. However, as I have attempted to show in detail in this chapter, examples of apparently free interchange between different morphemes is widespread even within a single context, and this is the case even in the most accurate textual witnesses that survive.[149] Accordingly, the interchanges cannot be simply ascribed to different linguistic strata, redactions or transmissions, since they often occur within a single statement in a single context in a single textual witness.[150]

An exception would perhaps be Levias's original position that the language of the Talmud underwent linguistic editing through the process of its transmission, and that these changes were only partially implemented. However, this argument is hard to accept regarding Geonic literature, for which we possess some excellent textual witnesses that were copied not long after the original works were composed, and which

---

reading is supported by EEMs **HPS** 114:16. Wajsberg, "Early Amoraim," p. 137, claims that the ית- morpheme is rare and primarily found in the pre-Amoraic period; however, it is also fairly common in Geonic writings, which would imply that the chronological factor is not decisive. See Morgenstern, "Geonic Responsa," p. 137. (In light of further manuscript study, I revise my conclusion presented there regarding the use of קטלית in the Talmud; I now agree with Kara, *Yemenite Manuscripts*, p. 143, that in the Talmudic sources, the ית- morpheme is rare.)

[148] Friedman, "Three Studies," pp. 58–64.

[149] Such interchanges are also found in the Aramaic magic bowls, as noted at several points in Morgenstern, "Non-Standard Spellings."

[150] Naturally, this does not mean that every linguistic form attested in late manuscripts has to be taken as reflecting the grammar of JBA written by native users. Although linguistic variation is integral to the idiom, it is not endless.

otherwise show few signs of linguistic interference.[151] It seems preferable to assume that the phenomenon of linguistic variation is integral to JBA texts, and does not result solely from sporadic changes introduced through the process of textual transmission, even though this may be *one* factor that accounts for it.

## 4.7.4 Oral Transmission

In light of these difficulties, in a 1993 article Morag suggested an alternative model to account for the linguistic variation found in Babylonian Rabbinic literature.[152] In Morag's opinion, the mixed language employed in Talmudic literature, with its widespread use of morphological doublets on the one hand, and the frequent interchanges of historical and phonetic spellings on the other, can best be explained by reference to the oral transmission of the Talmud. Morag compared the transmission of the Talmud to the literary idiom of Baghdadi Jews, as described in an article by Haim Blanc.[153] Blanc had noted that this idiom matches neither the spoken language nor the written standard, but contains elements of both. Morag proposed that the language of the Talmud may be best understood in this manner too:

> It seems preferable to explain the wide distribution of morphological doublets in light of the assumption that the Talmud was transmitted over several generations as an oral lecture. As we have seen, the degree of fixedness and measure of unity of idiom of oral lecture[154] are considerably lower than the degree of fixedness and unity of written idiom, since the former may incorporate more widely characteristics and elements from different periods—some relatively early and some relatively late, and some, of course, belonging to the period of the oral lecturer's spoken language. From the linguistic-typological perspective, this combination is not foreign to the language of oral lectures, and examples of the issue have already been presented above from the literary Judeo-Arabic of

---

[151] There are some exceptions to this, even among the Geniza fragments; see below.

[152] Morag, "Oral Transmission." On p. 341, Morag noted the synchronic difficulties in assuming that dialectal distinctions account for the distribution of forms.

[153] Blanc, "Literary Idiom."

[154] Morag clearly employed the term הרצאה here to mean an unwritten oral presentation in contrast to a written text, though in modern Hebrew it could theoretically also refer to the public reading of a written lecture.

Baghdad. When the scribes came to write down the text of the
Talmud in its entirety, after it had been transmitted orally over
generations, perhaps "some of it in writing and some of it orally,"[155] the phenomenon of morphological doublets was already a
permanent element in the linguistic fabric of the Talmud as it had
been transmitted orally, and the scribes saw no reason to be sur-
prised by it.[156]

Morag correctly rejected a simplistic explanation based upon dialect
changes which cannot explain the linguistic variation within any individual source. As we have seen, these variations cross source boundaries.
However, Morag's explanation, which was based entirely upon evidence
from the Talmud, does not take into account the fact that this phenomenon occurs in *all* RBA documents, including those that were written long
after the Talmud was committed to writing. This challenge to Morag's
theory is particularly strong when we consider the case of the Geonic
responsa, which are evidently written documents addressed to specific
recipients, and of which we possess copies from the Cairo Geniza that
are close in both time and location to the original recipients. It would be
difficult to claim that the variant forms in these texts result from oral
transmission.

Furthermore, from the manuscript evidence from the Cairo Geniza it
emerges that grammatical change continued to affect the language of
RBA literature during the period of its transmission in writing. If we take
for example a responsum by R. Natronai Gaon (no. 123 in Brody's edition), we find it has been preserved in two forms in the manuscripts. Ms
TS G1.87 retains the early Geonic orthography and forms, while Ms

---

[155] Citation from R. Judah Bargeloni (b. 1070), commentary on *Sefer Ḥayyeṣira*, ed.
Halberstam (Berlin, 1885), p. 187.

[156] נראה יותר להסביר את תפוצתם הרבה של כפלי התצורה לאור ההנחה, שהתלמוד היה
מועבר במשך כמה וכמה דורות בדרך הרצאה בעל-פה. כפי שראינו, מידת קביעותה ושיעור
אחידותה של לשון ההרצאה פחותים הם באופן ניכר ממידת קביעותה ואחידותה של לשון
הכתיבה, שכן הראשונה עשייה לשלב ברקמתה בהיקף נרחב יותר קווים ויסודות שהם בני
תקופות שונות—מהם קדומים ומהם מאוחרים ביחס, ומהם, כמובן, בני תקופת לשון
הדיבור של מרצה ההרצאה. מן הבחינה הבלשנית-הטיפולוגית אין שילוב זה זר ללשון
ההרצאה, וכבר הודגם העניין לעיל מן הערבית היהודית הספרותית של בגדאד. וכשבאו
הסופרים לכתוב את נוסח התלמוד בשלימותו, לאחר שהועבר בעל-פה במשך דורות, אפשר
"מקצתו בכתב ומקצתו בעל פה"', כבר היתה תופעת כפלי התצורה יסוד של קבע במארג
הלשוני של התלמוד כמות שנמסר בדרך ההרצאה, ולא ראו הסופרים לתמוה עליו. Morag,
"Oral Transmission," p. 341–42.

Kaufmann 193 is closer in style to the European manuscripts. The following examples demonstrate the characteristic differences:

| MS T-S G1.87 | MS Kaufmann 193 | Gloss |
|---|---|---|
| אילא | אלא | Or not |
| ראבה | רבא | Rabba |
| אסרה ... לריפתיה למיכלה | אסרה ... למיכליה לריפתיה | "He forbade his bread to be eaten"[157] |
| אותיביה | איתיביה | "He replied to him" |
| ניבי להי הסיקא | ניעביד להי הסקה | "He shall heat them" |
| חושין | חוששין | "are concerned" |

This is not to say that the Kaufmann text does not retain early elements. In several cases it is not possible to determine which reading is earlier, e.g.:

| MS TS G1.87 | MS Kaufmann 193 | Gloss |
|---|---|---|
| ולא קשיא אהדאדי | ולא קשיין על הדאדי | "They are not difficult for one another"[158] |

In this case, the participle is in the feminine plural, and the form על is characteristic of Geonic style. However, we do find feminine plural verbs with the -ā ending (apocopated *nun*), and אהדאדי is also employed by the Geonim. Yet overall the language of the Kaufmann manuscript differs from the language of the Geonim. It shows that even responsa may undergo editing, and that this editing has nothing to do with their original oral transmission. The evidence of the Geonic responsa reminds us of the role of secondary editing during textual transmission in determining a text's language.[159] This must be borne in mind when we consider Morag's next point.

---

[157] The Kaufmann manuscript reading is not logical; the direct object of אסרה is feminine and must refer to the bread, not the infinitive. An infinitive cannot be the object of a verb with a proleptic suffix.

[158] I.e., the two traditions do not necessarily contradict one another.

[159] I shall return to this issue in a future study of the Epistle of R. Sharrira Gaon. Meanwhile, see Epstein, *Amoraim*, pp. 610–15.

## 4.7.5 Change in Orthographic System?

Morag suggested that in the oral presentation, the pharyngeals were generally (though not always) pronounced, since the idiom of oral lecture was a classicizing elite idiom that brings honor and prestige to its user.[160] He argued that this form of the language is reflected in the majority of Talmudic manuscripts:

> When the scribes came to write the Talmud they practiced in their orthography what their ears heard in the language of lecture and discussion in the Academies, not according to the spoken Aramaic language of their time, nor even of the orthographic practices that were common in the Geonic period.[161]

In contrast to this, Morag claimed, the Yemenite manuscripts are characterized by widespread loss of the pharyngeals. He explained this distinction as stemming from different orthographic practices that existed from the moment that the Talmud was written, and that the *Urtexten* of the Yemenite manuscripts "came from a unique scribal school":[162]

> It is possible that the difference in orthographic systems between [the Yemenite manuscripts] and the other manuscripts points to different stages of consolidation in the orthography of the Talmud. The stage of orthographic consolidation of the Yemenite manuscripts is surely connected to the period of the Talmud's transmission to Yemen, i.e., its written transmission. The connections between Babylonia and Yemen in the Geonic period are well known, and it is also well known that Yemenite Jewry preserved much of the cultural wealth of Babylonian Jewry. It is certain that the Yemenite community sought acquaintance with the Talmud, the report of which reached them. For this purpose, chapters and complete tractates were written down for them—we do not know if it was the entire Talmud, since the Yemenite manuscripts that

---

[160] לשון שהיא תפארת ויוקרה לנוהג בה בהרצאתו. Morag, "Oral Transmission," p. 343.

[161] כשבאו סופרים לכתוב את נוסח התלמוד נהגו בכתיבם בו לפי מה ששמעו אוזניהם בלשון ההרצאה והדיון בישיבות, לא לפי הנהוג בלשון הדיבור הארמית בזמנם, ואף לא לפי דרכי הכתיב שהיו רווחות בתקופת הגאונים. Morag, "Oral Transmission," p. 343. On Morag's claim regarding the orthography of Geonic literature, see below.

[162] כתבי-יד אלה (כלומר, לא הם עצמם, שהרי הם בני המאות הט״ז והי״ז, אלא הנסחים המקוריים, טקסטי-האב, אשר מהם הועתקו, במספר שלבי העתקה שאינם ידועים לנו, כתבי-היד המצויים עמנו) מאסכולה מיוחדת של סופרים יצאו. Morag, "Oral Transmission," p. 344 (emphasis in original).

have reached us contain only parts of the Talmud—perhaps by scribes who were requested to do so, or by students who came to the Babylonian academies from Yemen. The method of writing was, orthographically, close to that customary in the contemporary literature. The method of transmitting Talmudic content orally continued in Babylonia even after the first Yemenite manuscripts were written and transmitted to Yemen; at a later stage, the orthography—that is the orthography that is found in other manuscripts—was consolidated in such a way that it reflects more closely the pronunciation used in oral presentation, a pronunciation in which, as we mentioned above, the pharyngeals were pronounced in the majority of words.[163]

However, Morag's view is based upon several questionable assumptions. The first is that the original orthography of the textual tradition upon which Yemenite manuscripts are based uniquely reflected Geonic orthography, while other, later manuscript traditions were closer to the "language of lecture and discussion." This assumption is not supported by the textual evidence. Already in 1981 Friedman demonstrated that the "Geonic" orthography—a term primarily connected to more widespread use of vowel letters and of phonetic spellings—is not unique to Geonic manuscripts but also characterizes the Talmudic text in its earliest stages.[164] Friedman published his findings prior to the completion of

---

[163] ייתכן, שההבדל שבדרכי הכתיב בינם לבין כתבי-יד אחרים מלמד על שלבי גיבוש שונים בכתיבו של נוסח התלמוד. שלב גיבוש כתיבם של כתבי-היד התימניים בוודאי קשור לזמן העברתו של נוסח התלמוד לתימן, וכוונתנו להעברה שבכתב. ידועים הקשרים בין בבל לבין תימן בתקופת הגאונים, אף ידועה העובדה, שיהדות תימן שימרה רבים מנכסי הרוח של יהדות בבל. ודאי הוא, שקהילות תימן ביקשו להכיר את התלמוד, אשר שמעו הגיע עדיהם. לשם כך נכתבו בשבילם פרקים של תלמוד ומסכתות שלימות—ואין אנו יודעים אם התלמוד כולו, שכן כתבי-היד התימניים שהגיעו אלינו, אין אלא חלקים מן התלמוד—אם על-ידי סופרים שנתבקשו לכך, אם על-ידי תלמידים שהגיעו מתימן לישיבות בבל. דרך הרישום היתה, מבחינת הכתיב, קרובה למקובל בספרות של אותה תקופה. שיטת העברתם של תוכני התלמוד בעל-פה נמשכה בבבל גם לאחר שנכתבו כתבי-היד התימניים הראשונים והועברו מבבל לתימן; בשלב מאוחר נתגבש הכתיב—הוא הכתיב הנוהג בכתבי-יד אחרים—בדרך שהיא משקפת במידה רבה יותר את ההגייה שנהגה בלשון ההרצאה, הגייה שבה, לפי ההנחה שהבאנו לעיל, נתקיימו הגאיים הלועיים במרביתן של התיבות .Morag, "Oral Transmission," pp. 344–45.

[164] Friedman, "Early Manuscripts," pp. 7–32; 48–51. See, for example, his overall assessment of MS **G1** (p. 13): הכתיב שבכ"י שלפנינו דומה דמיון מפליא לכתיבו של ספר הלכות פסוקות כ"י ששון ולשאר כתיבים הידועים מספרות הגאונים ומהבאות התלמוד שבה. כלומר, הוא שייך לאותו סוג של כתבי-יד מעולים, המוסרים בדייקנות צורות לשוניות

Kara's doctorate on the Yemenite manuscripts, and indeed Kara cites widely from Friedman's work in order to confirm the antiquity of many of the distinctive linguistic features he found in his corpus.[165]

Furthermore, the features that characterize the early manuscripts are generally not unique to them; rather, it is generally their *scope* that is unusual.[166] For example, phonetic spellings reflecting the loss of word-final phonemes are found in all RBA textual witnesses, including printed editions. However, while in printed editions this phenomenon is restricted to specific words and forms (e.g., imperfect/imperative forms of אמ״ר, and forms of קו״ם), in early manuscripts it affects a much wider range of words. In particular, the elision or apocopation of root consonants becomes increasingly more restricted in the later textual witnesses, though even forms that are regarded as rare occasionally show up in late Ashkenazic manuscripts, e.g., אזא "he went" (e.g., *BM* 103b [**V**115]; *Bech* 8b [**V**120]). Similarly, a brief glance at the words beginning with *ʾaleph* or *he* in Sokoloff's *Dictionary of Jewish Babylonian Aramaic* will suffice to produce numerous entries wherein the ʿ*ayin* and *ḥet* have shifted to laryngeals, and the majority of these are preserved in the later manuscripts and printed editions of the Talmud.

The following representative examples are all found in the printed edition of the Talmud (Vilna 1880–83). I have marked with an asterisk the only example in this list for which the etymon is not actually attested in JBA or cognate dialects.

---

רווחו בזמן הגאונים, והוא מסוג כתבי־היד עליו ביקשו החוקרים להשתית תיאור לשוני מהימן של הארמית הבבלית. "The orthography of the present manuscript is remarkably similar to the orthography of *Halachot Pesuqot* MS Sassoon and to other spellings known from Geonic literature and the Talmudic citations therein. That is to say, it belongs to that class of superb manuscripts that accurately transmit linguistic forms that were current in the Geonic period, and is of the class of manuscript upon which researchers have sought to base a reliable linguistic description of Babylonian Aramaic." Note that the manuscript in question is *not* a Yemenite manuscript.

[165] It sometimes appears that either Morag ignored the latest manuscript findings, or at least did not adapt his views to accommodate the new data. For example, in his *Yemenite Tradition*, p. 167 n. 27, he describes the form אמא as "found in Geonic literature but not in the Talmud (at least not in the printed editions)." However, both Friedman, "Early Manuscripts," and Kara, *Yemenite Manuscripts*, had demonstrated that such forms are not characteristic of Geonic literature, but rather of the early eastern manuscript tradition in general.

[166] See §2.12.2.7.

א- "upon" (עַל, common); אבא "thicket, forest" ( < עבא, BM 107b, San 39b); אדלא "before" (< עד דלא, common); אוגיא "furrow" (< עוגיא, Ber 6a); אומצא "piece, morsel" (< עומצא, e.g., Ber 45a); אורזילא "gazelle" (< עורזילא, BB 73b); אטמא "thigh" (< עטמא, e.g., Eruv 29b); איזלי "nets" (< עיזלי, MQ 11a); בר אמודאי "diver" (< עמוראי, RH 23a, BB 74b);[167] אקושא "hard, stale" (< עקושא, e.g., Qid 62a); אקרוקתא "frog" (< עקרוקתא, BB 73b); ארבא "boat, ship" (< ערבא, e.g., Ber 56a); ארבלא "sieve" (< ערבלא, e.g., BM 26b); ארדי "mushrooms" (< ערדי, e.g., Ket 61a); ארדא "mast" (< ערדא BB 73a);[168] ארזלא "hammock" (< ערזלא, ʿEruv 25b).[169] Sporadic "rare" examples from the verbal system even survived into the early printed editions, e.g., איביא להו "they asked" (Bech 27a [Venice printed edition]).

הברא "darkness" (< חברא, Tam 32a); היגי "thistles" (< חגי, e.g., Suk 13a); הדייק "to fit tightly" (< חדייק, e.g., Shab 53b); הדייר "to return, surround" and related noun forms (< חדייר, regular); הוצא "palm leaf" (< חוצא, e.g., Shab 77b); הורדי "reed mat" (< *חורדי, e.g., BB 6a).[170]

As stated, this list is partial, containing only lexemes of certain derivation in which an initial pharyngeal has shifted to a laryngeal. It does not include any cases of interchange of medial pharyngeals, even though these are similarly widespread in the printed editions, e.g., האידנא "now." However, even these examples should suffice to demonstrate that phonetic spellings of the etymological pharyngeals are common in the printed editions of the Talmud, and are certainly not unique to the Yemenite manuscripts. Even if we accept that the distribution of non-historical spellings is wider in the Yemenite manuscripts than in the later European sources, this does not mean that this necessarily reflects a difference in phonetic realities. Above, in chapter 2, I argued that there is

---

[167] In both of these cases the *dalet* of אמודאי has been mistakenly replaced with a *resh*. However, this does not alter the fact that the original ʿayin has been lost. For BB 74b, the Spanish MS H165 reads אמודאי.

[168] The editions erroneously read אדרא, while MS H165 reads ארדא. Cf. previous note.

[169] The printed edition reads אורזילא; I have followed the printed commentary of R. Shelomo b. Aderet (1235–1310), and early other commentators. Again, the question of the noun pattern does not affect the issue at hand.

[170] The *ḥet* is found in the Akkadian etymon and sometimes in the loaned Arabic form. See Sokoloff, *DJBA*, p. 374.

morphological evidence to suggest that the *ʿayin* had often been totally elided.

Moreover, contrary to Morag, who assumed that right from the outset the orthography of the Yemenite tradition differed from that of other manuscript traditions, Friedman's findings demonstrate that at the earliest stages of its transmission in writing, the Talmud text shared many of the features that Morag regarded as characteristic of and unique to the Yemenite manuscripts. The distribution of non-historical spellings is no more widespread in the Yemenite manuscripts than, for example, in MS G1 of *Bava Mezia*. The Yemenite manuscripts are unusual in having preserved at a relatively late date many of these spellings which were partially lost in the European (Sephardic and especially Ashkenazic) traditions, in particular the elision of the third radical in verbal forms;[171] but this is an issue of textual transmission, not of original encoding.

The evidence of the EEMss indicates that such spellings were originally more commonplace, and, as I have emphasized in this chapter, no textual witness of RBA literature is written in a wholly phonetic or wholly historic orthography. All of the textual witnesses employ both orthographic systems, and, as the examples cited in this chapter demonstrate, it is not rare for both early and later forms to appear side by side. However, it would seem that during the process of textual transmission, the phonetic spellings were often removed in favor of etymological spellings which are usually easier to interpret. The generally conservative nature of the Yemenite textual tradition meant that fewer such substitutions of this kind entered the Yemenite manuscripts.

## 4.7.5 Toward a Solution

This still leaves us with the problem of how to explain the widespread use of variant forms, even within the same context. In my opinion, there is no *single* explanation which can account for all of these phenomena, and we must assume that several factors are involved, most of which have been mentioned in the discussion above:

### 4.7.5.1 Chronology

It is possible that the earlier strata of Amoraic literature were formulated in distinctive literary forms. Wajsberg has sought to identify such fea-

---

[171] As noted above, forms of the roots קו״ם, and the imperfects and imperatives of אמ״ר constitute exceptions, as even in the printed editions of the Talmud they commonly occur with the third radical elided.

tures,[172] though, as I have stated, his reliance upon late and unreliable textual witnesses undermines the strength of his arguments.

### 4.7.5.2 Dialect

The existence of different local dialects is mentioned in the Talmud, and given the large geographic expanse in which Babylonian Jewry lived, it is reasonable to assume that dialectal variations existed. Evidence for such dialectal forms is cited in the Talmud.[173] With the possible exception of Palestinian dialectal forms, at present, it does not seem possible to ascribe particular forms to particular dialects.

### 4.7.5.3 Register

More formal and less formal forms of speech and writing seem to have coexisted. Sokoloff noted the distinction between the different levels of language in *Halachot Pesuqot* (Talmudic, Geonic, legal formularies), Friedman remarked on the use of the *yod* prefix in blessings, and of archaic forms employed in the "language of claims." In my own work on the language of the Babylonian Geonim, I was able to identify several registers and occasionally determine features of personal style.[174] Many of the supposedly Geonic forms in fact characterized only their more formal writings.

### 4.7.5.4 Literary Idiom or Lack Thereof

Connected to the issue of register is that of literary idiom. Much of Rabbinic Babylonian literature appears to have been formulated in an informal idiom reflecting many elements of the spoken language. However, as we have seen, certain sections of this literature are cast in a more conservative idiom, and this is particularly true of Geonic writings and the six tractates which were not studied in the Babylonian academies (see above). These conservative forms were presented in Epstein's *Grammar* as "Dialectal and Geonic." However, as previously noted, the Geonim do not employ these forms alone, but also make free use of Talmudic

---

[172] Wajsberg, "Early Amoraim."

[173] Cf. Epstein, *Grammar*, p. 14.

[174] Morgenstern, "Geonic Responsa," pp. 11–17, especially pp. 13–15.

forms.[175] Recently Breuer has shown that MS **O** of *Karetot*, one of the most important textual witnesses for the "unique" tractates, often employs the conservative forms interchangeably with the standard Talmudic forms, and that it is often in the relative distribution of these forms that the language of *Karetot* differs from that of other tractates.

Furthermore, Breuer has adduced additional support for the supposition that the language of the "unique" tractates is a purely literary idiom: the texts written in this form of Aramaic do not show the natural progression of intermediate forms, but only classicizing forms alongside non-classicizing ones.[176] The corollary of such an interpretation is that those parts of Babylonian Rabbinic literature which are formulated in the more conservative, literary language were deliberately encoded in this idiom for some literary effect. We cannot ascertain whether this encoding occurred during the stage of oral transmission or at the time that the text was committed to writing. All we can conclude from the evidence is that a higher, more conservative literary idiom was occasionally employed in Babylonian Rabbinic works, and that this idiom appears to have been favored—though not employed exclusively—by the composers of the *Nedarim*-like tractates and of some Geonic works. It is important to emphasize that this idiom is distinctly Babylonian in nature, and differs significantly from the standard Aramaic of Targum Onqelos.[177]

### 4.7.5.5 Prosody

Above I have alluded to a possible prosodic explanation for some of the interchanges. In some cases, this explanation might hold true only of the individual textual witness rather than of the *Urtext*; we have seen, for example, that interchanges between apocopated and unapocopated forms occur between different textual witnesses, and hence even this criterion remains somewhat arbitrary. Nevertheless, I believe that this is a factor worthy of further consideration, as far as the textual evidence allows for such an undertaking.

---

[175] A rare exception appears to be the 2 m.pl. perfect morpheme ‏תו-‎, which is standard in Talmudic manuscripts and citations, but which the Geonim do not employ in their own writings. See Morgenstern, "Geonic Responsa," p. 141.

[176] Breuer, "Karetot," p. 20, §1.4.2. I believe that the evidence of the magic bowls supports Breuer's contention: in that corpus, we find much greater linguistic variety, apparently reflecting the interplay of literary forms with a wide range of forms current in the spoken idiom. See Morgenstern, "Non-Standard Spellings," passim.

[177] See Morgenstern, "Geonic Responsa," p. 11.

#### 4.7.5.6 Orthographic Systems

The lower register in which much of RBA literature is composed never achieved a high degree of standardization, particularly in regard to its spelling. Accordingly, historical and phonetic spellings frequently interchange. Contra Morag, I believe that these frequently do not reflect phonetic realities. As argued in §3.3.1.1.2, the presence of an historical ʿayin in the orthography often seems to reflect an attempt to preserve historical spellings, whereas morphological changes indicate the true nature of the pronunciation. A spelling such as **תבעיי לא** "it (f.s.) **did** not **demand**" (*BQ* 111a [G1]) cannot reflect a form in which the ʿayin is preserved in pronunciation, since if this were the case, the analogy to the III-*yod* class would not have occurred.

The lack of uniformity in the orthography may account for some of the examples of variation in the manuscript traditions, though clearly not all. It cannot, for example, explain all the interchanges between the different pronouns or verbal morphemes.

#### 4.7.5.7 Textual Transmission

The manuscript evidence of the Talmud and Geonic literature indicates that already by the twelfth century, considerable linguistic and textual changes had entered the Aramaic literary product of Babylonia. Comparison of this evidence with that of the earliest manuscripts implies that scribal changes—errors and deliberate alterations—played a considerable role in this process.[178] The linguistic editing of the Talmud continued up until modern times.[179] We shall return to this issue in the final chapter.

### 4.8 Conclusion

Common to all of these explanations is the fact the Babylonian Rabbinic tradition lacked a single literary standard in which its Aramaic literary

---

[178] Sometimes, the attempt to standardize the language led to confusion; cf. Friedman, "Rabbah and Rava."

[179] One may also say that the linguistic editing of Geonic literature continued in the same fashion. A large number of the errors in Assaf's and Ginzberg's editions of early Geonic Geniza fragments arose through the imposition of grammatical forms familiar from the printed editions of the Talmud on the less familiar but more accurate forms found in the early manuscripts.

product was recorded. The interpretation of the evidence here suggests that while this literature was generally composed in an idiom relatively close to the spoken form of the language, this idiom had no fixed orthography and hence historical and non-historical spellings interchanged. Alongside this more colloquial idiom, the tradents, redactors, scribes or copyists (we cannot establish which) also employed a more conservative, formal idiom, which was preferred in certain contexts but was generally not employed exclusively in any literary work.[180]

---

[180] I say "generally" since Breuer's findings suggest that certain forms may have been employed exclusively in the non-standard tractates, e.g., אהכי(ן) "therefore." See Breuer, "Karetot," pp. 12–13 and tables 1–3.

CHAPTER 5

# The Direct Object in
# Rabbinic Babylonian Aramaic:
# Text, Structure, and Semantics

## 5.1 Background

In the previous chapters we have seen the importance of basing our description of RBA on the most accurate sources available. It was argued that since the publication of Epstein's *Grammar* in 1960, advances in research have led to the identification of a small group of early and accurate manuscripts, the EEMss, which are the only surviving sources that preserve the language of Rabbinic Babylonian literature in its pristine form. It was also indicated that while linguistically more conservative than the European manuscripts, the Yemenite manuscripts have nonetheless been subject to texual change, and accordingly, evidence adduced from them must be assessed in the light of the findings from earlier sources.[1]

In this chapter, I aim to demonstrate that the necessity to restrict the study of RBA to the small corpus of eastern manuscripts is true even in the field of syntax, which, in contrast to orthography and morphology, is sometimes regarded as one of the more stable elements in textual transmission.[2] It will be shown that study of the direct object constructions found in the eastern manuscripts—**HPS** and selected portions of Yemenite MS J—leads us to conclusions different from those found in the literature published to date. The internal evidence of these sources is highly consistent regarding the use of *lamed* as a direct object marker and the use of agreement pronouns; there are only a minute number of exceptions. However, when we compare these findings with the evidence of

---

[1] Cf. especially chapter 3 above.

[2] Kutscher, for example, felt that it was not necessary to include syntax in a grammar of Babylonian Aramaic, since it had been sufficiently dealt with by Schlesinger, *Satzlehre*. See Kutscher, "Review," p. 152 (reprinted in *Studies*, p. 230). However, as noted in chapter 2, n. 29, Kutscher himself disagreed with some of Schlesinger's conclusions, in light of his findings from manuscript sources.

the Spanish manuscript of *Neziqin* (H165) or later European sources, we find that the system that obtains in the early manuscripts has been lost, and that the *lamed* is employed more freely to mark the objects.

## 5.2 The Direct Object in RBA: Schlesinger's Description

According to Schlesinger, the direct object—whether noun or pronoun—may be indicated by the accusative *lamed*. Schlesinger records eight structures for the direct object:

1. עבדיה
2. עבד ליה
3. עבד מילתא
4. עבד למילתא
5. עבדה למילתא
6. עבד לה למילתא
7. מילתא עבדה
8. מילתא עבד לה

Since 7 and 8 in Schlesinger's scheme are examples of *casus pendens*, their core structures identical to 1 and 2, I shall not discuss them here, but shall rather concentrate on 1–6. Schlesinger was aware of the fact that the structure עבד לה was more common with the participle, because the participle itself does not take the direct object:

> Der Adverbialskasus bezeichnet zunächst ein von der Verbalhandlung affiziertes Object.
>
> Dieses kann in Form eines Pers.-Pron. suffigiert sein, . . . oder in Form eines nackten Substantivs hinter dem Verb stehen. Ist der Akkusativ determiniert, so kann er außerdem durch die Präposition ל׳ deutlich gemacht werden. Besonders häufig geschieht dies beim Part., das als ursprüngliches Nomen den nackten Akkusativ offenbar noch nicht gern regiert. Niemals ist das Part., abgesehen von ganz wenigen, z. Teil unsicheren Fällen, mit einem Personalsuffix versehen (s. Levias §§772, 723, 780), sondern es regiert das Pers.-Pron. durch Vermittlung von ל׳.[3]

---

[3] Schlesinger, *Stazlehre*, p. 101, §68. I have cited his words at length to emphasize the precision of this careful scholar. It is likely that had the resources available today been at Schlesinger's disposal, his conclusions would have been similar to those reached in this chapter.

A similar but briefer description appears in the teaching grammar of M. Margolis,[4] and both he and Schlesinger cite numerous examples that would appear to support the latter's description of the direct object constructions employed in RBA. However, examination of the most accurate manuscripts suggests that Schlesinger's description is in need of some revision. For the current survey, I have systematically examined extensive portions of several important Babylonian Aramaic manuscripts. Two are EEMss, and one is the best representative of the Yemenite manuscript tradition:

- *Halachot Pesuqot* Sassoon, according to the facsimile edition published in 1971.[5] The work is cited by page and line of the facsimile edition. When the text comprises a Talmudic citation, the original Talmudic source is noted. In the representative examples cited below, I have generally favored Talmudic citations.
- MS **G1** of *Bava Mezia*, including the unpublished sections, according to the photographs published by S. Friedman and other photographs held at the Microfilmed Manuscript Institute of the Jerusalem University and National Library. The manuscript contains the text of *Bava Mezia* from fol. 70a to fol. 85b.[6]
- In addition, I have examined the Yemenite manuscript of *Sanhedrin* and *Taʿanit* held by the *Yad HaRav Herzog*.[7] The chapter *Ḥeleq* (*Sanhedrin* 90a–113b) and the long Aramaic passage of *Taʿanit* (20b–25b) have been checked extensively.

---

[4] Margolis, *Manual*, pp. 84–85, §61.

[5] On this manuscript, see §2.14.2.1.

[6] See Friedman, "Early Manuscripts." On this manuscript see chapter 2.

[7] See Y. Kara, *Yemenite Manuscripts*, p. 8–9. Kara notes, ‏למרות שאב הטיפוס של כתב‎- ‏יד זה נעתק במאה השמינית לספירה נקי הוא משיבושים המאפיינים את יתר כתבי-היד‎ ‏התימניים, והוא המשובח שבהם. כתב-היד שלפנינו הוא היפה שבכתבי-היד התימניים‎ ("Even though the *Vorlage* of this manuscript was copied in the eighth century CE, it is free of the errors that characterize the other Yemenite manuscripts, and is the best among them. The present manuscript is the finest among the Yemenite manuscripts.") The textual tradition of the manuscript has been discussed in detail by Sabato, *Yemenite Manuscript*. See also Breuer's important comments in "Sabato," and my comments in chapter 2.

Occasionally, I have supplemented these examples with additional ones drawn from other EEMss, in order to clarify some of the finer points of usage.

## 5.3 Summary of Findings

From these accurate sources, it emerges that five syntactic structures are employed in RBA sources to express the direct objects of transitive verbs:[8]

| Participle | Finite Verb/Infinitive |
|---|---|
| עבד עובדא/עאביד עובדא (A) | |
| עאביד ליה (B2) | עבדיה (B1) |
| עאביד ליה לעובדא (C2) | עבדיה לעובדא (C1) |

Several points are worth emphasizing here:
1.  As Schlesinger already concluded, the structures of the participles differ from those of other verbal forms, in that the participles do not take enclitic object pronouns.[9]

---

[8] I do not deal here with the syntagm קָטִיל לֵיה "he killed," which lies beyond the scope of the present study. On this structure, see Kutscher, "Two Passive Constructions," and Goldenberg, "Aramaic Perfects," and Bar-Asher, "qətil li."

[9] In the entire corpus of material I have checked, I have found almost no examples of the participle with an object pronoun. In Morgenstern, "Geonic Responsa," p. 342, I incorrectly interpreted לא מחייביה (TGAs28 xvii 2a 5) as מחייב "he requires" + obj. יה- "him." However, upon rereading the context of this exceptional form, it became apparent that although written in the manuscript as one word, this should be read מחיי ביה "I did not protest against him." (On this use of the prepositional ב- cf. Sokoloff, DJBA, p. 655 s.v. מחיי#1.) This leaves only the forms תֹּאלֹה "he teaches it" (RH 29b [HPS 25:19]) and תאנה (MQ 8b [HPS 275:10]; BM 117b [HPS 145:15]), which according to the convincing interpretation suggested by Boyarin, "Studies," p. 175, should be interpreted as a participle with pronominal suffix. However, this appears to belong to a formal terminological level of RBA, rather than to the living language.

Kara lists occasional examples, though not all are certain; for example, עבדיה לאילו "he did [sacrificed] his ram" (Yom 71a [JTS1623]; Kara, Yemenite Manu-

In RBA, the infinitive takes the pronominal suffixes of the verb.[10] Accordingly, the structures here form a complementary distribution, and should be presented as such. Incidentally, we may note that there is some evidence to suggest that the prepositional *lamed* was often affixed to the participle, in which case in terms of underlying structure, the two complementary forms would be very similar.[11] For example, פרקיה "redeem it (imper.)" and פריק ליה "he redeems it" would be *pirqeh* (verb+pronoun) and *pāriqleh* (verb+*l*+pronoun).

2. Contra Schlesinger, I have not found that the participles prefer constructions with a *lamed* when the object is not pronominal. The use of the *lamed* in these cases is dependent upon the definite or indefinite status of the object. See below, §5.6.2.

3. The overwhelming evidence suggests that the pattern עבד למילתא (or participle עאביד למילתא) is not a legitimate construction in this dialect, but results from textual error. See below §5.7.

## 5.4 Representative Examples

Below I cite examples of all of these constructions on the basis of accurate manuscripts. Since constructions A and B are extremely common, I have cited only representative examples, though the restricted corpus upon which this chapter is based has been examined in its entirety. In contrast, I have cited extensively the examples of construction C, with the intention of establishing the precise use of this construction.[12]

---

scripts, p. 321) may be a perfect, referring to the past activity of Aaron about which the verse cited speaks. Particularly notable is the interchange of the unexpected מפקיה "they will bring him out" (*Pes* 91a [JTS1623] Kara, *Yemenite Manuscripts*, p. 187) for the more regular מפקי ליה (*Pes* 91a [O23, Col]).

[10] As Avinery, "Pronominal Objects," demonstrated, this is also the common form in the Syriac of the Peshitta. In Targum Onkelos and Jonathan, infinitive forms take the suffixed pronouns of the nouns, and this may have been the case in some forms of Babylonian Aramaic. See Morgenstern, "Unpublished Parallels."

[11] For the affixed *lamed* see now Morgenstern, "Mandaic."

[12] I have highlighted the relevant constructions in bold characters. In the English translation, only the lexical element of verbal action and direct object have been highlighted; accordingly, the highlighted verbs of the English do not correspond

## 5.4.1 Structure A: עבד עובדא/עאביד עובדא

A non-pronominal direct object is unmarked.

### 5.4.1.1 Perfect

*EEMss Talmudic*: מר זוטרא **קבע סעודתיה** עילויה "Mar Zuṭra **set his meal** around it" (*Ber* 38a [HPS 16:9]); **בערו חמירא** דבני חילא "They burned **the** soldiers' **leaven**" (*Pes* 5b [HPS 9:8]); **שדר** לה **גיטא** לדביתהו "He sent her **a divorce deed**" (*Git* 34a [HPS 92:8–9]); רב כהנא **יהב זוזי** אכיתנא "R. Kahana **gave money** for cotton" (*BQ* 103a [HPS 72:13]); **בנו** להו **ספסלי** "They **constructed benches** for them" (*BM* 84b [G1]); **קביל** עליה **איסורי** "He **took chastisements** upon himself" (*BM* 84b [G1]); **איתו** ליה שיתין **עבדי** "They **brought** him sixty **slaves**" (*BM* 84b [G1]); **איתו** לקמיה שיתין **מיני דמא** "They **brought** before him sixty **types of blood**" (*BM* 84b [G1]); **חזי ריחשא** דקא נפיק מיאוניה "I **saw an insect** coming out of his ear" (*BM* 84b [G1]); **אמ'** מר **מילתיה** "One scholar **said his piece**" (*BM* 84b [G1]); רב פפא **זבן ארעא** "Rav Papa **bought land**" (*BB* 106a [HPS 149:12]).

*EEMss Geonic*: אי **קביל** עליה ישראל **נטירותא** "If a Jew **takes** upon himself [the responsibilities of] **guarding**" (HPS 8:9); מאן **דקדיש** **איתתא** "A person who **betrothed a woman**" (HPS 168:9–10); והיכא **דעיילת** ליה **דהבא וכספא ומאני לבושא** וכו' "If she **brought** to him [as a dowry] **gold and silver and items of clothing**, etc." (HPS 180:11).

*Yemenite MS J*: **תלא נפשיה** "He **hung himself**" (*Tan* 21a); **שדרו דרון** לקיסר "They **sent a gift** to the Emperor" (*Tan* 21a); **גזר תעניתא** "He **enacted a fast**" (*Tan* 21b); **שדר** אביי זוזא מרבנן "Abbaye **sent a pair** of Rabbis" (*Tan* 21b); **דיהב** מארי דיוראי **עיניה** בגוה "whom the official[13] **set his eye** upon"(*Tan* 22a); **איתאי דורדיא** דחמרא "I **brought** wine **sediments**" (*Tan* 22a); **חזא** ההוא **גוברא** "He **saw a certain man**" (*Tan* 23a); לא **נהגו** ביה **יקרא** "They did not **treat** him with re- spect" (*Tan* 23a); **הבו** ליה **שלמא. לא אסבר** להו אפי. **דרא טעוניה** אחד כתפיה **וגלימיה** אחד כתפיה "They **gave** him **greetings**. He did not **show** them **a friendly face**... he **took up his load** upon one of his shoulders and **his cloak** on one of his shoulders" (*Tan* 23a–23b);

---

exactly to the highlighted verbs of the Aramaic original in which wider linguistic information is embedded in the verb.

[13] The precise meaning of this term is uncertain. See Sokoloff, *DJBA*, p. 708 s.v. מרי דיורא. Sokoloff suggests that, in the context, this term refers to the chief war- den of a prison.

**יהב** ליה לחד ינוקא **ריפתא** ולחד ינוקא **תרתי** "He **gave a piece of bread** to one child, and to one child **two**" (*Tan* 23b); בצנעה בלא **זוטרי איתי** דעתיהו "He secretly **brought small ones** without their knowing" (*San* 93a); על **חזא כולה ירושלם** "He **saw all of Jerusalem**" (*San* 95a); להההוא ביתא **ואשכח תרין מלאכי** "He entered that house and **found two angels**" (*San* 96a); **ושדא פרטאתא** בביתיה "He **left a rift** in his family" (*San* 96b); **איתי** ליה **משחא** במאנא ושף "He **brought** him **oil** in a vessel and he anointed [himself]" (*San* 101a); **איתי תורנגלא** "He **brought a chicken**" (*San* 105b); **שדא דהבא וכספא** קמיה "He **put gold and silver** before him" (*San* 107b).

## 5.4.1.2 Imperfect

*EEMss Talmudic*: **ליעבדו סכה** התם וליתיבו "Let them **make a sukka** and sit" (*Suk* 26a [HPS 39:19]); לא **נקני** ליה איניש **הושענא** לינוקא "A person **should not transfer ownership of a lulav bundle** to a child" (*Suk* 46b [HPS 47:12]); **מאי איבי** "**What** should I **do**?" (*BM* 84a [G1]);[14] **ניתי כסא** דכספא "Let him **bring a silver cup**" (*BM* 84a [G1]).

*Yemenite MS J*: **נעביד עסקא** "Let us **do business**" (*Tan* 21a); מן **נשדר**?! **נשדר** בהדיה **נחום איש גם זו** "**Whom** should we **send**? Let us **send** with it Naḥum of Gamzo" (*Tan* 21a); **ניברי** בהו מר **נפשיה** "May Sir **cure himself** with them" (*Tan* 21b); ולא **נחזיק טיבותא** לנפשן "Let us not **take credit** for ourselves" (*Tan* 23b); **ליקרי קרית שמע** "Let him **read the Shema**" (*San* 94a); בר ברך **קירא לזבון** "May your grandson **buy bitumen**"[15] (*San* 95a); אמאי לא תיתי **תשקול מזונך** "Why don't you come and **take your food**?" (*San* 108b); דאית ליה תורא **לישקול** "May he who has an ox **take** one hide. May he who does not have an ox **take two hides**" חד **משכא** דלית ליה תורא **לישקול** תרי **משכי** "May he who has an ox **take one hide. May he who does not have an ox take two hides**" (*San* 109b).

## 5.4.1.3 Imperative

*EEMss Talmudic*: **איתו** לן **חמירא** מבני חילא "**Bring us leaven** from the soldiers" (*Pes* 30a [HPS 12:15]); **חזai מאי** קא עביד "**See what** he is doing" (*BM* 84b [G1]); **הבא** לי **פלגא** רואחא **ופלגא** קרנא "**Give** me **half profit, half capital**" (*BM* 105a [HPS 93:14]); זיל **זבון** לי **ארעא** "Go and **buy** me **land**" (*BB* 169b [HPS 103:16]); כי היכי דלא **ליפגום שטריה** "that he should not **damage his deed**" (*BB* 172a [HPS

---

[14] A phonetic spelling for historical אֶעֱבִיד.

[15] Traditionally "wax." See Sokoloff, *DJBA*, p. 1015 s.v. קירא #1.

**שליפו פזמקכו** וחותו לדינא (104:9])); "**Remove your shoes** and go down to judge" (*Shev* 31a [HPS 194:15]); **יהוב מתנאתא** לכהנתא "**Give the prebends** to the priests' daughters" (*Hul* 131b [HPS 58:10, 61:11]).

*EEMss Geonic:* **אוסיף** עליהו **חומש** דידהו "**Add** to them **one-fifth** of their own" (HPS 57:14); **איכול פלגא** ברואחא **ודרי תלתי** תרי בזיאנא "**Enjoy half** as profit and **bear two-thirds** as a loss" (HPS 94:2); שקול מאניך והדר **איתי** לי **אגראי** "Take your vessel and **then bring** me **my wage**" (HPS 126:10); **הבא לי כתובתאי** "**Give** me my *ketubba* payment" (HPS 156:13).

*Yemenite MS J:* **איתו מאן הב** לן **מיטרא** "**Give** us **rain**" (*Tan* 23b]); דבעיתו בהדיכו "**Bring whomsoever** you wish with you" (*San* 93a); זיל **איתי** לי **מספרא** דאגיזך "Go and **bring me scissors**, that I may cut your hair" (*San* 96a).

## 5.4.1.4 Participle

*EEMss Talmudic:* דיתובי **מיתבא דעתה** "that she **calms her thoughts**" (*Shab* 128b [HPS 1:6]); אנא **חדתאתא עאבידנא** "**I make new ones**" (*Pes* 30b [HPS 12:20–21]); להנהו **דמזבני אסא** "to those who **sell myrtle**" (*Suk* 34b [HPS 45:10]); דקא **מגמר** ליה **שיקרא** "For he is **teaching** him falsehood" (*Suk* 46b [HPS 47:15]); דהוה **מזבין** **ארעא וזבין עבדי** "who used to **sell land and buy slaves**" (*Git* 52a [HPS 80:18–19]); הוה **מפקי** מיניה **דקולי דקולי** דתרבא "They **took out** of him **baskets and baskets** of fat" (*BM* 83a [G1]); **יהיבנא לך אחתאי** "I will **give** you **my sister**" (*BM* 84a [G1]); כי הוה **אמנא מילתא** "when I would **say something**" (*BM* 84a [G1]); **ומפריקנא** ליה עשרין וארבעה **פרוקי** "And I [would] **explain** for him twenty-four **explanations**" (*BM* 84a [G1]); הוה **מייכי** ליה שיתין **נמטי ונגדי** מיתותיה שיתין "They would **spread** for him sixty **bed coverings** and would **draw** from under him sixty **bowls** of blood and pus" (*BM* 84b [G1]); הוה **ראמי כיסתא** לחֵיותא "He would **throw fodder** to the animals"(*BM* 85a [G1]); אי **ידעיתו זימנה** כיתבוה בזמנה "If you **know its time**, write it at its time" (*BB* 172a [HPS 103:20]).

*EEMss Geonic:* **מבריך ברכת** המזון **ושתי כסא** דבירכתא "He **recites the grace** after meals and **drinks** from **the blessing cup**" (HPS 16:1–2); איתתא **דיריתת ממונא** מן בית נשה "A woman who **inherited money** from her father's house" (HPS 77:3–4)

*Yemenite MS J*: הוה **משדר שליחא** "He would **send a messenger**" (*Tan* 20b); הוה **כריך רפתא** "He was **taking bread**" (*Tan* 21a); כל דקא **דמשייל לי מילתא** "Anyone who **asks** me **something**" (*Tan* 21a); ואסרנא **מושיל מרא וזבילי** "He **lends a hoe and basket**" (*Tan* 21b); **גבריא** לחודיהו **ונשיא** לחודיהו "I **imprison the men** separately and **the women** separately" (*Tan* 22a); **רמינא פיראי** "I **set my bed**" (*Tan* 22a); כי **חזינא בת ישראל** דיהבי גוים עה **מסרנא נפשאי** עיניהו "When I **see a Jewess** whom the gentiles have **set their eyes** upon, I **endanger my life**" (*Tan* 22a); לא **מחתת חוטי** "**You** do not **put laces**"[16] (*Tan* 22a); כי **חזינן איניש** דעציבא דעתיה "When we **see a sad man**" (*Tan* 22a); טרחינן **ועבדינן** להו **שלמא** "We take great efforts and **we make peace** between them"(*Tan* 22a); דקא **נטע חרובא** "who was **planting a carob tree**" (*Tan* 23a); דקא **מנקיט חרובא** "who was **gathering carob**" (*Tan* 23b); הוו **שאדו אגרה** אגבה "They **would put its fee** on its back" (*Tan* 24a); אבישי בן צרויה הוה קא **חייף רישיה** "**Avishai** son of Seruyah was **washing his hair**" (*San* 95a); והוו **קאטחני קשיאתא** "And they were **grinding [date] stones**" (*San* 96a); אנן קא **מתנינן** "We **teach** four **orders**" (*San* 106b); יומא הוה יתיב וקא **ארבעה סדרי** "One day he was sitting and **splitting up a pomegranate**" (*San* 108b).

## 5.4.1.5 Infinitive

*EEMss Talmudic*: **לאיתויי מאי לאיתויי הא** דתנו רבנן "To **include what**? To **include this** [teaching] that the Rabbis taught" (*Suk* 8b [HPS 32:17–18]); **לאיתויי מאניה** "to **bring his clothes**" (*BM* 84a [G1]); מצוה **מימנא יומי**. ומצוה **למימנא שבועי** "It is a commandment to **count the days**, and a commandment to **count the weeks**" (*Men* 66a [HPS 17:6]).

*EEMss Geonic*: אסיר **למילש מצה** "It is forbidden to **knead unleavened bread**" (HPS 14:16); **למימנא** שבעה שבועי "to **count** seven weeks" (HPS 17:3); ובאעי **למיכל סעודתיה** בסכה "He wants to **eat his meal** in the *sukka*" (HPS 40:21); **לאיתויי לי זוזי** "to **bring me** *zuzim*" (HPS 98:20); **למיכתב גיטא** לאיתתיה "to **write a divorce deed** for his wife" (HPS 203:2).

*Yemenite MS J*: **לאיתויי ביזרא** דאספסתא "to **bring** alfalfa **seeds**" (*San* 93a).

---

16 Or "tie fringes."

## 5.4.2 Structure B1 עבדיה (Non-participle)

The direct object is a suffixed pronoun.

### 5.4.2.1 Perfect

*EEMss Talmudic*: תרגמה "He **explained it**" (*Shab* 150b [HPS 4:10]);
לתקוני **שדרתך** "I **sent you** to remedy [things]" (*Git* 42b [HPS 83:3]);
שקל **זבינתה** "She took [it] and **sold it**" (*Git* 52a [HPS 81:4]); לא
**אתנחתינהו** ידענא היכא "I don't know where I **put them**" (*BM* 42a
[HPS 126:11]); **תפסוה** "They **seized him**" (*BM* 83b [G1]); **זקפוה**
"They **hung him**" (*BM* 83b [G1]); שמעתיה **דביתהו** "His wife **heard
him**" (*BM* 84b [G1]); **טהרינהו** "He **declared them pure**"(*BM* 84b
[G1]); **אגניתיה** בעיליתא "I **laid him down** in the upper story" (*BM*
84b [G1]); **ואסקוה ואמטיוה** למערתא דאבוה "They **took him up** and
**brought him** to his father's cave"(*BM* 84b [G1]); **אסיקונהו** "They
**took them up**" (*BM* 84b [G1]); **שבקוה ייסורי** (*BM* 85a [G1]) "The
chastisements **left him**" (*BM* 85a [G1]); **ובטילנֵיה** "We would **cancel
it**" (*BM* 85a [G1]); מינך **זבנתיה ואכלתיה** "I **bought it** from you and
**ate it**" (*BB* 30a [HPS 135:4]); **ומלייה** מיא **וארתחיה** "He **filled it** with
water and **boiled it up**" (*ᶜAZ* 76b [HPS 16:17]); **חיביה** רב נחמן "R.
Nahman **found him liable**" (*Hul* 132b [HPS 60:20]).

*EEMss Geonic*: **אפייה** "He **baked it**" (HPS 16:11); **שמעינון** דקא וכד
**שבקינון** מדלגין "When he **heard them** skipping [text], he **let them
alone**" (HPS 51:11–12); **נסביך** "He **married you**" (HPS 156:14);
**ואצרכוהי** גיטא "They **required** a divorce deed **of him**" (HPS 169:7);
**וקבילתיה** גט **דקדשה** ההוא לה דיכתב היכא "If the one who 'sanctified' [married] her wrote her a divorce deed and **she accepted it**"
(HPS 237:13–14).

*Yemenite MS J*: **חזונהו** "They **saw them**" (*Tan* 21a); **וכבשוה** "They
**captured it**" (*Tan* 21a); **אוכלינהו ואשקינהו** "He **fed them** and **gave
them to drink**" (*Tan* 21b); **שקלונהו** בהדיהו **ואפקינהו** לשוקא "They
**took them** with them and **brought them out** into the street" (*Tan*
22a); **קריתך** דכי "that when I **called you**" (*Tan* 22a); מאן חרובא האיי
**שתליה** "This carob tree—who **planted it**?" (*Tan* 23a); **הימנוה** לא
"They did not **believe him**" (*Tan* 23a); **אשכחוה** "They **found him**"
(*Tan* 23a); **שבקיה** "He **left him**" (*Tan* 23b); **אשכחיה** "He **found
him**" (*Tan* 24a); **דסבעין** "He **satiated us**" (*Tan* 24a); **דשקלינהו** "that
he **took them**" (*Tan* 24a); בהדיהו **ושדיוה אתיוה** "They **brought him**
and **threw him down** with them" (*San* 93a); **קלינהו** "They **burned
them**" (*San* 93a); אבוה לגבי **שדרתינהו** לגבה אתו כי "When they came
to her **she sent them** to her father" (*San* 93a); **שאלתינהו** "I **asked**

them" (*San* 93a); פתק ביה גירא ולא **מטייה** "He fired an arrow at him, but it did not **reach him**" (*San* 95a); **משכיה** עד **דאמטייה** למחנה פלשתים "He **drew him** on until he **brought him** to the Philistine camp" (*San* 95a); **חזיתיה** "She **saw him**" (*San* 95a); **וקטלתינהו** "You **killed them**" (*San* 95b); ולא **ענייה** "They didn't **answer him**" (*San* 101b); **שקלה כרכה** בשיראיי **ואותבה** בסיפטא "He **took it**, **wrapped it in silks**, and **placed it** in a casket" (*San* 104a); ושמעון בן שטח **אטמרתיה אחתיה** "Shimeon ben Shaṭṭaḥ—his sister **hid him**" (*San* 107b); **אלבשוה וכסיוה ועיילוה** לבי גנאזיה דמלכא "They **outfitted him** and **brought him in** to the royal treasury" (*San* 108b); **אשכחוה שפוהא** דובשא **ואוקמוהא** אאיגרא דשורא "They **found her**, **daubed her** in honey, and **set her up** on the top of the city wall" (*San* 109b); **בלעתנון** ארעא "The earth **swallowed them up**" (*San* 110a).

## 5.4.2.2 Imperfect

*EEMss Talmudic*: **לשהיינהי** "Let him **leave them**" (*Pes* 30a [**HPS** 12:18]); **ליקנייה** "Let him **acquire it**" (*Suk* 30b [**HPS** 41:15]); **לקנינהו** ניה ליה אגב ארעא "Let him **transfer their ownership** to him along with land" (*BM* 46a [**HPS** 96:21]); תא **אגמרך** היכי תיבי "Come, let me **teach you** how you should act" (*BM* 83b [**G1**]); **ונימלייה** פרצידי דרומנא סומקא "Let him **fill it** with seeds of a red pomegranate" (*BM* 84a [**G1**]); **ונתביה** בין שמשא לטולא "Let him **put it** between the sun and the shade" (*BM* 84a [**G1**]); דלא **נדיחקוה** "that they should not **press him**" (*BM* 84b [**G1**]); כהיכי דלא **נקריוך** מפסיד עיסקי "so that they **should** not **call you** a business loser" (*BM* 105a [**HPS** 93:10–11]); ניזיל **נשיילינהו** "Let us go and **ask them**" (*ᶜAra* 21b [**HPS** 188:5]).

*EEMss Geonic*: וכד פישי תרי לא **נישחוטינהו** עד למחר "If two remain he should not **slaughter them** until the next day" (**HPS** 61:17–18); **נודעיה** שלשים יום מיקמי **דליפקיה** "He should **inform him** thirty days before he **removes him**" (**HPS** 107:20); והדר **ליכתביה** "And then he should **write it**" (**HPS** 205:15).

*Yemenite MS J*: **וליתביה** לעניים "Let him **give it** to the poor" (*Tan* 20b); **ולישדייה** לבהמה "Let him **throw it** to an animal" (*Tan* 20b); תא **ונישדייה** עילאווייהו ולא ליזבניה "Let him not **buy it**" (*Tan* 20b); **ונקטלינהו** "Come, let us **throw it down** on them and **kill them**" (*Tan* 21a); **לישקלינהו** מר "May Sir **take them**" (*Tan* 22a); לא **ניחשדון** "They should not **suspect me** over bread" (*Tan* 24a); **ניסבעך** אריפתא "May he **satiate you**" (*Tan* 24a); סברא דליפול עליה **וניקטלניה** "She thought that it would fall on him and **kill him**" (*San* 95a); זיל איתי

לי מספרא **דאגיזך** "Go bring me scissors that I may **tonse you**" (San 96a); אי הכי לא **ליכתביה** כלל "If so, let him not **write it** at all" (San 103b); כי מטיא ההיא שעתא **אילוטיה** "When that moment comes I shall **curse him**" (San 105b); ואנא נמי **אצעריה** "Shall I also **aggrieve him**?" (San 108b).

### 5.4.2.3 Imperative

*EEMss Talmudic*: בהדי דאתית **איתינהו** ניה לי "When you come **bring them** to me" (BQ 104b [**HPS** 97:16–17]); **תִּיפְסֵיה** "**Seize them!**" (BM 83b [**G1**]); **אגניין** "**Lay me down**" (BM 84b [**G1**]); **שבקינהו** "**Leave them!**" (BM 85a [**G1**]); זיל את **זבנה** מינה "You go and **buy it** from her" (BB 169b [**HPS** 103:17]).

*Yemenite MS J*: **שבקינו** "**Leave them**" (Tan 21a); **אגמרן דאידרשה** משמך "**Teach me**, that I may **expound upon it** in your name" (San 102b); **קבלן** "**Accept me**" (San 107b).

### 5.4.2.4 Infinitive

*Talmudic*: איכתש **לפרוקיה** "He strove to **save him**" (BM 83b [**G1**]); איתבעי לך **לאודעון** "You needed to **inform me**" (BM 101b [**HPS** 108:7]); דניחא ליה **לקרוביה** "It satisfies him to **bring him** into the family" (BB 168b [**HPS** 101:21]); לא הוה איפשר **לאפוקה** מיניה "It was not possible to **take it** from him" (BQ 112b [**HPS** 124:8]).

*EEMss Geonic*: ולית יה למאריה **למישקליה** "and its owner is not around to **take it**" (HPS 8:5); **לבעוריה** "to **destroy it**" (HPS 8:10); כל כמא צריך **למיפרקיה** "He needs to **redeem it**" (HPS 50:14–15); דלא מטבלין שרי **לזבוננהו** "As long as they do not immerse themselves it is permitted to **sell them**" (HPS 64:20); והיכא דקא באעי למיתן מתנה זוזי לחבריה וליתיה גביה **למיתבינון** ליה במשיכה "If he wants to give as a gift coins to his friend and he is not with him to **give them** by taking physical possession" (HPS 96:20–21); שטרא דמתאחר ולא כתבוהי בזימניה ובעו **למיכתביה** בתר הכי "A deed which was delayed and which they did not write at the time, and they wish to **write it** afterward" (HPS 99:11–12); לית ליה רשותא **לאשבועה** כלל "He has no right to **adjure her**" (HPS 180:20).

*Yemenite MS J*: בעא **למקטלינהו** "He tried to **kill them**" (Tan 21a); דלא מצו **למכבשה** "They were unable to **capture it**" (Tan 21a); שדר אביי זווא מרבנן **למיבדקיה** "Abbaye send a pair of Rabbis to **test him**" (Tan 21b); שקלונהו בהדיהו ואפקינהו לשוקא **לזבונינהו** "They took them with them and brought them out into the street to **sell them**" (*Tan* 22a); **בעינא למבדקינכו** "I want to **test you**" (*San* 93a).

### 5.4.3 Structure B2: עאביד ליה (Participle only; direct object is a pronoun affixed to object marker)

*EEMss Talmudic*: **משכחת ליה** "you **find it**" (*Suk* 32b [HPS 44:1]); חזינא ליה לרב כהנא **דמסדר להי** כולהי אכסא דקידושא "I see R. Kahana **recites them** all over the cup of sanctification" (*Suk* 46a [HPS 37:17–18]); היכי **יכלת להו** "How do you **overcome them**?" (*BM* 83b [G1]); ר' יוחנן לא קא **חשיב ליה** "Rabbi Yohanan—He does not **count him**" (*BM* 84a [G1]); את קא **מיתית להו** עלך "You are **bringing them** upon yourself" (*BM* 84b [G1]); עגלא דהוה קא **ממטו ליה** דההוא למשחטה "for a certain calf that they **were bringing** in order to to slaughter it" (*BM* 85a [G1]); והוה קא **כנשא להו** "And she was **sweeping them up**" (*BM* 85a [G1]); לא **ידענא לך** "I do not **recognize you**" (*BM* 39b [HPS 109:6]); דאינהו אשבחו **מסלקינן להו** "that they improved [the land]—we settle their claim [lit., **remove them**]" (*BM* 110b [HPS 83:11]); **כתבא ליה** ניה ליה "She would **write it** over to him" (*BB* 151b [HPS 88:8–9]).[17]

*EEMss Geonic*: **מבטיל ליה** "He **annuls it**" (HPS 6:19); **וחאזי ליה** "He **sees it**" (HPS 7:1); **מזבין ליה** לגוים "He **sells it** to the gentiles" (HPS 8:7); **שריף ליה** "He **burns it**" (HPS 8:8); **תרי ליה** ... **ואכיל ליה** "He **soaks it** ... he **eats it**" (HPS 16:4–5); כד **בצע לה** "When he **breaks it**" (HPS 16:12); שקיל דמי מתנות ומשדר להו להיכא דאיכא כהן "He takes the value of these gifts and **sends them** to wherever there is a priest" (HPS 61:7); **פלגין להון** בתלתה חולקין "They **divide them** into three parts" (HPS 84:19); **מגבנן להו** מיניה "We **collect them** from him" (HPS 162:1); **ובדקינן ליה** "We **inspect him**" (HPS 239:16).

*Yemenite MS J*: **מפקין ליה** בגוהרקא דדהבא "They would **take him** out in a golden carriage" (*Tan* 20b); הוה **סתר לה** "He would **demolish it**" (*Tan* 20b); אי אפשר ליה למרה באני לה "If its owner could, he **would build it**" (*Tan* 20b); **זאבין ליה ושאדי ליה** לנהרא "He would **buy it** and **throw it** into the river" (*Tan* 20b);[18] כולהו מצינא **מקיימנא**

---

[17] For this example of ליה (direct object) and ניהליה (indirect object) together, cf. מי יאמר דמזבני לה ניהליה "Who would say that they would sell it to him?" (*BM* 16b [Hark 178:5]); ויהבין לה ניהליה "They give it to him" (Hark 1:29); בעינא דמחוית ליה ניה לי "I want you to show him to me" (*San* 39a [J]).

[18] Note the differing uses of the preposition in this sentence.

**להו** "All of these—I can **do them**" (*Tan* 20b); **מלביש לה** "He would **dress her**" (*Tan* 21b); **מסרנא נפשאי ומצלנא לה** "I endanger my life and I **save her**" (*Tan* 22a); **ומבטלי לה** "And they **cancel it**" (*Tan* 22a); **ונקטין ליה** בשיפולי **יכילנא ליה** "I can **overcome him**" (*Tan* 22a); "Grasping him at his skirts" (*Tan* 23b); וקא **חשיב ליה** בתר הכי "He **counts him** afterward" (*San* 93a); אלהא רבא **קריתון ליה וכתביתון ליה** לבסוף "You call him the Great God but **you write him** at the end?" (*San* 96a); אנא **מפייסנא ליה** "I shall **convince him**" (*San* 96b); **ומיתו ליה** "They will **bring him**" (*San* 96b); מילט קא **לייטת לי** "You curse me" (*San* 99a).

### 5.4.4 Structure C1: עבדיה לעובדא (Non-participle)

An objective core argument is non-pronominal, marked with *l-*, and is anticipated by agreeing obj. suffix.

### 5.4.4.1 Perfect

*EEMss Talmudic*: רב אשי **אשכחיה לרב כהנא** "R. Ashi **found R. Kahana**" (*Suk* 7a [**HPS** 32:2]; *Suk* 19a [**HPS** 35:5–6]); לישנא **שחיוה** כולי עלמא **לפרדיסייהו** לחולו דמועדא **אפקריה** רבי ינאי **לפרדיסיה** "The next year everyone **kept his vineyard** waiting till the festival week; R. Yannai **renounced ownership of his vineyard**" (*MQ* 12b [**HPS** 279: 14–15]); **דאשכחינהו** שמואל **לתלמידי** דרב "Shemuel **found the disciples of Rav**" (*Qid* 25b [**HPS** 107:12]); אפקורי **אפקריה** רחמנא **לזרעיה** "The Merciful One **declared his progeny ownerless**" (*Yev* 98a [**HPS** 63:9]); אתא בעל חוב **טרפה לחדא** וקא אזיל **טרפה לאידך** "The creditor came and **seized one**, and went and **seized the other**" (*Ket* 91b [**HPS** 77:18–19]);[19] דגרועי **גרעה לנטירותיה** "He is reducing its protection (*BM* 36b [**HPS** 126:2]); **דאנסוהי לכולהי ארעאתא** דגזלן "that they **seized all the** thief's **lands**, and also **ואנסוה** נמי **לדידה** "also seized his" (*BQ* 116b [**HPS** 128:18])[20]; **שמטיה לקועיה** "He tore out his windpipe" (*BQ* 117a [**HPS** 129:19–20]); **אגביה** רב נהמן **לאפדניה** מניה "R; Nahman **exacted payment** from him **from his estate**" (*BM* 35a [**HPS** 125:19]); **אשכחוה לעכנה** "They **found a snake**" (*BM* 84b [**G1**]); **דחזיוה להילל** דהוה עדיף מינייהו "For they **saw Hillel** was greater than they" (*BM* 85a [**G1**]); **קבריה לרישיה** בכנפיה דרבי "It **buried its head** in Rav's folds (*BM* 85a [**G1**]); ההוא דיאנא **דאחתיה**

---

[19] MS Firk187 reads: אתא בעל חוב טרפא לחדא מינייהו. הדר אתא וקא טריף לה לאידך. The printed editions read: הדר קטריף לאידך.

[20] On this reading, see §3.5.2.7.1. MS H165 reads: דאנסוה לכולהו ארעאתא דיליה ואנסוה נמי להא ארעא בהדיהו.

למלוה לניכסי דלוה מיקמי דניתבעיה "A certain judge who **allowed the lender** to take possession[21] of borrower's property before he would sue him" (*BB* 174a [**HPS** 73:21–22]); ההוא ערבא דיתמי **דפרעיה** "A certain guarantor of orphans who **paid the lender** before he would would sue the orphans" (*BB* 174a [**HPS** 74:3–4]); פסקה אבוהו **למילתא** "Their father definitively expressed his statement" (*BB* 175a [**HPS** 75:11–12, 13]); אזל **שקלינהו** **לאיגריה** דבי "He proceeded to **remove the horizontal portions** of the [letter] *bet*" (*BB* 167a [**HPS** 100:7]); אימיה דרב זוטרא בר טובייה **כתבתנהו לניכסה** לרב זוטרא "R. Zutra son of Tuviah's mother **wrote over her property** to R. Zutra" (*BB* 151a [**HPS** 186:4–5]).

*EEMss Geonic*: מאן **דאוזפיה לחבריה** דינרי "one who **lent his companion** dinars" (**HPS** 65:20); **חזיתיה לגברא** פלניא דטבע "I **saw Mr. X** drowned" (**HPS** 231:3–4).

*Yemenite MS J*: שמעיה ר׳ יוחנן **למלאך** "R. Yohanan **heard the angel**" (*Tan* 21a); **שקלוה למא** דהוה בסיפטיה "They **took what** was in his caskets" (*Tan* 21a); **שרינהו לסיפטי** "He/they **opened the caskets**" (*Tan* 21a) // **שרונהו לסיפטי** "They **opened the caskets**" (*San* 109a); איילינהו לבי גנזא דמלכא **ומלונהו לסיפטי** "They brought him into the king's treasury and **filled his caskets**" (*Tan* 21a); **קטלונהו לכולהו** הני "They **killed all** those villagers" (*Tan* 21a) // **קטלינהו לכולהו** דיוראי "He/they **killed them all**" (*San* 109a); **חזייה לההוא גברא** "He saw the man" (*Tan* 23a); **שמעינהו לרבנן** "He heard the Rabbis" (*Tan* 23a); **דלינהי למאניה** ... **אחתינהו למאניה** "He lifted his clothes ... he lowered his clothes" (*Tan* 23b); **אודענהו לר׳ יוחנן ולריש לקיש** "They informed R. Yohanan and Resh Laqish" (*Tan* 24a);[22] **שמעינהו להנך** "He **heard the clouds** saying" (*Tan* 25a); **חזייה** **ענני** דקא אמרי "He **heard the clouds** saying" (*Tan* 25a); **קלייה לאלהיה** בנורא "He **saw his daughter**" (*Tan* 25a); **לברתיה** **burned his god** with fire" (*San* 93a); הינו האיי **דקטליה לגלית** אחי "This is the one who **killed Goliath** my brother" (*San* 95a); **רכביה** **לפרדיה** "He **rode his mule**" (*San* 95a); **חזייה לערפה** אימיה "He saw Orpa his mother" (*San* 95a); **פסקתיה לפילכה** "She **cut off her spindle**" (*San* 95a); **דעציה לניסכא** בארעא **ופתקיה לדוד** לעילא "He **stuck the lance** in the ground and **threw David** aloft" (*San* 95a); **אוקמיה** **לדוד** בין שמיא לארעא "He **set David up** between the heavens and the earth" (*San* 95a); **דאיתיתנהו לבניהו** "whose **sons** you **brought**" (*San* 95b); אלהא רבא **דשיזביה לנח** מטופנא "The Great God who

---

[21] Literally, "sent him down."

[22] Cf. והא לא אודעו, the direct object.

**saved Noah** from the flood" (*San* 96a); אתא גבריאל **וקרביה לשליחא**
גביה "Gabriel came and **brought the messenger near**" (*San* 96a);
**חזייה לדמא** דזכריה דהוה קא רתח וסליק "He **saw** Zechariah's **blood**
seething and rising" (*San* 96b); כד **שמעונהו לנביאי** דקא מינבו
אחורבנא דירושלם "When he **heard the prophets** were prophesying
about the destruction of Jerusalem (*San* 96b); **אשכחיה** ריב׳׳ל **לאליהו**
"Rabbi Yehuda b. Levi **found Elijah**" (*San* 98a); **חזנהו למלאכי** השרת
דקא מנסרין "He **saw the ministering angels** sawing" (*San* 100a);
אע׳׳ג **דגנזוה לספרא** דבן סירא "Even though they '**hid' the Book** of
Ben Sira" (*San* 100b); **שקליה לארעיה** מינך "He **took his land** from
you" (*San* 103b); **דכבשינהו לאפיה** מניה "He **hid his face** from him"
(*San* 104a); עבדא **זכייה למריה** "The slave **defeated his master**" (*San*
107a); **מנעינון לרבנן** מבי מדרשא "He **precluded the rabbis** from the
house of learning" (*San* 107b); **איתייה** קב׳׳ה **לאברהם** "The Holy One
**brought Abraham**" (*San* 108b); **שכבינהו לתורי** "He **killed the oxen**"
(*San* 109a); **דטרקיה לגליה ואבדיה למפתחיה** לגברא "to a man who
**locked his door** and **lost his key**" (*San* 113a).

### 5.4.4.2 Imperfect

*EEMss Talmudic*: מאן ניזי **נייתבה לדעתיה** "Who should go and **put
his mind** at ease" (*BM* 84a [**G1**]); **ניגרשה לדביתהו** "Let him **divorce
his wife**" (*BQ* 174b [**HPS** 75:7]); איזיל **איגיזריה לדיקלא** דפלניא "I
shall go and **cut off the fruit** of X's palm tree" (*BB* 33b [**HPS**
137:2]). איזיל **איקטליה לדיקלא** דפלניא "I shall go and **cut down** X's
**palm tree**" (*Shev* 46a [**HPS** 125:8]);

*EEMss Geonic*: **לגבהיה להדס** וליבריך "Let him **lift up the myrtle**
and bless" (**HPS** 48:9); **לכוליה** עיסקא הלואה **נשוייה** "He should
**make the entire deal** a loan" (**HPS** 69:12–13); לא **תיקטרינין לראשי**
צוציאתה "Let her not **tie the tips** of her curls" (**HPS** 215:11);
**דליחייבינון לעבדיו** "that he should **obligate his slaves**" (**HPS**
240:15).

### 5.4.4.3 Imperative

*EEMss Geonic*: **עיליה להאיי מידי** לחצר "**Take this thing** into the
courtyard!" (**HPS** 126:4).

### 5.4.4.4 Infinitive

*EEMss Talmudic*: **חיוביה לטבחא** איבי ליה "He should have **found
the butcher liable**" (*BQ* 99b [**G1**]).

*EEMss Geonic*: אסיר להון **למילשה לעיסה** "It is forbidden for them to **knead the dough**" (HPS 15:5); שרי ליה **למינסבה להא** דקדיש "He is permitted to **marry the one** he has betrothed" (HPS 231:17); ליה **ליבומה ליבמתו** "He is permitted to **contract the levirate marriage**" (HPS 231:18).

*Yemenite MS J*: **לאעוליה לדוד** קא אזיל "He is going to **attack David**" (*San* 95a).[23]

## 5.4.5 Structure C2: עאביד ליה לעובדא (Participle Only)

An objective core argument is non–pronominal, marked by *l-*, and is anticipated by agreeing 3 obj. suffix attached to preposition *l-*.

*EEMss Talmudic*: **הוה מבריר לה למילתא** "He would **clarify the matter**" (*Bes* 27a [HPS 5:9]); **חזינא ליה לראבא** דלא עביד כשמועתיה "I **see Rava** does not act according to his tradition" (*Suk* 46a [HPS 39:1]); **חזינא להו לרבנן** דבי רב פפא "I **see the Rabbis** of R. Papa's house" (*Suk* 46a [HPS 39:2]); הוה **עבר ליה לקליהו** קליה "His cry would **surpass their cry**" (*BM* 85a [G1]);[24] מאשי מיא עליון אזלי **ומזקי ליה לתחתון** "[When] the upper one washes with water, it goes and **damages the lower one**" (*BM* 117a [HPS 145:1]); **מפיקנא ליה לטבלא** מאוניך "I shall **remove Tavla** from your ear" (*Hul* 132b [HPS 60:21]); **כבישנא ליה לשטראי** "I shall **suppress my deed**" (*BB* 40b [HPS 140:4]); **מקיים ליה לתנאיה** "He **fulfills his condition**" (*Shev* 41b [HPS 199:10]); אי **מהדרנא לה לארעא** "If I **return the land**" (*BB* 33a [HPS 191:3]).

*EEMss Geonic*: בתר דגמר לה לסעודתיה בסכה **מפיק להון למאניה** מן סכה לביתיה "After he **finishes his meal** in the *sukka* he **removes his vessels** from the *sukka* into his house" (HPS 40:12); **פסיל לה לסכתו** ויתיב בה "He **renders his *sukka* unfit** and sits in it" (HPS 40:13–14); מידלא **קא תאני ליה לרבי אליעזר בן יעקב** במתניתין "Since he does not **teach R. Eliezer ben Yaᶜakov's opinion**" in the [lit, "our"] Mishna" (HPS 82:10); ומאן **דגרע ליה לרישיה** אף על גב דקא שקיל ליה כוליה מחיב "A person who **shaves his head**, even though he cuts it all, is guilty" (HPS 219:10); אלתר **שרנן לה לאיתתיה** "We immediately **permit the woman**" (HPS 231:5); עד **דמקביל ליה לגיטא** אבוה "until her father **receives the deed** of divorce" (HPS 237:16–17); **דחליץ**

---

[23] For this idiomatic translation, see Sokoloff, *DJBA,* p. 866 s.v. עלל *af'il.*

[24] H165 reads: הוה עבר קלא לקליהו.

**להי לתרוייהי** מספיקא "He **performs the** *haliṣa* **ceremony on both of them** on account of the doubt" (HPS 244:15); **דחי לה** רגל **לאבילות** "The festival **postpones the mourning**" (HPS 257:17).

*Yemenite MS J*: **וסאייר** לה לכולה מאתא "And would **inspect the entire town**" (*Tan* 20b); הוה **פתח ליה לדשא** "He would **open the door**" (*Tan* 20b); אי **שליפת ליה לאחרינא מחריבנא ליה לעלמא** "If you **draw the other one** I will **destroy the world**" (*Tan* 24b); השתא קאיינא עלך **ובעיטנא בך ופשיטנא לה לעקמומיתך** מינך "**Now I shall stand over you, kick you, and straighten out your crookedness from you**" (*San* 91a); דר' יוחנן **קארו ליה למאניה** מכבדותי "R. Yohanan—**they call his clothes** 'my honorers'" (*San* 94a);[25] אי אמינא ליה לחזקיה **דמיתינא ליה לסנחריב** וסיעתו ומסרנא ליה בידך "If I say to Hezekiah, 'I shall **bring Sennacherib** and his followers and give him into your hands'" (*San* 94b); **מקריב להו לתרין בניה** קמיה "He [euphemism for I] will **sacrifice his [my] two sons** before it" (*San* 96a); ואילא **סריקנא להו לבסריכו** במסרוקי דפרזלא "Otherwise I shall lacerate your flesh with iron combs" (*San* 96b);[26] לכי **חאפי להו** חשוכא "when darkness **covers those people**" (*San* 99a); נפק **להנך אינשי** "when darkness **covers those people**" (*San* 99a); מינה עמלק **דמצער להו לישראל** "From him came Amalek who **oppresses Israel**" (*San* 99b); כל דהוה **חאזי ליה לאברהם** אמ' : האיי יצחק. "Whoever would **see Abraham** would say 'This is Isaac," and whoever would **see Isaac** would say 'This is Abraham'" (*San* 107b).

## 5.5 Complementary Distribution

### 5.5.1 Representative Examples

The distinction between the structures of the participle and non-participle forms is pronounced in those contexts wherein the two forms appear side by side, as in the following representative examples:

> אמ' ר' אבא אמר שמואל הני צריפי דאורבאני כיון שהתיר ראשי מדנין
> שלהן כשירין. והא אגידי מיתתאי. אמ' רב פפא **בדשרנהו**. רב חונא בריה
> דרב יהושע אמ' אף על גב דלא **שארי להו** כל איגד שאינו עשוי לטלטלו לא
> שמיה איגד.

---

[25] Parallel texts (e.g., *BQ* 91b [H165]) read ר' יוחנן קרי להו למאניה מכבדותי "R. Yohanan called his clothes 'my honorers,'" which is probably a superior reading.

[26] But in parallels in European manuscripts: ואילאו סריקנא לבישרייכו במסרקי **סריקנא לבשריכו** במסרקי דפרזלא (*BM* 86a [H165]). *Git* 57b [V130]). דפרזלא (*BM* 86a [H165]).

R. Abba son of Shemuel says: "Those huts of papyrus reeds, once
he unties the tops of their knots, are permissible." But they are tied
from below! R. Papa says: "When he **untied them** [perfect]." R.
Huna son of R. Yehoshua says: "Even though he does not **untie
them** [participle], any tie that is not made for transportation is not
a tie." (*Suk* 13b [**HPS** 33:16–19])

אמ' רחמנא **פרקיה** והדר **איכליה**. כד הוה מקיים בית המקדש הוה **פריק**
**ליה** ומסיק **אכיל ליה** בירושלם. השתא **פריק ליה וקלי ליה לידמיה** והדר
מישתרי ליה **למיכליה** [מקור] בשתא חמישיתא.

The Merciful One says: "**Redeem it** [imperative] and then **eat it**
[imperative]." When the temple stood, one would **redeem it** [parti-
ciple] and take it up and **eat it** [participle] in Jerusalem. Now, one
**redeems it** [participle] and **burns** [participle] **its blood** and then it
becomes permissible for him to **eat it** [infinitive] in the fifth year.
(**HPS** 50:8–11)

מאן ד**שקלין ליה** מלכותא **לארעיה ולמייה** אי בדינא דמלכותא אישתקילת
ומיזדבנא שרי ליה לבר ישראל **למיזבנה לההיא ארעא** דלימחר מישתניא
מלכותא ומשכח דינא **ומפיק ליה לארעיה**.

A person whose **land and water** the regime **takes** [participle][27], if it
was taken and sold according to the law, it is permissible for a Jew
to **buy** [infinitive] **that land**,[28] because in the future the govern-
ment will change, he will attain justice and **recover** [participle] his
**land**. (**HPS** 72:10–12)

מידלא **פסקה למילתיה** סבר אידכר הוא ... אי לאו דהוה דכיר שפיר לא
**הוה פסיק לה למילתה**.

Since their father did not **definitively express** [perfect] **his statement**, [the Rabbi] assumes that the man remembered... had he not

---

[27] The singular proleptic object ליה refers only to the land. Similarly, in the continuation only the land is referred to. For this use of the ostensibly masculine
form ליה for feminine, see §4.6.3.
[28] On the use of Structure C1 when the object is modified by a demonstrative
pronoun, see below, §5.6.2.3, where further examples are cited and this example
is analyzed in greater detail.

remembered well, he would not have **definitively expressed** [participle] **his statement**. (*BB* 175a [**HPS** 75:15–17])

איתו לי שהדי **דאיסלקיה** דאמ' חונא חברין מישמא דרב, האיי אפטורפא דמפסיד **מסלקינן ליה**.

Bring me witnesses that I may **dismiss him** [imperfect], for R. Huna our colleague said in the name of Rav, "A guardian who causes a loss—we **dismiss him**" [participle]. (*Git* 52b [**HPS** 82:5–6])

אמ' ראבא האיי מן דשאיל מידי מיחבריה ובאעי דליפטר נימא ליה **אשקיאן** מיא בהדי דאתית דהויא שאלה בבעלים ואי חכים אידך לימא ליה משוך ברישא והדר **משקינא לך**.

Rava says: "The person who borrows something from his friend and wishes to be free of responsibility should say to him, **'Give me** [imperative] water as you come," for this is borrowing along with the owner. If the latter is wise he should say to him, "First take and then I'll **give you** [participle] [a drink]'." (*BM* 97a [**HPS** 113:10])

אמ' ראבא האיי מן דיגזל חביתא דחמרא מיחבריה מיעיקרה בעידנא **דגזלה**[29] הוה שויא זוזא לבסוף שויא לה ארבעא. **שתיה** או **תברה** משלים ארבעה. מאי טעמא. כיון דאי איתה הדרא בעינה למארה וההיא שעתא דקא **שאתי לה** או דקא **תבר לה** ההיא שעתא כמאן דקא **גזיל לה**.

Rava says: "A man who stole a barrel of wine from his friend, initially—at the time that he **stole it** [perfect]—it was worth a *zuz*, and subsequently it was worth four. If he **drank it** [perfect] or **broke it** [perfect], he pays four." Why? Since if it exists, it returns in its original state to its owner. And at that moment that he **drinks it** [participle] or that he **breaks it** [participle]—at that moment it is as though he **steals it** [participle]. (*BM* 43a [**HPS** 128:5–9])

והילכתא: היא אמרא אנא **מונקאנא ליה לבראי** והוא אמר **משלימנא ליה** למוניקתא לדידה שמעינן. בעל אמר לה לאיתתיה **אונקיה לבריך** והיא אמרא **משלימנא ליה** למוניקתא **מותבינן לה לאיתתא** גבי נשי אחרניאתא **ומהדרינן ליה לינוקא** על הנך נשי כולהי. אם **ידע לה לאימיה מוכפינן לה**

---

[29] The two words בעידנא דגזלה "at the time that he stole it" are not found in the Talmudic manuscripts, and may be a Geonic interpretative gloss.

**דמונקא ליה** מפני הסכנה. והני מילי בגו תלתה ירחי אבל לבתר תלתה ירחי
ודאי **ידע לה לאימיה** ולא צריכא בדיקה **ומוכפינן לה דמונקא ליה**.

The Halacha is: She says, "I shall **nurse** [participle] **my child**," and
he says, "I shall **hand him over** [participle] to the wetnurse," we
listen to her. The husband says to to his wife "**Nurse** [imperative]
**your child!**" and she says "I shall **give him over** to the wetnurse,"[30] we **seat** [participle] **the woman** with other women, and
**take the child** [participle] **past** before all those women. If the son
**recog-nizes** [participle] **his mother**, we **force** [participle] **her** to
**nurse him** because of the danger. This applies within three
months, but after three months he certainly **recognizes** [participle]
**his mother**, and there is no need for a test. We **force** [participle]
**her** to **nurse** [participle] **him**. (HPS 174:20–175:5)

דלמא מאיית האיי גברא בתרא **דניסבה לאימיה** ... וקא **פטר לה לאימיה**.

Lest the latter man who **married** [perfect] **his mother** should die...
and will **release** [participle] **his mother**. (HPS 230:17–20)

ואמר **דחזיתיה לגברא** פלניא דטבע במים ... **שרינן לה לאיתתיה**.

And he says, "I **saw** [perfect] **Mr. X** drowned in the water...we
**permit** [participle] **his wife**" (HPS 231:2–4).

לעינין **אפוקה** מיגברה לא **מפקינן לה**.

But regarding the matter of **removing her** [infinitive] from her
husband, we do not **remove her** [participle]. (HPS 209:130)

איהו **אסרה**. איהו **שרי לה**. הרי עריות **דאסרנהי** ולא **שרי להי**.

He **bound her** [perfect]; he **releases her** [participle]. But note the
consanguineous relations, **whom** he has **bound** [perfect] but
**whom** he does not **release** [participle]. (*Qid* 13b [**HPS** 164:17])

---

[30] Cf. §3.4.6.4.1.

כי **מעיילת ליה** לבי מדרשא **עיילוה** בפיתחא דיסמיך לשוקא. **עייליה.**

When you **bring** [participle] **him** into the study hall, **bring** [imperative] **him** in through the entrance close to the market. He **brought** [perfect] **him** in. (*Tan* 24b [J]).

אי **ענית לי ענית לי.** ואילא השתא אמרי. איהו נמי כותיהו. מיד **ענייה.**

If you **answer me** [participle], you **answer me [participle]**; but if not, they will now say "He is like them." Immediately he **answered him**. (*San* 101b [J])

גליא וידיעא קמך דאי בעי **למיכפיה** ליצראי הוה **כייפנא ליה.**

It is revealed and known before you that if it were required to **suppress** [infinitive] **my inclination**, I would **suppress** [participle] **it**. (*San* 107a [J]).

## 5.5.2 Conclusion

From the examples gleaned from the more reliable manuscripts of RBA it emerges that the use of the *lamed* to mark the direct object is restricted to certain syntactic constructions. The most common use of the *lamed* occurs after the participle when the direct object is a pronoun (structure B2). Beyond this, **the *lamed* marks the direct object only when that is accompanied by an anticipatory object pronoun**. I have not found any distinction between examples drawn from Talmudic materials and those in post-Talmudic writings.

## 5.6 The Use of the Agreement Pronoun and Object Marker

### 5.6.1 Introduction

In the following discussion, I shall consider Structure C, i.e., the use of the anticipatory pronoun and *lamed* object marker, in closer detail.

First, it must be clarified that when the only direct object is a personal pronoun, the constructions עאביד ליה ליה* or עבדיה ליה* are not employed; instead the structure עבדיה לדידיה is used, as in the following examples:[31]

**וכל** בני דילידת עבדי נינהו. וצריכין למיהדר **לשחרורינהו לדידהו** "And all the children to whom she gave birth are slaves, and they have to go back and **release them themselves**" (HPS 64:18). In other EEMss: **ונימנינהו לדידהו** "Let him count **them themselves**" (Yom 22b [Hark 156:31]); **לשיילנהו לדילהו** "Let him **ask them themselves**" (Nid 12b [HGP 50a:21]). With the fronting of the main direct object: **שבקה** **לדידה** וקדשה לאחתה "He **left her** and betrothed her sister" (HPS 231:10). Other EEMss: כגון **דאודעיה לדידיה** ואודעינהו לשהדי "For example that he **informed him** and informed the witnesses" (BQ 102b [G1]); הולכך **לדידהו קנסינן להו** "Accordingly, we **fine them themselves**" (BQ 111a [G1]); משום הכי **קנסוה לדיליה** בנכסי דילה "For that reason they **fined him himself** regarding her property, and **fined her herself** regarding his property" (Hark 35:26–27); **משמע לן** אעי"ג דלא דקדיק סופר אילין דקדוקי לא **לדילן** בדליכא ערעורא דבעל לא דינא מן ודין ולא חוכא כדלא תליא כראא "Even though the scribe was not punctilious regarding these fine points, it does not **mean to us**—when there is no legal appeal by the husband—'judgment' from ודין [plene spelling of 'and this'] nor 'laughter' if he does not suspend the leg of the he." (Hark 130:8–9)[32]


However, if the direct object is a *demonstrative* pronoun, then structure C may be used, e.g.:

השתה **דשמעתה להא** דר' חנינא.

Now that I have **heard this** [statement] of R. Hanina. (BQ 87a [G1])

**ומפיק לה להא** דקדיש בגיטא.

---

[31] Cf. Nöldeke, MG, §233.

[32] It is worth noting here the superiority of the EEMss over the Yemenite manuscripts. In a Talmudic citation, **HGP** reads: חד אמ' לדידי אוזפן ברביתא וחד אמ' קמי דידי אוזיף ברביתא "One says 'He lent to me with interest' and one says 'He lent before me with interest'" (San 25a [HGP 39a:13–14]) maintaining the use of the agreement pronoun (the *nun* of אוזפן) and the direct object לדידי, while J reads (with the common interchange of the two parts of the statement): חד אמר קמאי דידי אוזיף ברביתא וחד אמ' לדידי אוזיף ברביתא, employing the unexpected לדידי as the direct object of the perfect אוזיף.

And he **removes that one** that he betrothed with a divorce deed
(HPS 231:14–15).

הב האייך **ושקליה להאיי**.

Give that one and **take this**. (*San* 113a [J])[33]

When there is more than one object, the suffixed anticipatory object pronoun agrees with the collective direct object and is followed by the individual nominal objects, each marked with *lamed*:

אשכחינהו לרב חונא ולחייה בר רב ולרב חלקיה בר טוב.

He found R. Ḥuna and Ḥiyya son of Rav and R. Ḥilqiyah son of
Tov. (*BM* 39b [HPS 139:13])

However, we also find at least one example in which only the first object
is marked with *lamed*:

כי **סמכונהו לר'** אמי ור' אסי.

When **they ordained R. Ammi and R. Assi** (*San* 14a [Hark 180:25,
J]).


## 5.6.2 Definite Status of Direct Object

### 5.6.2.1 Introduction

From the examples cited here it emerges that the *lamed* is primarily employed when the direct object is definite. However, as Geoffrey Khan has
noted in his valuable study of object markers (OM) and agreement pronouns (AP), "the definiteness of the nominal is not a sufficient condition
for the co-occurrence of an O.M. or A.P., i.e. they do not occur with all
definite nominals. Moreover definiteness is sometimes not even a necessary condition, i.e. an O.M. or A.P. may occur also with indefinite nominals."[34] However, Khan has emphasized that definiteness is a value relative to the "the individuation of the nominal," by which he meant "the
distinctness or salience of the nominal from its own background and,

---

[33] Direct objects with appositional demonstrative pronouns and quantifiers such
as numerals or -כול "all" also employ structure C. See examples cited above, and
discussion below.
[34] Khan, "Object Markers," p. 469.

with regard to a verb complement nominal, also its distinctness from the subject."[35] According to this understanding of definiteness, even the pronominal objects marked by a *lamed* in structure B2 (wherein the *only* object is a pronoun) are definite, since a pronoun generally refers to a particular antecedent already individualized in the context of the discourse. It is worth recalling in this context that in RBA, the final *-ā* noun-marker has entirely lost its historical function as a definite article, and therefore cannot be used as a marker of definiteness.

### 5.6.2.2 Personal Names

In light of Khan's analysis, in particular his emphasis on indi-viduated referents, we can understand the propensity for employing the *lamed* marker and agreement pronoun before personal names, e.g.:

אמ' רב אשי **חזינא ליה לרב כהנא** דמסדר להי כולהי אכסא דקידושא.

R. Ashi says, "I **see R. Kahana** recites them all on the *kiddush* cup."
(*Suk* 46a [**HPS** 37:17–18])

**דחזיוה להילל** דהוה עדיף מיניהו.

For they **saw Hillel** was greater than they. (*BM* 85a [**G1**])

כי הא דההיא אשיתא רעיעתא דהואי בנהרדעא דלא הוה חליף מר שמואל
תחותה אע''ג דקם תליסר שנין. יומא חד איקלע רב ושמואל ורב אדא בר
אהבה להתם. אמ' ליה שמואל לרב: ניתי מר נקיף. אמ' ליה: האידנא איכא
רב אידא בר אהבה דינפישא זכותיה. רב חונא הוה ליה חמארא בההוא
ביתא דהוה רעיע. בעא לפנויה. **משכיה לרב אידא בר אהבא** בשמעתא עד
דפנייה.

As in the case of that broken down wall that was in Nehardea, that Mar Shmuel would not pass under, even though it had stood for thirteen years. One day Rav, Shmuel and Ida son of Ahava happened upon the place. He said to him—Shmuel to Rav: "Let Sir

---

[35] Khan, ibid.; see bibliography ad loc.

come and circumvent."[36] He said to him: "Now Ida son of Ahava is here, whose merit is great." R. Huna had wine in that broken down house, and sought to remove it. He **delayed R. Ida son of Ahava** with legal traditions until he removed it. (*Tan* 20b [J])

## 5.6.2.3 Modifying Demonstrative Pronoun

Another level of individuation is the specificity provided by a modifying pronoun, either demonstrative or possessive. Let us begin with the demonstrative pronouns. A study of the corpus reveals that objects accompanied by a demonstrative pronoun are almost invariably marked by a proleptic suffix and an object marker.

היכי **לידייניה** דיאני להאי דינא.

How can the judges **try this case**? (*BB* 34a [HPS 137:9])[37]

**חזיוה להההוא גברא** דהוה קא דלי דולא.

They **saw a certain man** who was drawing water. (*MQ* 4a [**HPS** 274:17])

דכולי עלמא לא פליגי דבאעי **לגרושה להההיא** דקדיש.

Nobody disagrees that he has **to divorce that one** whom he betrothed. (**HPS** 246:7)

ולסוף לא **מקימא ליה לההוא תנאה.**

But in the end she does not **fulfill that condition.** (**HPS** 64:17)

מאן דאית ליה הלואה אי פיקדון גבי איניש. ואית ליה ברתא, ואית לה בעל. **ופקדיה להההוא הלואה או לההוא פיקדון** לברתיה. ושכיב הוא ושכיבת ברתיה. אף על גב דלא מטא לידה מיחיה ירית ליה בעל לההוא ממונא.

---

[36] Or, "Let us circumvent." The address מר "sir" is often accompanied by a 3rd person singular verb; however, it is possible that the second verb here is in the 1st person plural.

[37] But in Rashbam's commentary: היכי **לידיינו** דייני **להאי דינא**

A person who has a loan or a deposit with somebody, and who has a daughter who has a husband; and he **entrusted that loan or deposit** to his daughter, and both he and his daughter died; even though it did not reach her when she was alive, the husband inherits that money. (**HPS** 76:15–18)

דכל פחות מארבע אמות אמרינן. **חזיה להאיי דופן** כמאן דמקרבא גבי סכך דאמי, וכשרה.

Because anything less than four cubits, we say **"regard this wall** as if it were close to the *sekak* [covering of *sukka*]" and it [the *sukka*] is permissible. (**HPS** 34:6–8)

הספידא יקרא דחיי הוא או יקארא דשכבי הוא. למאי נפקא מינה. דאמר. **לא תספדוה לההוא גוברא.**

Is a eulogy an honor for the living for an honor for the dead? What is the practical difference? If he said "Do not **eulogize that man** [i.e., me]." (*San* 46b [J])

אותו היום שמת בו אחז שתי שעות היה. וכי חלש חזקיהו ואיתפח **אהדרינהו** קב״ה **להנך עשר שעי** ניה ליה.

That day on which Aḥaz died was two hours [long]. When Hezekiah fell ill and recovered, the Lord **returned those ten hours** to him. (*San* 96b [J])

In many of these cases, the demonstrative pronoun is cataphoric:[38]

רבי **חזייה לההוא גברא** דהוה קאים בבית הקברות.

Rabbi **saw a certain person** who was standing in the cemetery. (*San* 5b [J])

ר׳ חייה בר זרנוקי ור׳ שמעון בן יהוצדק הוו קא אזלי לעבר שנה באסיא. איטפל בהדיהו ריש לקיש. אמי: איזיל אחזי היכי עבדי הלכה למעשה. בהדי

---

[38] This cataphoric use of the distant demonstrative pronouns to modify a noun that will play a central role in the ensuing narrative is particularly common in JBA.

דקא אזלי **חזייה להההוא גוברא** דקא כריב. אמ' ליה: כהן וחרש? אמרו ליה.
יכול לומ'. אגוסטעין אני בתוכה. תוא **חזייה להההוא גוברא** דקא כסח. אמ'
ליה: כהן וזמר? אמרו ליה: יכול לומ' לך. לעקל בית הבד אני צריך.

R. Ḥiyya son of Zarnoqay and R. Shimeon son of Yehoṣadaq were
going to intercalate [a month into] the year in Asia Minor. Resh Laqish joined them, saying: "Let me go [and] see how they apply the
*halacha* in practice." As they were going, he **saw a certain man** who
was plowing. He said to him: "He is a priest and is plowing!?"[39]
They said to him: "He can say, 'I'm just a hired worker'." Then he
**saw a certain man** who was pruning [his vines]. He said to him
"He is a priest and pruning!?" They said to him: "He can say to
you, 'I need [it] for an olive press bale'." (*San* 26a [J])

רבי חגא הוה קא אזיל וסליק בדרגא דבי רבה בר רב שילא. **שמעיה להההוא**
**ינוקא** דקא אמי. "עדותיך נאמנו מאד" וג'.

R. Ḥaga was ascending the ladder to the house of Rabba son of Rav
Shila. **He heard a certain child** reciting "Your testimonies are very
sure." (Ps. 93:5) (*San* 111b [J])

יומא חד הוה קא אזיל באורחא **חזייה להההוא גברא** דקא נטע חרובא.

One day he was going along the way. He **saw a certain man** who
was planting a carob tree (*Tan* 23a [J]).

ר' חייה בר לולייני **שמעינהו להנך ענני** דקא אמרי. ניתי ונישדי מייא בעמון
ומואב.

R. Ḥiyya son of Lulyani **heard the clouds** saying "Let us go and
cast water upon Ammon and Moab." (*Tan* 25a [J])

Exceptions are rare:

אמור אסוקי דהוה מסיק ביה מיעיקרה והשתא פרעיה. או נמי אמ' ליה:
**בחר לי הני זוזי**. או נמי שדריה בשליחותא ואמ' ליה: זיל **אמטי** ליה לפלניא
**הלין זוזי**.

---

[39] The man was plowing in the sabbatical year, when such activity is forbidden.
Resh Laqish's astonishment arises from the fact that priests were regarded as
being more punctilious about aspects of ritual law.

Say that initially he had a claim against him and now he paid him;
if he said to him: "**Choose these** *zuzim* for me"; or if he sent him
on a commission and said to him: "Go and **give these** *zuzim* to X."
(**HPS** 120:5–7)

וכד אכיל מצה צריך מיזגא ומיכל. מאי טעמא? בההוא יומא הונן חרי. וכד
שאתי נמי הני ארבעה כסי דחמרא צריך הסיבה.

When he eats the unleavened bread he must recline and eat. What
is the reason? On that day we were free. And also when **he drinks
the four cups of wine** he needs to recline [lit., reclining]. (**HPS**
14:4–6)

כל מאן דשמע חבריה דקא מבריך כל ברכה בין המוציא לחם בין ברכת היין
בית ברכת הפירות בין ברכת המצות. כל ברכה דשמע איניש מחיב למימר
הוא. אמן. ואף על גב דלא אכיל ולא קא עביד הך מצוה.

Any man who hears his fellow recite any benediction, whether it
be "Who brings forth bread," or the blessing over wine, whether it
be the blessing for fruit or the blessing over the commandments;
any benediction that a man hears, he must say "Amen," even
though he does not eat or **do that commandment**. (**HPS** 292:16–19)

זקינו דר' פרידא אשכח ההיא גלגלתא דהוה שדיא בשערי ירושלים והוה
כתי' עלה. זאת ועוד אחרת.

R. Preda's grandfather **found a certain skull** that was cast in the
gates of Jerusalem, on which was written: "This and one more."
(*San* 82a [J])[40]

## 5.6.2.4 Possessive Pronoun

A direct object marked with an agreement pronoun or an object marker
is often rendered definite by a possessive pronoun, or stands in a genitive relationship (construct or analytical genitive) with another noun
bearing a possessive pronoun, e.g.:

---

[40] However, in a parallel story in the same manuscript: זקינו דר' פרידא אשכח
גלגלתא דהות שדיא בשערי ירושלם "R. Preda's grandfather found a skull that was
cast in the gates of Jerusalem" (*San* 104a [J]), without the demonstrative pronoun.

אמי ורדינאה הוה בדיק בכרי דבי נשיאה. ביומא טבא לא הוה בדיק. אמ׳
רבי אמי. שפיר עביד דלא באדיק. והא ר׳ אמי גופיה דבדיק. רבי אמי
מאיתמל הוה בדיק ולמחר הוה מבריר לה למילתא. כי הא דההוא דאתא
קמיה דראבא לאהויי בכרא אפניא דמעלי יומא טבא. הוה קא חייף רישיה.
**חזייה למומיה.** [41] אמ׳ ליה. זיל הידאנא ותא למחר. למחר אתא אמר ליה.
אימ׳ לי איזי גופיה דעובדא היכי הוה. אמ׳ ליה. הוה מנחן שערי אחוריה
דחוצא **ועייליה לרישיה ופרטה לשפתיה.**

Ammi of Wardena used to inspect the firstlings of the Nasi's house.
On a festival he would not inspect. R. Ammi said: "He acts properly in not inspecting." But R. Ammi himself inspects! R Ammi
would inspect the day before and on the next day clarify the matter. As in this [case] that a certain person came before Rava to show
him a firstling on the eve of a festival toward evening. He was
washing his hair. He **saw its blemish**, and said to him: "Go now
and come tomorrow." On the next day, he said to him, "How then
did it happen?" He said to him: "Barley had been put on the other
side of the fence, and it **stuck its head in** and **split its lip**." (*Bes*
27a-b [**HPS** 5:7–13])

מאן **דמאחי ליה לאיתתא דחבריה** ומפלא, אמרי ליה: הבהנה ליה
דליעברינה לך.

Somebody who **hit the wife of his companion** and she aborted—
they would say to him, "Give her to him[42] that he may impregnate
her for you." (*San* 109b [**J**])


### 5.6.2.5 Anaphoric Definiteness

In some cases, the direct object is not specifically marked as definite by a
pronoun, but is inferred to be definite by previous mention in the discourse.

ההוא גברא דאמ׳ להו: ניכסאי ליבנאי. הוה ליה ברא וברתא. מי קארי
איניש לחד ברא בני **ולסלוקה ליברתא** מיעיסור ניכסי קא אתי. אי לא קארי
איניש לחד ברה בריה בני **ולמשיכה ליברתא** במתנה אתי.

---

[41] So printed edition, but MS **Gö3**: חזייה למומא
[42] For הבהנה ליה see §3.5.2.3.2.

A certain man who said: "My property [goes] to my sons," and had
a son and a daughter; does a person refer to one son [as] "sons,"
hence he intends to **remove the daughter** from the tenth of the estate? Or does a person not refer to his one son [as] "sons," hence he
intends to **include the daughter** in the gift? (*BB* 143b [HPS 185:11])

ההוא [ב]זיבנא[43] דאתא לקמיה דאביי. אמ' ליה: נהוי לי מר חתימות ידיה
דכי אתו רבנן איתו לי דיסקא מימר אידע. איתי אביי מגלתא. הוה קא מהוי
ליה ארישיה[44] דמגלתא. הוה קא **מתח לה למגלתא**. סבר לכתוב תתאי. אמ'
ליה. כבר קדמוך רבנן.

A certain customs collector came before Abbaye. He said to him:
"May Sir demonstrate for me his signature so that if the Rabbis
come and have brought me a document from Sir, I shall know."
Abbaye brought a sheet, and was demonstrating for him at the top
of the sheet. He [the collector] was **pulling at the sheet**, thinking:
let him write at the bottom. He [Abbaye] said to him: "The Rabbis
already anticipated you!" (*BB* 167a **[HPS** 100:16–19])

ההוא דשכיב ושבק ערבא. אתו בני מלוה **וקא תבעי ליה לערבא**.

A certain person died and left a guarantor. The lender's children
came and **sued the guarantor**. (*Shev* 48b? **[HPS** 198:7])[45]

תרין קינסי יבישי וחד רטיבא **אוקדוה** יבישי **לרטיבא**.

Two dry twigs and one wet one—the dry ones **set fire to the wet
one**. (*San* 93a [J])

אליעזר עבד אברהם איקלע להתם. פדעוה. אתא לקמי דיאנא. אמ' ליה: זיל
הב ליה אגריה דעבד לך אסותא. שקל גלאלא, **פדעיה לדיאנא**.

---

[43] The MS apparently reads כזיבנא with a *kap*. For this word and its etymology,
see Sokoloff, *DJBA*, p. 194 s.v בזבנא.

[44] *Sic*. On this use of the 3 m.s. pronoun instead of the regular 3 f.s. הַ- see
§4.6.3.2. However, above the second *yod* of ארישיה a *miptaḥ pummā* sign has been
added. I assume that this is intended to "emend" the reading from ʾarrēšēh to
ʾarrēšah.

[45] The words in bold are not found in our editions of *Shev* 48b.

Eliezer, Abraham's slave, happened upon that place. They bruised him. He came before a judge. He [the judge] said to him: "Go and give him his pay, since he cured you." He picked up a stone and **bruised the judge**. (*San* 109b [J])

אילו מאן דשוי שליחא למיכתב גיטא לאיתתיה, ואזל וכתב. ומן קמי דלימטי גיטא לידה אמי׳ ליה לשליח. לא תיתין לה גיטא דלא בעינא לגרושה. **ובטליה לגיטא** קמי שהדי. ובתר **דבטליה לגיטא** אזל שליח ויהב לה גיטא. ואזלת ההיא איתתא ואיתקדשת לגברא אחרינא. ההוא גיטא לאו גיטא הוא. דכיון דבטליה מיקמי דלימטי לידה בטיל ליה.

Whereas a person who appoints an emissary to write a divorce deed for his wife, and he went and wrote [it]; and before the deed reaches her hand says to the emissary "Do not give her the deed, because I do not want to divorce her," and **annulled the deed** in front of witnesses, and after he **annulled the deed** the emissary went and gave her the deed; whereupon that wife went and got betrothed to another man—that deed is not a [valid] deed; because since he had annulled it before it reached her hand, it was annulled. (**HPS** 203:2–6)

### 5.6.4.6 Entailed Definiteness

In some cases, the object is referred to by another name, but its identity is definite by virtue of previous mention. Above we saw the example רבי **אמי מאיתמל הוה בדיק ולמחר הוה מבריר לה למילתא** "R. Ammi would inspect the day before and on the next day **clarify the matter**" (*Bes* 27a [**HPS** 5:9]). "The matter" in question is the result of the previous day's inspection, which, while not mentioned explicitly, is implicitly understood from the context and hence definite.

Even less explicit is the following example. The Talmud discusses the biblical passage: בָּעֵת הַהוּא שָׁלַח מְרֹדַךְ בַּלְאֲדָן בֶּן בַּלְאֲדָן מֶלֶךְ בָּבֶל סְפָרִים וּמִנְחָה אֶל חִזְקִיָּהוּ וַיִּשְׁמַע כִּי חָלָה וַיֶּחֱזָק "At that time, Merodach-baladan son of Baladan, the king of Babylon, sent letters and a gift to Hezekiah, [for] he had heard that he had fallen ill and recovered" (Isa 39:1). Although the act of sending is central to the ensuing narrative, the messenger himself is not mentioned in the biblical verse or in the lengthy Talmudic discussion.[46] Nevertheless, when the messenger finally appears in the narrative, he is syntactically marked as definite: **אתא גבריאל וקרביה לשליחא** גביה "Gabriel came and **brought the messenger** near him" (*San* 96a [J]), since his existence is implied throughout the story.

Sometimes we can only guess as to definite status. In the following case, it is possible that the word ניסכא "lance" represents an interpretation of the Hebrew קֵינוֹ "his spear" in 2 Sam 21:15, the verse upon which the story in which it appears is based: **דעציה לניסכא** בארעא ופתקיה לדוד לעילא "He **stuck the lance** in the ground and threw David aloft" (*San* 95a [J]).

### 5.6.4.7 Unmarked Hebrew Noun

In RBA the agreement pronoun and *lamed* are sometimes employed to incorporate a Hebrew word into the sentence as the direct object:

מיתבעי ליה **לשוויה לסכה** קבע.

He has to **make the *sukka*** [Tabernacle] permanent. (**HPS** 39:8)

והיכא דלא **אתנחיה ללולב** בערב יום טוב בהושענא מתנח ליה ביום טוב.

When one did not **leave the *lulav*** on the eve of the festival on *Hoshana* one may leave it on the Festival. (**HPS** 43:6–7)

**לגבהיה לאתרוג** וליבריך **לגבהיה** להדס וליבריך.

**Let him lift up the citron** and bless; **let him lift up the myrtle** and bless. (**HPS** 48:9)

אזלו יתיבו תותי ההיא אשיתא רעיעא. הוו קא כרכי ריפתא. **שמעיה** ר' יוחנן **למלאך** דקאמ' ליה לחבריה: תא ונישדייה עילאויהו ונקטלינהו, דמניחין חיי עולם ועוסקין בחיי שעה.

They went and sat under a certain damaged wall. They were eating bread. R. Yohanan **heard an angel** who was saying to his fellow: "Come, let us cast it down upon them and let us kill them, because they are disregarding eternal life and busying themselves with day-to-day life. (*Tan* 21a [J])

---

[46] The NJPS translators were sensitive to this omission, and added "Sent [envoys with] a letter and a gift."

Perhaps in this case "angel" is definite since it governs the verb of the subordinate clause.

### 5.6.5 Loss of Personal Pronoun?

Examples that do not fit into one of these categories are rare, and it is possible that at least some of them may result from errors that entered the text during its copying and transmission. For example, in *Tan* 21a we read שקלוה למא דהוה בסיפטיה "They took what was in his caskets," and then later in the passage שרינהו לסיפטי, which would appear to mean "they opened the caskets." Theoretically, it would be possible to explain the use of the agreement pronoun and object marker as marking a direct object that is definite by virtue of having already been mentioned in the discourse. However, it is not impossible that the form סיפטי is definite by virtue of a 3 m.s. possessive suffix, but that the pronoun was not pronounced because the final -*h* was apocopated, neutralizing the distinction between *sipṭeh* "his caskets" and *sipṭe* "the caskets." The loss of word-final *h* in the possessive pronoun ה-י— -*eh* is common in all textual witnesses in כולי "all of it," and is sporadically attested in other forms in the best manuscripts, e.g., הני מילי היכא דלא קי לי בגוה ; מר קי לי בגוה "This applies when one is not fully acquainted with it. Sir is fully acquainted with it!" (*BB* 106b [**HPS** 149:15]). Examples are also found in the Jewish Aramaic magic bowls.[47]

In some cases it is possible to trace this process within the manuscript tradition. For example, the common Talmudic expression **אפקעונהו רבנן לקידושיה** "The Rabbis **annulled his betrothal**" appears in this form, i.e., with the direct object rendered definite by the possessive pronoun, in the most accurate textual witness, **HPS** 10:20.[48] In that manuscript we find the same expression with the older form of the direct object pronoun, also in a Talmudic citation: אפקעונון רבנן לקידושיה "the Rabbis annulled his betrothal" (*BB* 48b [**HPS** 168:12]). In both cases the object is definite by virtue of the poss. pronoun. However, in less accurate manuscripts of Talmudic literature, the situation is different. The expression appears in several places in the Talmud, and I shall here cite the textual witnesses for *Yev* 90b and *Ket* 3a:

---

[47] See Morgenstern, "Non-Standard Spellings," p. 253.

[48] Cf. אפקעינהו רבנן לקידושיה "ibid." (*BB* 48b [**HGP** 3a:11]).

| Yev 90b | | | |
|---|---|---|---|
| M95 | לקידושי | רבן | ואפקעינהו |
| V114 | לקידושי | רבן | ואפקעינהו |
| MG1017 | לקדושי | רבן | ואפקיעינהו |
| Other manuscripts | לקדושי | רבן | ואפקעינהו |

In this case, none of the complete manuscripts preserves the suffixed pronoun.

| Ket 3a | | | |
|---|---|---|---|
| V130 | לקידושיה | רבן | ואפקעינהו |
| M95 | לקידושיה | רבן | ואפקעינהו |
| G O2674 | לקידושיה | רבן | ואפקעינהו |
| G TSAs76.97 | לקידושיה | רבן | ואפקעינהו |
| V112 | לקידושי | רבן | ואפקעינהו |
| V113 | לקידושין | רבן | ואפקעינהו |
| G Kö 760 | לקידושייהו | רבן | ואפקעינהו |

In this case, the majority of the manuscripts have preserved the pronoun. In **V112**, it has been lost, while in **V113** it has been substituted by the plural morpheme of Rabbinic Hebrew. In the Geniza fragment from Köln, the original pronoun has been exchanged for the possessive pronoun of the 3 m.pl.

## 5.7 עבד למילתא: Legitimate Construction or Textual Error?

Above I have sought to demonstrate that the *lamed* marks a nominal direct object only when it is preceded by an agreement pronoun and that, in this respect, RBA differs from classical Syriac which does mark the direct object without employing an agreement pronoun.[49]

---

[49] Nöldeke, *SG*, §288, e.g., ܘܚܙܐ ܝܘܚܢܢ ܠܫܡܝܐ ܕܐܬܦܬܚ "And John saw the skies opened." The evidence for Mandaic is less certain; Nöldeke, *MG*, §270 (p. 391, end) writes "Viel seltner ist das blosse ל als Objectzeichen ohne Begleitung eines Personalpronomens," and notes that alternative readings for some of the examples in which the agreement pronoun is absent. To Nöldeke's discussion we may

If this is correct, how are we to explain the examples that Schlesinger and Margolis cited of the structure עבד למילתא? First of all, we must note that the examples that Margolis cited are not even found in the printed editions of the Talmud. Examination of the Talmudic sources reveals that Margolis reworked his citations in order to make them fit the structure that he wished to present.

By contrast, Schlesinger's examples are indeed found in the standard printed editions of the Talmud. Neverless, it appears that they result from inaccurate transmission of the Talmudic text:

1. לא **סבר להא** דנהרדעי "He does not **accept this [opinion]** of the Nehardeans" (*Bes* 6a); so already in the early printed editions of Bomberg (Venice), but in all the manuscripts and the Soncino printed edition of 1484: לא **סבר לה להא** דנהרדעי.[50]

2. הוה **מחי לבנו הגדול** "He was **hitting his** eldest **son**" (*MQ* 17a); however MS **M400** reads דהוה קמחי ליה לבנו הגדול. The agreement pronoun also appears in **V108**, **V134**, but as Schlesinger himself noted, **M95** reads מחי בנו הגדול.

3. ליפסלוהו לדידיה **לא ליפסלו לזרעיה** "Let them declare him unfit himself; let them not **declare his progeny unfit**" (*Mak* 2a). But in MS **J**: ליפסליה לדידיה ולא לפסליה לזרעיה, according to Structure 3a above.

4. לא חציף איניש **לשוייה לשמא** דאבוה סימנא "No man would be so presumptuous as to **make** his father's **name** a sign" (*Git* 87b). As cited by Schlesinger, this example does not belong to the structure עבד למילתא, but rather to the pattern עבדיה למילתה, i.e., structure 3a above. Presumably, Schlesinger intended to cite the form of this statement found in the Vilna edition, which reads לשוייה לשמא. However, **V130** reads לא חציף איניש **לשווייה לשמיה** דאבו' סימנא, i.e., with the agreement pronoun, and it is also found in **V140** and **M95**.

---

add the following two points. Nöldeke did not note that ᶜl syprᵓk qlyᵓ bnwrᵓ "Burn your books with fire" (GR 212:3) is paralleled by syprᵓk qlynwn bnwrᵓ "Your books—burn them with fire" (GR 211:16). Secondly, one of the examples adduced by Nöldeke is better understood as an indirect object: lkwn qᵓrynᵓ wmpᵓryšnᵓ "I call you and instruct you" (GR 278:1). In any case, this is a participle, which in RBA similarly employs the l- object marker before pronouns.

[50] In MS **L400**: לא סבר לה להא שמעתא דנהרדעי; MS **Gö3**: לא סבר לה מר להא; לא סבר לה להא דנהרדעי. These readings are drawn from the synoptic edition in Tal, *Besa I*.

5. הוה **מקנה לאודנייהו** לעכו"ם "He **transferred ownership** of their ears to idolatry" (*Bek* 3b); but in **V**120: הוה **מקני להו** **לאודניהו** לגוים, according to Structure 3b above. The agreement pronoun also appears in **M**95.

It thus emerges that none of Schlesinger's examples is supported by the best textual witnesses.[51] However, it would not be true to say that the structure עבד למילתא is not found in the manuscripts; in fact, it is only the very best manuscripts that consistently conform to the scheme presented above with almost no exceptions.

## 5.8 Is MS Hamburg 165 a Primary Textual Witness?

As mentioned, the scheme laid out above, in which the use of each of the direct object structures is presented, is based upon the findings of the best sources of RBA, the EEMss. However, such textual witnesses are available for only a small proportion of Talmudic and post-Talmudic Rabbinic literature. Hence, several attempts have been made to identify other sources that may provide a basis for the study of the language and literature of the Babylonian Talmud.[52] As stated in chapter 2, I believe it is essential at this stage of research to restrict our studies to the best textual witnesses and not attempt to present studies based upon the whole of the Talmud text, dependent by necessity upon later manuscripts which have been subject to secondary changes.[53]

An interesting example that may indicate how complex these issues are is that of the Hamburg manuscript of *Neziqin*, **H**165. In his review of Epstein's *Grammar*, Kutscher suggested that this manuscript, while not of Babylonian provenance,[54] may serve as a sound basis for research. However, since Friedman published his findings on MS **G1** of *Bava Mezia*, which is close in style to what had previously been regarded as "Geonic" language, it has become apparent that **H**165 represents a secondary text that has undergone fundamental linguistic editing. Friedman convincingly established that **H**165 may be grouped with other Spanish

---

[51] Naturally, we do not have EEMss for all of these sources.

[52] See, for example, Wajsberg, "Principles."

[53] Naturally, this luxury applies only to grammatical study; in a dictionary it is necessary to include all the words in the corpus, whether attested in primary or secondary manuscripts. I have indicated some of the difficulties inherent to this approach in §2.10.1.

[54] Kutscher, "Review," p. 175 (reprinted in Kutscher, *Studies*, p. 253).

manuscripts that do not preserve the characteristics of EEMss.[55] The present study confirms Friedman's findings regarding H165. In not a few cases we have find that the EEMss maintain the structures of the direct object presented above, while in H165 they were lost.

Let us begin with examples from the sixth chapter of *Bava Mezia*. As mentioned above, this chapter of *Bava Mezia* survives in its entirety in an early eastern Geniza fragment. Alongside the other textual witnesses, the fragment has been published by Friedman in his synoptic edition under the lemma גו (here: **G1**).[56]

| BM 83a[57] | | |
|---|---|---|
| **G1** | לגלמיהו | שקליה |
| **H165** | גלימיהו | קבל |
| **E** | לגלימייהו | שקליה |
| **Soncino** | לגלימיהו | שקל |
| **V115** | לגלימיהו | ושקלינהו |
| **V117** | לגלימיהו | ושקלוה |
| **G5** | גלימיהו | שקל |
| **M95** | לגלימיהו | שקלו׳ |
| **Fl8** | גלימיהו | שקל |

In this case, we can witness the process through which the original structure was lost. In MS **M95**, the proleptic pronoun is missing but is marked by an apostrophe. The apostrophe was omitted from the later printed editions, creating the reading שקל לגלימיהו.

---

[55] See Friedman, "Typology," especially his conclusions on pp. 181–82.

[56] In Chapter 1 I emphasized my support of Friedman's assertion of the importance of synoptic editions for textual study. See in particular Friedman, "Variant Readings." Thanks to these editions, it was possible to gather these examples with relative ease.

[57] All the data from *Bava Mezia* in these tables are drawn from Friedman, *Bava Meziᶜa Text*. The Geniza fragment numbering follows that of Friedman, ibid, pp. 57–62.

| BM 76b | | | |
|---|---|---|---|
| G1 | לשליחותיה | שליח | דאקרה |
| H165 | לשליחותיה | שליח | דעקר |
| G3 | לי?של?יחותיה | .>ל<.. | [חסר] |
| Esc G-I-3 | לשליחותיה | | דעקר |
| Soncino | לשליחותי׳ | שליח | דעקר |
| V115 | לשליחותיה | שליח | דעקר |
| V117 | לשליחותיה | שליח | [דקא עקר] |
| Macerata | לשליחותיה | שליח | דע(י)קר |
| Fr107 | לשליחותיה | שליח | דעקר |
| M95 | לשליחותי׳ | | דעקר |
| Fl8 | לשליחותיה | שליח | דעקרה |

In this case, the proleptic pronoun has been preserved only in MS **G1** and in MS **Fl8**. In MS **H**, it is missing.

| BM 76b | | | |
|---|---|---|---|
| G1 | מיאורתא | לארעיה | דסארה |
| H165 | מאור׳ | לארעה | דסיירה |
| G3 | מאורתא | לארעא | >...<יירא× |
| Esc G-I-3 | מאורתא | לארעא | דצייר |
| Soncino | מאורתא | לארעיה | דסיידה |
| V115 | מאורתא | לארעיה | דסרה |
| V117 | מאורתא | לארעיה | דס[יי]רה |

| Macerata | מאורתא | לארעא | דסיירא |
| Fr | מאורתא | לארעא | דסיירא |
| M95 | מאורתי' | לארעא | דסיירי' |
| Fl8 | מאורתא | לארעיה | דסיירה |

In this example, MS Hamburg and other manuscripts also preserve the original structure. In some manuscripts, the final *he*, representing the proleptic suffix, has been substituted with an *ʾaleph*. Thus an ostensibly 3 f.s. verb form was created. The suffix has been entirely lost in MS **EscG-I–3**. In the Vilna edition of the Talmud, which serves as the basis for most of the reprints of the Talmud today, we find the reading דסיירא לארעיה מאורתא.

Comparison of H165 with the EEMss reveals additional examples of this phenomenon:

**ושמעי לקלא** נחותי ימא "The sailors **hear the sound**" (*BM* 85a [H165]), but **שמעו ליה לקליה** נחתי ימא (*BM* 85 [G1]).[58]

דאתא זיקא **ודלי להו למאניה** "That the wind came and **lifted up his clothes**" (*BQ* 86b [H165]). This would appear to be the use of a proleptic *lamed* not in the participle; however, in the EEMss: דאתא זיקא **כרכינהו למאניהו** (*BQ* 86b [G1]).

## 5.9 Exceptions

In the corpus examined for the purposes of this study, there are almost no exceptions to the direct object structures laid out in §3 above. For example, I have found no exceptions in MS **G1** of *Bava Mezia*. In the whole of **HPS**, I have found only three exceptions:

---

[58] This example is a little surprising, since we would expect שמעי "they hear" rather than שמעו "they heard." The context is also better suited to the participle. Two possible explanations suggest themselves: (1) that שמעו is a copying error for שמעי; (2) that the III-ʿayin root is conjugating according to the pattern of the III-*yod* roots, with the -*ū* morpheme for 3 m.pl. participle. However, since, as noted in §3.4.6.3.1, this phenomenon is rare with participles, I would cautiously suggest a copying error has occurred, perhaps encouraged by the distance of the participle here from the preceeding הוה, which renders it a past tense.

אמ' נקוטו לי זימנא **דמיתינא לשהדי** ומרענא ליה לשטרא.

He said: "Specify a time for me that I should **bring the witnesses** and undermine the validity of the document. (*BQ* 112b [**HPS** 123:14–15])

However, in this case MS Hamburg reads: ואי אמ' : קבעו לי זמנא **דמיתינא** [לשטרא] **סהדי ומרענא ליה**, while a slightly rewritten version in *Halachot Gedolot* reads: [59] ואי אמ' קבעו לי זמנא דאזיל **איתי שהדי** דמרענא **ליה לשטריה** (**HGP** 16b:36–37). We would thus be justified in assuming that the agreement pronoun has been omitted in **HPS** through homoioteleuton.[60]

ואי **משילין לאימיה**.

"And if they **ask his mother**." (**HPS** 223:7)

This section of *Halachot Pesuqot* does not appear to have survived in any other manuscripts, and it cannot be determined if this is also a case of homoioteleuton.

אמר להו לפועלים אזלו **סיירו לה** ניה ליה.

"He said to the laborers: 'Go [and] **inspect it** for him.'" (*ʿAra* 21b [**HPS** 188:8])

In this case too, there appear to be no surviving parallel fragments of *Halachot Pesuqot*, and the Talmudic manuscripts of this tractate are all late European manuscripts of low linguistic value. However, the same Talmudic citation survives in *Halachot Gedolot*, for which we find several readings. Hildesheimer's edition reads: אמ' להן לפועלים זילו **סיירוה** ניהלי "He said to the laborers: 'Go [and] **inspect it** for me'," [61] while Geniza fragment Antonin 494 reads: זילו סילו **וסיירוהא** ניהלי.[62] On another badly

---

[59] The *he* of this word is damaged, but visible in the photograph.

[60] Lengthier examples of this phenomenon have been noted by Danzig, *Introduction*, pp. 511–546, passim. Cf. further Danzig, *Introduction*, p. 508, wherein he cites examples of homoioteleuton as one of the causes of differences between **HPS** and other manuscripts of the same work.

[61] This is also the reading in the printed editions of Rashi's commentary and of the Tosefot.

[62] I do not know how to explain the second word.

worn Geniza fragment, T-S F6.12, one may discern the words **סירוה** זלו
נילי.63

Exceptions are slightly more common in the Yemenite manuscript:

יומא חד אתא לקמיה. אשכחיה דהוה קא קארי קרית שמע. **אחד ליה**
בידיה.

One day he came before him. He found that he was reading the
*Shema*. He **took him** by his hand. (*San* 107b [J])

However, the parallel texts read **אחוי ליה** בידיה "He **indicated to him**
with his hand," which is a contextually superior reading. We can easily
understand how in the Hebrew script the combination וי could have become a ד.

יתבא איהי אבאבא **וסתרא למזייה.**

She sat at the gate and **disheveled her hair.** (*San* 110a)

However, once again the other textual witnesses conform to the grammatical patterns that we have established according to the best manuscripts, and read **וסתרתה למזייה.**64

קא **מצערת לבריאתא.**

**You** are **aggrieving mankind.** (*Tan* 24a)

However, the early Pisaro printed edition of the Talmud reads מצערת להו
לברייתא, a reading also found in our editions, while **M95** reads קא מצערת
ברייתא without the lamed. MS **O366** and **V134** support the reading of the
Yemenite MS **J.**

הוה קאימנא אגודא דנהר פפא **חזינא למלאכי** דאידמו למלאחי.

---

63 ניל- is a rare variant of the indirect object marker -ניהל. See Kara, *Yemenite
Manuscripts*, p. 50.
64 So MS **F19. M95:** וסתרתי למזייה. MS **K9:** וסו(ו)תרה למזייה. Barko printed edition:
וסתרתיה למזיה.

I was standing on the bridge of the Papa River and **saw angels** that looked like sailors. (*Tan* 24b)

However, the Ashkenazi textual tradition reads חזאי מלאכי "I saw angels" (**V134; M140**).

Theoretically, it could be argued that these examples preserve the early use of the object marker without the agreement pronoun. However, as we have seen, this structure is almost entirely absent from the earliest and most accurate textual witnessess, most notably **HPS**. Furthermore, of the three attested cases in **HPS**, one is not supported by other early manuscripts, and one appears to be wholly corrupt, leaving only one example which cannot be supported or rejected on the basis of other sources.

## 5.10 Conclusion

In this chapter we have examined the structures of the direct object found in eastern manuscript sources of RBA. Analysis of these eastern sources, particularly the EEMss, presents a picture that differs from that found in the presently available reference works. In particular, there are strong grounds for doubting that in this dialect of Aramaic the *lamed* may be employed freely as a direct object marker before a definite object. Analysis of the direct object structures found in the most reliable textual witnesses for Babylonian Rabbinic literature indicates that the *lamed* serves in this function only in certain syntactic structures, and that these structures serve to highlight the definite status of the object.

It was also suggested that the few exceptions found in the best manuscripts may result from inaccurate textual transmission, particularly from homoioteleuton. This hypothesis is strengthened by the fact that such exceptions are almost non-existent in the best manuscripts, while they become more frequent as one moves down the manuscript tradition. As I attempted to show, this topic has once again reaffirmed S. Friedman's assessment that MS H165 is not to be regarded as a primary source for textual research but reflects a reworked text that has undergone secondary linguistic editing.

## 5.11. Wider Implications

The discussion of the direct object structures presented in this chapter indicates that, just as in the study of phonological and morphological topics, so in the study of syntax, a sound textual basis is a prerequisite for accurate philological work. Since the vast majority of the manuscripts of RBA literature are not of the highest quality, these should be employed for linguistic study only with caution. Expanding the corpus to include less accurate manuscripts reduces, rather than increases, the veracity of our findings.

CHAPTER 6

# Conclusions

Throughout this book, I have sought to demonstrate the importance of founding a future grammar of RBA solely upon the small corpus of accurate linguistic witnesses. The call for a more stringent methodological approach toward Babylonian Aramaic philology, specifically regarding its grammatical description, lay at the heart of E. Y. Kutscher's seminal review of Epstein's *Grammar*. In my opinion, the methodology he outlined remains valid forty years later. The main emphasis of research must be the identification and linguistic description of the most accurate textual witnesses.[1] We must not lose sight of this central aim, even though (or precisely because) the majority of manuscript sources at our disposal do not belong to the category of primary textual witnesses.

In chapter 2, I outlined the development of research and sought to assess its achievements and needs. I argued that advances in research since Kutscher's review have facilitated the identification of such primary textual witnesses, which I have dubbed the EEMss, and which are drawn predominantly, though not exclusively, from the Cairo Geniza. I contended that these sources alone reflect RBA in a form close to that employed in Babylonia during the Talmudic and Geonic periods, and that external evidence may be found to support this contention in the Jewish Aramaic magic bowls.[2] The linguistic data of the EEMss provided the basis for the studies in this book.

As mentioned, the most pressing need is to classify the large number of Geniza fragments of Babylonian Rabbinic literature (especially the Talmud fragments) and to identify which fragments originally belonged to the same manuscript. Those manuscripts must then be categorized on the basis of linguistic, codicological, and textual criteria. Much of this work is already underway under the auspices of the Friedberg Geniza Project, and it is certain that when this process is complete, the material gathered will make a significant contribution to the study of RBA. We may hope that further manuscripts of the early eastern type will be

---

[1] Accuracy here is defined as linguistic accuracy, rather than accuracy in terms of content. For this distinction, see chapters 1 and 2 n. 128.

[2] I have presented the evidence from these bowls in several studies; see Morgenstern "Magic Bowl," "Moussaieff Collection," and, particularly, "Non-Standard Spellings."

located, and it is in order to facilitate the identification of such manuscripts that a checklist of their characteristic features was provided toward the end of Chapter 1. In particular, it is hoped that further Talmudic (rather than Geonic) manuscripts of this nature will be identified.

In chapter 3, I considered the claims made for the historical reliability of the Yemenite traditions of Babylonian Aramaic, i.e., the written
manuscript tradition and the oral reading tradition. A comparison of the
Yemenite manuscripts with the EEMss and the language of te Jewish
Aramaic magic bowls indicated many points of contact, as well as several points of divergence. The evidence suggests that while the Yemenite
manuscripts are indeed unique in preserving many phonetic spellings
long after they had become rare in the other textual traditions, the
Yemenite textual tradition itself was open to external influences. These
influences stem particularly from the language of Targum Onqelos, but
also from the later developments in the language of the Talmud found in
the North African and European textual traditions. Regarding the
Yemenite reading tradition of the Babylonian Talmud, while it is undoubtedly Babylonian in origin, in its present form it has been greatly
influenced by the adoption of the European printed editions of the Talmud, by the language of Targum Onqelos, and by internal analogies.

Accordingly, while the Yemenite manuscripts remain an important
source of linguistic data, these data must be verified from other early
sources before being accepted as reflecting genuinely Babylonian features. The Yemenite reading tradition, though historically rooted in the
reading traditions of Geonic Babylonia, often contradicts the grammar of
Babylonian Talmudic Aramaic as it emerges from the earliest and most
accurate sources, and cannot therefore be regarded as an historically reliable source for the reconstruction of the dialect.

In chapter 4, I considered the complex issue of variant forms, i.e.,
phonological and morphological variants that serve the same grammatical function within RBA. By citing many examples wherein the variant
forms are used interchangeably within a single context in a single textual
witness, I have tried to show that there is no simple solution for this
puzzling situation. The variants often cannot be explained by reference
to chronology, dialect, style, register, or textual transmission alone. It appears that all of these factors may have been involved in producing the
·linguistic mix that we find in our sources, and, as was emphasized, this
mix is characteristic of all surviving sources, including the most accurate
ones. It therefore cannot be ascribed to inaccurate textual transmission.

In the same chapter, I also sought to refute claims regarding the
unique nature of the phonetic spellings found in the Yemenite manuscripts. I argued that such spellings are found in all textual witnesses of

RBA literature, and that the phonetic spellings in those manuscripts are not fundamentally different from those of other early eastern manuscript sources. Furthermore, since in all manuscript sources of RBA (including the Yemenite ones), phonetic and historical spellings interchange, there are no grounds for claiming that the Yemenite manuscripts reflect a textual tradition that from the start—i.e., the moment of encoding the Talmudic text in writing—differed from that of the other manuscript sources. The present distribution of forms in Talmudic manuscripts is better explained by assuming that later manuscripts reflect secondary linguistic editing, which sometimes "restored" historical forms (particularly in the verbal system) and sometimes imposed secondary forms on the original Talmudic language.

In the final chapter, I sought to show how reliance upon primary textual witnesses alone is likely to lead us to reconsider basic topics in the grammar of RBA. Close scrutiny of the direct object structures employed in the EEMss indicated that their use differs significantly from the accounts of the direct object found in the presently available reference works. In particular, the EEMss differ from the later editions in their suppletive system of marking pronominal objects, and in their consistent use of agreement pronouns before non-pronominal objects marked with the *lamed*. It was shown that the later manuscript sources—including the relatively conservative Spanish manuscript M165—have lost these systematic distinctions. Accordingly, I maintain that the natural desire to widen the scope of our textual base must be counterbalanced by the frustrating recognition that few primary textual witnesses survive. By expanding our textual base to include later and less accurate manuscripts, we expose ourselves to the risk of introducing numerous forms and structures that are not authentically Babylonian, but are rather the products of later textual transmission. The number of such forms in the later European sources is considerable, and they cannot be regarded merely as a marginal phenomenon, as I have suggested regarding the Grade B EEMss.[3]

My aim throughout this work has been to emphasize the importance of systematic research carried out on the best manuscript sources. It is only by examining and recording all of the examples of a given phenomenon according to the most accurate sources that we can hope to present an accurate linguistic description. This book is not intended to be the final word on this dialect, and it is my hope that this volume will encourage other researchers to investigate the linguistic riches of RBA. I hope that the methodology and findings presented here will be of use to

---

[3] See §2.14.3.

them in their work, and that future discoveries will enable us to determine, refine, or correct those aspects of RBA grammar for which the answers still lie buried in unpublished manuscript sources.

— סליק —

# Bibliography

## A Note on the Hebrew Titles

Many of the studies cited here were published in Hebrew. Wherever possible, the titles and references cited here are those provided on the Latin-character title page. In the rare case that no title in Latin characters was available, I have provided the original title in Hebrew and translated it into English.

## Studies

Abramson, *Inyanot*—S. Abramson, עניינות בספרות הגאונים [*Topics in Geonic Literature*] (Jerusalem: Mossad Harav Kook, 1974; Hebrew).

Amit, *"Pesahim* IV"—A. Amit, "An Edition and Comprehensive Commentary of Chapter IV of Tractate *Pesahim* in the Babylonian Talmud," MA Thesis, Bar Ilan University, 1999 (Hebrew).

Amit, "Yemenite Manuscripts"—A. Amit, "The Place of the Yemenite Manuscripts in the Transmission-History of b. *Pesahim,*" *HUCA* 73 (2002), pp. 31–77 (Hebrew section).

ʿAmr—R. Yosef b. Aharon Halevi, התלמוד הבבלי המנוקד על פי מסורת תימן עם כל המפרשים [*The Babylonian Talmud Vocalized According to the Yemenite Tradition with all of the Commentors*] (Jerusalem, 1980–) (Hebrew).

Assis, "Linguistic Aspects"—M. Assis, "Linguistic Aspects of Chapter 143 of R. Shmuel ben Hofni Gaon's Introduction to the Talmud," *Leš* 56 (1991), pp. 27–43 (Hebrew).

Avinery, "Pronominal Objects"—I. Avinery, "Pronominal Objects in Old Syriac (The Pĕshiṭta Translation)," *Leš* 38 (1973–74), pp. 220–24 (Hebrew).

Bar-Asher, "Contextual and Pausal Forms"—M. Bar-Asher, "Contextual and Pausal Forms in Mishnaic Hebrew According to MS Parma B," *Language Studies* 4 (1990), pp. 51–100 (Hebrew).

Bar-Asher, *L'hébreu mishnique*—M. Bar-Asher, *L'hébreu mishnique: études linguistiques* (Orbis/Supplementa 11; Leuven and Paris: Peeters, 1999).

Bar-Asher, *"qtil li"*—E. A. Bar-Asher, "The Origin and the Typology of the Pattern *qtil li* in Syriac and Babylonian Aramaic," in A. Maman et al. (eds.), *Shaʿarey Lashon: Studies in Hebrew, Aramaic, and Jewish Lan-*

*guages in Honor of Moshe Bar-Asher* (Jerusalem: The Bialik Institute), vol. II, pp. 360-92 (Hebrew).

Bar-Asher, "Traditions"—M. Bar-Asher, "The Different Traditions of Mishnaic Hebrew," in D. M. Golomb (ed.), *Working with No Data: Semitic and Egyptian Studies Presented to Thomas O. Lambdin* (Winona Lake, Indiana: Eisenbrauns, 1987), pp. 1–38.

Bar-Asher, "Vatican 32"—M. Bar Asher, "A Preliminary Study of Mishnaic Hebrew as Reflected in Codex Vatican 32 of *Sifre Bemidbar*," in M. A. Friedman et al. (eds.), *Studies In Talmudic Literature in Post-Biblical Hebrew and in Biblical Exegesis* (Teʿuda III; Tel Aviv: University Publishing Projects, 1983), pp. 139–65 (Hebrew).

Ben-Asher, "Conjugation"—M. Ben-Asher, "The Conjugation of the Aramaic Verb in *Hălakot Pěsuqot*," *Leš* 34 (1970), pp. 278–86; 35 (1970), pp. 20–35 (Hebrew).

Ben-Ḥayyim, *Studies*—Z. Ben-Ḥayyim, *Studies in the Traditions of the Hebrew Language* (Madrid: Instituto Arias Montano, 1954).

Ben-Ḥayyim, "Word Studies"—Z. Ben-Ḥayyim, "Word Studies III," *Tarbiz* 50 (1981), pp. 192–208 (Hebrew).

Blanc, "Literary Idiom"—H. Blanc, "Notes on the Literary Idiom of the Baghdadi Jews," in *For Max Weinreich on his Seventieth Birthday* (The Hague: Mouton, 1964), pp. 18–30.

Blau, *Grammar*—J. Blau, *A Grammar of Mediaeval Judaeo-Arabic* (second edition; Jerusalem: Magnes Press, 1980; Hebrew).

Blau, "Structure"—J. Blau, "The Structure of Biblical and Dead Sea Scrolls Hebrew in Light of Arabic Diglossia and Middle Arabic," *Leš* 60 (1997), pp. 21–32 (Hebrew).

Boyarin, "Codex Hamburg"—D. Boyarin, "The Babylonian Aramaic Verb According to Codex Hamburg," MA Thesis, Columbia University, 1972.

Boyarin, "Final Consonants"—D. Boyarin, "The Loss of Final Consonants in Babylonian Jewish Aramaic (BJA)," *AL* 3 (1976), pp. 103–7.

Boyarin, "Kara"—D. Boyarin, [Review of] Kara, *Yemenite Manuscripts*, *Leš* 51 (1987), pp. 252–56.

Boyarin, "Low Vowel System"—D. Boyarin, "The Low Vowel System of Gaonic Aramaic," *IOS* 8 (1978), pp. 129–41.

Boyarin, "Marcus"—D. Boyarin, [Review of] Marcus, *Manual*, *JNES* 42 (1983), pp. 297–98.

Boyarin, "Reading Traditions" — D. Boyarin, "On the History of the Babylonian Jewish Reading Traditions: The Reflexes of *a and *ā," *JNES* 37 (1978), pp. 141–60.

Boyarin, "Studies" — D. Boyarin, "Studies in Babylonian Aramaic," *Leš* 40 (1976), pp. 172–77 (Hebrew).

Boyarin, "Talmudic Lexicon III" — D. Boyarin, "Towards the Talmudic Lexicon III," in M. A. Friedman and M. Gil (eds.), *Studies in Judaism* (*Teʿuda* IV; Tel Aviv: University Publishing Projects, 1986), pp. 115–28 (Hebrew).

Breuer, *Hebrew* — Y. Breuer, *The Hebrew in the Babylonian Talmud according to the Manuscripts of Tractate* Pesaḥim (Jerusalem: The Hebrew University Magnes Press, 2002; Hebrew).

Breuer, "Karetot" — Y. Breuer, "The Babylonian Aramaic in Tractate *Karetot* According to MS Oxford," *AS* 5 (2007), pp. 1–45.

Breuer, "Sabato" — Y. Breuer, [Review of] Sabato, *Sanhedrin*, *Pe'amim* 88 (2001), pp. 157–67 (Hebrew).

Breuer, "Yemenite Tradition" — Y. Breuer, "The Noun Pattern in the Aramaic of the Babylonian Talmud according to the Yemenite Tradition," *Leš* 65 (2003), pp. 121–41 (Hebrew).

Brock, "New Syriac Documents" — S. Brock, "Some New Syriac Documents from the Third Century AD," *Aram* 3 (1991), pp. 59–67.

Brockelmann, *LS* — C. Brockelmann, *Lexicon Syriacum* (second edition; Halle: Max Niemeyer, 1928).

Brody, *Geonim* — R. Brody, *The Geonim of Babylonia and the Shaping of Medieval Jewish Culture* (New Haven and London: Yale University Press, 1998).

Chwat, "Menahot" — נוסח חלופי מימי הגאונים למנחות פרק י"ג [E. Chwat, "An Alternative Version of the Thirteenth Chapter of *Menaḥot* from the Geonic Period"], *Maʿalin Be-Qodesh* 2 (2000), pp. 143–55.

Dalman, *Grammatik* — G. Dalman, *Grammatik des jüdisch-palästinischen Aramäisch* (Leipzig: J. C. Hinrichs, 1905).

Danzig, *Introduction* — N. Danzig, *Introduction to Halakhot Pesuqot with a Supplement to Halakhot Pesuqot* (second, revised and augmented edition; New York and Jerusalem: The Jewish Theological Seminary, 1999; Hebrew).

DeCaen, "Distribution"—V. DeCaen, "On the Distribution of Major and Minor Pause in Tiberian Hebrew in the Light of the Variants of the Second Person Independent Pronouns," *JSS* 50 (2005), pp. 321–27.

Dodi, "I-aleph"—A. Dodi, "A Morphological Study of Verba Primae ʾAlef in Targum Onkelos," *Massorot* 3–4 (1989), pp. 73–86 (Hebrew).

Dodi, "Grammar"—A. Dodi, "The Grammar of Targum Onkelos According to Geniza Fragments," PhD Dissertation, Bar-Ilan University, Ramat Gan, Israel, 1981 (Hebrew).

Drower–Macuch, *MD*—E. S. Drower, and R. Macuch, *A Mandaic Dictionary* (Oxford: The Clarendon Press; 1963).

Epstein, *Amoraim*—J. N. Epstein, *Prolegomena ad litteras Amoraiticas* (Jerusalem: Magnes Press, 1962; Hebrew).

Epstein, *Der Gaonäische Kommentar*—J. N. Epstein, *Der Gaonäische Kommentar zur Ordnung Tohoroth: Eine kritische Einleitung zu dem R. Hai Gaon zugeschriebenen Kommentar* (Berlin: Mayer & Müller, 1915).

Epstein, "Die Rechtsgutachten"—J. N. Epstein, "Die Rechtsgutachten der Geonim, ed. Cassel nach Cod. Berlin und MS. Michael," *JJLG* 9 (1911), pp. 214–304; 10 (1912), pp. 372–80.

Epstein, "Gloses"—J. N. Epstein, "Gloses Babylo-Araméennes," *REJ* 73 (1921), 27–58; 74 (1922), 40–72.

Epstein, *Grammar*—J. N. Epstein, *A Grammar of Babylonian Aramaic* (Jerusalem: Magnes Press and Tel Aviv: Devir, 1960; Hebrew).

Epstein, "Notes I"—J. N. Epstein, "Notes on Post-Talmudic Aramaic Lexicography I," *JQR* 5 (1914), pp. 233–51.

Epstein, "Notes II"—J. N. Epstein, "Notes on Post-Talmudic Aramaic Lexicography II: *Sheeltot*," *JQR* 12 (1922), pp. 299–390.

Ford, "Mandaic Incantation Bowls"—J. N. Ford, "Notes on the Mandaic Incantation Bowls in the British Museum," *JSAI* 26 (2002), pp. 237–72.

Fraenkel, "Recension"—S. Fraenkel, "Recensionen: Levias, C., *A Grammar of the Aramaic idiom contained in the Babylonian Talmud*," *Zeitschrift für hebræische Bibliographie* 5 (1901), pp. 92–94.

Frank, *Dayqa Nami*—Y. Frank, דיקא נמי—דקדוק לתלמוד הבבלי ולתרגום אונקלוס [*Dayqa Nami: A Grammar of the Babylonian Talmud and Targum Onkelos*] (third, expanded edition; Jerusalem: Feldheim, 200l; Hebrew).

Frank, *Grammar*—Y. Frank, *Grammar for Gemara: An Introduction to Babylonian Aramaic* (second, expanded edition; Jerusalem: Ariel United Israel Institutes, 1997).

Friedman, "Ancient Scroll"—S. Friedman, "An Ancient Scroll Fragment (*b. Hullin* 101a–105a) and the Rediscovery of the Babylonian Branch of Tannaitic Hebrew," *JQR* 86 (1995), pp. 9–50.

Friedman, "Akiva Legend"—S. Friedman, "A Good Story Deserves Retelling: The Unfolding of the Akiva Legend," *JSIJ* 3 (2004), pp. 55–93.

Friedman, "Avodah Zara"—S. Friedman, "*Avodah Zara*, Cod. JTS—A Manuscript Copied in Two Stages," *Leš* 56 (1993), pp. 371–74 (Hebrew).

Friedman, *Bava Meziᶜa Text*—S. Friedman, *Talmud Arukh, BT Bava Meziᶜa VI: Text* (New York: Jewish Theological Seminary, 1996; Hebrew).

Friedman, "Brief Notes"—S. Friedman, "Brief Notes on Babylonian Aramaic," *Leš* 58 (1994–5), pp. 49–57 (Hebrew).

Friedman, "Early Manuscripts"—S. Friedman, "Early Manuscripts to Tractate *Bava Metzia*," *Alei Sefer* 9 (1981), pp. 5–55 (Hebrew).

Friedman, "Rabbah and Rava"—S. Friedman, "Orthography of the Names *Rabbah* and *Rava*," *Sinai* 110 (1992), pp. 140–64 (Hebrew).

Friedman, "Three Studies"—S. Friedman, "Three Studies in Babylonian Aramaic Grammar," *Tarbiz* 43 (1974), pp. 58–69 (Hebrew).

Friedman, "Typology 1"—S. Friedman, "A Typology of the Manuscripts of the Babylonian Talmud Based upon Orthographic and Linguistic Features," *Leš* 57 (1993), pp. 123–24 (Hebrew).

Friedman, "Typology 2"—S. Friedman, "The Manuscripts of the Babylonian Talmud: A Typology Based upon Orthographic and Linguistic Features," in M. Bar-Asher (ed.), *Studies in the Hebrew and Jewish Languages Presented to Shelomo Morag* (Jerusalem: The Hebrew University and The Bialik Institute, 1996), pp. 163–90 (Hebrew).

Friedman, "Variant Readings"—S. Friedman, "Variant Readings in the Babylonian Talmud: A Methodological Study Marking the Appearance of 13 Volumes of the Institute for the Complete Israeli Talmud's Edition," *Tarbiz* 68 (1999), pp. 129–62 (Hebrew).

Garr, "Targum Onkelos"—W. R. Garr, "*\*ay* > *a* in Targum Onkelos," *JAOS* 111 (1991), pp. 712–19.

Geller, "Tablets"—M. J. Geller, "Tablets and Magic Bowls," in S. Shaked (ed.), *Officina Magica: Essays on the Practice of Magic in Antiquity*

(Institute of Jewish Studies, Studies in Judaica 4; Leiden, Boston: Brill, 2005), pp. 53–72.

Glatzer, "Early Babylonian Manuscripts"—M. Glatzer, "Early Babylonian Hebrew Manuscripts," *Books & People* 11 (1997), pp. 8–13.

Golinkin, *Ginzei Rosh Hashana*—D. Golinkin, *Ginzei Rosh Hashanah: Manuscript Fragments of Bavli Rosh Hashanah from the Cairo Genizah: A Facsimile Edition with a Codicological Introduction* (New York and Jerusalem: The Jewish Theological Seminary of America, 2000).

Golinkin, *"Rosh Hashana"*—D. Golinkin, *"Rosh Hashanah* Chapter IV of the Babylonian Talmud (part 2)," PhD Dissertation, The Jewish Theological Seminary of America, 1988 (Hebrew).

Häberl, *Khorramshahr*—C. G. Häberl, *The Neo-Mandaic Dialect of Khorramshahr* (Wiesbaden: Harrossowitz, 2009).

Harviainen, "Karaite Bible Transcription"—T. Harviainen, "A Karaite Bible Transcription with Indiscriminate Counterparts of Tiberian *qameṣ* and *ḥolam* (MS Firkovitch II, Arab.-evr. 1)," in A. Dotan (ed.), *Proceedings of the Eleventh Congress of the International Organization for Masoretic Studies* (IOMS), Jerusalem, June 21–22, 1993 (Jerusalem: World Union of Jewish Studies, 1994), pp. 33–40.

Hoftijzer–Jongeling, *DNWSI*—J. Hoftijzer and K. Jongeling, *Dictionary of the North-West Semitic Inscriptions* (Handbook of Oriental Studies: The Near and Middle East 21; Leiden: Brill, 1995).

Jastrow, *Dictionary*—M. Jastrow *A Dictionary of the Targumim, the Talmud Babli and Yerushalmi, and the Midrashic Literature* (London: Luzac and New York: Putnam, 1903).

Juusola, *Linguistic Peculiarities*—H. Juusola, *Linguistic Peculiarities in the Aramaic Magic Bowl Texts* (Studia Orientalia 86; Helsinki: Finnish Oriental Society, 1999).

Kara, "Megilla"—Y. Kara, "Babylonian Aramaic in the Tradition of Yemen According to the Diacritical Punctuation of Rav ʿAmar in Two Editions of the Tractate *Megilla*," *Tema* 3 (1993), pp. 5–28 (Hebrew).

Kara, "Unity"—Y. Kara, "Tradition yéménite de l'araméen babylonien: unité et diversité," *Massorot* 2 (1986), pp. 79–102 (Hebrew).

Kara, "Preservation"—Y. Kara, "The Way of Preserving the Yemenite Tradition," in *Proceedings of the Sixth World Congress of Jewish Studies, 1973* (Jerusalem: World Union of Jewish Studies, 1980), vol. IV, pp. 175–82.

Kara, *Yemenite Manuscripts*—Y. Kara, *Babylonian Aramaic in the Yemenite Manuscripts of the Talmud* (Jerusalem: Magnes Press, 1983; Hebrew).

Kaufman, "Review"—S. Kaufman, [Review of] S. Morag, *Babylonian Aramaic: The Yemenite Tradition [Aramit Bemasoret Teman: Leshon Ha-Talmud HaBavli]*, *JAOS* 112 (1992), pp. 543–44.

Kaufman, *Akkadian Influences*—S. Kaufman, *Akkadian Influences on Aramaic* (The Oriental Institute of Chicago Assyriological Studies 19; Chicago and London: The University of Chicago Press, 1974).

Khan, "Object Markers"—G. A. Khan, "Object Markers and Agreement Pronouns in Semitic Languages," *BSOAS* 47 (1984), 468–500.

Kutscher, "Hermopolis Papyri"—E. Y. Kutscher, "The Hermopolis Papyri," *IOS* 1 (1971), pp. 103–19.

Kutscher, *Isaiah Scroll*—E. Y. Kutscher, *The Language and Linguistic Background of the Isaiah Scroll (1Q Isaa)* (Studies on the Texts of the Desert of Judah 6; Leiden: Brill, 1974).

Kutscher, "Mishnaic Hebrew"—E. Y. Kutscher, "Mishnaic Hebrew," in S. Lieberman et al. (eds.), *Henoch Yalon Jubilee Volume* (Jerusalem: Kiryat Sefer, 1963), pp. 246–80.

Kutscher, "Neutralization"—E. Y. Kutscher, "Neutralization of Gender and Number of the Third Person Perfect in Babylonian Aramaic?" *Leš* 35 (1970–71), pp. 36–38 (Hebrew).

Kutscher, "Review"—E. Y. Kutscher, [Review of] Epstein, *Grammar*, *Leš* 26 (1962), pp. 149–83, reprinted in Kutscher, *Studies*, pp. 227–55 (Hebrew).

Kutscher, *SGA*—E. Y. Kutscher, *Studies in Galilean Aramaic* (Ramat Gan: Bar Ilan University, 1976).

Kutscher, *Studies*—E. Y. Kutscher, *Hebrew and Aramaic Studies* (Jerusalem: Magnes Press: 1977; Hebrew and English).

Lane, *Lexicon*— E. W. Lane, *An Arabic-English Lexicon* (London: Williams and Norgate, 1863–93).

Lerner, "Sheʾiltot"—M. B. Lerner, "The Geniza Fragments of Sheʾiltot de-Rav Ahai in the Munich Library," in M. A. Friedman (ed.), *A Century of Geniza Research (Teʿuda* XV; Tel Aviv University, 1999), pp. 161–88.

Levene, *Corpus*—D. Levene, *A Corpus of Magic Bowls: Incantation Texts in Jewish Aramaic from Late Antiquity* (London, New York, and Bahrain: Kegan Paul, 2003).

Levene, "Moussaieff 164"—D. Levene, "'If You Appear as a Pig': Another Incantation Bowl (Moussaieff 164)," *JSS* 52 (2007), pp. 59–70.

Levene–Bhayro, "Bring to the Gates"—D. Levene and S. Bhayro, "'Bring to the Gates . . . upon a good smell and upon good fragrances': An Aramaic Incantation Bowl for Success in Business," *AfO* 51 (2005/2006), pp. 242–46.

Levias, *Diqduq*—*A Grammar of Babylonian Aramaic* (New York: The Alexander Kohut Memorial Foundation, 1930; Hebrew).

Levias, *Grammar*—C. Levias, *A Grammar of the Aramaic Idiom Contained in the Babylonian Talmud* (Cincinnati: The Bloch Publishing and Printing Company, 1900).

Lewin, *Otzar Ha-gaonim*—B. M. Lewin, *Otzar ha-Gaonim: Thesaurus of the Gaonic Responsa and Commentaries following the Order of the Talmudic Tractates* (13 volumes; Haifa and Jerusalem, 1928–1944 [published by the editor]).

Liebermann, *Das Pronomen*—A. Liebermann, *Das Pronomen und das Adverbium des babylonisch-talmudischen Dialektes* (Berlin: Mayer & Müller, 1895).

Luzzatto, *Elementi grammaticali*—S. D. Luzzatto, *Elementi grammaticali del caldeo Biblico e del dialetto Talmudico babilonese* (Padua: A. Bianchi, 1865).

Macuch, *Handbook*—R. Macuch, *Handbook of Classical and Modern Mandaic* (Berlin: De Gruyter, 1965).

Malone, "Observations"—J. L. Malone, "Observations of Linguistic Similarity between the Babylonian Aramaic of the *Hălaḵot Pĕsuqot* and Mandaic," *Leš* 37 (1973), p. 161–64 (Hebrew).

Malter, *Taʿanit*—H. Malter, *The Treatise Taʿanit of the Babylonian Talmud* (New York: American Academy of Jewish Research, 1930).

Marcus, *Manual*—D. Marcus, *A Manual of Babylonian Jewish Aramaic* (Washington, D.C.: University Press of America, 1981).

Margolis, *Manual*—M. Margolis, *A Manual of the Aramaic Language of the Babylonian Talmud: Grammar, Chrestomathy and Glossaries* (Clavis linguarum Semiticarum 3; München: C. H. Beck'sche Verlagsbuchhandlung and New York: G. E. Stechert, 1910).

McCullough, *Incantation Bowls*—W. S. McCullough, *Jewish and Mandaean Incantation Bowls in the Royal Ontario Museum* (Toronto: University of Toronto Press, 1967).

Montgomery, *AIT*—J. A. Montgomery, *Aramaic Incantation Texts from Nippur* (The Museum, Publications of the Babylonian Section, Vol. III Philadelphia: University of Pennsylvania, 1913).

Morag, "Diphthongs"—S. Morag, הערות לסוגיית הדו-תנועות בארמית הבבלית ["Notes on the Topic of Diphthongs in Babylonian Aramaic"] in M. Bar-Asher et al. (eds.), *Hebrew Language Studies Presented to Professor Zeev Ben-Ḥayyim* (Jerusalem: Magnes Press, 1983), pp. 337–58 (Hebrew).

Morag, "Geniza"—S. Morag, "Some Notes on the Grammar of Babylonian Aramaic as Reflected in the Geniza Manuscripts," *Tarbiz* 42 (1972–73), pp. 60–78 (Hebrew).

Morag, "Kethib and Qere"—S. Morag, "*Kethib* and *Qere* in Post-Biblical Literature" in Y. Ratzaby (eds.), *Boʾi Teiman* (Tel Aviv: Afikim, 1967), pp. 26–45 (Hebrew).

Morag "On the Yemenite Tradition"—S. Morag, "On the Yemenite Tradition of Babylonian Aramaic," *Tarbiz* 30 (1961), pp. 120–29 (Hebrew).

Morag, "Oral Transmission"—S. Morag, לעניין העברתו בעל-פה של התלמוד הבבלי ["On the Oral Transmission of the Babylonian Talmud"] in M. Bar-Asher and D. Rosenthal (eds.), *Meḥqerei Talmud II: Talmudic Studies Dedicated to the Memory of Professor Eliezer Shimshon Rosenthal* (Jerusalem: Magnes Press, 1993), pp. 334–48 (Hebrew).

Morag, "Phonology"—S. Morag, "Notes on the Phonology of Babylonian Aramaic as Reflected by the Vocalization of *Hălakot Pĕsuqot*," *Leš* 32 (1968), pp. 67–88 (Hebrew).

Morag, "Strong Verb"—S. Morag, "The Strong Verb in Babylonian Aramaic according to the Yemenite Tradition," in S. Lieberman et al. (eds.), *Henoch Yalon Jubilee Volume* (Jerusalem: Kiryat Sefer, 1963), pp. 182–220 (Hebrew).

Morag, *Studies*—S. Morag, *Studies in Hebrew, Aramaic and Jewish Languages* (Jerusalem: Magnes Press, 2003; Hebrew).

Morag, "Vocalisation"—S. Morag, "On the Vocalisation of the Babylonian Talmud in the Geonic Period," in *The Fourth World Congress of Jewish Studies, 1965* (Jerusalem: The World Union of Jewish Studies, 1967–1968), vol. 2, pp. 89–94.

Morag, *Vocalised Manuscripts*—S. Morag, *Vocalised Talmudic Manuscripts in the Cambridge Genizah Collections, Volume I: Taylor-Schechter Old Series* (Cambridge: Cambridge University Press, 1988).

Morag, "Vowel System"—S. Morag, "Notes on the Vowel System of Babylonian Aramaic as Preserved in the Yemenite Tradition," *Phonetica* 7 (1962), pp. 217–39.

Morag, *YT*—S. Morag, *Babylonian Aramaic: The Yemenite Tradition: Historical Aspects and Transmission, Phonology, the Verbal System* (Jerusalem: Ben Zvi Institute, 1988; Hebrew).

Morag–Kara, *BAYTN*—S. Morag and Y. Kara, *Babylonian Aramaic in Yemenite Tradition: The Noun* (Jerusalem: Magnes Press, 2002; Hebrew).

Moreshet, *Lexicon*—M. Moreshet, *A Lexicon of the New Verbs in Tannaitic Hebrew* (Ramat Gan: Bar Ilan University Press, 1980; Hebrew).

Morgenstern, "BM 91767"—M. Morgenstern, "The Jewish Babylonian Aramaic Magic Bowl BM 91767 Reconsidered," *Le Muséon* 120 (2007), pp. 5–27.

Morgenstern, "Geonic Responsa"—M. Morgenstern, "Jewish Babylonian Aramaic in Geonic Responsa: Studies in Phonology, Verb Morphology, Pronouns and Style," PhD Dissertation, The Hebrew University of Jerusalem, 2002 (Hebrew).

Morgenstern, "Magic Bowl"—M. Morgenstern, "Notes on a Recently Published Magic Bowl," *AS* 2 (2004), pp. 207–22.

Morgenstern, "Mandaic"—M. Morgenstern, "Jewish Babylonian Aramaic and Mandaic: Some Points of Contact," *Aram* 21 (2009), pp. 289–302.

Morgenstern, "Moussaieff Collection"—M. Morgenstern, "Linguistic Notes on Magic Bowls in the Moussaieff Collection," *BSOAS* 68 (2005), pp. 349–67.

Morgenstern, "Non-Standard Spellings"—M. Morgenstern, "On Some Non-Standard Spellings in the Aramaic Magic Bowls and their Linguistic Significance," *JSS* 52 (2007), pp. 245–77.

Morgenstern, "Noun Patterns"—M. Morgenstern, "Notes on the Noun Patterns in the Yemenite Tradition of Jewish Babylonian Aramaic," *REJ* 168 (2009), pp. 51–83.

Morgenstern, "Review of Muraoka–Porten"—M. Morgenstern, [Review of] T. Muraoka and B. Porten, *A Grammar of Egyptian Aramaic* (first edition), *JSS* 48 (2003), pp. 140–47.

Morgenstern, "Risqué Pun"– M. Morgenstern, "A Rather Risqué Pun in Jewish Babylonian Aramaic," in C. Cohen et al. (eds.), *Birkat Shalom: Studies in the Bible, Ancient Near Eastern Literature, and Postbiblical Judaism Presented to Shalom M. Paul on the Occasion of His Seventieth Birthday* (Winona Lake, Indiana: Eisenbrauns, 2008), pp. 877–86.

Morgenstern, "Segal"—M. Morgenstern, [Review of] Segal, *Catalogue, IEJ* 55 (2005), pp. 121–22.

Morgenstern, "ZHS"—M. Morgenstern, [Review of] C. Müller-Kessler, *ZHS, JSS* 55 (2010), pp. 280–89.

Müller-Kessler, "Die Stellung"—C. Müller-Kessler, "Die Stellung des Koine-Babylonisch-Aramäischen auf Zauberschalen innerhalb des Ostaramäischen," in N. Nebes (ed.), *Neue Beiträge zur Semitistik* (Jenaer Beiträge zum Vorderen Orient 5; Wiesbaden: Harrossowitz, 2002), pp. 91–103.

Müller-Kessler, "Die Zauberschalensammlung"—C. Müller-Kessler, "Die Zauberschalensammlung des British Museum," *AfO* 48/49 (2001/2002), pp. 115–45.

Müller-Kessler, "Muraoka–Porten"—C. Müller-Kessler, [Review of] T. Muraoka and B. Porten, *A Grammar of Egyptian Aramaic* (first edition), *BSOAS* 63 (2000), pp. 285–86.

Müller-Kessler, "Targum Onqelos"—C. Müller-Kessler, "The Earliest Evidence for Targum Onqelos from Babylonia and the Question of Its Dialect and Origin," *Journal for the Aramaic Bible* 3 (2001), pp. 181–98.

Müller-Kessler, ZHS–C. Müller-Kessler, *Die Zauberschalentexte in der Hilprecht-Sammlung, Jena und weitere Nippur-Texte anderer Sammlungen* (Wiesbaden: Harrassowitz, 2005.)

Müller-Kessler–Kwasman, "Incantation Bowl"—C. Müller-Kessler and T. Kwasman, "A Unique Talmudic Aramaic Incantation Bowl," *JAOS* 120 (2000), pp. 159–65.

Muraoka–Porten, *Grammar*—T. Muraoka and B. Porten, *A Grammar of Egyptian Aramaic* (second, revised edition, Leiden: Brill, 2003).

Naveh–Shaked, *AMB*—J. Naveh and S. Shaked, *Amulets and Magic Bowls, Aramaic Incantations of Late Antiquity* (Jerusalem: Magnes Press, 1987).

Naveh–Shaked, *MSF*—J. Naveh and S. Shaked, *Magic Spells and Formulae, Aramaic Incantations of Late Antiquity* (Jerusalem: Magnes Press, 1993).

Nöldeke, *MG*—Th. Nöldeke, *Mandäische Grammatik* (Halle: Buchhandlung des Waisenhauses, 1875).

Nöldeke, *SG*—Th. Nöldeke, *Kurtzgefasste syrische Grammatik* (second edition, Leipzig: Tauchniz, 1898).

Rabbinovicz, *Variae lectiones*—M. N. N. Rabbinovicz, *Variae lectiones in Mischnam et in Talmud Babylonicum* (Munich: Roesl and Huber, 1867–86).

Rosenberg, *Das aramäische Verbum*—J. Rosenberg, *Das aramäische Verbum im babylonischen Talmud* (Marburg: Oscar Ehrardt, 1888).

Rosenthal, *Die Sprache*—F. Rosenthal, *Die Sprache der palmyrenischen Inschriften und ihre Stellung innerhalb des Aramäischen* (Leipzig: J. C. Hinrichs, 1936).

Rülf, *Lautlehre*—G. Rülf, *Zur Lautlehre der aramäisch-talmudischen Dialecte. I. Die Kehllaute* (Leipzig: J. C. Hinrichs, 1879).

Rybak, *"Nedarim"* —S. F. Rybak, "The Aramaic Dialect of *Nedarim*," PhD Dissertation, Yeshiva University, 1980.

Sabar, *Homilies*—Y. Sabar, *Homilies in the Neo-Aramaic of the Kurdistani Jews on the Parashot Wayḥi, Beshallaḥ and Yitro* (Jerusalem: Israel Academy of Sciences, 1984; Hebrew).

Sabato, *Yemenite Manuscript*—M. Sabato, *A Yemenite Manuscript of Tractate Sanhedrin and Its Place in the Text Tradition* (Jerusalem: Yad Izhak Ben Zvi, 1998; Hebrew).

Schlesinger, *Satzlehre*—M. Schlesinger, *Satzlehre der aramäischen Sprache des babylonischen Talmuds* (Leipzig: Asia Major, 1928).

Segal, *Catalogue*—J. B. Segal, *Catalogue of the Aramaic and Mandaic Incantation Bowls in the British Museum* (London: British Museum Press, 2000).

Shaked, *"Food"*—S. Shaked, "Between Iranian and Aramaic: Iranian Words Concerning Food in Jewish Babylonian Aramaic, with Some Notes on the Aramaic Heterograms in Iranian," in S. Shaked and A. Netzer (eds.), *Irano-Judaica V: Studies Relating to Jewish Contacts with*

*Persian Culture Throughout the Ages* (Jerusalem: Ben-Zvi Institute, 2003), pp. 120–37.

Shaked, "Magic Bowls"—S. Shaked, "Magic Bowls and Incantation Texts: How to Get Rid of Demons and Pests," *Qadmoniot* 129 (2005), pp. 2–13 (Hebrew).

Sharvit, "Lack of Contrast"—S. Sharvit, "Lack of Contrast between *qameṣ/ḥolam* and between *segol/pataḥ*" in E. Y. Kutscher et al. (eds.), *Henoch Yalon Memorial Volume* (Jerusalem: Kiryat Sefer, 1974), pp. 547–55 (Hebrew).

Shetreet, "Aramaic Verb"—T. Shetreet, הפועל בארמית הבבלית על פי כתב-יד פירנצה 7–9 ["The Babylonian Aramaic Verb according to MS Florence II I 7–9"], MA Thesis, The Hebrew University, Jerusalem, 2009.

Shremer, "Lishana Aharina"—A. Shremer, "Fragments of *Lishana Aharina* of Bavli *Moed Qatan* from the Geniza," *Sidra* 9 (1993), pp. 117–61 (Hebrew).

Shweka, "Studies"—R. Shweka, "Studies in *Halakhot Gedolot*: Text and Recension," PhD Dissertation, The Hebrew University, Jerusalem, 2008 (Hebrew).

Sokoloff, "Aramaic Verb"—M. Sokoloff, "The Aramaic Verb in *Hălakot Pĕsuqot*," *Leš* 35 (1971), pp. 235–42 (Hebrew).

Sokoloff, *DJBA*—M. Sokoloff, *A Dictionary of Jewish Babylonian Aramaic of the Talmudic and Geonic Periods* (Ramat Gan: Bar Ilan University Press and Baltimore and London: The Johns Hopkins University Press, 2002).

Sperling, "Aramaic Spousal Misunderstandings"—S. D. Sperling, "Aramaic Spousal Misunderstandings," *JAOS* 115 (1995), pp. 205–9.

Sussmann, "Talmud Fragments"—Y. Sussmann, "Talmud Fragments in the Cairo Geniza," in M. A. Friedman (ed.), *Cairo Geniza Studies* (*Teʿuda* I; Tel Aviv University and Ha-Kibbutz Ha-Meuhad, 1980), pp. 21–31 (Hebrew).

Tal, "Beza I"—A. Tal, "The Geniza Fragment Antonin 891 to the Chapter '*Beza*', Tractate *Yom Tov*, Babli—Characterisation and Tradition," MA Thesis, The Hebrew University, Jerusalem, 2000 (Hebrew).

Wajsberg, "Early Amoraim"—E. Wajsberg, "The Aramaic Dialect of the Early Amoraim," *Leš* 60 (1997), pp. 95–156 (Hebrew).

Wajsberg, "Palestinian Traditions"—E. Wajsberg, "The Aramaic Dialect of the Palestinian Traditions in the Babylonian Talmud," *Leš* 66

(2004), pp. 243–82; 67 (2005), pp. 301–26; 68 (2006), pp. 31–61 (Hebrew).

Wajsberg, "Principles" — E. Wajsberg, הצעת העקרונות לקביעות בחנים לשוניים להערכת כתבי-היד של התלמוד הבבלי ["A Proposal of Principles for Establishing Linguistic Criteria for Assessing the Manuscripts of the Babylonian Talmud"], *Minutes of the Academy of the Hebrew Language* 28–29–30 (1981–83), pp. 338–45.

Wajsberg, "Taxonomy" — E. Wajsberg, "The Contribution of the Forms רי כאיזה צד and שמעון בן לקיש to the Taxonomy of Talmudic Manuscripts," *Leš* 55 (1991), pp. 367–82 (Hebrew).

Yeivin, *Babylonian Vocalization* — I. Yeivin, *The Hebrew Language Tradition as Reflected in the Babylonian Vocalization* (Jerusalem: The Academy of the Hebrew Language, 1985; Hebrew).

Yeivin, "Yiqtolennu" — I. Yeivin, "The Verbal Forms יקטולנו ,יקטולנו ,יקטולנו in the DSS in Comparison to the Babylonian Vocalization," in B. Uffenheimer (ed.), *Bible and Jewish History: Studies in Bible and Jewish History Dedicated to the Memory of Jacob Liver* (Tel Aviv: Tel Aviv University, 1971, pp. 256–76 (Hebrew).

# Grammatical Index

Note: numeration refers to section number unless otherwise specified.

## ORTHOGRAPHY

*ā* with *mater lectionis* in general: 4.3.1; following *waw/yod*: 4.3.1.4; f.pl. morpheme: 2.12.2.1; 4.3.1.3; medial *ʾaleph* in G participles: 2.7.2; 4.3.1.1; nominal forms: 4.3.1.2; numerals: 4.3.2.3; grammatical particles: 4.3.2.4; final *ā* vowel in 3 f.s. participles: 4.3.2.1; III-*yod* perfect 3 m.s.: 4.3.2.2

Final *ā'ā*: 4.4.2.2

Historical *śin*: 4.3.4

Historical *bet* written with *waw*: 4.3.5

*i* with *mater lectionis* in closed syllable: 2.12.2.1; 4.3.3.1; in syllables closed by gemination: 4.3.3.2

Medial *ay* written with single *yod*: 2.12.2.1

Non-historical *ḥet* for *h*: 3.3.1.2.1; 4.4.1.2

Non-historical *ʿayin*: 3.3.1.1.1–2

## PHONOLOGY

*\*a > i* in closed syllables: Ch. 3 n. 159

Anaptyxis : 2.12.2.1; 3.3.2; 4.4.5.5

Assimilation: 2.12.2.1; third radical: 3.4.6.2; *t*-morpheme: 3.3.3; 4.4.5.2.2; at word boundaries: 4.4.5.3

*\*b > w* 4.3.5

Dissimilation: 4.4.5.4

Elision of word-final consonants in general: 2.12.2.1; Ch. 2. n. 173; 4.4.3. *dalet*: 2.3.3; *gimel*: 2.7.2; *taw* in perfect verb morphemes: 3.4.1.1

*\*i > a* before the consonants החעייר: 2.7.2; 3.3.2.2

Interchange of *ʾaleph* and *he*: 4.4.2.1

Interchanges of *nun* and *lamed* 4.4.4

Prosthetic *ʾaleph*: 3.3.3

Reflection of historical *\*ā*: 2.6.4; 2.12.2.1.5; 3.1;

*Shewa* after unstressed *ʿayin*: Ch. 2 n. 171; before *yod* vocalized *i*: 3.3.1.1.2

Shift *\*āʾe > āye* in gentilics: 2.12.2.1; 3.3.1.1.2

Weakening of pharyngeals in general: 3.3.1; of *ʾaleph* in juncture: 4.4.2.2; of *ḥet*: 3.3.1.2; 4.4.1.2; 4.7.5; of *ʿayin*: 2.3.3; 2.12.2.1; 3.3.1.1; 4.4.1.1; 4.7.5

## PRONOUNS

Demonstrative: 4.6.5

Indirect object ניהל-: affixing to verb: 2.7.2; 3.5.2.3.2
ניהלהו/ניהליהו: Ch. 3 n. 309

Object
    1 c.s.: 3.5.1.1
    2 m.s.: 4.6.1

# green press
## INITIATIVE